SALMON FISHING

We thank you on behalf of
Lloyds Bowmaker for your support
over the years and wish you every happiness
in your retirement

Stephen Moran

Alan Glass.

Peter Iton.

David Baggaley

PLATE 1 *Frontispiece*

The Author

SALMON FISHING

A PRACTICAL GUIDE

by

HUGH FALKUS

*Illustrated with numerous
photographs and diagrams
and nine colour plates*

H. F. & G. WITHERBY LTD

First published in 1984 by
H. F. & G. Witherby Ltd.
14 Henrietta Street,
London WC2E 8QJ

Reprinted with some revision, November 1984
Reprinted with minor amendments, February 1985
Reprinted with further revision, September 1985
Reprinted with minor amendments, February 1986
Reprinted, January 1987
Reprinted, October 1987
Reprinted, October 1988
Reprinted, June 1989

Dedicated to
ANTONY WITHERBY

ISBN 0 85493 144 9

Filmset in Monophoto 11pt. Ehrhardt
and printed in Great Britain by
BAS Printers Limited, Over Wallop, Hampshire

Preface

No creature on earth treats the dogmatist more sternly than *Salmo salar* the Atlantic salmon. Anyone writing about this extraordinary fish enters a literary minefield—each unconsidered sentence threatening to blow up in his face.

That comparatively few authors complete their journeys unscathed is not surprising. Contradictory in everything he does, *Salmo* cannot be tied down by dogma. Almost every statement demands to be qualified.

Essential to the wildlife films I used to make, a good deal of my working life was spent observing the behaviour of animals. All those hours were exciting and instructive, but none more so than the time spent on river banks observing salmon. In addition to providing days of rare enchantment, it taught me that much of what I had read about *Salmo*'s behaviour was pretty dubious. Often, the fish I was watching seemed a different creature from the one encountered in print. And over the years it began to dawn on me that far from being fact, a lot of what I had hitherto taken for granted was indeed fallacy; that most authors had written about what they *thought* salmon did, not what they had *seen* them do.

Since then I have tested certain of their statements, some of which will be found among these pages: assertions by acknowledged experts and regarded as Gospel—but unsound. Most of the accepted tenets of salmon fishing started as conjecture; but gradually, parroted by writer after writer, part of this conjecture became "fact".

The examination of such "fact" led to much observation and experiment. As a result, this book—which for years had been forming in my mind—eventually came to be written.

Based on my own experience, it is intended simply as a practical guide that I hope may increase the reader's enjoyment of salmon fishing—and his appreciation of what is surely the most fascinating animal on earth.

Acknowledgements

For their contributions to the text of this book I wish to thank my friends: Dr Roger Burns, Peter Curtis, Michael Daunt, Esmond Drury, Dr Bob Gartside, Dr David Goldsborough, Mike Kendall, Derek Knowles, Eric Robb, Dr Jimmy Skene and G. H. N. "Briggy" Wilson.

I must also thank Dr Christopher Harpley of the North West Water Authority for permission to extrapolate from his research into river movements of salmon; and his colleague R. F. Prigg together with those members of the NWWA Scientists Division responsible for the report of acidification of the Cumbrian Esk.

For their kind help I wish to record my thanks to Ron Coleby, Dr Eric Edwards, Dr Alwyne Wheeler and Laurence Murray; also to Leslie Stout for his interesting letter quoted on page 89.

Without the generosity of friends who over the years have made their fishing available to me, this book could not have been written, and it is in deference to their wishes that many places I have fished remain unnamed. But I am glad of the opportunity to thank Alan Shipman for his great hospitality on Deeside, and Jim Miller, Chairman of Hardy Bros., for many splendid days on Tweed and Tay. I must also express my gratitude to those eminent all-round sportsmen G. H. F. Chaldicott, Moc Morgan and Tim Thomas, among other friends in Wales who have made me so welcome on their delightful rivers.

For frequent happy visits to Speyside I am indebted to Nigel Grant of The Seafield Lodge Hotel, Grantown, and to that great angler Arthur Oglesby—not least for the many excellent pictures he has so kindly provided for this book.

For additional photography I wish to thank Fred Buller, *The Birmingham Post and Mail* (page 358), Michael Daunt, Esmond Drury, Sandy Leventon, Moc Morgan, Reg Scaife, Alan Shipman and Malcolm Taylor.

ACKNOWLEDGEMENTS

I wish to thank Sean Morris and Peter Parks of Oxford Scientific Films for their colour photographs on plate 2; the paintings of Capelin and Sand-eel on this plate are by Henning Anthon (reproduced in *Fishes in Colour* (Danish edition Politikens Forlag). For other colour plates I am indebted to Arthur Oglesby, Alan Shipman, and Alan C. Parker whose expertise is displayed in the four depicting flies.

For the flies themselves I am grateful to Steve Riding of 135 Church Street, Preston, from whom all patterns mentioned in this book can be obtained.

I also wish to thank Leslie George, most knowledgeable of Dee gillies, for access to his father's record of A. H. E. Wood's fishing at Cairnton; and Tod Millard for permission to publish the picture of his magnificent Wye fish.

I wish to make acknowledgement to the following works for short excerpts quoted: *Salmon* by Arthur Oglesby (Queen Anne Press), *Salmon and Trout* by Dr Derek Mills (Oliver and Boyd), *The Atlantic Salmon* by Lee Wulff (Nick Lyons/Winchester Press, U.S.A.), *Letters to a Salmon Fisher's Sons* by A. H. Chaytor (John Murray), *Rod Fishing for Salmon on the Wye* by J. Arthur Hutton (Jonathan Cape), *A Salmon Fisher's Odyssey* by John Ashley-Cooper (Witherby), *Salmon Fishing* by Eric Taverner: A. H. E. Wood extracts (Seeley Service), *Casts from a Salmon Reel* and *Salmon and Trout in Moorland Streams* both by Major Kenneth Dawson (Herbert Jenkins), *Ghosts at my Back* by Tom Rawling (Oxford University Press), *Fly Fishing for Salmon* by Richard Waddington (Faber and Faber), *Torridge Fishery* by L. R. N. Gray (Nicholas Kaye), *The Great Salmon Rivers of Scotland* by John Ashley-Cooper (Gollancz), *Fishing Fantasy – A Salmon Fisherman's Notebook* by J. Hughes-Parry (Eyre and Spottiswoode), *Salmon and other Things* by Henry Nicoll (Methuen) and *Angling on Lomond* by Bill McEwan (Albyn Press). I am indebted to Richard Walker for the quotation on page 182. For their patient proof-reading I must applaud those accomplished flyfishers Dr Jo Rippier and R. N. Booth whose keen eyes spotted so many of my mistakes. Some of the more complicated drawings were kindly prepared by Kenneth Jessup. For advice on bibliographical details my thanks are due to David Beazley and Ron Coleby.

Like Penelope's web, the completion of this book has seemed a never-ending task. It is with much gratitude that I acknowledge the unfailing help of my old friend and publisher, Antony Witherby.

Contents

Colour Plates

Prehistoric relief carving of *Salmo salar* from a little shelter (Abri de Poisson) in the Gorge d'Enfer at Les Eyzies, one of the earliest records of man's association with the salmon.

You must not use this aforesaid artful sport for covetousness, merely for the increasing or saving of your money, but mainly for your enjoyment and to procure the health of your body and, more especially, of your soul.

Attrib. Dame Juliana Berners, *A Treatyse of Fysshynge wyth an Angle*, 1496.

Introduction

The big salmon was lying in three feet of water on top of a rock just above the pool tail. The rock was wide and flat and smooth, and against its pale grey surface, undulating slightly as he kept station in the current, the fish flickered like a streamer of weed.

From a cliff-path thirty feet up, Kathleen and I stood watching him. Two-thirty in the afternoon. From the fishing hut we had started upstream straight after lunch, finally reaching our pool via a narrow path that ran along the cliff side like the track of a mountain-goat. Now, after a long scramble, we stared down into the summer-low, limpid water of that beautiful little Scottish west coast river. There were no other salmon in sight. Just this one big fish. But one was better than none.

On the opposite bank the rocky face of the gorge fell sheer into the pool. On our side, in a small bay at the foot of some rickety steps, a ledge extended for a few yards underwater making a sort of casting platform from which it seemed possible to cover the fish.

"You stay up here and watch", I suggested. "I'll go and give him a fling."

Kathleen perched herself on the crumbly gravel of the path while I picked my way gingerly down to the pool. Waist deep on the ledge, I lengthened line.

"Now", I called up. "See what happens."

The line sang in the air. The size eight Blue Charm looped out across the water, touched down, dipped and started to swing round towards the rock . . . suddenly the line tightened and a I felt a tiny pluck.

There was a squeak from the cliff. "He took! I saw him!"

"I know", I said. "I felt him. He just *nipped* the fly!"

I retrieved some line and cast again . . .

Nothing happened.

Another cast . . .

Nothing.

I cast again . . .

Again, no response.

"Is he still there?" I asked.

"Yes."

"In the same place?"

"Yes."

"All right, fish", I thought. "I'll try you with something smaller."
To change down in size after a salmon tweaked was my usual drill.

Knowing that the exact amount of line needed to cover the lie was
already stripped off, I didn't move my feet or touch the reel: simply
pulled in the line, cut off the size eight fly, tied on a size ten, allowed
the current to take out the slack straight downstream and then cast again.

No response.

After half-a-dozen casts with the size ten, I thought: "Very well, I'll
just change that size ten for a size six." To bump up the size of fly
when a potential taker is playing hard-to-catch is a dodge that works
sometimes.

Not this time.

Five minutes later, feeling rather desperate, I changed back to the
original size eight. Perhaps by now he was prepared to be more positive.

He wasn't.

I looked up at Kathleen perched on the cliff-path. "Is he still there?"

"Yes."

I stood where I was, thinking. There seemed little point in making
another change of fly. Might as well carry on with what I had. After
all, he had come to it once. So, I just went on casting.

And on and on.

I knew that every cast must be covering the fish. I had neither altered
the length of line nor moved my feet.

"He's still there", Kathleen volunteered, after another fifteen minutes
of this. "Why don't you try something else?"

That thought had already occurred to me. "Yes", I agreed. "It's about
time!"

Again, without shifting position, I stripped in line and, for the fourth
time stuffed the rod-butt down inside my breast waders. Then, after
cutting off the fly, I exchanged the nine feet of 14 lb monofil leader for
a length of 20 lb. On the end of this I tied a weighted prawn—which
happened to be occupying a tobacco tin in my pocket.

"That's more like it", said Kathleen approvingly. "Now we'll see."

I held the stripped line in loose coils and shot it as I swung the prawn out across the pool. The bait splashed down and started to fish. I was dry-mouthed, tense with anticipation.

As the prawn crossed the lie, a squeak from the cliff coincided with a sharp tug . . . then the line went limp.

"Hell!" I said. "He took!"

"I know, I saw him go for it", shouted Kathleen. "Why didn't you hook him?"

"God knows!" I said, pulling in line. "They behave like that sometimes." I looked at the prawn. The front part of the head had been sliced off—as though with a knife.

"Look!" I said, holding it up. "Whiskers gone! How the devil can a salmon *do* that without getting hooked?"

I was sweating slightly. Here was a fresh-run twenty pounder that had risen twice: first to fly, then to prawn. Success seemed so tantalizingly close—and yet . . . what next? Would that fish come a third time?

I looked up. "Is he still there?"

"Yes. What are you going to do?"

"Just keep at it. As long as he stays there we're in with a chance."

I examined my decapitated prawn. Would it still be acceptable? The only way to find out was to go on fishing it. Anyway, I had no other bait ready-mounted; the salmon would have to make do with what was left of this one. I would fish over him, I decided, until either he moved away or the prawn fell to pieces. After giving the thin copper-wire that bound the prawn to the hook-mount a twist or two to tighten it, I started to cast again—letting the bait swing round exactly the same arc as before . . .

After more than a hour of this I was getting tired. So was the prawn, which by now looked decidedly frayed at the edges. But the salmon was still there.

I fished doggedly on, a running commentary from the cliff-path keeping me informed. During cast after cast, as the bait swung round its unvaried arc, the fish simply moved slightly to one side or the other to avoid contact. He showed no further interest in it.

Eventually, fatigue called a halt. I stood there, waist deep, loops of stripped line hanging in the current, the prawn dangling. Now what? Was there any point in moving elsewhere? The river was dead low, chances in other pools unlikely to be any brighter. Here was a good fish; a potential taker who had already risen twice. Why leave him? Unable to think of any profitable alternative, I resolved to stay where I was.

"I'm getting bored with this," said Kathleen.

She had my sympathy. And had she spoken a few minutes earlier I would probably have packed it in and given that salmon best. As it was I had made up my mind. "Hang on", I said. "Just for a bit longer."

The sun had moved round throwing most of the pool into shadow, so that I seemed to be casting into a darkening tunnel. Downstream, late afternoon sunlight flashed on the lip of the pool, lighting up a cloud of insects that danced over the river where it cascaded into the run below. How long did I go on fishing? Kathleen says for at least another hour, and she may be right. But if we say forty-five minutes it's still a hell of a time to spend covering the same lie—a lie that had already been hammered for over an hour-and-a-half. However long it was, my arms were aching. I was using an old fifteen foot split-cane rod of my father's vintage and it weighed heavy. I must have been making nearly my last cast when, suddenly, the salmon took!

For a moment I thought I had hooked the rock. There was an astonished shout of triumph from the cliff. The salmon leaped in a shower of spray. My rod bent and bent as I held the fish on the very lip of the pool. Then he swung round and shot upstream . . . and I breathed again.

Ten minutes later he was on the bank. He weighed $22\frac{1}{2}$ lb—and what remained of the prawn was halfway down his throat!

*   *   *

Altogether, I think you will agree, an interesting experience. For well over two hours I had flogged away in the same place for the same fish; first with fly, then with prawn. And after giving that prawn a tweak first time round, the salmon had taken no further interest—until suddenly, after this battered bait had swung past his nose a hundred times, he tried to swallow it!

Of course, had someone not been up top watching the fish and assuring me he was still in residence he would not have been caught. I would have made another two or three casts and moved on—as most anglers would have done, if they had been fishing "blind"; unable to see what was happening in the river. Nevertheless, the incident raises a couple of points.

First of all, what was I, keenest of fly-fishers, doing with a prawn in my pocket? Secondly, even though I knew the fish was still there, by casting time after time in the same place didn't I think I might be overfishing the lie?

No. I didn't.

The vexed question of salmon reaction to a prawn is dealt with in detail in its appropriate chapter. Sufficient here to say that, according to the rules of the beat, I could fish what I liked provided only a fly-rod was used; and that my observations of salmon behaviour had shown the prawn to be less of a villain than is often claimed. Equally, I had learned that *provided it is covered properly and the fish is not scared, a salmon lie cannot be overfished.*

To any angler whose enthusiasm is unmatched by success, the significance of this statement is of enormous importance. It points a great truth; a truth frequently obscured by the mistake of treating salmon fishing as an offshoot of trout fishing and binding it with a similar code of behaviour.

Despite close relationship to the trout, the salmon is an entirely different animal. He has his own unique characteristics, and his capture with rod and line demands its own highly original philosophy. As we shall see later, the history of salmon fishing is clouded with misconceptions. And confusion still exists, so that the sport is riddled with curious conventions and strange fallacies, not least of which is the notion that, like the lies of most other species, a salmon-lie must not be fished too hard and will benefit from being "rested".

It will indeed—though not in the way most anglers would wish.

To forbear from fishing a pool will certainly benefit any salmon it holds because, if left alone long enough the fish will simply run on out of it before getting caught. This scarcely benefits the angler who arrives to fish that water.

The mistake is commonplace. Some fisheries, on the grounds of resting pools for an hour or so during lunch, make it compulsory to vacate the water at one o'clock preparatory to changing beats at two o'clock. This in my opinion is plain stupid. Whatever the benefit to anglers wanting time to sit down and eat, it does nothing to improve their chances of catching fish. A salmon may take the first lure he sees; he may take, say, the hundredth; he may not take at all. During spring and late autumn, to rest pools at lunchtime in the hope that salmon will take better in the afternoon merely deprives us of an hour's fishing—often, in cold weather, during the best part of the day. It is a time, moreover, when in certain months of the year on some of the bigger rivers we can *expect* to encounter "taking" fish.

This means that by the end of a week we have squandered nearly a whole day's fishing, during all of which we had excellent chances of hooking salmon—which is more than can be expected during the course of an average day.

I must make it clear that my advice regarding this mid-day fishing period is by no means categorical. As described and explained in Chapter III, there are times when, by fishing straight through the late morning and afternoon, we certainly *shall* be giving ourselves a good chance of catching salmon. There are times when we shall *not*.

These times depend on three conditions:
1. The type of river.
2. The height of water.
3. The time of year.

Spate rivers, with their rapid rise and fall, are a law unto themselves and will be considered separately in due course. For the moment I am referring to the big spring-run rivers in which, from the start of the season until roughly the end of May, it is foolish not to be fishing throughout the middle of the day.

When May is out it is often sensible to stop fishing some time during the morning and not re-start until the evening. Except for those flat, shallowing pool tails which, in summer, are best left until dusk, this has nothing to do with resting the water. It is simply to rest the angler.

During June, July and August, there is a much better chance of catching salmon by fishing in the early morning and late evening than when the sun is high—especially in the conditions of hot, bright weather and low water that these months so often bring. It is common sense to conserve our energy for the times that give us the best opportunities. In the heat of high summer, except when the river is up, the would-be successful salmon angler will be fishing very early in the day and very late, and he is wise to adjust his times of eating and sleeping.

In this he is simply following the example of the experienced sea trout night fly-fisherman—who knows that because some of his best chances are likely to occur in the early hours of the morning, he must fish through to daybreak and not pack up at midnight. And plans accordingly.

Just like the sea trout, which has its own specialized behaviour, the Atlantic salmon is a fish all by itself whose behaviour is vastly different from that of any other species. Alas, during the past couple of centuries, partly due to the parrotry of angling writers, confusion has been heaped upon confusion and much misinformation has resulted. In consequence, it is not surprising that much of what I have read about this fish conflicts with my experience. The exhortations, enshrined in the literature, to "rest" the salmon—in other words, treat it as we might a trout—is an example. One eminent authority of yesteryear states categorically:

> Salmon get tired of seeing the same lure and when the novelty has
> worn off they are not likely to take.

A single sentence containing more dogmatic falsehood would be hard
to find—as anyone will confirm who has spent much time on the river
observing salmon and how they really behave. And yet, judging by the
books I have read and the number of anglers who have discussed it with
me, it is a common belief.

On what grounds is such advice so blandly given and accepted?
Simply, I think, because it *sounds* good. And with the passing years
copied by one writer from another, the imaginary becomes "real".

I am by no means implying that "dogging" a fish is always the right
thing to do. But what is at issue here is not the best tactics for any particular moment but the truth about salmon behaviour. And when we come
to form our fishing strategy it is fact, not conjecture, that matters. On
so *many* occasions have I caught salmon, that could be seen and identified, after casting the same lure to them time after time.

In a way it seems a shame that virtue is not always rewarded; that
the angler derives no benefit from his self-discipline, especially as it is
all so plausible. For hour after hour salmon see all sorts of lures swinging
over their heads. Surely, an angler thinks, it must be beneficial to give
the fish a rest.

I am sorry to disappoint him. But as I have seen many, many times,
with few exceptions "resting" a lie will not help him catch the salmon
it holds. Quite the reverse in fact.

A classic example of how salmon can sometimes react to what is so
often condemned as "overfishing a lie", occurred one June day when
my friend Peter Curtis went to fish the River Inver. Here in his own
words is what happened:

> There had been three weeks with no rain and the shores of the loch
> showed several yards of dry mud. The river itself was low and clear
> and looked unlikely to be holding fish in the upper reaches. However,
> I thought there might be a chance of some fish in the rocky gorge
> a mile or so below the loch. And sure enough, when I looked down
> from some twenty feet above the stream I found five fish. They were
> lying one behind the other in a narrow pool no more than four yards
> across and ten or twelve yards long.
>
> There was no way down the steep cliff, so the cast had to be made

from above. Not so much a cast; more a flop, a float and a draw—the latter lasting only a second or two across the lie. I went on putting the fly over those salmon cast after cast. Nothing happened. I could see the fish clearly, and there wasn't a movement. Not even the restless shifting of fish that might have been disturbed. So I just went on and on casting over them; lengthening and shortening line; dapping the fly, sinking it, changing it from time to time. And still there wasn't a movement. But since I had found no fish anywhere else, I stuck to my quarry.

By now my fishing had become automatic—out, down and across; out, down and across. And the salmon just lay there in line ahead. Five of them. Unmoving.

I must have cast over those fish at least a hundred times when, to my astonishment, with a flick of his tail, Number Four fish suddenly started to move forwards and upwards towards the surface. There was hardly time for me to realize that he was actually coming for my fly—a size six Shrimp Fly—when he had opened his mouth, taken it, turned over with it and gone back down towards his lie. It was so quiet and leisurely, like watching a film sequence in slow-motion.

I tightened and he was on, solid. Down the falls he went to the bottom pool, where ten minutes later he came to the net.

The moment I knocked him on the head must have been a good two hours after my fly first went over him!

Returning upstream, I found the remaining four salmon still motionless in the same pool. I fished on for another hour, but with no further result. By then I had had enough, and packed up, more than content with my fortune. But I often wonder what might have happened had I persisted for yet another hour.

And now another example, taken from many similar experiences of my own.

A long time ago, while managing a stretch of Scottish river as a parergon to my writing, I had the golden chance of fishing for or observing salmon on nearly every day of the season. In late spring I would sit on a high bank overlooking a pool and watch salmon coming up from the sea. One by one they would appear over the lip of the pool tail, run slowly through the pool and disappear into the fast water at the pool neck. Every now and then, however, a fish would rest in the pool. There was a particular rock about two-thirds of the way down and, favoured by serendipity, I made the happy discovery that any fish lying

Spring fish from Tweed caught on fly by concentrating on one known taking lie.

beside this rock was frequently a ready taker. So, I would leave a rod assembled at the water's edge. When, sitting up there in my eyrie, I saw a fish occupying this lie I went down to the pool and cast for him. Quite often he took at once. Sometimes, however, not for perhaps ten or fifteen minutes, and it dawned on me that to overfish that lie was impossible. Provided I made a careful approach and didn't scare the fish, he remained catchable no matter how many times I had covered him.

There was another point. A fish would sometimes inhabit that rock lie for only half-an-hour or so before moving on again. To have rested the lie would, therefore, merely have resulted in missed opportunities. I think that most salmon anglers miss many more opportunities than they realize. Certainly in springtime. After all, most of us are fishing "blind" for an unseen quarry and have only the vaguest notion of what is happening beneath the surface.

Anyone eager to increase his chances of catching fish would be sensible to spend less time fishing, and more—much more—time observing what these extraordinary creatures get up to.

Accurate observation, as I know well, can be exceedingly difficult. In many rivers owing to the depth or colour of the water, fish are hidden from view and, except for rare glimpses, remain so. Nevertheless, there are some clear-running rivers, spate streams mainly, where fish *can* be seen and where a stealthy observer may spend many profitable hours. He should do so preferably in company with a friend prepared to help carry out various angling experiments of the nature described in this book. I can promise him some exciting moments.

For many years, in addition to having my own stretch of fishing, it was my good fortune to live within easy reach of several clear-water salmon rivers, in each of which fish could be observed. And, as the fol-lowing chapters endorse, I took full advantage of this. During day after day, when the water was low, I watched the reactions of salmon to every type of lure I could think of. In this I was lucky sometimes to have the help of friends, all skilful anglers, who could present an assortment of attractions to particular fish—while I lay on the river bank with a pair of polaroids. Far from being the dull, rather stupid automaton he is sometimes dubbed, the salmon showed himself to be highly complex, full of strange quirks and fancies.

These observations, carried out over a number of years, led me to re-think much of what I had hitherto accepted. I learned, for example, that if I really wanted to catch salmon the last thing to do was to leave them alone.

Obviously, it is sometimes a different matter in the heat of summer with dead low, gin-clear water, for those conditions make it very difficult to fly-fish without causing excessive disturbance. Even so, the qualifying "sometimes" used in the previous sentence cannot be dispensed with. As stated in the Preface, *salmon behaviour cannot be tied down by dogma.* And the more we discover about this fish the brighter the truth of that axiom shines forth.

Now, I am not suggesting that to stand in a river and put cast after cast over the same place is either the best or the most enjoyable way of fishing for salmon. It would be dull and often unprofitable. It would, if someone else wanted to fish that water, be inexcusable. All the same, its potential—based on an appreciation of the taking behaviour involved—is worth some thought, because I know from experience that the antics of those salmon I have described are by no means unusual. Indeed, they represent the sort of reactions we may frequently expect. Typical of the salmon's strange habits, they show that no matter how often a fish is covered, *provided we don't frighten him* he may still take. And I predict that anyone who understands what is implicit in this advice and knows when and how to make use of it—particularly, as explained later, when fishing the dry fly—in addition to approaching the sport with fresh interest and confidence, will undoubtedly increase his catch.*

Before the angler can take advantage of this, however, he must acquire a thoroughly sound technique based on stealth, water-sense and accurate casting, so that he can approach and cover fish without scaring them. He must then learn to present his lure, be it bait or fly, in a manner likely to *attract* those fish.

To help him do so is the object of this book.

The author fly-fishing tidal water on a small north-country river. Conditions are ideal: the tide ebbing and the river in high spate. The rod in use is a fifteen-footer—which may seem out of proportion on a stream that could be covered with the shortest trout rod. But the notion that a long rod need never be used on a narrow river is a common myth. Here, reed beds on a slope too deep to wade make it impossible to get near enough to the water's edge to control the fly properly with a short rod. A long rod allows the line to be hung well clear of the bank and the fly fished right round to the dangle—where salmon often take.

*For example, see "Two-Way" fishing, p. 296.

For Salmon being Fish of Prey, and great Feeders, Nature directs them to the salt Waters, as Physick to purge and cleanse them, not from their Impurities after Spawning, but from all their muddy terrene Particles and gross Humours, acquired by their extraordinary, excessive Feeding all the Summer in fresh Rivers . . . And when they are fatted and glutted with their long excessive Feeding in fresh Rivers, and have spawn'd in the latter end of the Year, repair to the Sea for Warmness, and to be purged from the gross Humours by the Calidity of the Saline Water; and when Winter is over, return to their Summer Habitations.

Robert Howlett,
The Angler's Sure Guide, 1706

I
The Fish

PART ONE: LIFE-STYLE

He comes in from the dark sway of the sea; from lonely reefs and wrecked ships hairy with weed. A wanderer of the ocean, returning to spawn in the river of his birth. The Greeks made no mention of him, but Britain's early invaders knew him well enough. He was leaping in the Thames when Caesar landed and in the wild Welsh streams when Agricola marched north. From the banks of so many rivers, from Gaul to the Scottish Highlands, the Romans glimpsed his flashing beauty and they named him *Salmo*—which means "The Leaper".

*   *   *

Any animal we wish to hunt successfully we must first study, and *Salmo salar* the Atlantic salmon is no exception. Although his life-style is well known to most anglers, a book on salmon fishing would be incomplete without some account of it. He is one of the most remarkable animals on earth, and since certain aspects of his biology are all-important to our fishing philosophy, it will be profitable to consider these before going into the ways and means of catching him.

Briefly *Salmo*'s origin is shrouded in mystery, but it is generally agreed that the several species of salmon, both the Pacific species and the Atlantic salmon, came from a common ancestor about 500,000 years ago. Whether this ancestor originated in fresh or salt water is uncertain. Biological evidence favours fresh, since most members of the Salmonidae are unable to breed in salt water.

Salmo's life-cycle starts in fresh water usually during November, December or January, when the hen fish lays her eggs in the gravel bed of some well-oxygenated and fairly fast-flowing stream. This can be the

23

head-waters of the parent river itself, or a feeder stream having the essential requirements of clean, unpolluted water flowing over a bed of small stones from which the hen can "cut" her nest, or redd.

Spawning starts this account of the salmon's life-cycle because although it is the climax of his return from sea, the end of a fantastic journey—and often the end of his life, for comparatively few salmon survive—the spawning redd is where and how it all begins.

Many times in my life I have lain full-length and watched the mating ritual of fish only a few yards from me. In the shallow, winter-clear water every stage of it can be seen, and it is fascinating.

Bit by bit, with flapping movements of her tail—having swum up into position against the current and turned on her side—the hen salmon prepares a trough in the gravel: a nest in which to lay her eggs. Nature makes provision for heavy losses. According to a recently published estimate by two zoologists, a hen spawns roughly eight hundred eggs per pound of her body weight.

As the stones are sucked up from the bottom by the flat of her tail they are carried downstream clear of the trough by the current. Over a period of several days she will cut several of these troughs and spawn in each of them—not all of her eggs being released during the first mating session.

When she is nearly ready to lay—and if the observer watches for this he will not miss the actual mating—the hen fish hovers over the redd and presses down with her anal fin, seemingly to test the depth of the trough. Shortly after this the cock fish, who has been in almost constant attendance, glides slowly up beside the hen, who is stationed over the trough, and encourages her to mate by making violent quivering movements. This quivering increases right up to and during the orgasm.

As the male's stimulation reaches its peak the female starts to extrude eggs, and the male responds by releasing his sperm (milt) that will fertilize the eggs.

During the orgasm the mouths of both fish gape wide open; a significant feature, precisely similar to the behaviour of trout. The milt from the male floats back with the current like a cloud of smoke and mingles with the eggs. Fertilization takes place immediately.

Afterwards, the female flips gravel over the eggs in the same way that she prepared the trough—swimming upstream, turning on her side and flapping with her tail from a position just upstream of the nest. Gradually, the current carries sufficient gravel downstream to cover the eggs, so that the completed redd has the appearance of a shallow grave.

PLATE 2

FOOD OF THE ATLANTIC SALMON at sea comprises mainly fish and crustaceans. Among the former most commonly reported are: herring; sand eel; sprat and predominantly, capelin. Also eaten are young pollack; cod; whiting and polar cod. Crustaceans known to be eaten include: euphausiid shrimps; prawns; gammarid amphipods and various crabs.

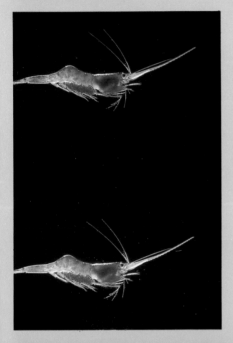

Among oceanic crustaceans eaten (or similar to species eaten) by Atlantic salmon, may be:

Top left: Ephausiid, *Meganyctiphanes*. An inch or so long. Common in northern waters. Important food item of baleen whales.

Middle left: Prawn, *Parapandulus richardi*. Found between 100–200 fathoms. Females carry their eggs on their legs until hatching; after which the young prawns migrate to feed at the surface.

At left: Deep Sea Prawn. *Acanthephyra* sp. The species shown is *c*. $2\frac{3}{4}$ in. long and bears a marked resemblance to the angler's boiled prawn bait. It should be remembered, however, that the creature's vivid red will appear black at depths beyond the reach of daylight.

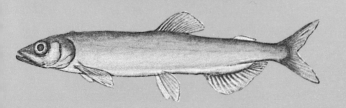

Among fish species, the capelin, *Mallotus villosus*, is known to be a major food item of Atlantic salmon. Although maximum length is said to be about $9\frac{1}{2}$ in., few are longer than 6–7 in.

Sand eel, *Ammodytes tobianus*.

PLATE 3

Helmsdale. Prolific east-flowing Sutherland river.

Towy. A lovely Welsh salmon river that runs into the western end of the Bristol Channel. Famous for its big sea trout.

PLATE 4

Tamar. One of the most beautiful of south-western rivers, it divides Devon and Cornwall and flows into the sea at Plymouth.

Eden. Like the Border Esk, this famous Cumbrian river joins the Solway Firth near Carlisle. Once renowned for its early spring run of big salmon, but now (like so many others) more of a back-end river.

PLATE 5

Spey. One of the greatest of British salmon and sea trout rivers whose spring salmon run has shown a marked decline in recent years.

Lune. A once prolific salmon river flowing into Morecambe Bay. The pool shown is where the salmon were caught at night (see p. 88).

Observation of salmon spawning shows clearly why a gravel bottom is essential. Only small stones can be sucked up by the flapping tail and swept down by the current into position.

Underneath the stones of a redd, salmon eggs lie protected from predators. But they depend on a supply of oxygen flowing through the gravel canopy. Forest thinning can block feeder streams preventing fish from reaching their spawning sites and causing heavy deposits of silt. Silt is also brought down into the stream from land-working on the slopes above. If a redd becomes covered with silt the eggs will not hatch. Today, losses due to this cause must be considerable.

After spawning, most of the cock fish and many of the hens die. But where left to themselves, undisturbed, the salmon eggs lie secure under the gravel. Gradually, provided they can obtain sufficient oxygen, baby salmon take shape inside.

After three or four months the little embryos become alevins—tiny translucent creatures with umbilical sacs hanging beneath their throats.

During the alevin stage of its development a baby salmon lives on the contents of its yolk sac—which contains upwards of a month's rations. And when the yolk sac has been absorbed the alevin becomes a fry.

Now, in company with others, the little salmon is forced to fend for itself, hunting actively for food and slowly acquiring a sort of camouflage in the shape of dark fingermarks along its sides. At this stage of its development it is known as a parr, and in looks is similar to a baby brown trout.

As parr, the tiny salmon feed on fly larvae, nymphs, minute crustacea and other forms of aquatic life, depending on the food supply available. In turn, they are preyed on by a host of enemies. In quiet backwaters the keen-eyed heron lurks like a sentinel at the water's edge—rising at the first hint of danger with its harsh cry of alarm. Feral mink hunt like small, fierce otters; cormorants, mergansers and goosanders dive in the pools, while in the shallower stretches the kingfisher plunge-dives for its living from some overhanging branch. "The secret splendour of the brooks", the poet called it. But it takes its toll of tiny fish.

Among piscatorial predators that sometimes share the water, pike, perch, chub, eels and other coarse species, have all been known to feast on young salmon; but of all the river's predators *salmo*'s cousin, the brown trout, is probably the worst. During one season of research, 134 tags originally attached to salmon parr were taken by freshwater biologists from the stomachs of 20 brown trout ranging in size from nine to thirteen inches long. Substantial evidence of the damage brown trout can cause to a salmon fishery.

When a parr is anything between sixteen months and four or five years old—usually two—certain physiological changes take place that fit the little fish for a new environment. Salt-excreting cells form in the gills, and the scales start to develop a silver coating. When the parr is fully silvered it becomes known as a smolt, a slender fork-tailed, sprat-like little fish about six inches in length. And now, during spring or early summer, in company with descending sea trout smolts, the salmon smolts swim downstream into the saltwater of the river estuary.

This seaward migration is imperative. Few if any rivers contain sufficient food to support a population of fully-grown salmon. Only by going to sea can these fish find enough to eat.

Like sea trout and other fishes that spend part of their lives in the sea and part in fresh water, the salmon when passing between these environments is able to adapt to changes in salinity by adjustments of the physiological processes regulating the water and salt contents of its blood. In salt water, the excess of salts is excreted through the special cells that have formed in the gills.*

In the new, intensely hostile estuarine world, the young salmon face further enemies: skate, cod, seals, porpoises, gulls, shags, pollack, coalfish, bass, congers and many more. But there is no lingering in the shallows. The smolts hurry on towards the rich feeding grounds of the ocean—and they go there in order to grow.

Female Sea Louse above anal fin of fresh-run salmon.

*But see also Young's *The Life of Vertebrates*, Second Edition 1962. "At the hind end of the spinal cord of fishes is a small lump, the urohypophysis. In function it appears to be connected with salt regulation".

A lucky escape! An incoming salmon photographed shortly after it was attacked by a seal close inshore. It wriggled free, and the seal's jaw mark can be seen on the fish's flank just below the dorsal fin.

In the sea, young salmon grow quickly, their growth rate, it is thought, being determined by the amount of food available to them during their first few months. By the end of their first year of migration they may be twenty to thirty times their original weight. After this the growth-rate lessens.

From the examination of fish captured at sea, the salmon's diet consists of large zooplankton organisms such as euphausiids and amphipods, together with capelin, herring, sprats, sand eels, whiting, squid and polycheate worms. And doubtless they eat a lot of other things as well. But it is interesting that according to a research project in Greenland waters, 86 percent of the salmon examined had been feeding on capelin.

Some salmon return to fresh water as grilse: fish of about 3 lb up to 10 lb (usually 4 lb to 6 lb) that have stayed little over one year at sea. Some fish return as "maiden" salmon after a sea-life of two or more years. Some may even return after an absence of four years—as maiden thirty to forty pounders. Indeed, several years may separate the home-coming of fish that left the river together. But at whatever age or weight they return—whether as grilse after one year at sea, or as maiden salmon of two sea years or longer—return they must, since they cannot spawn in salt water.

The recapture of tagged fish offshore indicates that returning salmon arrive from the Atlantic at many different points, but after reaching

SALMON'S HEAD

SEA TROUT'S HEAD

Note the difference in appearance of salmon and sea trout heads. The sea trout usually has a blunter snout with less receding forehead. Its maxillary bone extends beyond a vertical dropped from the rear edge of the eye, whereas the salmon's is level with it. (For other distinguishing characteristics, see *Sea Trout Fishing* pp 22–28.)

coastal waters swim close inshore up or down the coast until they reach their destined rivers.

Although a small percentage explore estuaries other than the ones they left, and ultimately find their way to the spawning redds of strange rivers (Nature's insurance policy at work), the majority return to spawn in the rivers of their birth.

Incoming salmon have a tendency to move from tidal water to fresh water at dusk, but will head straight upstream at any time if the river is in spate.

That salmon can find their way back from the distant ocean to the coast is a staggering feat of navigation, and although it is thought possible that they use the stars, no one is quite certain how they do it. On one point, however, science is assured: experiments have established that once a salmon *reaches* the coast he finds his own particular river by sense of smell. From all other rivers he can detect the odour of his *own* river—the river he left behind when he went down to sea as a smolt.*

Salmon have a very acute sense of smell. They are, for instance, able to detect certain predators by scent. Fish running up a Canadian river have been seen to scatter when a bear put its paw into the water upstream. And it is not without interest to anglers that the odour of human skin can certainly affect salmon. Even when extremely diluted it has caused fish to show alarm reactions lasting for several minutes.

In addition to possessing what is, to us, an almost incredible sense of *smell*, the salmon has excellent *sight*. Beneath the surface in clear water a fish can probably see the approach of a lure a dozen or so yards away. Perhaps much further.

There is no doubt that the salmon can distinguish colour, although to what extent is not known. It has been suggested that they may become colour-blind after their return to freshwater. This seems unlikely. Generally speaking, the colour red when worn by male animals in the breeding season has an important function as a signal: attracting females of the species; repelling other males. Many species bear witness to this. The male salmon—like the male stickleback—turns red in preparation for spawning, presumably to help attract a mate and to warn-off other males. This change of coloration would seem pointless if colour-blindness prevented the others from "reading" the signal.

The sense of *touch* is conveyed by sensitive nerve organs scattered over the skin, particularly around the head and lips.

*Recent research suggests that a salmon navigates from the Atlantic by means of a magnetic indicator situated in the front of the head.

Taste is probably unimportant. Like most fish, the salmon is said not to masticate or chew food, but to gulp it straight down. As discussed later, however, the fish's behaviour when "toying" with and squeezing a worm, makes one suppose that there are exceptions to this.

The sense of *hearing* is made possible by the otoliths in the brain. These enable a fish to align its position in relation to the vertical, and so remain upright. They may also respond to vibrations.

As well as these five senses, the salmon like other fish has a sixth sense made possible by the lateral line. All the functions of this line are not known, but its main purpose is monitoring the flow of current passing round the fish. It may also be used to detect obstacles, by picking up the reflection of water-waves in the way of an echo-sounder. So, too, it may detect vibrations caused by the movements of other fish.

The lower the position of an animal in the evolutionary scale, the higher its pain threshold. In the fish this is very high indeed. A recent scientific enquiry has announced that fish can feel pain. This may be so. But commonsense based on observation dictates that there is no comparison between pain as we know it and pain as may be experienced by a hooked fish.

Most interesting of all from an angler's point of view is that the incoming salmon bring their rations with them. Having stopped feeding during the return from sea, they enter a river with sufficient food reserve in their tissues to sustain them for upwards of twelve months, in addition to supplying the food necessary for their developing milt and ova. They arrive, therefore, in a state of fasting and, during the whole of their stay in freshwater, have no need to hunt for food.

This is not to imply that food items are never taken. Sometimes they are. (After all, our lures are sometimes taken, and they are not the only "creatures" in the river that move differently from inanimate debris!) Like many people, I have observed occasional salmon sucking-in surface flies and nymphs—in addition to grabbing parr and small trout, and a host of other items. There are examples on record. For instance, as quoted in my book *Sea Trout Fishing*, Sir Richard Levinge's letter to *The Field*, which describes an experience on the River Boyne during the mayfly hatch:

An apparently great trout was rising steadily to mayfly all of one day, just out of casting reach from the bank. The following afternoon I came back to the river, equipped with breast waders to find the fish still sucking down mayflies.

I waded out close enough to cover it and was, I remember, disappointed to find it was only a salmon of 6 lb. Not only was its stomach packed full, enough to fill two cupped hands, with mayfly nymph and dun, but it also had a broken cast and a bedraggled mayfly in its gullet.

In a previous year, an eminent Dublin surgeon enjoyed a great evening with the mayfly on the same beat, taking two trout of 8 lb. and 4 lb. and a salmon of 12 lb. The following year on the Deel, a tributary of the Boyne, I saw a large salmon, 15 lb. or more, sucking down mayfly as hard as it could go.

But if feeding is defined as "the taking of nourishment in order to sustain life", such examples, apart from their isolation, do not turn migrating adult salmon into active feeders.

A moment's thought places the matter in perspective. While in the sea, the fish feed greedily. Few rivers can provide such meals. Many of the smaller, spate rivers, rocky, barren and acidic, hold barely enough food to support a tiny resident population of diminutive brown trout, let alone an adult migratory population with normal appetites. If nature had not removed their need for food during the spawning run, these returning fry-devouring fish would long-ago have exterminated themselves.

The salmon's abstinence from food while waiting to spawn is of great significance to the angler, and this will be followed up in the next chapter. For the time being we shall complete the salmon's life-cycle and glance at some of his behaviour after the return from sea.

Not all salmon face the same period of fasting, since they do not enter freshwater all at the same time. In what seems to be one of Nature's "insurance policies", there is a twelve-month staggering of salmon arrivals. During every month of the year, fresh salmon are running into one or other of our rivers, and whereas fish that run during winter and early spring wait in freshwater for many months before spawning, others spawn only a comparatively short time after their late summer or autumn arrival.

As with all fish, water temperature is a critical factor in the life of the salmon, since change of temperature affects reproduction as well as growth rate and respiration. Salmon (*stenotherms*) will mate only in cold water, hence their winter spawning season. As distinct from *eurytherms* (carp and others), which spawn only during the summer months when the water is warm.

Water temperature is one of the factors that govern salmon river migration, important in the downstream migration of smolts and the upstream migration of adult fish on their return from sea. Salmon do not adapt easily to a sudden drop in temperature. Water temperature affects a fish's metabolism. Enzymes do not work so efficiently in cold water. Fish returning to some of the big salmon rivers in January and February are inhibited from running far upstream if the water is too cold, especially if there is any obstacle to be passed. Conversely, if the weather is mild, considerable distances may be covered—always provided there is sufficient height of water to encourage a run.

Hitherto, the complex problem of early season salmon migration in rivers has been somewhat controversial. Many people have queried the importance of water temperature. But now, thanks to the research of Dr Christopher Harpley, Fisheries Officer, North, of the North-West Water Authority, together with the records of other scientists who have studied this problem, the matter is beyond reasonable doubt:

> Extremes of water temperature certainly have a limiting effect on salmon migration. Although salmon will enter a river from the estuary at a temperature as low as 1° C. (34° F.), they will not run far upstream until the temperature has risen above 5° C. (41° F.). Between this temperature and a temperature of 20° C. (68° F.), their movements are not affected. When the temperature rises beyond the upper limit, movement is again inhibited and fish will lie doggo in the pools. There is no evidence that air temperature plays any part in salmon migration. It is water temperature alone that affects this movement, provided light intensity and water levels are congenial.

It is interesting to compare these conclusions with those of Arthur Oglesby who, in his fine book *Salmon*, writes with day-to-day experience of his own beat on the River Tweed:

> There is no doubt that a mild spell in January induces many fresh fish to run into our more noted salmon rivers. If the weather stays mild and water temperatures rise correspondingly, the fish will tend to run up fast. If a cold spell either continues or intervenes, it has a slowing-down effect on running salmon. The old rule about warmer water making the fish run faster, is a good old basic; and the knowledge of these facts often enables the angler to intercept a run of fish on a particular beat of the river; always provided, of course, that he has access. Let us look at the Tweed for examples.

In a normal year, it was almost unknown for fresh fish to be as far upstream as Makerstoun during February. Beats below Kelso, and down to Lennel, were having the cream of the sport. Then, since 1963, we have had a succession of comparatively mild winters. The beats at Lennel have had a lean time; whereas those around Floors, and higher upstream, have been taking fish earlier than ever before. I regularly fish the Upper Hendersyde water, immediately below Kelso . . . I have taken this beat regularly during the first two weeks of February. Examination of the records over the past ten years, during what is considered to be the most productive period, show that sometimes salmon have not come up in any number if there has been a cold spell in January; and that the bulk have gone through if January has been mild . . . I recall that when I was on this same beat during the bitter February of 1963, there was hardly a fish in the river. For the most part the river was an ice rink; but I was fortunate enough to have access to the same beat during the third week of March, by which time the thaw had arrived and our pools were full of fresh-run fish.

Water temperature also plays a major part in the angler's approach to his sport. As the temperature changes so, too, does the salmon's behaviour in relation to a lure. In early spring, when the water is down in the thirties and low forties (Fahrenheit), salmon tend to accept only a large lure fished deep. After mid-April or thereabouts when the water warms up to, say, fifty degrees and above, the fish are intent mainly on a small lure fished close to the surface. There may be other reasons for these changes in behaviour; but whatever else affects them, the salmon's reactions to a lure undoubtedly coincide with changes in water temperature.

But I anticipate. These matters are discussed more fully later on.

With reference to migration, there are factors other than water height and temperature that affect the salmon's upstream movements. Many rivers have stretches beyond which for no accountable reason the fish, for a time, refuse to run. And sometimes places where, during certain months, migrating fish refuse to stop. On a northern river I fished regularly for several years there was a pool in which, during the early part of the season, I failed to hook a single fish.

"You won't", said the local oracle, whose opinion I sought. "That pool never holds fish until August."

Nor did it. Fish came up into the pool through the fast shallows below and ran straight through. I would sit on the bank and watch them. But during and after August it proved one of the best taking pools in the beat.

The reason for this curious behaviour? Only the fish themselves could answer that. An examination of the pool in low water, and comparison of water temperatures, offered me nothing in the way of clues.

As an enigma it reflected a pool on my own little river in the days when we had fine runs of fish. Neither sea trout nor salmon would stay in this pool until about mid-season. Before that they would run through and lie in the pools above; in fact, as holding water the next pool upstream was one of our best. After mid-season, however, that hitherto virtually empty pool downstream would start to fill up with fish. By autumn they would be lying there in shoals. This was no isolated instance, it happened every year. A reminder of the mystery that forever surrounds our migratory fishes—and of how little we really understand about them.

Wye salmon leaping a weir. Fish will not jump obstacles at night or in poor daylight.

During their long journeys up river towards the spawning redds, driven on by a ripening sexual urge, salmon force their way past the most formidable obstacles. And what they cannot swim over they try to jump. As an early writer noted:

In spawning time, when they repair from the sea up the river, scarce anything can stop their progress. They have been seen to leap up cataracts or precipices many yards high.

It was not without good reason that the Romans dubbed them "The Leapers", but even less than a couple of hundred years ago the question of how *Salmo* managed to perform the leap was hotly argued. According to one school of thought:

The salmon will throw herself over cataracts or waterfalls by taking her tail in her mouth and bending her backbone downwards, till the letting it go all at once gives her strength enough to throw herself over the cataract at a leap.

But a more astute observer wrote:

I very much question the truth of this fact, as to the *manner*—namely, the taking hold of her tail, for neither does the salmon's mouth, which is small and weak, nor the tail, which is large and slippery, allow the thing in itself. But that they *will* leap, or throw themselves out of the water perpendicularly is certain, and I affirm that I have seen a very large salmon leap as near as I could judge five or six feet high—and some say they leap much higher. But so high as mentioned I can assert from my own knowledge.

He was right. The leaping of salmon has often been exaggerated, but the truth is sufficiently dramatic. A perpendicular leap of twelve feet has been measured over the Orrin Falls in Scotland.

But that early writer with his tail-in-the-mouth theory may be forgiven his mistake. In much more recent times, we were nearly as far from the truth. Until a few years ago it was taken for granted that a salmon needs to start his leap deep down, perhaps from the very bottom of the pool below a waterfall.

Having watched comatose salmon lying in a pool suddenly "come to life", aim at an angle of about 75° and come shooting up out of the water, it never occurred to me to think they did otherwise when faced with an obstruction to be jumped. It came as a surprise when I learned that this is *not* how *Salmo* jumps his fences. Instead, having first assessed the height to be cleared—by swimming to the surface and looking at it—he approaches the take-off point in a quite leisurely way. Then, with sudden and tremendously powerful strokes of his tail, he makes his leap from just below the surface. Jumping salmon, it seems, aim at the division between light and shade at the top of an obstruction, and so stop leaping at dusk or when the sky becomes heavily overcast.

Casual observers, or anyone interested in river improvements, should remember that although the salmon's take-off run is from only a shallow depth, the overall depth of the pool must still be sufficient to dissipate turbulence caused by the waterfall, and so reduce the entrained air: i.e., air bubbles, which otherwise would lower the water density and make it difficult for the salmon's tail to "get a grip".

By November many of the salmon have arrived in or close to those parts of the river, or the feeder streams, where they are going to mate. And from then until about mid-January most of the spawning takes place.

Now, with the late autumn leaves drifting overhead, the salmon's silver streamlined beauty has quite vanished. The once sleek females are dark, almost black, with bulging bellies; the males rust-red, their heads ugly and misshapen, with huge pointed kypes curving upwards from the lower jaws.

After a period of exploratory wandering, the female prepares the spawning bed. Meanwhile, the male fish waits nearby, ready to drive off any intruders. Eventually, perhaps after days of preparation, the male joins the female on the bed . . .

Despite all his efforts to protect his nuptials, the cock salmon sometimes fails to do so. Male parr frequently haunt the redds. Precocious little creatures, at the *moment critique* they will often nip in behind the adult male fish—and fertilize the eggs themselves!

It has been found that up to 75 percent of male parr become sexually mature and it seems certain that they make a substantial contribution to the successful fertilization of the eggs. This remarkable fact may be another form of biological insurance, since the parr's ejection of milt goes deep into the gravel; whereas, in a strong current, some of the adult's milt may get dispersed.

By the time spawning is finished the salmon are emaciated and very weak. These spent fish, or "kelts", are little more than two-thirds of their original weight. The once juicy pink flesh is pale and flaccid, and often enough their hollow-flanked and ragged-finned bodies are smothered in fungus.

For reasons unexplained (except that, knowing something of Nature's cunning, we might expect it) the surviving females greatly outnumber the surviving males. Very few males spawn more than once. And it is interesting to note that these survivors do not all leave the river

A well-mended ♀ salmon kelt. Note the fish's "parallel" appearance; the size of the head in comparison with the diminished body; the sunken belly just forward of the vent. Another sign of a kelt, hidden of course in this picture, is the probable presence of gill maggots.

together—even when seemingly able to do so—but in staggered order over a period of several months. Again, as with the incoming fish, Nature seems to insure against total disaster. Were all fish to enter a river during the same week or month, some catastrophe such as river blockage, drought or disease, might wipe out a complete annual run. As it is, those fish still at sea destined to make their homecoming during a later month, or even a later year, form an insurance against total loss.

And so it is even with the "mended" kelts that are heading seawards. Should some meet with disaster—perhaps seals or porpoises lurking at the river mouth—there are others to follow, and there are the fish that have gone ahead.

Those salmon that regain the rich feeding grounds of the ocean recover their condition surprisingly quickly, and it is strange that on their subsequent return to fresh water for a second spawning, their fat content is as high as or, in some cases, even higher than that of virgin fish.

Very few salmon return for a third spawning, and only an exceptional fish survives to spawn a fourth time.

*   *   *

This, then, is *Salmo*—the creature we propose to catch on rod and line.

Brief though it is, the foregoing account holds sufficient clues to make anyone suspect that this is not going to be easy. Indeed, one might imagine that after reading it even the village idiot would scratch his head—and think salmon fishing a rather weird if harmless form of insanity.

On approaching freshwater the salmon stops feeding and will not feed again until it returns to salt water as a spent fish or kelt, which may be six months to a year or more later. Fortunately, this phenomenon makes little difference to the angler as salmon, for some inexplicable reason, take anglers' lures into their mouths although not feeding.

Dr Derek Mills, *Salmon and Trout*, 1971

All logic points to a loss of appetite or nausea which Nature induces for the benefit of the species and adjusts for in her special way. To this moment it is beyond our understanding.

Lee Wulff, *The Atlantic Salmon*, 1983

II
The Fish

PART TWO: TAKING BEHAVIOUR

Description

Let us imagine for a moment that *Salmo* was a species entirely unknown to you, and that I had invited you to come and fish with me for this strange creature. Our conversation might well take these lines:

"This salmon", you ask. "Is it worth catching?"

"Oh, yes", I say. "Indeed it is."

"A strong fighter?"

"Very strong."

"Good to eat?"

"Most excellent to eat."

"You tell me they return from sea to spawn in freshwater, and that we fish for them on their way up the river."

"That is so."

"On rod and line?"

"Yes."

"Splendid! Now, let me see . . ."

And at this point, in order to learn what sort of bait or lure to use, you would undoubtedly pose the one really important question:

"What does this salmon *eat* in freshwater?"

And I reply: "Nothing."

"Nothing! You mean it doesn't *feed*?"

"That is precisely what I mean."

Well—after this little exchange you might be excused for thinking me a lunatic. After all, how on earth can anyone expect to catch such a fish on rod and line?

And yet that is the problem confronting every salmon angler, for what in effect he is trying to do is to hook a fish that, while lying in the river

39

waiting to spawn, lives on the supply of nourishment stored in its tissues and has no need of food. What is surprising is not that salmon are hard to catch, but that any are caught at all.

After all, why should this non-feeding fish *ever* take? Often of course he doesn't. But what we usually mean by a "taker" is a fish prepared to accept the particular fly we happen to be using at the time. If we catch nothing we say there were no takers. But is this necessarily true? Far from it. There is nothing to suggest there were no fish in that water prepared to take some other offering: worm, spinner, prawn or shrimp, let alone another type of fly.

Anyone who has not done so, but has sufficient interest to experiment, should obtain the fishing on a stretch of water clear enough for salmon to be observed, and fish it as and when conditions permit day after day, week after week, with all sorts and manner of lures. He will soon find out for himself how capricious these fish can be.

But from experience, having done this for many years on water of my own, I think it unlikely that more than a small percentage of fish are potential takers at any given time. To the chance of encountering one of this small number can be added the vagaries of the salmon's response to the multitudinous lures we have available, on all of which a fish may be caught, but from which we can choose only one at a time. We talk of fishing "bait", but there is little similarity between the appearance of, say, a Devon minnow and a mepps, or between a Kynoch killer and a bunch of lobworms. To this, add the number of different ways each type of bait or lure may be presented.

To all this can be added the likelihood that each salmon is an individual with his own characteristics. Furthermore, that each river breeds its own strain of fish, among which a small number of wanderers from other rivers appear each season. And then, on top of this strange creature's unpredictability, if we try to take into account his differences in reaction caused by weather, temperature, height of water and time of year, as well as the length of time he has been in the river, we may grasp the magnitude of the task confronting anyone who sets out to catch him with rod and line—let alone has the temerity to write about his behaviour!

A hundred years ago, George Kelson, an experienced, puzzled but honest old salmon-fisher, wrote:

There is no accounting for the humour of a salmon. You do not know when he will take it into his head to rise. The angler must make up his mind to have many blank days . . . and never be put out by failure.

Well—despite all the books that have been written since then and despite all our fine theories, we are not much further forward today. Admittedly, modern tackle and techniques have made salmon fishing more refined. Certainly they have made it easier. The multiplier and fixed-spool reels with nylon lines have revolutionized spinning. Fast-sinking lines have improved our chances when we fish big flies in early spring. The floating line and small fly—or "greased-line" technique—has made the fly rod fun to fish with even in the height of summer. But for all our advance in tackle and technique, we still don't know why or when a salmon will take our lure. And in this context, to avoid tedious repetition, I use the term "lure" to cover any of the spinners, plugs, prawns, shrimps, worms and other baits we offer salmon, including the so-called fly—"so-called", because nobody knows what this thing we call a salmon-fly represents. As to what the salmon think it is, we are as much in the dark as old George Kelson long ago.

Nevertheless, salmon *will* sometimes take a lure. This was discovered hundreds of years ago when, thinking that the returning salmon fed avidly like trout, the few anglers who fished for salmon used similar lures and baits to catch them with. And, although in very small numbers, catch them they did.

At the time all this seemed natural enough, but as soon as it was realized that, on their arrival in the rivers salmon had stopped feeding, the angler's approach changed dramatically: it was no longer a question of why salmon did not take a lure more frequently, but why they should ever take one at all. A riddle that has baffled everybody ever since.

Over the years, various reasons for this anomalous behaviour have been suggested. Most popular of these is that the salmon takes from *habit*: the feeding habit he has indulged during his life at sea, and also, perhaps, during his earlier river life as a parr. This habit, it is thought, is triggered-off by the appearance of something that not only seems to be alive but resembles food the fish has been eating in the past: flies and fly larvae when the fish was a parr; worms, small fish, crustacea and other marine organisms eaten during his year or two in seawater—some of which are reflected in the baits and lures we offer salmon, and which salmon sometimes accept.

It seems a logical reason and, at least in part, it has my support. But although I think that *habit* is a good working hypothesis, it does not account for all the variations in salmon taking-behaviour.

I suggest that in order to discover the salmon's taking motive, we must first find out *how* he takes—and the answers to that are staring at us from the river. "Answers" in the plural, because no single answer fits all the facts. As I have learned during many hours spent watching salmon, a fish may take in any of several very different ways.

The mistake of thinking there is only one taking response, and that the fish intends to seize a lure firmly every time he makes an approach is quite common, and has been expressed as follows by a well-known angling writer:

> I do not believe that a salmon ever goes for a fly, or bait for that matter, without having a firm intention of taking it. And by "taking it", I mean catching hold of it in its mouth and carrying it back to its lie . . . once he takes it in his mouth he has done everything that he can do to offer himself up to you. If you now fail either to hook him or to land him the blame is yours, not his. There is, to my mind, no such thing as a fish which "comes short" or which is "only playing".

I have a high regard for the man who wrote that passage; he is a good writer and has given much to the sport. But theories are barren if not married to experiment. If he had shared some of my observations of salmon taking-behaviour he would, I am sure, have qualified this.

Within each species there must be an enormous pool of behaviour that enables the species to adapt to changing conditions, although only a minute part of this behaviour repertoire is called into play at any time. What behaviour pattern in the non-feeding salmon is elicited by, say, the sudden appearance of a small tube-fly is a matter of conjecture. But, as we shall see later, this pattern can differ, and differ dramatically.

What I have seen of their behaviour has convinced me that *salmon have more than one way of taking a lure*—and that more fish react and move to a lure, without taking it, than many anglers realize. Sometimes, a fish really *does* "come short"—that is to say, approaches a lure with *no immediate intention of seizing it*. Furthermore, he may do so time after time if given the opportunity. As suggested later, if this behaviour is suspected such a fish may sometimes be *induced* to take.

Salmon observation indicates that there are at least six different types of "take", for which (in rough order of likelihood) the following I think are responsible:

1. Feeding Habit—Strong.
2. Aggression.
3. Inducement.
4. Curiosity.
5. Irritation.
6. Playfulness.

Diagrams illustrating this taking behaviour will be found on pp. 234–237

These are the names I have given them. The reader may prefer to coin his own.

1. *Feeding Habit.* By far the most usual take, motivated I think by the salmon's feeding response as already described. The fish moves to the lure, sucks it in, closes his mouth on it and returns with it to his lie. This form of take will be discussed at length in the chapters on fly fishing. All that need be said here is that the salmon's behaviour is very gentle but very positive; provided the angler *does not strike*, the fish is nearly always well hooked.

2. *Aggression.* "Got you!" The "*Crunch*" take. An instant and seemingly automatic reaction to a lure that appears unexpectedly inside the fish's territory.

Judging by what I have seen in pools where fish are not overcrowding, a salmon's territory is an area with a radius of two to three feet all round extending like an inverted truncated cone towards the surface.

Usually, a *Crunch* take occurs when a big sunk lure suddenly and unexpectedly invades this territory deep down; but there are exceptions. Sometimes a fish, moving with great speed to the surface, will seize a lure the moment it hits the water. The salmon has excellent vision, and I have seen a fish flash up from deep water to grab an unweighted prawn almost before it actually landed. A typical take of this sort occurs sometimes when a spinner, caught in overhanging branches, is jerked free, falls vertically into the water on a slack line and is taken at once. I have seen a salmon in shallow water instantly grab a tiny trout-fly that landed immediately above his nose.

It is the sudden *overhead* appearance of a lure that seems to trigger off this crash-surface take: the fish has not watched the lure's gradual approach as the angler fished his way slowly down the pool. For this reason I think it is sometimes better, when conditions permit, to fish a salmon or sea trout pool by "backing-up" rather than fishing down in the usual way (see p. 298). Time and again at night I have caught sea trout when backing-up a pool, straight after fishing it down without an offer. And often by day I have caught salmon in the same way.

Sometimes of course backing-up a pool is impracticable owing to wad-

43

ing difficulty, or the uneven nature of the river bank. Nor is it sensible to back-up a pool when fish are lying close-in and may be disturbed by the angler before his lure appears. But backing-up is a useful ploy to remember, for when conditions are suitable it may result in provoking a fish to take: a fish that might otherwise not have been caught.

Like the take ascribed to *Feeding Habit*, the *Crunch* take usually results in a well-hooked fish. But how different these takes are. The contrast between them—the gentleness of the former, the aggressiveness of the latter—is beautifully illustrated in this account written by that fine salmon angler Dr Jimmy Skene of Windermere:

> While spinning the River Eden, on a beat very familiar to me, I threw my minnow to the far side of some streamy water. I declared at the time that a salmon saw it coming and came out of the water to meet it! But perhaps I exaggerated, and the bait did just hit the surface before the surge of the salmon engulfed it. Never had I seen such a sudden and savage assault.
>
> Some little time later, during the early summer, I was again casting on the self-same run, but this time with a fly. I fished steadily downstream—with no success, until, becoming bored I tucked my rod under my armpit, found my cigarettes and matches in my pocket and lit a cigarette.
>
> Recovering my rod, I positioned myself for a fresh cast—only to find my fly stuck in the bottom. Or so I thought, until a salmon moved away! Like its predecessor, it was very well hooked, and duly landed.

Two salmon caught from the same pool, but what a gulf in their taking-behaviour!

A dramatic example of the salmon's ability to seize an object *above* the surface was witnessed recently by Peter Curtis on the River Feshie:

> I was lying on a rock just below Feshie Bridge watching a salmon. He was large by Feshie standards—twelve pounds, perhaps—lying some four feet down and quietly keeping station in the smooth draw, which empties out of the bubbling pot below the bridge. The water was gin clear and I could see every scale on his grey back and silver flank.
>
> As I watched, racking my brains as to what means I might employ to apprehend such a prize, the fish suddenly thrust forwards and upwards with his powerful tail. And then, with his nose clearing the surface by a good eighteen inches, came straight up out of the water

All-round sportsman Brigadier J. H. P. Curtis M.C. of Inshriach
with a sixteen-pounder caught on his beat of the River Spey.

at an angle of about forty-five degrees, opened his big white mouth
and engulfed a small sedge-fly, which had been hovering overhead.
Down he went again; this time into the deeper part of the pool. And
there he stayed. Whether he caught sight of me when he rose to the
fly, I don't know. But watch for him though I did, he never returned
to his former lie.

3. *Inducement.* There seems to be no direct connection between the *Induced* take and the usual, more positive, "feeding response". It is more like a reaction to something that (presumably thought to be alive), is "getting away": some erstwhile prey species escaping across or towards the surface, often almost at the water's edge. Like the kitten that chases after an "escaping" ball of wool jerked across the lawn, the fish is impelled to follow. Although it is usual for the fish to refuse, there are many exceptions. There was an example of this recently when a friend of mine was deliberately pulling a worm with little movements across the current, trying to tempt a salmon that had already followed the bait as it was being drawn in. After several excursions the fish took, turned away with the worm, hooked itself in the scissors—and came to the net five minutes later. This struck me as a most intelligent piece of fishing. Had the bait not been manoeuvred in such a way, I am sure that salmon would not have been caught.

It is commonplace for a fish to follow close behind a lure, taking only when this attractant is on the point of being withdrawn from the water. Sometimes as a lure swims across the pool a salmon will follow and make several passes at it, swinging right round each time as though to intercept, but at the last moment turning away. I have heard it said that when this happens the fish has accidentally missed the lure. But I don't believe that for a fish to *miss* grabbing something he really wants can happen often. Such a mistake must, surely, be rare.

Why, then, does the fish not take the lure?

It may of course be our own fault. There may be something in the lure's behaviour that destroys the illusion—some breakdown in attractiveness; in life-like movement—but in most cases I think it much more probable that the fish is not sufficiently motivated. (After all, as already suggested, a salmon's refusal to take should cause no astonishment. What is surprising is not the fish that doesn't take, but the fish that does!)

Sometimes a salmon can be induced to take by casting upstream, or squarely across the river, according to the strength of current, allowing the lure to sink and then, as it comes over the fish's lie, drawing it up quite smartly in a nymph-like manner towards the surface. As described in Chapter XIII, I have caught salmon like this when fishing a very small fly on floating line. The same chapter also includes a description of salmon reaction to the various ways of presenting a dry fly. These methods, I feel sure, *induce* a fish to take.

4. *Curiosity.* "What *is* this?" Here there seems to be no aggression, no chasing after an escaping prey. It is all so gentle. The fish just *nudges*

the lure. All the angler feels is an infuriating little tweak—as he does when the prawn gets nipped, or loses its whiskers, or the fly gets pulled a foot or two, before the line goes slack. The fish that behaves like this is never well hooked, if hooked at all. The angler, who often blames himself and wonders what he has done wrong in failing to hook such a fish, can spare himself the hair-shirt. There is nothing he could have done. The only possible mistake he may make after meeting such a fish is to rest it.

Occasionally, as illustrated by the incident described in the Introduction, if one persists, this salmon may be goaded into a more positive reaction, so that the take of Curiosity becomes a take of Aggression.

Two of a kind. At first glance, alike as two peas. But a closer look soon reveals differences. They represent about ten percent of the fish present at the time they were caught. What induced them to take? Or, to put it another way, what prevented the other ninety per cent from doing so? (See the Goldsborough Hypothesis, p. 59)

47

5. *Irritation*. This is the take of a fish that seems to become more and more agitated as the lure approaches down the pool—until, finally, he has a snatch. Sometimes he will grab it first time past; sometimes not until it has crossed his lie a number of times. He appears to attack the lure and, to the angler, such a take seems very definite. But, as I have seen, a fish will often take when heading downstream, turning on the lure after it has passed him, and in consequence is nearly always poorly hooked. I think the lure is nipped with the very front of the mouth.

There is no mistaking this fish. You feel a sudden snatch at the lure; a yard or two of line is drawn out, and then goes limp. The weight of the fish is seldom if ever felt.

I have an idea that a fish sometimes reacts like this when the lure is being fished too slowly down the pool—that is to say, the *angler* is fishing too slowly, by moving too short a distance between casts. I once watched a salmon becoming more and more agitated during an experiment when a friend was purposely fishing like this. Eventually, after the lure had reached the salmon's lie and crossed it several times, the salmon swung round with the current, seized the lure and darted downstream with it for a yard or two before blowing it out again. My friend, who had been aware only of the sudden snatch at his line, was downcast, thinking himself incompetent to have missed hooking the fish. Having seen what had happened, I was able to reassure him. As I am happy to reassure any of my readers who may, with a nagging sense of loss, recall a similar experience. The fish that takes like this is rarely hooked—and even more rarely landed.

6. *Playfulness*. To suggest that a salmon may take a lure for fun probably invites ridicule from the traditionalists. Nevertheless, I can only describe such behaviour as being "playful" because I have watched some extraordinary salmon capers, and no other explanation makes much sense.

In fact, if my observations have been accurate, the fish that behaves like this doesn't really *take* at all; he simply sucks the lure into his opened mouth, holds it there on a cushion of water and then blows it out again. And, as I say, I think he does this for fun.

The objection may be made that my concept of a fish "enjoying" himself is unduly anthropomorphic. All the same, this is what I believe. I believe, furthermore, that a good deal of the seemingly pointless leaping and sloshing and splashing about that goes on in the pools is a form of play, which the salmon "enjoys". And I think there are probably many other things he enjoys doing, too.

48

To the behavioural scientist for whom all animal characteristics must be interpreted in terms of survival value, my views are almost certainly anathema. So be it. I will content myself by suggesting that territory, a mate, hunting ability and so on, cannot be the only essentials in animal life any more than in our own. Play, humour, enjoyment, in however primitive a form, must surely have their survival value too, for animals as indeed for us.

Much of my working life, while researching my wildlife films, has been spent observing animals—so much of whose behaviour has seemed to reflect my own that, when describing it, I do not shirk the use of subjective terms. My three Labradors, when not working or sleeping, spend most of their time romping about and playing with simple toys with every evidence of enjoyment. After their long day is done, the cawing rooks that swirl and tumble across the sky like smuts blown from a chimney in the dusk, are surely enjoying a brief playtime—before swooping down into the silence of their winter roost. And that family of ravens doing those breathtaking aerobatics on the flank of the crag behind my cottage, zooming upwards in tight v-formation, before breaking away and curling downwards in a plume of black—can anyone really think that those birds are not "enjoying" themselves?

And if, as I believe, birds and mammals experience (however crudely by our standards) a sense of fun, why not fish? Yes, I know. Fish are a much lower order of animals. But what of that? It was once claimed that all animals were mere reflex automata, slaves of the outside world. But as one of the world's greatest zoologists, has said: "Things are not so simple . . . an animal's behaviour must be controlled from within as well as from the outside." And there can be little doubt that he is right. Thus, the concept of piscatorial individuality containing in addition to a sense of danger a sense of playfulness, albeit extremely remote from that of the higher orders, is not at all unlikely.

An old work-mate of mine, Michael Kendall of the B.B.C. Natural History Unit, a fine naturalist and highly-skilled observer, has told me of some interesting fish behaviour he witnessed while working at the London Zoo. Over a period of six years he spent many hours watching "Clarissa", the famous 44 lb carp caught in 1952 by my friend Richard Walker and which lived in the aquarium for nineteen years. In his own words, Mike relates how this great fish seemed frequently to be "thoroughly enjoying herself":

One example of play-behaviour, often seen, was when she would swim round in mid-water intercepting and sucking-in a morsel of meat, then blowing it out again. She would do this repeatedly, always in a very leisurely and contemplative manner, seeming to "enjoy" the slow rhythm of the "game". Sometimes she would spend some time snapping at the air bubbles from the aerator, flicking from one bubble to another in a continuous movement, as though playing with them. Regularly she would have a game with one of her keepers, rising to the surface and then, with her mouth wide open and right out of the water, thrusting forward to push and suck the hand that fed her. Over all the years I watched her the impression she gave me was one of playfulness. I know this sounds far-fetched, but she seemed to know when she was being watched and appeared sometimes to "put on an act", to be swaggering and showing-off. That fish, I am convinced, was "having fun" and enjoying herself hugely.

Some of Clarissa's antics bear an uncanny resemblance to *Salmo*'s behaviour in the river. Whatever his place in the hierachy *Salmo*, of all creatures, is one of the most astonishing. And anyone ignorant of it will know why by the end of this book. Meanwhile, those of my readers who still doubt *Salmo*'s capacity for play may care to digest the following blow-by-blow report of a droll encounter between a salmon comedienne and Fred J. Taylor.

I was lying on a high, steep-to river bank in midsummer, watching a hen salmon who, judging by her recent behaviour, looked to be a potential taker. On the opposite bank, slightly upstream of me, with his rod and a tin of worms—Fred.

Now, of all the worm fishers I know, Fred is one of the most skilful, and on this occasion was on peak form. He couldn't see the fish, of course, so was casting to instructions: throwing the worm upstream with unfailing accuracy to just the right point from which it could float downstream, sinking as it went, and finish by drifting a few inches from the bottom right past the salmon's nose.

The river was low with very little current, so that each cast was quite a lengthy business. In that crystal-clear water I could see the worm as it came drifting down—and every movement of the fish. She was lying straight down below me in about six feet of water a yard or two out from the bank.

Fred had been working on this fish for nearly an hour. Each time down, as the worm drifted towards her, the salmon showed signs of agitation: the pectoral fins would start to quiver, the fish give tiny shuddering movements . . . then, at the last moment, just as the worm seemed likely to hit her on the nose, she would sidestep and let it go wriggling past. Sometimes it looked as though she purposely contrived to let the worm make contact—so that it slid along her flank.

This pantomime continued for cast after cast. Fred was quite happy, sitting half on the bank with his feet in the water, throwing the worm out and letting the gentle current strip line off the reel spool while I gave him a running commentary on what was happening in the river. Which was very little—until all of a sudden, as the worm floated down yet again, doing from what I could see exactly what it had done before, the fish swam a yard or so upstream and stopped it.

She did this by opening her mouth and hanging there, slightly tail down, with the worm cushioned, as it were, in front of her. Presumably she held it in position by puffing at it. Even if he had realized what was happening, Fred had no chance of hooking that fish. Never once did she close her mouth.

Fred felt no movement on his line because from the moment the salmon intercepted his bait she had been drifting backwards tail first with the current, her white mouth open, the worm still positioned just ahead.

And then very quickly, far quicker than I can describe it, came the "one-hundred-and-eighty" throw. Still keeping the worm glued to her nose the fish turned a complete figure-of-eight and then stood on her tail, bolt upright, like a seal with a ball. After this, she swivelled round and round two or three times, still upright, finishing the act by blowing the worm away and sinking slowly back to her lie.

While this was going on I had been speechless. Across the river, Fred was winding-in preparatory to another cast.

"Did you feel anything?" I shouted.

He shook his head.

"*Nothing?*"

"Well . . . I *did* feel a little tremor." He looked up. "Why?"

"Fred", I said. "You're not going to believe this. But . . ."

Fred listened in silence. When I had finished he just sat there, shaking his head.

"Well . . ." he said at last. Well . . .!" What he said after that was expressive, but not so expressive as the way he said it. He sat there for quite a long time, muttering and shaking his head.

Now, what do you make of that fish? Does its behaviour qualify as a "take"? I think it does, and I would call it the "Playful" take. After all, if that pirouetting hen salmon wasn't *playing* with the worm, what the devil *was* she doing? The extraordinary thing about it was that she did it with no tightening of the line. All Fred felt was "a little tremor". And that from one of the most sensitive worm anglers I know. How often, I wonder, does something of the sort happen while we are fishing?

Fred and I tried for that fish again next day. I took another friend along with me to watch her give a repeat performance. But of course she didn't!

*   *   *

In attempting to categorize salmon taking-behaviour in the six ways listed above I am almost certainly guilty of over-simplification. These cannot, I feel sure, be the only ways in which a salmon may take a lure. Nor is it likely that my six examples are always so clear-cut in practice. Inevitably, there must be some blurring at the edges; some overlap of behaviour.

But although my interpretation of this behaviour may be questionable, there is one point about which I am in no doubt: a salmon does not take a lure for one reason alone. This to the angler is very important, because if he believes it he will spare himself a great deal of anguish. As I know from the frequency with which I hear people discussing it, many an angler, exasperated by the number of fish that tweak his lure, wonders in desperation what he has done wrong and how on earth he has failed to hook them.

Compounding his misery, angling writers have suggested that failure is due to faulty presentation. And of course at times it may be. But I maintain that far more often it is nothing of the sort. Nineteen times out of twenty when a salmon nips or tweaks or nudges a lure, it is not the behaviour of the fisherman that is to blame, but the behaviour of the fish. The frustrated and baffled angler can take heart. As suggested in a later chapter, he can stop tormenting himself over whether he should have struck. A salmon that behaves like this is almost impossible to hook, for the simple reason that almost never is the hook inside the mouth.

Confusion surrounding the general concept of salmon taking behaviour stems from the belief (already quoted) that every time a salmon approaches a lure he intends to seize it firmly and return with it to his lie. This I know to be a fallacy. I have watched salmon nibble lures, tweak them with a shake of the head, pull them, nip them, suck them in and blow them out again, toy with them, nudge them and even roll on them. Such fish are "twitchers".

Dr David Goldsborough double-Spey casting in a strong wind on Upper Floors, River Tweed. The picture illustrates the *safety* of this casting method, as described in Chapter X. The three-inch brass-bodied tube-fly can be seen on the point of leaving the water well downstream of the rod; there is no chance of its striking the angler's face or body—an accident that can happen all too easily when a heavy lure on quick-sinking line is fished with an overhead cast.

53

Of my six listed reactions to a lure, only three are likely to result in a hooked fish.

In neither of the takes I have dubbed *Curiosity* and *Playfulness* does the fish return to his lie with the lure. In the former he merely nips the lure with the front of his mouth. In the latter he seems only to suck the lure inside on a "cushion" of water and hold it there without closing his mouth. In both instances the lure is released, or blown out, before the fish re-occupies his lie.

The acrobatics of the salmon that played with Fred Taylor's worm were probably exceptional, but the customary "*Playful*" behaviour I have watched is no more conducive to success: a fish simply opens his mouth and either lets the bait drift inside, or sucks it in, and then, without having closed his mouth, blows it out again. On several occasions I have watched salmon intercepting maggots that have been drifted down on the current, sucking them in and puffing them out—as if playing blow-football! I once saw three salmon in a row do this one afternoon to a "greased-line" fly a friend of mine was fishing. In no case was he aware of it. He felt nothing. There was no pull, no movement of his line.

It is difficult to see quite what an angler can do to hook fish that are "taking" like this.

Nor do I think an angler can do much about hooking a salmon that takes through *Irritation*. From what I have seen, this take, too, is quite different from what I have termed *Feeding Habit*. The fish nips the lure with the front of his mouth, often swimming downstream with it. I have seen a salmon turn round and nip a small brown trout, or a parr, that seemed to have annoyed him, then releasing it before swinging round and swimming slowly back upstream. (It is interesting that "nipping" in fish is thought to be a mild expression of aggressiveness.)

In the *Aggressive* or *Crunch* take, when a lure suddenly and unexpectedly appears inside a salmon's territory, the fish seems to attack the lure—not, I think, to take it back to his lie, but to drive it away. One salmon I was watching grabbed a parr that by darting suddenly across his lie had (presumably) strayed too close. The little fish was seized broadside on with the front of the mouth, held for a moment or two while the salmon drifted backwards downstream, and then spat out. Nevertheless the fierceness of the take usually ensures a well-hooked fish.

I am not sure whether a salmon having been *induced* to seize a lure always intends to return with it to his lie. Probably he does, and I will concede this as a positive take. The "induced" fish is usually well hooked,

54

though not always. I have noticed that the quick snatch a salmon makes at an "escaping" underwater lure can result in a poor hook-hold in the front of the mouth. On the other hand, as we shall see, the fish that rises to and sucks in a dry fly skittering across the surface is frequently well hooked.

From an angling viewpoint the salmon's most positive reaction is when he sucks the lure firmly inside his mouth and *does* return with it to his lie. Unless the angler makes an ass of himself by striking too soon, a high proportion of fish that take like this are well hooked and, in consequence, landed.

*　　　*　　　*

While writing this chapter I happened to discuss the variation in salmon taking-behaviour with my friend Dr Bob Gartside who is an all-round angler of considerable experience. I was intrigued to learn that Bob, who lives in Rochdale and has fished several of the clear-water North Country rivers well known to me, had himself made some fascinating observations. At my suggestion he jotted down a few notes—from which, with his kind permission, I quote the following:

Some of the salmon behaviour I have seen is very interesting, but I have never read about anything like it in the books on salmon fishing.

These observations which may, perhaps, go part of the way towards helping us to understand why on some occasions our lures are taken, were mostly made when I have been fishing shrimp or worm. I have noticed that when swimming a worm down towards a salmon in its lie, the worm is often mouthed and pulled-at by parr and small trout. But when the worm gets within, say, a yard or so of the fish, the small fry will usually leave it alone. I have seen them stray too close to the salmon and get a very aggressive snap of the salmon's mouth for their trouble, though I haven't actually seen one get eaten. This surely must be in defence of the salmon's lie, and similar in effect to the way a spinner or a large fly gets taken in spring or autumn.

When a bait stops close to a salmon, the fish either ignores it completely or seems to get very excited and upset by its presence so close. The excited fish starts to quiver and make little movements backwards and forwards in rapid sequence, often opening and shutting his mouth, for all the world like a dog barking at the bait! But, again, there are two reactions here: one is merely to take the tiniest hold of the bait, with the "lips" only, and nip it. Another reaction is to swallow it really deep down the gullet. This fish is very well hooked indeed.

Sometimes a fish will roll on the bait with his side, like a hen fish cutting a redd.

When a bait is left lying on the bottom a yard or so in front of a fish, there is often no reaction. But if the bait is lifted a little so that the current washes it down towards the fish, three types of behaviour are possible:

1. The fish ignores the bait.

2. He moves forward and gulps the bait—in these circumstances always deeply—or, without seeming to move at all, sucks the bait in as it comes towards his nose and then turns away with it.

3. He gets rather agitated and, instead of picking up the bait, leaves his lie and goes on a tour of the pool for a while—often whizzing round at great speed, seemingly quite terrified, sometimes jumping whilst on tour, but usually well away from the lie. This reaction is caused equally by worms and shrimps.

I have formed the impression that some lies are "preferred" to others and that if a fish is in one of the premier lies it is more reluctant to leave it, whereas those fish in what seem to be less favoured lies will leave them more readily.

If a fish leaves a prime lie, it is not long before another will move into it. Sometimes I have seen the original occupant return to his lie and show aggression on finding it occupied.

Generally speaking, I think that the larger fish occupy the prime lies—but not always.

Everything that Bob describes I, too, have seen at some time or other, so I can vouch for the accuracy of his observations. His account of the salmon snapping at the parr that ventured too close is particularly interesting. Large sea trout, too, will occasionally attack parr in this way. But parr usually keep their distance from sea trout when these fish are on the take, seeming to know when this is likely. Often, when sea trout fly-fishing at twilight time, I have noticed that if parr are active—grabbing the fly cast after cast as they are apt to do sometimes during the hour of dusk—I catch no sea trout. But as soon as the sea trout "come on" the parr activity ceases.

In this section I have described some of the salmon's taking behaviour. By my reckoning, if a fish takes because of aggression, or a strong feeding response he is likely to be well-hooked and there is a good chance of landing him. If not, if the angler is unfortunate enough to encounter fish whose feeding response is more depressed, he is doomed to suffer those infuriating little tugs and tweaks and nudges—about which there is very little he can do.

At the same time it is important to remember that however frustrating this behaviour, it may still be turned to advantage. After all, unlike all the salmon that have totally ignored our lure, the tweaking fish has at least shown an *interest* in it—and such a fish is a potential taker. Believing this, and knowing where he lies, we can go to work on him, either then or later on. As my own experience has shown, it is sometimes possible to goad this fish into taking "properly". (See the "Hamlet" fish, Chapter XIII.)

*   *   *

As a rough guide all this is valid and I am confident that anyone who puts it into practice will increase his chances of success. I must, however, emphasize that it *is* only a rough guide. When reflecting on the moods and fancies of these strange and unpredictable creatures, I realize only too clearly how little I have grasped of their behaviour.

But in spite of a lifelong association with salmon, my failure to understand them does not surprise me. For I believe that within their specific range of behaviour these fish are individuals with individual characteristics.

If natural selection is to play its part as life evolves, no two members of any class can be exactly the same. A certain dissimilarity there *must* be.

Although in a given set of circumstances we may predict that the members of any species (like the atoms in Heisenberg's famous *Principle of Uncertainty*) will *on average* behave in a certain way, such behaviour cannot be expected from any single member of that species taken by itself. This applies equally, I suggest, to *salmo*. And after all it is the problem of how any particular salmon is likely to behave at any given moment that concerns us as anglers.

As we soon learn on the river, each salmon, within the confines of his specific identity, is very much a law unto himself. And it is small wonder that we find his variation in taking-behaviour so bewildering. As for rationalizing it, I am reminded of Eric Taverner's words:

> The last thing I should expect to find in any solution is completeness and simplicity, or that one explanation will cover all the difficulties with which, to our endless delight, the whole problem bristles.

An example of what the "whole problem" includes happened years ago on a stretch of fishing owned by a friend of mine. In the middle of this beat was a pool that attracted the attention of a cormorant. The salmon in this pool were exceedingly dour, and everyone agreed that these fish wouldn't take because the cormorant disturbed them. One afternoon my friend went down to the pool with his gun and waited for the cormorant. When it turned up he shot it. He tossed the empty cartridge case into the pool. As the case hit the water, a salmon rose and grabbed it.

Now, I am not suggesting that shooting cormorants and baiting with empty cartridge cases is an infallible way to success, but there is a moral to be drawn. It emphasizes that in salmon fishing almost anything is possible. If an angler persists, he is always in with a chance—whatever the time of day; however hopeless the conditions may seem; however bizarre his tackle or technique. Indeed, the curious incident of the cartridge case is not so singular as it may seem. It illustrates the *Crunch* take—already described—which happens from time to time when spinners, tube-flies and other objects inadvertently drop into the water over a salmon's head, and are immediately grabbed. Moreover, it opens up a new method of salmon fishing—in which a specially designed lure is cast so that it drops vertically into a salmon's lie.

This technique of "Overhead Fishing" can be very exciting. And since its potential has never to my knowledge been explored, I pass on the notion with my compliments to any reader who feels inclined to experiment. It may help him while away an hour or two when conditions seem hopeless and fish impossible to catch. (The lure I recommend for this form of fishing—the Dee Special Nymph—is discussed in Chapter XIII.)

Salmon frequently seem impossible to catch. Earlier, I suggested that what is so remarkable about these fish is not that they are fickle takers, but that they ever take at all. And of course during most of the time we cast to them they *won't* take. They just lie there, refusing everything we offer—until suddenly one of them will treat the lure like a long-awaited snack and half-swallow it. Or—as if this behaviour were not by itself sufficiently surprising and illogical—a fish will suddenly decide to suck the thing in and puff it out again, or tweak it, or chin it, or slap it with his tail, or roll on it, or stand-on-end and balance it on his nose.

Truly, this enigmatic animal we try to catch with rod and line seems one of nature's great eccentrics. Indeed, the newcomer to salmon fishing might be forgiven for thinking that what he is after is not a fish at all, but a creature from another age, whose characteristics lie somewhere between those of a reluctant virgin and a performing seal.

*   *   *

Explanation
But the salmon's extraordinary pattern of taking-behaviour cannot happen by chance. There has to be a reason for it—and the answer must surely lie within the fish.

As my observations have proved, a salmon may respond to our lure in one of several very different ways, his degree of interest varying between total disdain and eager acceptance. When seeking an answer to the riddle of why it is possible to catch this non-feeding fish on rod-and-line, the diversity in his taking-behaviour might seem to be a complication. Paradoxically however, this variability not only simplifies the matter but leads to a single explanation covering all Eric Taverner's "difficulties with which the whole problem bristles".

The solution is propounded by my friend Dr David Goldsborough, keen salmon fly-fisherman, and lecturer in physiology. At my cottage in front of a log fire during many a long winter evening we have discussed the puzzle of *Salmo*'s taking-behaviour. As a result, here in tabulated form is *The Goldsborough Hypothesis*.

1. Atlantic salmon are known to stop feeding during their return from sea.

2. The return of these migratory fish, usually to their rivers of origin, is a necessary function for spawning and the procreation of their species. It would therefore seem reasonable to suppose that the "sex drive" is significant in the mediation of this and associated changes in behaviour.

3. It is possible that such behavioural changes are induced:
First. By the *pituitary*: the major "administrative" or governing hormone gland in the brain, which controls changes in the hormone secretion of several glands.
Secondly. By the *hypothalamus*, which is an anatomically and functionally closely-related "automatic" part of the brain, known to exert influence on behavioural characteristics such as fear, aggression and appetite. This association is often referred to as the pituitary-hypothalamic axis. (See fig. 1.)

4. The suggestion is that the salmon's cessation of feeding is due to appetite suppression caused by the hypothalamus, and that some return-

Fig. 1   LONGITUDINAL SECTION OF SALMON'S BRAIN.
A schematic representation of the pituitary hypothalamic axis, (area A in photo on p. 64).

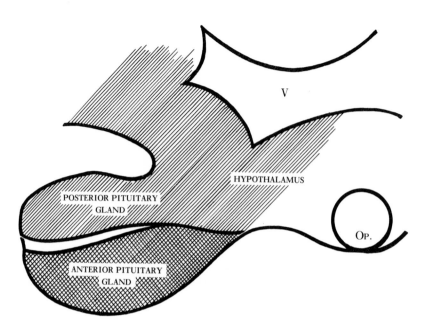

V = Ventricle (a fluid filled brain space).
Op. = Optic chiasma or cross-over of optic nerves.

Hypothalamus and posterior part of pituitary gland/neuro-hypophysis, influencing behavioural responses, including:
1. Thirst
2. Appetite
3. Fear
4. Aggression

Anterior part of pituitary gland/adenohypophysis (Rathke's pouch), influencing hormone production, including:

1. Gonadotrophins, which stimulate sex glands (sex drive)
2. Pigment changes. Melanophore or pigment cells responsible for cyclical colour change, (silver to red; red to silver, etc.)
3. Body growth
4. Metabolism: e.g. thyroid activity

(*N.B.* The urohypophysis situated at the caudal end of the spinal cord, thought to be concerned with salt regulation probably has no connection with this hypothesis.)

ing fish do not experience 100 percent appetite suppression.

5. It is a biological fact that total appetite suppression in 100 percent of returning migratory fish is not to be expected, and that the degree of appetite suppression should follow the normal distribution curve found generally in biological phenomena. (See fig. 2.)

Fig. 2   NORMAL DISTRIBUTION CURVE

In this instance the curve is applied to the height or weight distribution of a normal human population.

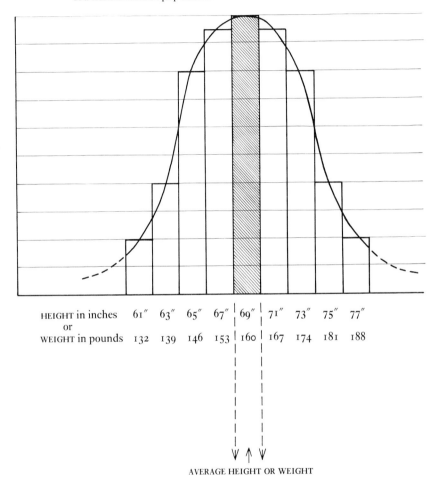

HEIGHT in inches	61″	63″	65″	67″	69″	71″	73″	75″	77″
or									
WEIGHT in pounds	132	139	146	153	160	167	174	181	188

AVERAGE HEIGHT OR WEIGHT

This type of Distribution Curve may be applied to *any* form of biological measurement, whether human or animal.

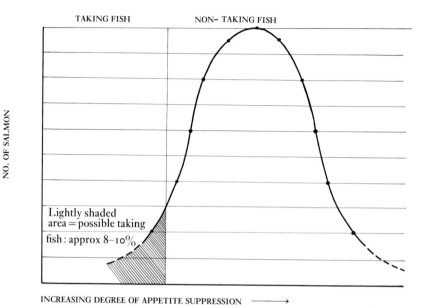

Fig. 3 (a)   NORMAL DISTRIBUTION CURVE. THEORETICAL
APPLICATION TO APPETITE SUPPRESSION IN SALMON.
("NORMAL" OR AVERAGE CONDITIONS)

TAKING FISH   NON- TAKING FISH

NO. OF SALMON

Lightly shaded
area = possible taking
fish : approx 8–10%

INCREASING DEGREE OF APPETITE SUPPRESSION ⟶

Fig. 3 (b)   As shown below, the Distribution Curve may shift to the right or left in
response to changes in environmental conditions, or within the fish itself. Such shifts
will reflect the angler's chances of success.

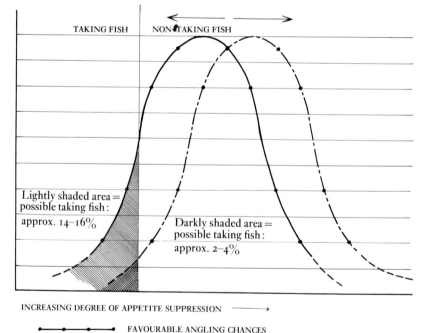

TAKING FISH   NON-TAKING FISH

NO. OF SALMON

Lightly shaded area =
possible taking fish :
approx. 14–16%

Darkly shaded area =
possible taking fish :
approx. 2–4%

INCREASING DEGREE OF APPETITE SUPPRESSION ⟶

●———●———●———● FAVOURABLE ANGLING CHANCES

●—·—●—·—●—·—● LESS FAVOURABLE ANGLING CHANCES

Note. These curves could equally apply to degrees of aggression.

6. The shape of the curve is constant, but its *position* may shift from side to side according to changes within the fish itself on return from sea; changes in water height and water temperature, and other environmental variants. (See fig. 3 (a) and fig. 3 (b)

Note. A fish cannot run from the sea with a fixed degree of appetite suppression. This degree must vary according to the salmon's physiological state.

7. This implies that there is a variable *reluctance* rather than an anatomical *inability* to feed. In other words, the salmon's gut has not shrunk—though in time "digestive system shrinkage", more accurately expressed as "disuse atrophy" may occur.*

8. Thus, incomplete suppression of appetite, varying in degree, would explain not only the observed incidence of a small percentage of "taking" fish, but the variation in taking-behaviour described earlier in this chapter.

9. The hypothesis, therefore, is that variation in salmon taking-behaviour is initiated by the pituitary-hypothalamic axis in increasing sex-drive via the gonadotrophins and associated steroid hormones, and behavioural changes—significantly appetite suppression, controlled by the hypothalamus.

10. This hypothesis—which is not proposed as a complete analysis of migratory fish behaviour—may be substantiated or refuted by the microscopic-histological and histochemical examination of the pituitary-hypothalamic axis, gonads, thyroid and adrenal glands of sexually-mature parr, departing smolts, fish returning after some life at sea, and surviving kelts.

If research proves it to be correct, David Goldsborough's hypothesis explains not only why a salmon takes a lure, but why on any given occasion only a few salmon are "taking" fish. It explains the variation in a salmon's degree of interest in a lure—which is reflected in the way the fish takes, and because of which we may sometimes fail to hook him. It explains why many fish will refuse our lure; why some will come and look at it; why some will give it a tweak—and why some will grab it.†

But even so, it is well to remember that although at last we may know the reason for *Salmo*'s taking-behaviour, we shall still not know for certain when any of it is going to happen. The vagaries of the

---

*The theory that a returning salmon stopped feeding because its gut had shrunk seems to have originated in a paper given by Dr C. W. Greene in *Transactions—American Fisheries Society*, 1911. Strangely, this notion has persisted ever since—even though at the time of Dr Greene's address it was agreed that no one had determined whether anatomical or physiological change came first!

†It is important to differentiate between appetite suppression and aggressiveness. Instances of aggressive behaviour—especially during or close to the mating period—are commonplace, and it is probable that this accounts for the increase in readiness to seize a lure in autumn as the spawning time approaches, although the fish may have spent many months in the river. Biological Distribution Curves (similar to those on p. 62), applying to aggressive behaviour, could of course be drawn.

Side view of head and brain of a 15 lb salmon

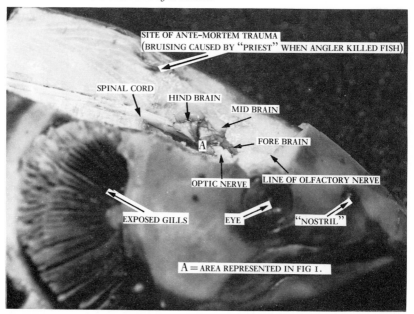

SITE OF ANTE-MORTEM TRAUMA
(BRUISING CAUSED BY "PRIEST" WHEN ANGLER KILLED FISH)

SPINAL CORD

HIND BRAIN

MID BRAIN

A

FORE BRAIN

OPTIC NERVE

LINE OF OLFACTORY NERVE

EXPOSED GILLS

EYE

"NOSTRIL"

A = AREA REPRESENTED IN FIG 1.

Dorsal view of salmon's brain showing olfactory and optic nerves.

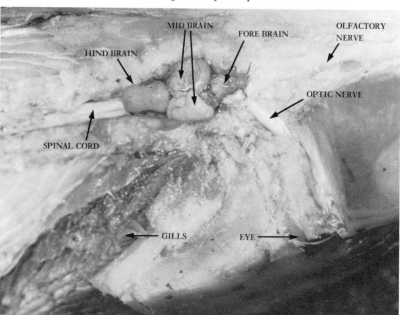

MID BRAIN

FORE BRAIN

OLFACTORY
NERVE

HIND BRAIN

OPTIC NERVE

SPINAL CORD

GILLS

EYE

The comparatively large size of optical and olfactory nerves reflects the salmon's astonishing acuity of vision and smell.

Close-up dorsal view showing size of brain from 15 lb salmon.

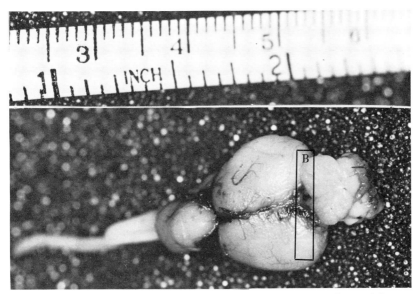

B = Portion of brain under investigation. The scale illustrates the smallness of the area relevant to the Goldsborough Hypothesis.

hypothalamus, transmuted into that golden moment when our line tightens, will continue to take us by surprise.

David Goldsborough writes as follows:

A unique opportunity of studying the control of appetite is provided by the Atlantic salmon, a species wherein a marked non-feeding state develops predictably during the life-cycle. This state, if the hypothesis is valid, could be described as that of anorexia.

Anorexia is *a physiological reluctance to swallow food, rather than an anatomical inability to do so*. That stomach content in salmon caught during the spawning migration is seldom found, despite a presumed variable degree of appetite suppression, is therefore not surprising. An anorexic fish, although taking food or presumed food—e.g. the angler's lure—into its mouth, would seldom complete the process of ingestion.

Throughout the world over many years there has been a great deal of highly sophisticated scientific research into appetite and weight control. This has been done primarily by investigating mammals and in part has been directed towards the effects of the experimental administration of a range of neuro transmitters in varying concentrations to the hypothalamus, and in correlating the observed changes in food consumption under controlled conditions. It is significant that calcitonin, a hormone found in many vertebrates *including the salmon*, has been used to induce a reversible state of anorexia in several other vertebrate species.

Following preliminary discussions on the basic hypothesis, scientific interest has been shown in the opportunity provided by Atlantic salmon during their presumed anorexic state. In cooperation with interested scientific groups, a pilot study is now being developed to investigate the suggested differences in hypothalamic-pituitary function between feeding and non-feeding salmon, using histological, histochemical and biochemical techniques within the limits imposed by a cold-blooded, aquatic vertebrate.

I imagine that most experienced salmon anglers have certain times of the day when they are most hopeful of meeting a fish, and other periods when the chances appear less propitious. These times vary with the individual to a quite considerable degree, but there would be, I feel pretty sure, a fairly large majority who preferred the hours before lunch to those after . . . When conditions are difficult, the last half-hour of daylight is probably as likely time as any.

Major Kenneth Dawson,
Casts from a Salmon Reel, no date [1948]

III
The Fish

PART THREE: RUNNING AND TAKING TIMES

When writing about salmon fishing it is easy to think only in terms of one's favourite method, applied to a favourite river or type of river. But this, of course, offers a far too limited view. Salmon rivers vary enormously, not only in character but in the length of time they are fishable. By selecting his rivers, an angler with the time and money to spare could be salmon fishing somewhere in Britain or Ireland for a full eleven months of the year. Any local angler on one of the big Scottish rivers could be fishing for almost as long whereas the season for the average spate stream angler extends for no longer than three to four months.

Several of Britain's biggest rivers have fresh salmon running into them all the year round. The spate rivers, scattered mainly down the western coastline, seldom have a run of fish before June at the earliest—a time of year when fishing in the big rivers is in the doldrums. As the graph on p. 70 shows, the spring run in the middle beats of the River Spey is tailing off by the end of May, and there is something of a lull in June— before the grilse run in July and August.

Why some rivers enjoy a spring salmon run while other rivers, seemingly as well endowed with what we might think were essential requirements, receive no fish until summer and autumn, is not fully understood. It seems to be just another example of Nature's insurance policy; that by staggering the runs of incoming fish the chance of total catastrophe is lessened. If all returning fish were to migrate during the same period it is just conceivable that some national disaster could wipe out the whole run for that year. But this, of course, is not a scientific explanation.

In the case of the spate river with its rapid rise and fall, seldom lake-fed and often suffering long periods of very low water during early summer, with only shallow stickles linking the pools, the absence of a spring run is understandable. But even when the rise and fall of a river is cushioned by lake water, it is no guarantee of an early run. That king of summer fly-rivers, the evenly-flowing Cumbrian Derwent, gets no salmon run of any consequence until July, although fed by both Bassenthwaite Lake and Derwentwater.

In terms of angling there is scant comparison between a small spate stream, foaming down from the hills, and one of the big salmon rivers with its more stately flow and comparatively slow rise and fall. Salmon rivers are so different: in size, in depth, in speed. Each has its own character, its own challenge; each requiring from the angler its own approach. To switch from river to river with any chance of immediate success demands exceptional all-round angling skill. To start with, even the best anglers need to lean heavily on local knowledge.

Often enough, however, it is technical ability that is lacking. I have seen anglers, highly competent on a big river, completely flummoxed when faced with the problem of catching salmon in a fast-running alder-lined spate beck. And I have watched the ineffectual efforts of a skilful spate-stream angler, highly successful on his local water, but unable to Spey-cast, struggling in vain to put out a long enough line from a steep-to bank of that famous river.

Each lie in each pool of each salmon river is a separate study in itself. No two rivers and no two pools in any river are the same. Each presents its own particular problems—to be solved anew each time we visit the water and try to anticipate how on that occasion the fish are likely to behave.

There is a vast difference (not always appreciated by the angler who usually fishes only the one or the other) between our approach to fishing a small summer spate river and a big spring-run river. They set quite different problems. Apart from the angling techniques involved, the times of day when salmon may be more likely to take are different. And, as we shall see, these demand their own strategies.

But despite the widely differing environments that harbour salmon on their return from sea, and although the hooking of a fish depends partly on chance, some anglers are consistently more successful than others. This is because, in addition to their ration of luck, they have the knowledge born of experience and the skill to apply it. They also contrive to be on the river at the right time.

From what we have learned about the salmon's life-style and behaviour, it is clear that the odds are stacked pretty heavily against us. It is equally clear that if we wish to be successful we must set about trying to reduce these odds. We can do this by:

1. Suiting our angling method to the prevailing conditions.
2. Using water-sense and stealth.
3. Applying technical ability.
4. Knowing what the fish are up to.

It is on the last of these that our overall salmon fishing strategy is founded.

The longer we are covering fish effectively, the more chance we have of meeting a taking salmon and hooking it. But, according to the time of year, certain times of the day offer slightly better chances than others, and since we need to stop fishing from time to time to rest, to eat, to study the water, and so on, it is sensible to choose times that seem less propitious.

This question of the best salmon taking-times has been hotly debated. Some people hold the opinion that no such times exist. Others claim a knowledge of them that borders on the supernatural. Both views are based on theoretical arguments. What is the truth?

The answer, I suggest, lies not in supposition but in observation. It is impossible to predict exactly what salmon will or will not be doing at any specific time, but it is fully possible to predict what they are *likely* to be doing.

It is when salmon are running fresh from sea that we have the best chance of catching them. During their long journey upriver towards the spawning redds they will, for varying lengths of time, occupy the various "taking lies". *It is when a fish is alert in such a lie—having just reached it, or being on the point of leaving it, that he is most vulnerable to the angler's lure.*

It has often been said that running fish are poor takers. A glance at the graph shown on the next page confutes this idea. As we can see, on the beat in question the maximum catch corresponds with the peak of the spring/summer run.

So—from the premise that it is the running fish that offers us the best opportunity, it follows that if we know the times when salmon are likely to be on the move, we shall know the times when we, too, should be in action.

Salmon migrate upriver according to the *time of year*, the *height of water* and the *time of day*. For reasons unknown, rivers show considerable

SALMON RUNNING BEHAVIOUR

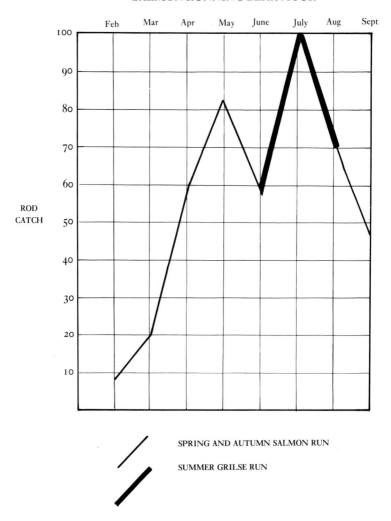

ROD CATCH

SPRING AND AUTUMN SALMON RUN

SUMMER GRILSE RUN

The graph shows the average monthly rod catch of salmon and grilse taken from a beat of the River Spey over a ten year period, from 1971–1980 inclusive.

In May at the peak of the spring run, catches are highest. After this, during the end of May and June, the catch decreases with the diminishing run of fish. Then, during July and August, come the grilse, and catches reach their highest peak.

A similar graph can be plotted for any particular fishery, and anyone planning a holiday can see at a glance when his best chances are likely to occur. But he will find these reflected in the weekly rents charged by the fishery owner!

70

variation in the timing of their salmon migrations. Ignoring the fluctuations of recent years, the Tay and Tweed with their traditional early and late runs will show a different overall picture from, say, the Awe or the Derwent. But as an example of what I mean, let us take one of the world's finest salmon fly-rivers, the Spey*.

According to the water temperature, salmon move into the river during early spring, their numbers swelling until a peak is reached sometime during May. By this time, fish are on the move pretty well throughout the length of the river. Some will even have arrived far up the valley in the headwaters of some of the feeder streams such as the Rivers Avon and Feshie.

This movement dwindles towards the end of May and during June— as reflected in the rod catches, which drop during June, until the arrival of the grilse run—which usually reaches its peak in July. (See graph opposite.)

Whether a spate stream or one of the big spring-run rivers is being fished, the factor that most greatly influences salmon taking-behaviour is the height of the water, for it is this, primarily, that dictates the time when salmon are likely to be moving.

Movement is at its highest when the river is falling, but salmon will also move during the early stages of a rise. If the water continues to rise, and becomes dirty, the fish stop running. They will not start again until the river begins to fall and clear. Maximum movement takes place when the water level has fallen to roughly a third of the height reached by an average spate. (See p. 82.)

It is during the start of a rise and the latter stages of the run-off that salmon fishing chances are at their best. The weather itself is comparatively unimportant. A. H. Chaytor comments on this in his *Letters to a Salmon Fisher's Sons*, 1910:

> Cold winds and wretched weather, which send the trout fisher home empty-handed, seem often to make little or no difference to the salmon. The wind and the weather do affect success in salmon fishing, but it is in a very uncertain and capricious manner. No day and no weather is hopeless if there are salmon in the pools ... Even bitter north and east winds do not prevent the fish from taking the fly, though they can make the fisher pretty miserable, and especially if on his

---

*Miserably aware of the Spey's disastrous spring run of recent years, I can only echo the prayer of every salmon angler that the return to glory of this great river will prove as sudden as its decline.

water they happen to be foul winds, that is to say, winds blowing up-stream or in his face. But salmon seem to dislike haze and gloom, and they seldom take well either in hot and hazy weather or in dull gloom. But if the air is clear and without mist the day may be as hot or as cold, as sunny or as dark as you will, and still you may have a very fine day's salmon fishing.

There is no doubt that salmon can anticipate weather change. But the effect of this on their taking behaviour is chiefly, I think, through its influence on the river. Despite all that has been written about the significance of barometric pressure, I have never been convinced that it means much to the salmon angler—except as a possible indication of rain. Rain can result in a rise of water, which to the waiting salmon is the stimulus to run—and chances of a taking fish extend from that.

Like sea trout, salmon seem able to predict this rise. Shortly before rain comes, especially when it follows a long spell of low water, there is sometimes great activity in the pools. Fish sling about; swim up and down, often flashing as they turn on their sides. While in this mood

14 lb. Aberdeenshire Dee spring salmon, caught on fly just after a heavy thunderstorm. Although fish are usually dour during the build-up of thunderstorms, they often take well once a storm has broken.

72

they are exceptionally dour and seldom take. But once the rain has come and the river begins to lift, fish are likely to start moving. Now, for a short time, fishing chances can be very good.

It should be remembered that a spate depends not on local rainfall but on what has fallen higher up the valley. This may come as a complete surprise. It is by no means uncommon for a cloudburst in the hills—perhaps twenty miles or so upstream—to cause a sudden rise of water in the stretch you are fishing, although not a drop of rain has fallen locally.

In addition to rainfall, snow-melt in the hills may bring about a mini-spate to which fish will sometimes react. But such taking periods are spasmodic and usually of short duration. To help you not to miss them, always mark the water level with a piece of stick before fishing starts. And keep an eye on it throughout the day.

I do not claim any originality for my remarks about the importance of water height and relative unimportance of weather. That keen salmon angler J. Arthur Hutton mentions it in his carefully observed *Rod-Fishing for Salmon on the Wye*, 1920:

> Our records of the weather do not seem to indicate that this has much effect on the catching of fish. We have caught them in quantities in all sorts and conditions of weather . . . The day on which I was lucky enough to catch my first forty-pounder—as a matter of fact he was 44 lb—was apparently a hopeless fishing day. The water was clear, there was not a cloud in the sky, and it was broiling hot.
>
> The conclusion we have come to is that temperature of water, height of barometer, state of the weather, etc., matters comparatively little. *The one thing that really matters is the height of the water*, and if there are fresh-run fish about and the water is at a good fishing level that is all they care about . . . I am also beginning to think that the pattern of the fly or the variety of minnow also matter very little.

Fishing is best when a river is falling almost certainly because that is when most salmon are engaged in their upstream migration. The length of this period depends on the type of river. On some of the big rivers with their comparatively slow rate of fall, water conditions can be suitable for fly-fishing during many days on end. On other rivers with quicker rise and fall, fly-fishing is profitable only for a day or two during the run-off. In the spate rivers with their violent fluctuation of water levels, the fly fisherman must choose not only the right day to be on the river, but even the right hour, so quickly do conditions change.

This taking period is what I call the "Magic Moment", and its timing is crucial. Readers of *Sea Trout Fishing* may remember the sad occasion during that long-ago Cumbrian spate when I declined my father-in-law's* invitation to go fishing. Thinking I had the water "all worked out", confident there would be no Magic Moment for at least another couple of hours, I let the old man wend his way to the river and got on with my writing.

At the time I felt rather sorry for him. The river was full of fish and I anticipated some excellent sport when the water had dropped a bit more. As it was, he had undoubtedly gone down too soon and would be exhausted by the time everything started.

When I arrived on the river as planned, he was certainly tired-out—being on the point of landing his third salmon, a sixteen-pounder. He had already accounted for a twelve-pounder and a nine-pounder, in addition to a five-pound sea trout. All with his single-handed sea trout rod, on a size 8 Peter Ross, from the same place, with just four casts.

I carried his fish up to the farm for him—and ran back to the river. It seemed in perfect nick, and I fished until dark.

Without an offer!

*   *   *

As I learned painfully on that never-to-be-forgotten afternoon, the taking period on these violent spate rivers can offer some fast and furious sport, but seldom lasts for very long. However intimate one's knowledge of the river, it is by no means easy to predict! After it has passed, the spate-stream angler can for the most part put aside his fly-rod, except of course for sea trout at dusk. Until another rise of water brings a run of fish upstream, almost his only chance at salmon will be with the bait— that is, unless he is lucky to have water suitable for fishing the surface fly, as described in Chapter XIII. If so, his chance of sport is far from being hopeless. Nor is he without hope of catching a salmon on the fly at night. But we shall come to all this in due course.

Time of Day
Apart from those conditions of rising water when the river is rushing down thick with mud and filth, a salmon may take at any time of the day. According to the time of year, however, certain times of day offer slightly better chances than others, for it is then that salmon are more likely to be alert and on the move.

Like that of most other animals, the behaviour of salmon is influenced

---

*Benjamin Armstrong of Cragg Farm, 1891–1982. A splendid angler. A splendid man.

by light intensity. Facts regarding their movements upstream in relation to daylight and darkness are illustrated by the graphs below. These data have been found by means of electronic fish-counters on a number of rivers over a period of years, during which the precise migration times of many thousands of salmon have been recorded. This research has shown that from about mid-May to October, salmon move upstream in greater numbers during darkness than in daylight. Conversely, from

DAILY SALMON MOVEMENTS

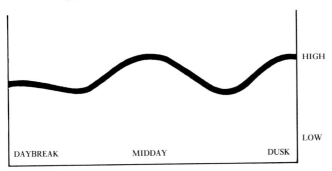

SPRING and AUTUMN

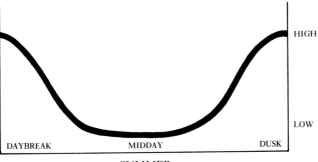

SUMMER

The curves give an indication of salmon migration day and night throughout the season, and show the difference in movement between summer and spring/autumn.

Salmon will not jump obstacles at night, or by day in poor light. But providing there are no obstacles to be passed they will travel upstream as freely by night as by day, and they will do so in lower water than by day. There is no significant difference in these water heights at different times of the year.

Although salmon tend to move in scattered groups, this is not to say that they start together, run for a distance and then pause together. Running fish pause individually, perhaps for hours perhaps for minutes, before setting off again and leapfrogging some of their erstwhile companions. In spring it is mainly on fish behaving in this manner that our sport depends.

75

October to mid-May, more fish move in daylight than in darkness.

These tendencies to move upstream at certain times are, I suggest, of prime importance to the salmon angler.

Exactly what it is that urges a fish to move at any moment is not known. Several theories have been advanced, prominent among them the suggestion that variation in light and temperature causes changes in the water's oxygen content which, in turn, stimulates the fish to move. This may be true. But at present it remains supposition, and so outside the scope of this book—which is intended simply as a practical guide.

In practice, according to the month, salmon are likely to be moving upstream during certain periods of the twenty-four hours, and it is sensible for the angler to ensure that during these periods he is on the river—and not in bed, or tucking into food, or standing at the bar.

I emphasize that these migration times are only an approximate guide. Nevertheless, although they guarantee nothing, a knowledge of them will in the long run help us to be more successful.

Not long ago on a chilly May morning, I had two fish on the bank before breakfast. Afterwards, although the weather had improved, I caught nothing. The following day, on the same water, I took my only salmon in almost pitch darkness with what was virtually my last cast of the evening.

This may seem rather strange. But the point I want to make is that from April onwards we can *expect* the chance of a taking fish in the early morning and late evening; for, as we have seen, at those times salmon are likely to be moving. Anyone fishing only during the conventional period—from after breakfast until five-thirty or thereabouts, when the gillie goes for his tea—is at a distinct disadvantage.

When the water temperature is low, from January until, say, the end of March, on rivers that hold fish as soon as this, salmon are slow to move early in the morning. At this time of year fishing chances are better when the day has become well "aired". But after about mid-April there is always the chance of a fish before breakfast. This chance improves as the water warms and the light intensity increases during May; until, in June, July and August, early morning becomes one of the two best fishing times of the day.

During spring and autumn there is also a tendency for salmon to migrate in the middle of the day (see diagram p. 75). It is to seize advantage of the "taking" opportunities created by the salmon's mid-day migrational movement that, in the Introduction, I suggested how silly we are to impose our normal meal-time routine on a day's fishing. Salmon behaviour is not so conveniently synchronized with human domestic arrangements.

Anglers sometimes are unaware of the significance of what is happening beneath the surface of the river; that salmon are running past them upstream at the very moment they are casting their lines. Often, when one or two fish are hooked in fairly quick succession, it is thought that they have suddenly "come on the take". They may have, but this is seldom the right answer. Apropos the Spey in springtime, John Ashley-Cooper makes the point in his evocative book *A Salmon Fisher's Odyssey*, 1982:

> A pool may be empty at one moment, and at the next be full of jumping fish, while a further ten minutes may see all quiet again, with the shoal moved on. A fisherman on the spot at the right moment may quickly take a couple of fish from those which pause for a minute in their passage, and perhaps fish blank for the rest of the day. To the inexperienced it may seem as though for a short time and for some unaccountable reason the fish in the pool all "woke up", and thus some of them took. This is usually a mistaken view. The truth is that a shoal is apt to arrive at one moment and be gone the next, or so it is in nine cases out of ten.

If you are fishing your own water, or water rented exclusively for your own use, you can of course (depending on your terms of agreement) please yourself how, when and where you fish. But on fisheries where individual rods are let by the day or week, you will almost certainly be sharing with several others. In which case you will probably fish each pool on the beat according to a roster. Pools usually change hands at lunch time. This entails meeting at the fishing hut—if the fishery boasts one—and spending an hour or so together before dispersing to the afternoon's water.

This arrangement is fine for the morale of the unsuccessful angler. A convivial munch, a heartening drink, a welcome rest. But it is also the waste of a valuable hour's fishing which, early or late in the season, occurs during one of the best times of the day. By most rods this is cheerfully accepted, on the grounds that "resting the water" after it has been flogged all morning, must be sensible.

So far as I am concerned, for reasons already given, it is foolish. And it is at such times that, for anyone who prefers fishing to chatting, the advantages of rod-sharing are shown to the full.

For two anglers to share a rod, taking it in turns to fish and rest, is a civilized and practical arrangement. It halves the cost of the fishing. It enables each angler to fish hard for a spell, then have a break. The lure can be kept in action all the time and no chances are missed—which can make all the difference between a fish and no fish on those frequent days when offers are hard to come by.

But of course there is more to rod-sharing than that.

Time spent in observation is never wasted. Sooner or later the "resting" partner will see things happening at the waterside that he would probably never notice while handling the rod. In addition, if he is lucky, he will witness for himself various aspects of salmon behaviour as the fish react to his companion's lure. He will probably find this more fascinating than the actual fishing.

Many of my friends have taken to sharing rods these days, as I have myself. It enables me to fish beats I could not otherwise afford, and gives me all the casting I want. A novice, fishing with an experienced companion, will find rod-sharing an easy way to learn some of the do's and don'ts of water-sense and stealth. Besides, gillying for a companion during one's periods of "make and mend" is good for the spirit and helps to prevent us from getting too greedy for fish. Dame Juliana, I feel certain, would have approved.

But no matter whether he is rod-sharing, anyone who wishes to derive maximum advantage from the amount of fishing time available, is wise to adjust his daily programme to suit the salmon's whims rather than his own. From early spring until the heat of summer, and again in late autumn, he will be silly to spend the mid-day hours sitting on the bank— a time when fish are likely to be stirring. On the other hand, during the summer months, in other than spate water, salmon seldom move much in daylight, and almost never when the sunlight is strong. It is mainly for this reason that fishing the middle part of the day in summertime is so unproductive. Salmon that have been creeping upriver in darkness and at daybreak, are lying in the deep pools. They will stay there while the sun is up; not moving again until the light begins to fade during that magic hour of dusk—when so often a fish is hooked.

The quiet movements of salmon that take place in the half-light should not be confused with the comparatively violent behaviour when they are running straight from sea in autumn, or after they have been penned-up for a time by low water. Fish running in these circumstances move up rapidly; showing frequently in the fast, shallow water between pools; then in the pool tail; again, perhaps, near the head of the pool, before hurrying on into the shallows leading to the pool above.

This rushing from pool to pool is similar in effect to the mass summer runs of sea trout at night in low water, when the fish come splashing up through the stickles sometimes only half awash, sounding in the darkness like a herd of cattle fording the river. A hair-raising experience for the nervous night fly-fisherman unversed in the habits of these fish.

Viewers may remember the run of sea trout splashing upriver in my film *Salmo the Leaper*, when the fish came zipping up through the shallows below the weir, sloshing over the top, and then slowing down on reaching the quiet, deeper water just above. As we managed to show on film, several of these fish hung in position for a while as though resting, before moving slowly on. It occurred to me at the time that these briefly resting fish might well have been potential takers.

An excellent example of the taking behaviour of running salmon in a similar location is sometimes afforded by a weir on the River Tamar. This water has been fished for many years by that great Derbyshire sportsman, Alan Shipman, to whom I am indebted for the picture shown below.

Spate water foaming from the weir pool on the River Tamar. Salmon, which run from the tidal water below the weir, usually when the tide is ebbing, tend to lie for a time in the smooth glide above the sill. These running fish frequently prove to be ready takers.

After making their way upstream from the estuary, through the weir-pool and then up one of the two salmon ladders on either side of the river, fish usually pause in the smooth, evenly-flowing water just above the weir. Here, in a clear, comparatively shallow glide, these fish—which often prove ready takers—can be watched from the moment they arrive. Sometimes a new arrival can be *seen to take*—thus removing any doubt that it was in fact a fish in the process of running.

Salmon travelling fast seldom seem to take while actually on the move. The fish that *does* take while moving is likely to be the quietly-running fish that is making his way slowly upstream and seldom showing himself. But it is certainly incorrect to claim that fast-moving salmon *never* take. Occasionally they do. As always, when discussing salmon behaviour it is wise to avoid the absolute—although I concede that the following example is probably exceptional.

Once, when a hectic run of fish was whizzing up through the beat a friend and I were fishing, just above the tidal water, on a Scottish west coast river, I decided to experiment and try to find out whether one of these fast-running salmon could be caught. Stationing myself at the end of a pool, I drift-lined a prawn across the very tip of the tail where the out-flow narrowed into a shallow glide. It was up this stretch of fast water that each migrating salmon had to swim. By wading deep and using the full length of the rod, I got the prawn to hang in the glide, moving slightly from side to side.

With an observer crouching among the rocks beside the glide, out of sight but close to the water's edge, I kept at it for about an hour. During this time, amid intense excitement, several salmon swam up past the prawn, but ignored it. And then, as my companion watched, a big salmon—which a moment or two before had shown in the broken water below—came swimming up, saw the prawn and grabbed it. Very exciting.

As it happened, I lost this fish. But the point had been made. Whether the fish would have taken a fly I shall never know.

There are of course other useful signs besides fish movement. In early spring I will not sit idly on the bank when a gleam of sun brings some warmth into the air. Nor, in summer, when clouds dull the bright sunshine; or a breeze springs up and ripples the water. On the other hand, if on a louring day I see fish flashing, I am content to rest my arms and wait for the rain—confident there will be a much better chance during the first few inches of rising water. But I will fish happily when a spate is falling; or on any day, warm or cold, with the river at a height that encourages salmon to run, for irrespective of air temperature it is the presence of fresh fish that provides the best chance of all.

The curves on p. 75 indicate the times when salmon are likely to be migrating; and so, the times when we may be in with a chance. But don't read too much into them. Nobody can predict accurately what salmon will do; they tend to swim upriver in loosely knit groups with delays between groups during which no fish will migrate, even under ideal conditions, which may account for those times when a rise of water fails to stimulate an expected movement. So—don't regard these "taking" times as infallible. They are not.

Nevertheless, although they guarantee nothing, they *will* help to reduce the odds. And of all these possible taking times, the most important in my opinion is the last hour of the day.

I have noticed that whatever the weather or the time of year, most anglers stop fishing too soon. Early in the season this is very understandable. After flogging away for hours on a cold April day, with a chill east wind blackening the river, people are tired and cold and disheartened. Gladly they succumb to the temptations of the bottle and a hot bath.

It is a mistake.

The chances are that by dinner time, just when they are all trotting in to feed, that bitter wind will have dropped. This is when they should be starting to fish. The river is cloaked in stillness. An "electric" feeling has come into the air . . . It is during this hour of fading light, at "sea trout time", that salmon are moving, and it is now that we have our best chance of catching one. Of all hours of the day, this is the most likely.

Gillies usually go for their tea at about five-thirty. And this is when so many anglers pack up. Have a break by all means. Like the gillies, go and eat a high tea. But come out again—and fish on into the darkening. It is not by chance that, according to the terms of lease, the gillies themselves so often fish in the evening for their estates. This is when they catch many of their salmon. Go and do likewise.

No one had ever told me about this and I learned it, as I did most of my fishing, in the hard school of experience.

On a bitterly cold February day thirty-five years ago I was spinning on the River Eden. By four o'clock in the afternoon the three of us had each caught a salmon. And now, in the late dusk, with a north-east wind howling outside, feeling rather pleased with ourselves we sat huddled in the fishing hut waiting for the fourth member of the party, who, so

Salmon movement and taking chances during an average spate

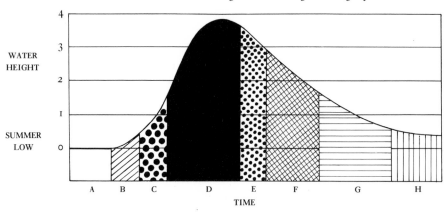

A ☐   Dead low water. No movement of fish upstream. Taking chances very poor.

B ▨   First six inches of rise. Fish moving. Taking chances good.

C ⬚   Water colouring up. Taking chances poor.

D ■   Water very dirty. No movement. Taking chances virtually nil.

E ⬚   Water starting to clear. Taking chances poor but improving.

F ▨   Fish starting to move more freely. Taking chances fair.

G ☰   Maximum movement. Taking chances good.

H ▥   Water height tailing off. Taking chances diminishing.

far, had failed to materialize. He turned up at last, emerging from the shadows with his rod and announcing his intention of having a throw.

Frankly, I thought he was wasting his time. So did the others. We waited impatiently, sharing the last of the bottle, while he went down to the water's edge and cast into the windy twilight.

Almost at once we heard him shout. He had hooked a twenty-pounder—which he landed in pitch darkness.

It shook me. I had not thought there could be the slightest chance of a fish so late in the day at that time of the year in such cold weather. It taught me a lesson I never forgot. And since then it has caught me a lot of fish.

At the end of the 1981 season on Tweed, in the gathering darkness of a very chilly day, fishing a three-inch tube on sunk line, I was taken by the biggest salmon I have ever hooked. In conditions reminiscent of sea trout fishing on a moonless night, save that the temperature was at freezing point, I played the monster as the river dissolved into darkness. Finally, the big fish wallowed in the shallows, and by walking backwards I drew him in to beach him. At the very last moment, the hook came away.

Numb with disappointment, I stumbled up the bank—to be consoled by my companion, who thrust a glass into my hand.

I swallowed the whisky and then, to his astonishment, took my rod and strode back into the river. But I was simply following my own advice. I lengthened line by letting the lure drift downstream, then roll-cast into the darkness. On that very first cast, as the lure swam round out of the current—the line tightened . . .

After the monster I had just lost, this salmon felt like a pygmy. But few fish have ever given me so much satisfaction in the manner of their capture. He weighed fourteen-and-a-half pounds, and we ate him smoked at the cottage Christmas party.

I do not think it a coincidence that the British record rod-caught salmon—Miss Ballantine's 64 pounder—was hooked at dusk (see p. 84.)

Whatever the time of year, when planning your day always make sure you will be fishing late. In trying to help you to catch salmon there is no better advice I can offer—although in doing so, I am aware of the inconsistencies in salmon behaviour. Not long ago two anglers who had been fishing at dusk in different pools on the same beat, came into the hotel after dark. One reported that his water had gone "absolutely dead" at about nine o'clock. The other brought in three beautiful fresh-run fish—caught between nine and nine forty-five. So—don't regard any

Miss G. W. Ballantine and her father beside her British Record rod-caught salmon. Weight: 64 lb. Length: 4′ 6″. Girth: $28\frac{1}{2}$″. Hooked in the Boat Pool, Murthly, on the Glendelvine beat, River Tay; 7th October, 1922. The fish was hooked at dusk on a dace trailed from a boat in the pool below.

Miss Ballantine's cottage beside the Boat Pool.

It is said that several salmon upwards of seventy pounds were hooked or netted in Britain during the last century, but no accurate records of these fish have survived. The official rod-caught record salmon is Miss Ballantine's.

84

salmon "taking time" as being infallible. There is no such thing.

Nevertheless, if I had to choose just one hour of the day—on any but a spate river—irrespective of the temperature or the time of year, spring, summer, autumn, it would without exception be the last hour of daylight.

*   *   *

Time of Night

Fishing for salmon at dusk leads us on naturally to fishing for them in darkness. Apropos of which, I have found very little in the literature—few writers having touched on the techniques of salmon night fly-fishing. Unlike his cousin the sea trout, *Salmo salar*, reputedly, is not a fish that takes a lure in the darkness.

In fact, salmon will take at night. I know, because I have caught them.

I cannot claim to have caught many. In all, between thirty and forty. But these, together with the fish landed by my friends, add up to well over fifty salmon I know to have been caught on the fly at night. Not a great total perhaps, but a significant number nevertheless.

I write "on the fly". What I really mean is on the *lure*: the big Sunk Lure—$2\frac{1}{2}$ to $3\frac{1}{2}$ inches long, as described in my Introduction to *Sea Trout Fishing*.

It must be emphasized that these are not fish caught in the twilight of mid-summer nights on Highland rivers. In every case they have been taken late on *dark* nights—one might say, *pitch* dark—and mostly in the early hours of the morning, between about one o'clock and three-thirty.

It was while night fishing for sea trout that I hooked my first salmon in the darkness. It happened quite by chance.

The mid-August night was black, with heavy cloud and a hint of rain. I had been fishing since dusk. To start with there had been a brief flurry of activity from the sea trout, after which they had gone off the take. And stayed off. By two o'clock in the morning, feeling chilled and tired, with the light from my cottage kitchen winking invitingly from the distant fell, I was debating whether to pack up. And then, suddenly: a heavy splash somewhere out in the darkness up near the head of the pool. I could guess where. By a sunken rock under the far bank was an age-old lie for a big sea trout.

I cut off the fly I had been using, and tied on a big Sunk Lure: a tenuous creation of peacock herl and blue, three inches long. (See plate 6)

Out in the river, well upstream of the lie, I started to lengthen line. When everything was going smoothly I moved downstream and put out the all-important cast that would cover the fish. The lure touched down and started to swing round . . . He took it at once.

There were no snags in that pool, but he felt a mighty good fish and I didn't take any chances.

Fifteen minutes later I had him in the net and carried him up the bank to the little fishing shelter. There, behind the bushes, I stretched him out on the grass and shone the torch. I had the surprise of my life. He wasn't a big sea trout. He was a fourteen-pound salmon!

This was the first salmon I had ever caught on "fly" late on a dark night. It was very exciting, and I sat there for a long time just gazing at the fish. I had been told that salmon wouldn't take on pitch dark nights, and I felt I was on to something . . .

Not long after that incident I was fishing a private stretch that had just been sold on a neighbouring river—like my local river a clearwater spate stream. The new owners had asked me over to demonstrate my sea trout night fishing lures and methods.

I started at dusk and by two-thirty in the morning had "gone through the card". Now, on the point of going home, we were sitting high up on the bank admiring the catch, drinking the last of the coffee and discussing the night's events. It was pitch black, with a dense ground mist. I have never known a darker night. It had also turned very cold.

Suddenly, just as we were leaving, there was a loud slosh in the pool below.

"Hold on", I said. "That could be a taking fish."

I took up my rod, waded in, and after three or four casts with the big Sunk Lure—I hooked him.

Of course, I cannot *prove* he was the fish that sloshed. But I am certain he was. He took just where I had heard him move and where I expected him to be.

When he took, I thought he was a big sea trout. After I had been playing him for a few minutes I wasn't so sure. When he was ready to land, since I had no intention of fishing again that night, we put the torch on him to help us to get him in the net. As an indication of how dark it was, the swirling mist made the fish almost invisible even when the torch was held only three feet from the surface. Anyway, we netted him and lifted him up into the light.

He was a nine-pound salmon.

Like the salmon caught on my own stretch of fishing shortly before,

86

this fish was a forerunner of the salmon I was to land in the darkness from time to time over the years. The similarity between each catch was quite uncanny. There seemed to be a distinct *pattern*. The lateness of the hour. The night often turning cold, sometimes with thick ground mist—in itself, odd, since the appearance of river-mist is never a good augury of taking fish and sends most night-anglers scurrying home. Then, the fish moving before it took: the slosh on the surface, at the head or tail of a pool, which was the signal for me to go into action. The instant acceptance of the big Sunk Lure. The gentle take. Then—pow!

Gentle take, yes. But very positive. I have lost few fish that took at night in this way. Of course, each time it happened I thought that what I had hooked was a big sea trout. Until, sometimes, it gave itself away by trying to sulk. After all, I only hooked them when I was fishing for sea trout. And indeed, this was how many of my big double-figure sea trout have been caught—by casting a big lure to them after hearing them move late at night.

But why, you may wonder, hadn't something of this sort happened before? Night fly-fishing for sea trout had been going on for a long time. Well, perhaps it *had* happened. After all A. H. Chaytor seems to have known about it. In *Letters to a Salmon Fisher's Sons*, he says:

... in the heavy streams and in big waters at dusk, or *when it has grown quite dark, you may use your very largest fly*, and may take fish that would not look at anything during the day. (My italics).

Even so, I think it hadn't happened often, because people were using flies that were much too small. It hadn't happened to me until I started to use the big Sunk Lure in freshwater as well as salt. Before that blessed flash of intuition most of my sea trout fishing at night, like that of other anglers, had been with the conventional sizes of fly.

Another reason may be that when sea trout go off the take around midnight, after the activity during what I call the "first-half", most sea trout anglers pack up and go home. At least, they did in those days. In other words, to catch these salmon I am talking about, which seem to take only a big lure late at night, anglers neither fished the right size of fly, nor persisted long enough.

The curious thing is that when salmon fishing at dusk in summer time I have always done best with small flies: sizes 10 to 14, whereas in the darkness, on those rare occasions when I caught one, the salmon would take nothing except a big lure—even though I have frequently used a size 12 or 14 Double as a switch from the big fly late at night when sea trout were hard to catch.

I remember catching a salmon with Sunk Lure one long-ago August night when fishing for sea trout with Arthur Oglesby on his lovely stretch of the River Lune. He was impressed. So, when we parted, I gave him the lure—with which, in the same pool the following night, he caught a salmon himself. During the same week, he took the late Ian Wood, then editor of *Trout and Salmon* magazine, fishing for sea trout, and lent him the lure. That night Wood, too, caught a salmon on it. The three fish taken on it that week weighing between ten and twelve pounds each.

Are these salmon we have caught at night *moving* fish? I think they must be. Provided there are no obstacles in their path, salmon will migrate as freely by night as by day. The place where these fish take best is not the deep part of a pool but the tail or the neck, and I think the fish that sloshes on the surface and then takes a Sunk Lure is a migrating salmon that is just going to move, or has just been moving. Why such a fish should refuse our small flies and take the big Sunk Lure, I have no idea.

What I have described here is pretty well all I can write about salmon night fly-fishing. It will interest only a few anglers, I expect. Many people are not enamoured of fishing at night. Only the dedicated sea trout man will face the long darkness.

After all, why should the salmon angler bother to fish at night? Unlike the sea trout angler on many rivers in low water, he can catch his fish in daylight, when he can see what is happening and do it all in comparative comfort. There is no need to make things difficult for himself by angling in the dark. But I have included these notes because catching salmon at night is exciting, and I have not read a lot about it in the books.

So—to anyone who may feel inspired to have a cast long after the light has gone, I pass on the little I know. From experience, I believe that any angler with sufficient energy left after fishing all day, who cares to try late at night with Sunk Lure, or something similar, on a sinking line or a floater with sink-tip according to the water, is in with a chance of catching salmon.

The salmon I have caught at night were nearly all hooked while I was fishing for sea trout in the months of July and August. What I should have done years ago was to try this method on one of the big spring-run rivers during the earlier part of the season, in April, May and June.

Alas, I never did. And now my opportunity of doing so is all too limited. I wish somebody young and with time on their hands would go and try.

Note: Amazingly, as this work was going to press, I received a letter relating to night fishing for sea trout in the River Tay, and Mr Leslie Stout, my correspondent, tells me:

"In five seasons—late May to October—I took a total of 11 salmon on the big Sunk Lure, the best being an autumn fish of 16 lb. I was purposely avoiding the known salmon lies for the benefit of estate guests the next day. I'm positive that if I had set out specifically to fish for salmon, the total would have been very much higher."

Alan Shipman playing a Dee springer at dusk.

If you follow the guidelines suggested in this chapter you will give yourself a slightly better shade of odds in your quest for salmon. But I emphasize yet again that they will do no more for you than that. In salmon fishing there is no magic substitute for water-sense, skilful presentation, and persistence.

However varied your experience; however promising the conditions on any occasion; whatever your chosen method, there are no certainties. You can tap the barometer, look at the sky and the wind direction and the height and colour of the river, measure the air and water temperatures, and say: "Today seems a good day. I will put on such-and-such a lure and fish down this pool and catch a salmon."

And maybe you will. And, no matter how well you know your water, maybe you won't. Very likely you won't.

Salmon can be very irritating creatures. No other fish have quite the same knack of making the expert look silly. They will obstinately refuse to co-operate on what appears to be a perfect occasion. And at some other time, seemingly hopeless, a fish will suddenly take—when we are simply casting for the fun of it.

A few years ago, Arthur Oglesby took his Grantown-on-Spey casting class to a wide, shallow outflow from a pool to explain the principles of salmon fly-fishing. He purposely chose this location because it was well out of everybody's way. He wasn't interfering with anyone fishing the beat. It was a place that offered no chance of finding a fish. He merely wanted to demonstrate.

"Tick-tock . . . This is how you make the overhead cast," he said, lengthening line and chucking out into the stony shallows.

"Now," he went on. "When you fish the fly you just let it swing round with the current . . . like this . . . and a salmon usually takes it when it gets to about *here*."

At that moment a salmon obligingly took it.

Watched by his admiring pupils, Arthur, stunned into silence, played and landed the fish. It turned out to be a sea-lice covered ten-pounder. The only fish, as it happened, to be caught on any of the beats that morning.

Later, I measured the depth of water where that salmon took. Fourteen inches. Nowhere in that stretch of shallows between the pools was it any deeper.

I have mentioned this incident to illustrate the absurdity of salmon fishing. Also, to make the point that where Arthur hooked his fish no one had ever *thought* of casting. And yet, *there* was a taker. Indeed, the *only* taking fish of the morning.

How long had this fish been occupying that particular spot? A very short time, I guess. Indeed, if he had been lying there when Arthur and his class marched down to the water's edge, he would surely have seen them and fled. I feel certain the fish was quietly making his way up through the stickles from the pool below when, suddenly, Arthur's fly swung overhead—and he grabbed it.

The running fish again. Whether he had paused momentarily, I don't know. But I doubt it. I think he was a true "runner", and on the move when he took.

But simply because our best chance at salmon happens when they are migrating fresh from sea, it doesn't mean that running fish are automatic takers. If that impression has been given, I hasten to correct it. If it were true, salmon fishing chances would be easy to predict. As we know only too well, they are anything *but*.

It is this very uncertainty of salmon fishing that provides such a limitless field of speculation and makes the sport so fascinating. I have known the only fish of the day to be hooked by an eleven-year-old schoolgirl who had never cast before and whose line had fallen in coils almost at her feet.

It may seem preposterous, it is nevertheless true, that although the Atlantic salmon is the hardest of fish to catch and over a season the expert will come out on top, the sedulous novice is always in with a chance of beating the expert *on the day*. I find this delightful.

But no matter whose line it is tied to, a lure that isn't in the water will never catch a fish. A glimpse of the obvious, maybe, but the best advice anyone can have—and, incidentally, just about the only unqualified statement it is possible to make about this irrational sport. The beginner is always in with a chance of hooking a salmon—if he keeps on plugging away. And the more he learns, the better he fishes his lure, the better his chance.

As already discussed at some length, according to the season of the year certain times of day offer better chances of catching salmon than others. For instance, in mid-summer I would much rather be fishing at daybreak and dusk than in the noon-day glare. Even so, I remember landing four fish on the fly in two hours just after lunch during a drought in flaming June, when my companions were asleep. The only reason I was on the water in the heat of that blazing afternoon was my having to leave the beat at tea-time. I couldn't stay on to fish late with my friends, and preferred casting a fly to twiddling my thumbs. To say the least of it, the result was unexpected. But in salmon fishing the unexpected so often seems to happen!

Again, on river big or small, I would a hundred times rather be fishing a falling water than a rising water—after the first six inches or so of the rise, that is. But (rather than go home in despair) I have caught salmon on Tweed from little "lay-bys" alongside the bank in what seemed hopeless conditions of raging flood.

Talking of rising and falling water: when fishing a beat within about ten miles of a spate river estuary, I have occasionally noticed a small run of fresh fish coming through two or three hours after the time of high tide. Such fish are often ready takers, particularly in places where they rest after swimming a fairly heavy stream. So—provided there is sufficient water in the river to encourage a run, a glance at the tide-tables is worthwhile. For example, if high water is at 10 a.m. I make certain I am fishing the beat in question between 12.30 and 2.0, and not sitting on the bank eating lunch! The presence of female tide-lice on fish I have caught confirms their freshness.

However well we know our river and its humours, we never know when that magic tightening of the line will happen. Many a salmon is missed through indolence, or faulty presentation. The best any of us can do is to persist, and make sure the lure is fishing attractively all the time it is in the water.

"Never be put out by failure", wrote George Kelson. They are wise words. If you allow yourself to get disheartened you will soon lose your concentration—in consequence of which you will almost certainly miss the opportunity when it comes. Sadly, though, you will probably not realize that your chance *has* come—and gone.

The difference between catching a salmon and not catching one can be infinitesimal. A fly faltering in a back-eddy; a clumsy cast; a heavy foot-fall; a silhouette against the sky; a line-flash during some foolish false-casting; a lowering of the spirits that made you stop fishing a moment or two before your one positive fish of the day was prepared to take. Any of these may send you home fishless, wondering not for the first time whether salmon fishing, for all its charm, is really worth the effort; the frustration; the nagging sense of defeat. Especially the defeat.

It is not easy to be philosophical after yet another blank day—which, with one thing and another, may have set you back a considerable sum of money; failure made no more bearable by the heavy humour of your wife and friends.

Take heart. There is no need to shoulder all the blame. Excuses for not catching salmon are legion. I do not agree with all of them; but here, taken mostly from the literature, are a few to choose from:

The weather was too settled, or unsettled. It was too hot, too cold, too bright. There was thunder about; lightning flashing; mist over the water; clouds on the hill. The sun was shining down the pool. There was a red sunset. The wind was too strong, or from the wrong direction, or there was no wind. The river was too high, too low, too coloured, too clear. There was foam on the surface. The fish were running through. There were no fish. The glass was falling. There was too much grue coming down. Air and water temperatures were all to hell. The pool had been disturbed by poachers, predators, canoe-ists, cattle, swimmers or the fellow on the other bank. You had forgot-ten your lucky charm.

There are times when you may think that only the last is valid.

On a blazing summer day beside a shrunken river many years ago I was gillying for two very experienced (and articulate) salmon anglers.

It was three o'clock in the afternoon; very warm, very bright, very still. The two experts had flogged the hours away with various patterns and sizes of fly, and now sat, exhausted, on a riverside seat, analysing their failure.

They were an argumentative pair. But on one point they were in com-plete agreement: the fish would look at nothing. Conditions, they con-curred, were impossible. The river was too low; the light too strong; there was no ripple; it was too hot; there was no movement; the fish were "potted". It was silly to think a salmon would take anything at that time of day, unless the sky clouded over, or a breeze came up, or it rained. There was a chance, just the faintest chance that a very small fly—a trout fly, perhaps—might get an offer at dusk. But until then, they agreed, it was hopeless. There was no point in fishing.

A boy appeared from behind some bushes on the opposite bank. He carried a cheap fibre-glass rod. From it, on stout nylon, dangled a three-inch blue-and-silver Devon. He released the bale-arm of his reel and swung the Devon out across the pool. A salmon took it at once.

The boy skulldragged the fish ashore. Knocked it on the head. Put a cord through its gills, slung it over his shoulder and disappeared in the bushes.

The speed at which he accomplished all this seemed highly suspicious. But let that pass.

From the two experts, who had been watching open-mouthed, came a brief but blinding flow of obscenity. After this they fell silent and sat staring across the sun-flecked water, each alone with his thoughts. For perhaps the first time in their respective forty-odd years of fishing, neither of them could think of anything else to say.

Of such glorious moments is the very stuff of salmon fishing composed.

That salmon-fishing, as practised from the boat on Tweed, is upon the whole a very agreeable recreation, affording exercise and some measure of joyous excitement to the person engaged in it, I do not mean to deny; but it is not, to my mind, nearly so pleasurable or satisfactory a sport as when pursued on foot.

Thomas Tod Stoddart, *The Angler's Companion*, 1853

IV
The Approach

PART ONE: ANGLING METHODS

Considering his indifference to food, the returning *Salmo* is a surprisingly accommodating fish. He can be caught on a huge variety of lures fished with every method known to the freshwater angler. In addition to fly-fishing, both wet and dry, and dapping, these methods comprise spinning, trailing, trolling, harling, drift-lining, trotting, long-trotting, stret-pegging, ledgering, float-ledgering and laying-on. As we shall see, each has its own technique; its own time and place. Of them all however, fly-fishing is the most graceful and, to my mind, the most delightful. (And I stress the point that my devotion to it verges on the fanatical.) Unfortunately, for a number of enthusiastic but unthinking followers this is not enough. By them, fly-fishing is frequently described as the most *sporting* method, other methods being considered less sporting, or in some cases even *unsporting*.

Clearly, there is a time and a place for every angling style, and it is unreasonable to suppose that, when properly used, one is more sporting than another. The vice or virtue of any form of angling lies not in the method but in the *man*. It is where and when and how it is *used* that makes a method "sporting" or "unsporting".

Whatever style he chooses, an angler, before starting to fish should ask himself three questions:

1. Am I harming the fishery?
2. Am I interfering with a fellow angler's pleasure?
3. With the tackle I propose to use, have I a reasonable chance of landing a fish?

If the answer to the first two questions is "No", and to the third "Yes", I say that irrespective of the method, his approach is as sporting as need be.

95

What is a "reasonable" chance of landing a fish? Each angler must answer that for himself. But he will not find it difficult if he accepts the following dictum:

To be broken by a fish is almost always his own fault, and is a disgrace.

Although, *when used in the right context*, all angling methods are of equal merit, all tackles are *not*. Here, bearing in mind our humane/sporting compromise, there is a distinct division.

Irrespective of lure or method, the use of tackle that is too thick and strong for the water in question is likely to be unprofitable, but certainly not unsporting. The use of tackle that is too weak and thin, while equally unprofitable, most certainly *is* unsporting. The chances are that salmon will ignore the former, but break and swim away with the latter.

The angler one sometimes hears boasting of fishing fine "to give the fish a chance" exposes himself as an idiot, insensitive to the fate of the animal he hunts, since the only "chance" he gives the fish is to let it escape with a hook in its throat, trailing a length of line.

Knowing that if he uses tackle too weak he is likely to get broken; if he uses tackle too strong he is unlikely to hook a fish; the sporting angler's compromise should always be to use the strongest tackle he can—consistent with giving him a chance to attract, hook *and land* a fish.

The American notion that the heavier the fish, the lighter the line, the greater the merit of a catch—which, alas, has made some headway in Great Britain—is a disastrous philosophy that can only bring angling into disrepute. The cult of using unnecessarily light tackle is a whim, and the days have gone (if they ever existed) when sportsmen can indulge in such whims at the expense of the animals they hunt.

So—whatever method he uses, the first point for the angling "sportsman" to remember is to fish with tackle of suitable strength.

*   *   *

I believe, and I hope I am right, that most anglers go fishing simply to enjoy themselves. Whatever their secondary motives; to catch a meal, to impress friends or camp followers, their primary object is not cash, but pleasure. To this end, each angler has his own favourite method or methods of fishing. He prefers these methods because he enjoys handling the tackle involved or because they are best suited to his temperament, or—most probably—because he finds they catch him most fish.

The angler who is ashamed of being broken, and so fishes with tackle of sensible breaking-strain; who suits his approach to the water he fishes and is sensitive to the pleasure of others, is a sportsman irrespective of the method he uses.

Whatever the reason, however, *provided he accepts the three conditions listed above*, he should be thought neither more nor less of a sportsman whatever method he chooses.

On many rivers, for much of the time, fly-fishing is a very pleasant and rewarding method of catching salmon. But not by any means on all rivers, nor for all of the time. In conditions of very low water, although it is frequently forbidden, worm-fishing is a more successful method. It is also more sporting.

There are two reasons for this:

1. It is more difficult.
2. It causes less disturbance.

Few anglers, however, are experienced in this form of fishing. Indeed the dexterity required by successful upstream low-water worm fishing (for which, incidentally, no rod other than the fly-rod need be used), suggests that due to lack of skill some of the more vociferous "fly only" men are making a virtue of necessity!

Much the same may be said of those anglers found on some rivers who, whatever the water conditions, use nothing but spinning tackle, priding themselves on being better sportsmen than those who fish the prawn—although sometimes without experience of presenting this much-maligned bait.

The biggest mistake any angler can make is to be too successful. The "Brotherhood of the Angle", a concept beloved by angling writers of a by-gone age (may they rest in peace) is largely a myth. Human frailty exists in all men. And in salmon fishing, as in all angling, jealousy is seldom absent. Regrettable though it may be, some anglers cannot bear to see another catching more fish than they are catching, and if his success derives from any method other than fly, he can be sure that it will soon come under attack.* On some fisheries, these grizzlers succeed in getting all other methods banned—in conditions other than flood water.

It is a pity when fisheries become clogged with unnecessary restrictions. One of salmon angling's most supreme pleasures is diminished in consequence—the delight of using other methods when one method fails. It was by fishing in this way, experimenting, offering all sorts of lures to fish under observation, that I gained experience of salmon

---

*I write "other than fly". A southern angler, fishing a border river, had the good fortune to land three salmon on fly when all the locals were unsuccessfully spinning. Later he heard one of them remark that some unmentionable visitor had been catching fish on "those tube flies". "That's right", said his companion. "So I heard. Things like that ought to be banned."

taking-behaviour.

It is ironical that the "holier than thou" attitude adopted by some fly-fishermen, which has its origins in the trout fishing dry-fly cult of Edwardian days, is based on a curious fallacy. At the time when dry-fly fishing gradually became popular, during the latter part of the last century, the dry-fly was acclaimed not because people thought it more sporting than the wet-fly, but because they found it was more practical. It caught more fish! Early reaction was not favourable. As John Waller Hills describes in *River Keeper*, the first angler known to have used the dry-fly—as distinct from the blow-line—on the Derbyshire Wye, James Ogden, in 1865, did so with such success that he was mobbed by other anglers and driven from the river.

By the end of the century, however, the method had become firmly established and the words "fly-fishing" began to exert a strange influence. Irrespective of the species to be caught, whether brown trout, sea trout or salmon, the fly-rod became the "sporting" tool of the middle and upper class angler, who tended to regard anything else as being slightly suspect.

So, to the present, when many salmon anglers harbour notions of fly purity and couple it with the ultimate in terms of sportsmanship. A blissful example occurred not long ago after lunch one early spring day beside a famous river.

On a bridge, just above the tidal reaches, I encountered a local riparian owner: a delightfully affable man in crumpled tweeds, sporting a Guards' tie and a large cigar.

"Are you fishing today, sir?" I enquired, after exchanging pleasantries.

"No, sir. Not today," he replied, waving his cigar towards a small cluster of huts on the far bank. "Just come to have a look at me nets."

"Nets?" I queried.

"Yes. Got a netting station over there. Going down to see what the men are up to." He peered at me in sudden recognition. "You're Falkus, aren't you?"

I murmured assent.

"That's right", he said, nodding with satisfaction at such total recall. "Read your books. Seen you on the box. You here to fish?"

"No", I said. "Just come to have a look."

"Ah", he said. "Pity. Rather busy. Got to go now. But tell you what, give me a ring sometime. Come and fish my water." He handed me a card and climbed into the waiting Range Rover. "Any time you like.

Delighted to have you."

He let in the clutch and started off across the bridge towards his nets. A sudden thought struck him. Stopping, he wound down the window and called back to me.

"Fly only, of course."

*　　　*　　　*

In the sense that an artificial "fly" is a simulated insect, there is almost no such thing in Britain as fly-fishing for salmon. It is nearly all lure fishing. Salmon *are* caught at times on artificial insects by trout anglers, both on the wet fly and on dry fly—several of my friends have hooked salmon on imitations of mayfly and sedge while fishing on the surface in the lower reaches of south-country chalkstreams. But generally speaking it is a rare occurrence.

This is not to say that salmon cannot be caught on what may loosely be called a "dry fly". A delightful method of doing so is described in Chapter XIII. But even so, the fly used—although fished on the surface—is a tiny *lure*. It represents no known species of living creature. So, wet or dry, what *is* a salmon fly and what should we call it?

This question was very well answered many years ago by Eric Taverner in the book we were all brought up on when I was young: *Salmon Fishing*, 1931:

> A modern salmon fly is not regarded as an imitation of the natural fly, upon which it may primarily have been based, in fact, the word *fly* is given by courtesy; it is a title earned by the manner of its construction and origin and academically is entirely wrong. But what else can it be called? The Scottish use of hook is ambiguous, as I once found out on Speyside when a fisherman taking out his fly-book, kindly said he would "tell me a good hook." We were at cross-purposes for a few minutes; but mutual understanding came at length and we agreed that *hook* was a very poor substitute for *fly*. So fly it will remain until the real word is born and better so, because every fisherman is aware of the fiction.

That was very well said, and so whether wet or dry "fly" it shall be called in this book. But, when sanctions are being mooted, let those responsible remember what the salmon fly really is beneath the masquerade, and that its use is nothing for anyone to get upstage about.

On most rivers, during any but exceptional days on exceptional beats, the salmon is quite difficult enough to catch without being hedged with unnecessary restrictions. Irrespective of the angling methods used, it is unlikely that a salmon river can be over-fished with rod and line. By removing their appetites, nature has afforded salmon considerable protection against anglers; only comparatively few at any time are taking fish. The angling catch is proportional to the number of salmon that run up the river. A big run results in a good rod catch; a small run, a poor catch. The river is self-regulating. It is this that makes salmon and sea trout fishing different from any other form of angling.

Does this mean that salmon fishing should be a free-for-all; that anglers should be able to fish any method they wish on any water at any time? Most certainly not! According to my definition of sportsmanship, *the methods we choose should depend on the type of water and prevailing conditions, so that they harm neither the fishery nor the chances of other anglers.* I have written of the need to avoid *unnecessary* restrictions. There are situations where I think control is essential. On waters unsuitable for it, spinning is an example.

Of all items of fishing tackle, a spinning rod and fixed-spool reel are usually the beginner's first choice. Nothing there to which one can take exception—except that, being inexperienced, the novice soon finds his bait fast in the bottom and as often as not breaks his line. This is less likely to happen in the deeper parts of big rivers such as Tweed or Tay, but is a frequent occurrence in the long, shallow pools of rivers such as the Spey or Aberdeenshire Dee. To spin those lower beats of the Spey below Grantown is something of an angling crime. Not because spinning in itself is an inferior or unsporting method, but because in the hands of so many inexperienced anglers the spinning reel carpets the river bottom with snagged baits and leaves yards of abandoned nylon trailing downstream—an evil that seems to have increased during recent years.

The truth is that on many rivers the spinning rod is not the best tool for a novice angler; he will do far less harm to the fishery with a fly rod. Almost anyone can learn to *cast* a spinner in under half-an-hour, but it takes many months, sometimes years, before most people can fish a heavy bait effectively without frequent loss. The resultant tangles of monofilament, lost with snagged spinners, can cause havoc. During a recent difficult season on the Spey, when salmon were exceptionally scarce, a friend of mine lost his only two fish of the week when both fish got ravelled up with tangles of nylon anchored to the bottom.

Of course, these big nylon losses while we are spinning can usually be avoided by fitting a leader of lighter breaking-strain than the main

Philip Lord, an excellent salmon and sea trout angler, holding a mass of nylon (spinner still attached) which cost him a fine salmon when he was fishing with me on the Spey. In his own words: "The fish, almost played out, suddenly went solid and would come no further in. Eventually, it wrenched itself off the fly, and after a struggle all I pulled in was this wretched tangle of nylon and weed."

line. Some anglers, however, ignore this obvious safeguard—with disastrous results.

On most fly beats spinning is permitted when the water is above a certain height. But, as explained in a later chapter, there is seldom any need to spin in such conditions. When the river is up, salmon tend to lie close to the bank. Most of the taking lies can be covered easily enough with fly.

There is a further point. In low water, with salmon densely congregated in the pools and unable to move upstream, fish after fish can get jagged by a spinner whirling through their ranks. Perhaps more than anything else, salmon *hate* being "jagged". It is reflected in their behaviour. Pricked fish do *not* become ready takers. As I have seen, they tend to get restless; show distinct alarm reactions when a line falls across the water and sometimes flee even at the approach of a small "greasedline" fly.

The following sentiment will not increase my popularity with those members of the tackle trade who thrive on lost spinners, but the fishery

On water such as this, spinning is a crime—however high the river. The Spey in summer.

manager who forbids spinning in low water conditions has my firm
support.

It depends on the type of water in question, but so far as fish-catching
is concerned many rivers offer excellent fly-fishing opportunities and
anyone restricted to fly-only need not feel unduly deprived. My friend
Brigadier George Wilson, one of the finest game fishermen I have ever
known, is responsible for angling arrangements on a beat of the River
Derwent. He comments as follows:

> As you know I get and collate the fishing returns from the local anglers
> who fish the beat on Fridays and Saturdays. They are restricted to
> *fly only*, whereas the Monday to Thursday rods are allowed to spin
> when the river height is up to the 2′ 6″ mark on the gauge.
>
> During the season there are always a certain number of Fridays
> and Saturdays when flood or near flood conditions prevail—when the
> level is over the approved "spinning height". It is a fact that the
> Friday/Saturday people, restricted to fly-fishing, do as well as if not
> better under these conditions than the Monday to Thursday people,
> who turn to their spinning rods the moment the water level reaches
> the spinning mark on the gauge!
>
> On several occasions I have had a fish myself on fly, when following
> someone who has been spinning (and by "following" I mean fishing
> down about twenty yards behind him). There must be a lesson in
> this somewhere.
>
> I believe the reason could be that one can make a fly move more
> slowly over the fish than a spinner. I have also noticed that in these
> conditions fish tend to lie (or at any rate to take) much closer in to
> the bank than at normal heights of water.

I wholeheartedly endorse everything George Wilson has said. The
beat he refers to happens to be one I visited regularly for many years.
Although I fished the water at all heights and never once used a spinning
rod, I managed to catch my share of the fish. It may also be of interest
that this was one of the beats on which throughout three successive years
I used only the three patterns of fly, one for each year, referred to on
p. 197.

I must repeat, however, that each stretch of fishing has to be treated
on its merits. For example, to attempt fly-fishing in spring on a deepwater
beat of that early river the Eden, is pointless. Here, the depth of water
in which most of the fish are lying makes a spinner obligatory. During
the first three or four months of the season, salmon prefer a big lure

sunk pretty much to their own level. In such deep, cold water, the fly-rod, even with high-density line, is not the best tool for catching them. Those abyssal, strong-flowing Eden dubs demand the spinning rod with a big bait—and very heavily weighted at that.

These examples illustrate how such a trusty old method as spinning may be top-of-the-bill on one river and shunned on another. Is there ever a time when fly-fishing becomes dubious?

Indeed there is. And when, moreover, it gives pride of place to the worm!

In the height of summer, some rivers have stretches where upstream worm is more sensible than downstream fly. And more sporting, too, since the water is not disturbed by the mechanics of fishing to the same extent. On such rivers, in these conditions, except for an hour or so at daybreak or during and after dusk, the fly should be used sparingly.

It is in their attitude to the worm that some fishery managers (not always experienced anglers themselves) tend to get it wrong. Almost invariably, even if it is permitted at all, the use of the worm is forbidden in low water—the very time when it comes into its own as a highly-skilled angling method.

And, as we shall see later, so does the shrimp.

Provided these baits are permitted, there are few conditions of water in summer when salmon cannot be caught by a skilful all-round angler. It has been said that their use causes harm to a fishery by disturbing the fish; and it is true that, at the approach of worm or shrimp, a salmon will occasionally leave his lie and charge round the pool—behaviour that is probably responsible for some of this criticism. But in my experience this rushing about does not necessarily deter the fish from taking later on. There is no comparison between this form of "disturbance" and the behaviour of a jagged fish.

In competent hands, both worm and shrimp are thoroughly sporting and successful low-water lures. Anyway, if they are catching fish it is not easy to understand what *harm* they can be doing!

Of all angling lures, prawn is the most controversial. Some anglers never fish it. At its very mention they throw up their hands in horror, declaring that it will drive every salmon from a pool. Others use it furtively, shuffling their feet and muttering when challenged.

Some, myself among them, who think all this is rather silly, enjoy fishing it unabashed—*always with the proviso that its use neither flouts the rules of the fishery, nor interferes with the pleasure of other anglers.*

My opinion, based on years of observation, is that the ill-effects of prawn-fishing have been exaggerated. Never once have I seen a prawn drive a salmon from a pool. I have sometimes seen fish leave their lies and whizz about on the approach of a prawn, but then I have also seen them do this when confronted with worm, spinner, shrimp and, in one or two cases, even fly. In every instance, the fish have been back in station within half-an-hour; usually within five minutes. I do not say it *never* happens. There is evidence that it does: several of my friends, as well as some of the well-known angling writers claim to have seen it. And I believe them. It is simply that I have never witnessed it myself. And since, over the years, I have spent very many hours watching salmon reactions to prawn, I think it cannot happen often.

Prawn-fishing is sometimes said to be unsporting, because it can interfere with fly-fishing; and indeed, if used at the wrong time, it may. But there is no need for it to do so. As with worm and shrimp, provided we use the prawn in its appropriate context (as defined in my analysis of angling sportsmanship), it cannot affect anyone's fly-fishing opportunities, for the reason that, when the time comes to fish it, chances with the fly are already next to hopeless. That is *why* we seek the use of bait. It is only when fly-fishing chances are so poor that we may need to try other methods.

On many of the smaller rivers during continued spells of low, clear water in the heat of summer, opportunities of casting a fly with any real chance of hooking a fish are almost nil. And they will not improve until a change of weather brings the long awaited spate.

It is unrealistic to equate fly-fishing on one of the big, classic salmon rivers, with the far smaller quick-up-and-down spate rivers. On rivers such as these, during the otherwise hopeless conditions of low water, an accomplished all-round angler may save a blank day, or even a blank week, by skilful use of worm, shrimp or prawn.

Which bait he uses will depend on a number of factors: depth of water, strength of current, nature of the river bottom, presence of weed beds and so on, and can only be decided at the waterside. But one thing is certain: in these conditions, whatever bait and method of fishing it he chooses, cannot affect anyone's chances with the fly and cannot, with reason, be dubbed either harmful or unsporting.

In my experience, to fish the prawn in low, clear water when one can angle for individual fish and observe their reactions, is fascinating and instructive, being full of surprises. In addition to providing salmon I would not otherwise have caught, it has given me hours of pleasure. And watching the behaviour of the fish has been a revelation.

Apropos of this, it is worth noting that the salmon we are fishing for in these exacting circumstances is for all intents and purposes a very different animal from the fresh-run springer.

When a salmon comes straight in from the sea, resting occasionally as he runs upstream, fishing is at its best; for it is during these periods of rest that the salmon is most likely to take a lure. When fish arrive at a holding pool where they are forced to lie-up for a time, or destined to stay for most of the summer, they soon become less responsive.

The length of time a salmon spends in a holding pool may depend on inclination. He has no urge to run further. He has, perhaps, reached a pool close to the feeder stream in which he is due to spawn. Or his term of residence may be because of exigency: the river has dropped and there is simply not enough water to make further upstream progress possible—a common occurrence in any spate river. But for whatever reason, the longer a fish spends cooped up in a pool during summer as the water temperature rises, the less interest he tends to show in a lure. In these conditions, intent only on a supply of oxygen, the fish goes into a state of torpor and becomes "potted".

Broadly speaking, salmon fishing consists of casting to two classes of fish:

1. The Runner. A fish that is migrating fresh from sea. Alert. Resting between spells of running, but still alert while resting, and a potential taker.

2. The Resident. A fish that for one reason or another has taken up residence in a holding pool and stays there for weeks, perhaps months on end. This fish soon becomes "potted", and reluctant to take.

The best chance of catching a salmon is when he first arrives in a pool. As time passes he becomes more and more difficult—until eventually, in desperation, during the long, hot, summer dog-days, an angler feels constrained to try some of the tricks he hopes may stir fish up, and induce a take.

These consist of fishing a big, flashy lure quickly down a pool, and then immediately fishing down again, or backing-up, with a very small lure.

Throwing a large flat stone into the water to cause as big a splash as possible.*

---

*I have recently been astonished to learn that this method of moving a salmon is in fact illegal, and that anyone using it is in breach of the criminal law—Section 1. (1) c, of the Salmon and Freshwater Fisheries Act 1975.

> ... no person shall ... throw or discharge any stone or other missile for the purpose of taking or killing or *facilitating* the taking or killing of any salmon, trout or freshwater fish. (My italics)

For pointing this out to me, my thanks are due to Mr W. Howarth, lecturer-in-law, University College of Wales, Aberystwyth.

Putting his dog across, or persuading a companion to have a swim.

Comatose fish, such as those described above, are much more likely to grab a lure after they have been "woken up" and compelled to take some exercise.

It is in these conditions of summer heat that I sometimes welcome the sight of a canoeist paddling past—always provided he carries on downstream and doesn't hang about too long circling round and round in the middle of the pool.

At times, I'm afraid, canoeists choose to do just this, in schools, seeming to relish the angler's discomfiture. It is so unnecessary. There are arranged stopping places, and failure to observe them is sheer bad manners. The result is to create bitter ill-feeling—injurious to anglers and canoeists alike.

*   *   *

At some time or other I have known each of the fish-catching gimmicks mentioned above to succeed—at least, I have caught resident fish soon after waking them up in this way. But to be truthful, such success comes only occasionally. And it is in these unhappy conditions of low water and summer heat, with pools full of apathetic salmon, that fly-fishing chances become so poor. This is the time when shrimp or worm or prawn fishing, judiciously applied, comes into its own.

The matter will be dealt with later on, but I might as well point out now that anyone relying on prawn to fill his deep-freeze is due for many disappointments. Salmon often ignore it. Totally.

Prawning technique and the salmon's reactions are discussed in Chapter XVI. For the time being I suggest that, when considering our approach to salmon fishing, what really matters is not so much the effect of prawn on the fish but its effect on other fishermen. No sportsman should wittingly spoil someone else's pleasure. If your companions believe that fishing prawn will interfere with their chances of catching salmon—then *don't use it*. If the rules of the beat forbid its use, observe them. After all, sportsmanship is largely a matter of good manners. Always, before starting to fish as a guest, enquire what the form is—an elementary precaution common to the shooting field. To bag a hen on a "cocks only" day, or a fox on a hunting estate where these animals are sacrosanct, will not brighten your chances of another invitation. So with salmon fishing. Unless your host is very enlightened, or just doesn't care, "the carriage" will soon be waiting if he comes down to fly-fish his favourite pool and finds you putting a prawn through it!

While on the subject of fishing manners, a word about behaviour in general might not go amiss.

No matter whether fishing spinner or fly, don't go in half-way down a pool, look round at the angler above in feigned surprise and say: "Oh, sorry! Didn't see you ... You don't mind if I have a dip in now I'm here, do you?"

This doesn't fool anybody.

The angler above *does* mind, whatever he may say. Having started first he has the right to fish down the pool ahead of you. If you want to fish it too, wait either until he has finished, or until he gives you the nod. Then go in behind him. *Never* in front.

And when you *do* start, move down the pool at a steady pace. Don't keep stopping in one place, casting away, holding everybody up—if other rods are waiting to fish.

Again, if you are fishing spinner from one bank with an angler opposite fishing fly, wait for him to get a reasonable distance down the pool. He will find it disconcerting to have your piece of ironmongery hooking his line or flying round his neck. If his fly hooked you in the ear you would be the first to whine. But he can't cast as far across the river as you can.

You think I paint too dark a picture? I don't! On much ticket and association water today, fishing manners are appalling. Plop, plop, plop, in go those spinners not a yard away from some wading angler on the other bank. And fly fishermen behaving just as badly—pushing in ahead without as much as "By your leave"!

And on the subject of thoughtless and selfish behaviour, who leaves our fisheries littered with empty tins, beer bottles, plastic bags, food wrappings and cigarette cartons? It is commonplace to find yards of discarded nylon draped along river banks—an enduring threat to the species of wildlife that share this environment with us.

The eye of man does not see things as the salmon does, and often, for no determinable reason, one pool holds salmon while another of seeming equality, equally well situated, does not. There can be no hard and fast rule for locating all the resting places for salmon in a given river save by actual experience, but there are certain general habits that give the angler a key to most salmon positions even in a river with which he is totally unfamiliar.

Lee Wulff, *The Atlantic Salmon* (revised edition), 1983

V
The Approach

Illogical though salmon fishing with rod and line may be, the hooking of these fish from time to time is not impossible. And surprisingly, although success seems infinitely haphazard, there is much more to catching salmon than mere chance. True, the angler is operating in the face of heavy odds. But, as we have seen, by judicious choice of angling method, and by ensuring that he is on the water during what seem to be the most propitious times, these odds can be slightly reduced.

If he acquires some skill in "reading" water, and approaches the sport stealthily like a hunter, he can reduce the odds still further. The beginner who starts to behave like a good hunter needn't worry about making a good angler; already he will be well on the way to being one.

But after we have been fishing for hours without an offer it is natural to wonder whether failure is due to choice of lure, the state of the river, the weather, or the behaviour of the fish. Usually we blame the fish. And usually we are right. But not always.

By no means always.

Despite the inherent reluctance of salmon to take a lure, failure to catch them is frequently our own fault.

Marching down to the river like a platoon of infantry. Bobbing about against the skyline. Clattering on the floorboards of the boat, or on the shingle. Rattling on a stony bottom with an iron-shod wading-stick. Unnecessary false-casting when fly-fishing, so that the line flashes to and fro just above the lies—sometimes, even, thrashing the water as it does so. Casting with a bright sun shining behind rod and line, whose flickering shadows precede us down the pool . . . All these may frighten salmon. And we cannot catch frightened fish.

Casting ability is often given precedence in the novice's preparation and approach to salmon fishing. Wrongly. Essential though long and accurate casting most certainly is, stealth is a pre-requisite. No matter how well we cast, it is profitless if, due to our incautious and insensitive approach to the waterside, the fish have fled.

Clearly, if a salmon has been frightened from his lie he cannot be caught. But to be rendered uncatchable (for a time, at least), it is by no means necessary for him to have moved away. Salmon do not always react as trout do and rush off the moment they see you. Unlike trout, they will frequently stay where they are in their lies—even though they are aware of your presence. Experience has taught me that to cast for such fish is to cast in vain. Indeed, these circumstances provide one occasion when a salmon lie may benefit from being rested!

Stealth, therefore, is imperative. Although to watch some people fishing one wouldn't think so. All too commonly the salmon is credited with the sensitivity of an ox. Anglers who will crawl about on all fours beside a chalk-stream, blunder up and down beside a salmon-river, their lines thrashing the water in a way that would horrify them if they were after trout.

Out of twenty salmon in a pool, just one, perhaps, may be a taking fish. We have no idea exactly where this hypothetical fish may be. He could be occupying any of the lies. So, if we are to have any chance of hooking him we must imagine that he is going to be covered by each cast we make. This means taking as much care over our first and last casts as over any of the others. If we do so, if we fish fluently and cannily through the pool, we will catch this salmon—provided he happens to be lying in a suitable position relative to the path and speed of our lure.

If nothing results, we will at least have enjoyed the satisfaction of fishing the water in good style. This is one of the rewards of fly-fishing, for the fly-rod is a joy to handle, and skilful casting gives pleasure whether we are catching fish or not.

I might mention in passing that anyone fishing the fly down this imaginary pool should have done so from start to finish without a single false cast. False-casting is the curse of fly-fishing. Watching the reactions of salmon while other anglers have been flicking their lines to and fro over the lies, has left me in no doubt about the disturbance it causes.

To cultivate a stealthy approach is the advice I offer to novices who come to me to learn their fishing; it is the way I go about the sport myself. I am quite certain that, together with confidence and persistence, stealth leads to success. It is one of the three golden rules of angling.

A lovely little Hebridean spate stream. The author, using a floating line, is fishing his fly across a possible taking lie; rod purposely kept low, a loop of his line held in the crook of the right forefinger ready to slide out at the slightest touch from a salmon. But why wear breast waders when fishing such a small river?

The picture has been posed to illustrate the point that wading deep is sometimes helpful on very small rivers as well as the very big ones. How much more stealthy an angler's approach if he *keeps off the skyline* and fishes down the pool thigh-deep, hugging the bank as shown in the second picture.

Another point: the place where a feeder stream flows into a river is often a good taking lie for a salmon. The line of outflow is clearly defined. It is somewhere along this line that a fish is likely to be lying.

Note: On more level ground the angler could gain concealment by standing well back from the water's edge. But in the instance shown, with rising ground behind and no background of foliage, little would be gained by doing so.

And what do they say about a rule? That exception proves it. Well—how about this:

In the days not long ago when the shrimping-net accompanied every group of happy holiday-makers whether on saltwater or fresh, I happened to be spending a hot summer afternoon beside a small salmon pool, researching for possible future wildlife filming.

As things turned out, there was very little movement of any sort until, at about three o'clock, a family outing materialized on the opposite bank. As I read it, the party comprised Mum, Dad, their three kids in rompers, plus Uncle.

Immediately, Dad sat down with the daily paper, while Mum set about preparing tea. Making a lot of noise, the kids got to work in the shallows with shrimping-nets. For a time, Uncle fiddled about fitting a fixed-spool reel to a short fibre-glass rod, then went to the waterside and flung in a four-inch Toby spoon.

After an hour or so of mixed family activity Uncle, who by now had lost several spoons, tired of fishing and joined the kids in skimming stones across the water. Eventually, even this began to pall and, summoned by Mum, they all had tea. Afterwards, they threw what remained into the river—together with an empty cocoa tin which, while Mum packed-up, an enlivened Dad, leading the rest of the family, followed down the pool, pelting it with stones. Shortly after this, sated with pleasure, off they all went.

Distance had scarce stilled their voices when an angler appeared on my bank. A perky little chap with a pronounced north-country accent.

"Good afternoon", I volunteered. "Much about?"

"Oh, aye", he said. "There's plenty of fish in here. They were splashing about all over this morning. Caught nowt though. Thought I'd go somewhere else after lunch and give the boogers a rest."

"Do you find that resting a pool makes much difference?" I ventured.

"Of course it does", he said sharply, making his way down towards the water. "If tha' wants to catch fish, that is. Stands to reason. Tha'll catch nowt else."

Uncertain of his blood-pressure, I felt it unwise to mention the recent visitation. Hopes of research had been long abandoned but, since I had nothing better to do and the riverside has always been my spiritual home, I stayed where I was and watched him fish.

His casting reminded me of an Australian I once saw in a film wielding a stock-whip. But after about half-an-hour of this he hooked and landed a twelve-pounder.

"There you are", he crowed, carrying his fish triumphantly up the bank and out of my life downstream towards the next pool. "I told you so! It pays to rest the water. Aye, it does that. It just goes to show."

It does indeed! But exactly what?

Was that salmon hooked in spite of, or because of those roistering happy holiday-makers? I don't know. But I have rather more than a sneaking suspicion that the latter could be true; that the fish had been brought into a taking mood through having been stirred up.

This possibility is referred to on p. 107.

Of course, the answer might be that the fish had just run into the pool, although, on reflection, I very much doubt it. The river was too low for that to be at all likely. I prefer to think of it as the *exception*—the fish that crops up from time to time throughout this book: the fish that illustrates the absurdity of ever trying to tie salmon fishing down to an inflexible set of commandments.

Do so, and invariably the tablets of stone will crack in your hands.

$$* \qquad * \qquad *$$

The ability to read a stretch of river and recognize, if not all, at least some of the probable taking lies—and, further, how best to cover them—is essential if we are ever to fish unfamiliar water successfully without the help of local advice. Few anglers are lucky enough to live beside a river, with the opportunity to study it in all its moods. Most people fish for salmon only at lengthy intervals and for comparatively brief periods. All the more important to them is this faculty of knowing where fish are likely to be lying, how to go about hooking them, and what to do once they are hooked.

There is nothing mystical about this. Like reading stories of animal behaviour from tracks and signs, reading water is simply a matter of experience allied to observation and commonsense. Naturally, it takes time to develop, it will not come all at once. But come it will, if the novice keeps an open mind and gives himself some elementary training in observation. Hence the importance of becoming a nature detective.

At first, like reading the stories of the waterside, trying to read the water itself seems like learning a new language—which, in a sense is what we are doing. But it is really quite simple, and we soon learn what to look for.

Most important of all when studying a pool for the first time is to decide on the "Taking-Strips". This is the name I have given to those bands of water—sometimes on one side, but usually on both sides of the river—in which salmon are most likely to be caught. Fish resting on their way upstream lie mainly in these strips. This is probably because in the band of river between strong current and moderate current, or between moderate current and slack, they find congenial resting conditions: sufficient stream for relaxed breathing, but also an easy lie.

As shown in the diagrams, the position and width of these Taking-Strips vary with the height of water.

Nearly all salmon pools have a shallow side and a deep side. When the deep side is pronounced, with the opposite side shelving down much more gradually, it is what I call a Soup-Spoon Pool. When a river cross-section is much flatter, it is a Tea-Tray Pool. These Spoon and Tray contours, together with the water height, control the width of a Taking-Strip.

No two pools are identical. Each is a study in itself, and it is in Taking-Strip recognition that our water-sense plays such an important part, for it is in those bands of water that many of our salmon will be hooked.

This means that having pin-pointed such a strip, we can present our lure to the best advantage, for each cast we make is to a possible taking fish of whose position (if he is in residence) we can be reasonably sure.

Elevation diagrams of Soup-Spoon and Tea-Tray Pools
Showing rough position of Taking-Strips at different river heights

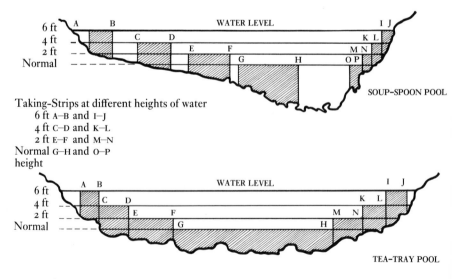

Taking-Strips at different heights of water
6 ft A–B and I–J
4 ft C–D and K–L
2 ft E–F and M–N
Normal G–H and O–P
height

Typical salmon pool showing both Soup-Spoon and Tea-Tray contours with
Taking-Strips from head to tail of pool

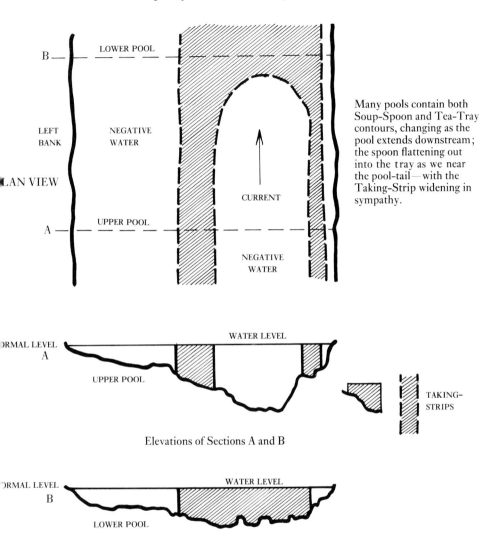

B ——

LOWER POOL

LEFT
BANK

NEGATIVE
WATER

PLAN VIEW

CURRENT

A ——

UPPER POOL

NEGATIVE
WATER

Many pools contain both
Soup-Spoon and Tea-Tray
contours, changing as the
pool extends downstream;
the spoon flattening out
into the tray as we near
the pool-tail—with the
Taking-Strip widening in
sympathy.

NORMAL LEVEL
A

WATER LEVEL

UPPER POOL

TAKING-
STRIPS

Elevations of Sections A and B

NORMAL LEVEL
B

WATER LEVEL

LOWER POOL

The width of a Taking-Strip is controlled by water height and underwater contours
of the pool. Generally speaking, the higher the river the narrower the Taking-Strip and
the shorter the line we need to cast. Conversely, the lower the water the wider the strip
and the longer the line.

117

It is not long before, instinctively, we are noting the various heights of water and how these affect the strength and set of the current, realizing that it is the current strength that governs our choice of fly-line, and whether we use a heavy, medium or light lure.

Drawings showing the same salmon pool at three different river heights with change of Taking-Strips. Angler fishes from left bank only.

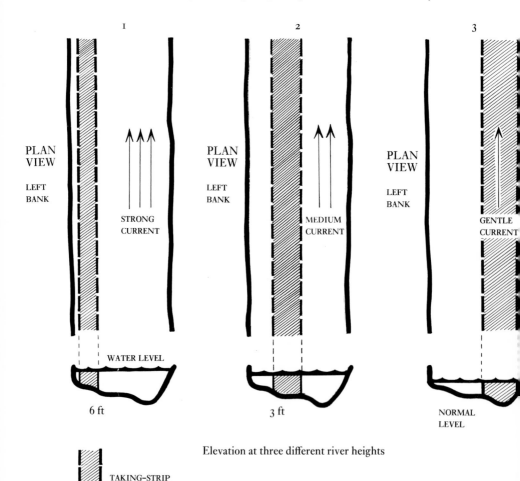

Elevation at three different river heights

A Taking-Strip moves across the river and widens as the water drops and the current slackens.

The angler, Dr Adam Price, is careful not to wade too deep; just far enough to allow him to control the fly's speed across the Taking-Strip as shown. The taking lies of salmon vary according to the height of water. Here, as the water level drops, the Taking-Strip will move across towards the centre of the river.

Water sense. Unless the angler reads this stretch of river correctly, he is likely to miss the chance of a salmon by failing to fish his lure far enough round. At this height of water, fish will be lying close in to the bank, along the Taking-Strip as shown.

From the surface swirls we note the position of sunken rocks, soon learning that salmon tend to lie in front of, beside or on top of blunt-ended rocks—but (because of water turbulence) seldom *behind*. These submerged rocks are likely taking lies. So too are those stretches of gentle flow between fast water and slack found somewhere on nearly every pool.

Sooner or later while conning the water we will see fish showing, and it is helpful to know whether they are resting or running through. A sideways jumper, or a fish that comes out at an angle and falls back flat on his side; a fish that makes a high leap ending with a belly flop; or one that lollups lazily out and drops back tail first: these are resting fish.

A running fish may show with a purposeful head and tail in the broken water below the pool, again some yards further upstream, and again in the pool tail; a fish that jumps clear of the water in a shallow arc straight upstream several times in succession but higher and higher up the pool (easily misread as being different salmon), he too is a runner.

As we glance down the pool we notice places where the current becomes refluent; where back-eddies and patches of slack water occur, often very close to lies for resting fish. And we must think carefully of how to fish them, for if our lure wanders uncontrolled into such places it will falter, lose its semblance of life and thus its attractiveness.

Conditions of dead low water are fine for reconnaissance because we can usually see any snags that may cause trouble when we hook a fish. And in preparation of such a contingency, we select suitable fish-landing spots, to which we can walk our salmon: preferably little bays of slack water with gently-shelving bank where the played-out fish can be safely beached.

When the river is low we also note any exposed rocks which, when covered by spate water, may provide lies for fish. Reaches close to the bank which have a bottom of fine, hard gravel, are also likely resting spots for fish during a spate. Such places may be high and dry when the river is at summer low, but taking lies that we shall be fishing when the river is in flood.

Other spots we look for are places on the bank where we can conveniently get in and out of the water when wading, and reaches where we can wade in safety, and where we can't: the position of large boulders; where the bottom shelves sharply away, or drops vertically from a shelf of rock.

Salmon may take anywhere on the edge of the current in this pool, but an obvious lie—in fact, the best in the water—is just ahead of, and beside, the submerged rock which is causing the ripple a few yards out from the two small leaning trees top right of picture.

Here, salmon may take all down the run of the stream on left of picture, but a good lie is that slight ripple which betrays a sunken rock centre stream and straight out from the nearest tree.

At the tail of this pool fish tend to lie just upstream and on both sides of the rock in right foreground. The sill of a run-off such as this is a very good cast for a salmon. It should be fished right to the very edge. Fish will sometimes take the fly just as it swings across the current almost on the reverse slope of the sill.

MENISCUS

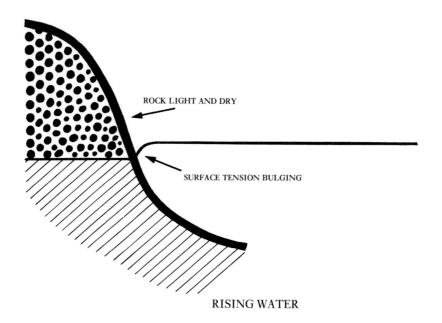

RISING WATER

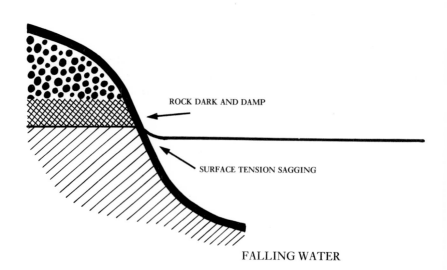

FALLING WATER

All the time we are at the waterside we keep an eye on the meniscus—the convex or concave surface of the water caused by capillarity—which tells us whether the river is rising or falling. This is an important sign if we have omitted to put in a stick as the day's water gauge, for if the river starts to rise unexpectedly as it sometimes does we may easily get into difficulties by wading too far along some underwater ridge, only to find retreat impossible against the extra water-level and strength of current.

In *Casts from a Salmon Reel*, Major Kenneth Dawson describes a West Country moorland river:

A stream which falls nearly 2,000 feet in about twenty miles is an awe-inspiring sight in high flood. Its voice is like that of an express train in a tunnel; its might irresistible. One summer night I was fishing for sea-trout from a patch of shingle in mid-stream. Presently I was conscious of a noise which I hadn't noticed before, and then that the water was lapping round my ankles where a few moments previously I had been on dry stones. Hastily I reeled up; the bank was not ten yards away, but by the time I reached it the flood was above my knees with enough force to make keeping a foothold very difficult.

There are many other aspects of river lore easily pointed out on the spot, and in his quest for knowledge the angler cannot do better than make the acquaintance of someone who really knows the water. Good angling books are of great value. They can stimulate interest and excitement, provide hours of enjoyment and a wealth of information. But when it comes to learning about *water*, and all that goes with it, a week with a first-class gillie* is worth a ton of books.

With a good gillie to help him the beginner can fish with confidence. Sooner or later, if he follows instructions and casts where he is told, he will catch fish. But most important of all, if he uses his wits and works out *why* he is doing this or that, and learns to recognize some of the likely taking lies for salmon, he will be starting to acquire some water sense. After this, it will not be long before he applies his new-found knowledge to another river and starts to catch fish by himself.

When he can do this he will no longer be a beginner.

---

*I am aware of the controversy that exists over the spelling of this word. Judging by the correspondence columns of the sporting press, acute distress is sometimes caused by the omission of the "h" from "ghillie". The authority for my spelling is *The Oxford Dictionary of English Etymology*: "Gillie—attendant on a Highland Chief: one who attends a sportsman. Gael. *gille*—lad, servant."

Now my theory is that the very successful anglers are those who habitually send out their magnetic impulses on the right wavelength to be received by the fish, whereas the not-so-successful people are the ones whose sets are not tuned-in right.

Major Kenneth Dawson, *Salmon and Trout in Moorland Streams*, 1928. Revised edition, 1947

VI
The Approach

PART THREE: THE "FEELING"

Most of this book is devoted to the practical hints that I hope will point the reader towards success. But although all roads lead to Rome, some may take him on a circuitous route. Paradoxically, for instance, it will help him to catch more fish if he understands that there is more to fishing than catching fish.

The early Chinese philosopher Chang Chi Ho is said to have spent most of his time angling, but used no hook—since his object was to enjoy the sport of fishing without actually landing anything.

I don't for a moment suggest that we should go all the way with Ho. But his delightfully idiosyncratic approach raises a point. We shall miss a great deal of pleasure if the catching of fish is everything and we can find no time to appreciate our surroundings. Salmon fishing takes us to some of the most beautiful rivers in the world, and an awareness of what is happening beside them lends a new dimension to our sport.

How barren our fishing would be without the brilliance of the kingfisher; the heron's harsh croak; the cheerful note of the chaffinch; the falling cadence of the willow warbler—to name but four of our many waterside companions. When I think back, so many of my fishing hours are remembered chiefly through the animals I met. There was that long, hot summer, years ago, when a badger took possession of one of my fishing shelters. I would go down to the river at dusk and find him sitting there. Enchanting.

Most of those nights, together with the fish I caught, are forgotten now. But not that badger. He seemed so totally unconcerned. Peering short-sightedly in my direction, he would scratch himself and sniff the air, before ambling off to start his nightly round. After a time I think he got to know me. As I discovered, by tracking him along the river bank, he spent the daylight hours in a temporary sett dug out of an old rabbit-hole.

Then there were the times at daybreak when I would stop fishing to stalk along the river and watch a pair of otters tumbling down their slide into the crystal-clear water. Once when I looked, I saw a shoal of sea trout and some salmon lying motionless not twenty yards away from the gambolling otters, seeming to sense that their enemies were only at play, and not hunting. That scene is unforgettable.

Sometimes when the light burst brightly above the fells and I switched from fishing sea trout at night to salmon in the sunrise, the curlews and sandpipers would add their magic to the morning. Then, perhaps, under the singing skylarks, roe deer would ford the river *en route* to their daytime haunt among the bog myrtle, or a hedgehog stumble past me, heading homewards through the dew-wet grass.

Anglers by the very nature of the lonely and beautiful spots they visit, are uniquely placed to witness the day-by-day happenings of the countryside. There is so much to be seen by those who wish to see. And for them it is more than captured fish that bring the rivers of yesterday to mind. Not long ago my friend Dr Jimmy Skene, on a visit to the Highlands, wrote to me of the time he chanced to stay overnight in the hotel at Inchnadamph by the eastern end of Loch Assynt:

> An evening walk revealed the presence of salmon running up the River Lonan. It was very late in the season and I only had with me a trout rod, but permission was freely given to me to try my luck ... The following morning I was delighted to hook and land three fish (all of which I returned, since they were very dark), but that was only the background of my day. While playing a salmon I became conscious of a strange hoarse sound reverberating round the hills—the roaring of the red deer stags at the beginning of the rut. Overhead, to complete the picture, a golden eagle circled in all his leisurely glory. Truly, a rare and unforgettable moment.

I too remember a wild spate river of the west, when my attention was seized by a golden eagle quartering the glen. As I watched, four ravens, like fighter planes in line abreast, came over the brow of the hill and swept down to attack. After minutes of aerial combat they drove the eagle to the far side of the glen. Whereupon, with honour seemingly satisfied, they reformed and disappeared whence they came. Whatever I caught on that dramatic day has long faded from my mind, but the excitement of that "dog-fight" lives with me still.

Note: Unbelievably, I had just written the foregoing paragraph when my wife, shortly returned from her morning walk with the dogs, interrupted to tell me of a hawk-like bird "like a big buzzard" circling overhead and being mobbed.

For a moment I sat dumbfounded. Such a coincidence was too absurd. Then I grabbed binoculars and rushed outside. Sure enough, there above the cottage was a golden eagle being attacked by four ravens!

As I watched, two of the ravens—this year's young, I fancy—broke off the attack. But the two parent birds continued to press home their dives with great determination, striking violently at the eagle's back. The eagle—also, I think, a young bird not long on the wing and inexperienced at dealing with such unprovoked assault—wisely concentrated on height, soaring higher and higher, until at last the ravens tired of the encounter. Setting their wings, and without a further wingbeat, they swooped at great speed right across the sky to join their young birds on the distant crag. A marvellous piece of theatre in itself. The eagle, meanwhile, had become a mere speck against the pale blue of the heavens, and very soon was lost to view.

Well—something of a digression from the subject in hand, and trivial in its interest. But amusing, perhaps, in the extraordinary degree of co-incidence involved. Certainly, whenever I re-read this passage the incident will be remembered with a smile—even though I was not salmon fishing at the time.

I *was* fishing, however—in Argyllshire, and wading deep—the day the otter surfaced just beside me. *That* was something I shall never forget. Vivid in memory is the penetrating stare from two beady eyes—before the little animal disappeared in a trail of silver bubbles.

As anglers we are lucky in what we have the chance to see. Even so, to understand much of what is taking place around us, we must apply the skills of the nature detective. When we do so, both water and water-side assume a new interest.

Human footprints are immediately recognizable as such. But man is not the only creature to leave behind clues to his identity. Animals, too, scatter clues from which they can be identified, and stories of their behaviour read. Tell-tale signs are everywhere: on bushes, plants, rocks, branches and the bark of trees. In wet grass, sand, mud, snow or soft earth are footprints, scrapes, scratches and scuffles. Even where the ground is too hard to register an imprint, there may be feathers, drop-pings, pellets, wisps of fur: clues from which we can deduce what creatures have been there before us, what they have been up to, and why.

Like badger and otter, the fox treads the river bank at night, and so does the heron and the water vole and stoat and squirrel and a host of other creatures. If we care to use our eyes, to find the signs they leave behind them, and our brains to interpret what we see, we can read stories of their behaviour that are as fascinating as anything the countryside has to offer.

In a work devoted to practical angling, a section on natural history and nature detection may seem incongruous. But my chief object in writing this book is to help you to enjoy success, and in my experience it is along these lines that, ultimately, success is most likely to result. A good nature detective has all the aptitudes of the good hunter, and a good hunter makes a successful angler.

Besides, there is a practical side to all this which any angler would be foolish to ignore. A knowledge of animal prints and signs can be very illuminating—as anyone will appreciate who by the side of a pool full of frightened fish finds fresh otter or mink tracks!

By practising some simple detective work and giving ourselves a chance to flex those buried hunting instincts which, like wizened muscles, have long become weakened by disuse, we start to sharpen our powers of observation. This growing awareness of what is happening in the natural world around us, does more than make us better naturalists. It heightens our instinctive understanding of the river itself—and eventually, perhaps, something of the fish it holds.

But this empathy, this sense of being "in tune" with our waterside surroundings, has an aspect of deeper significance; for it is, I believe, chiefly from this that what I call *The Angler's Feeling* springs.

Years back, in the first edition of *Sea Trout Fishing*, I mentioned the strange faculty of sometimes knowing beforehand when a fish was going to take. "Recently", I wrote, "this odd prescience has become more and more pronounced, especially after long, quiet periods of fishing when nothing has been moving." I pointed out that it manifested itself by a sudden "tingling of the senses": a vague feeling that *now* was the time to concentrate; that somewhere close by was a taking fish. Even when sitting on the bank, I might suddenly "get the message" to pick up the rod and start casting at once. And sure enough, almost immediately the line would tighten—and there was the fish!

As explained in the book, I thought this weird intuition a part of my "water-sense"; an atavistic survival from the hunting instinct of ages past. What brought it about, I suggested, was a subconscious assessment of some change in conditions: a change so slight as to be almost imperceptible; sufficient, nevertheless, to bring a fish into a taking mood.

That is the gist of what I wrote about this rather off-beat subject over

Fresh otter print, found in riverside sand.

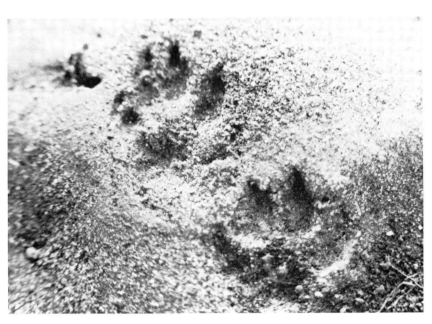

Fresh mink tracks. Like the otter print above, found beside a pool on the Aberdeenshire Dee, March, 1983.

twenty years ago, since when I have experienced the "feeling" on many occasions. It has been just as strong, just as accurate. But although I am no nearer to understanding it, I have discovered that this uncanny sense of awareness is not felt by me alone. Several of my friends have told me that they too experience something similar.

As examples of what I mean, here are two incidents that occurred during recent years on Speyside. They are purposely chosen, because in both instances there is corroborative evidence of something rather strange.

The first happened at about one o'clock in the afternoon of a bitterly cold April day. The morning had been punctuated by intermittent squalls of hail and sleet, with an east wind blackening the river— miserable conditions for wildfowling, let alone fly-fishing!

Although I had been doing my best at Number Two Burn on Castle Grant, there had been little pleasure in it. The gusty wind had made casting very difficult. No fish had been showing. None had been caught. Now, at a few minutes to one o'clock, having fished since breakfast, I was tired—and anyway, it was time for lunch.

Without reluctance I wound in my line and waded ashore. Coming up on the bank and looking towards the fishing hut thirty yards away I could see anglers from the other pools already at the trough. Among them the familiar figure of Arthur Oglesby. He had, as it happened, been there for nearly half-an-hour.

I mention these details to emphasize the fact that just then neither Arthur nor I felt the slightest urge to start fishing again. With the little calor-gas fire burning, it was snug inside the hut. Arthur was quite happy sitting there, chatting, and my only ambition at that moment was to join him and curl my frozen fingers round a glass.

On legs stiffened with cold after several hours of wading, I hobbled to the stile and put one foot up to climb over. Then I stopped. I had a sudden irrational but overpowering notion that I was being silly; that I shouldn't be up there on the bank at all; that I ought to be fishing— casting to the salmon lie which, at that height of water, existed off the fence-end . . .

As though in a dream (I can only describe it thus) I found myself walking back into the river. Waist deep, I lengthened line and cast across the blustery wind. A sudden, harder gust caught my leader and blew the fly upstream. Immediately, I let the wind put a big mend in the line and held the rod-point right down on the surface, with a yard of slack trapped in the crook of my forefinger. The fly swung round on the current. And then, when it had almost reached the dangle, as though programmed, there was a tiny pluck and the loop of line slid out. I raised the rod . . . and felt the slow tug-tug of a salmon.

Conscious of an extraordinary sense of fulfilment I backed in towards the bank. As I came up out of the water, Arthur appeared at the fence above me, rod in hand.

"Gosh!" he said, seeing my bending rod. "You've hooked him!"

When you come to think about it, that was an astonishing thing to say!

Later, having heard his story, I realized that at what must have been the very same moment I felt a compulsion to go back into the river and start fishing, Arthur, too, had sensed the chance of a fish! That feeling must have been very strong. He was quite comfortable where he was inside the fishing hut. Conditions outside were anything but inviting. And yet, suddenly, he had put down his gin-and-tonic, left the communal snug, got his rod from his car and walked down to the river bank—only to meet me backing-up from the water with a salmon on. "The" salmon!

Do you not think that an extraordinary incident? Quite independently two people received a similar "message" at the same time. Indeed, so strong was this "feeling" that both reacted accordingly—even though hitherto the day had been entirely unproductive. The point is: *how did we both know there was a salmon there?* And if it is argued that we *didn't* know; that we only felt we *ought to be fishing*, what inspired us both to head for *the same spot at the same time?* Was it really just a fantastic coincidence?

I don't know. But I feel certain it was not.

Here is the second equally baffling incident. It happened at Polchrain, a pool on the same beat, in the month of May.

During the morning I had been filming some fly-casting and river scenics for my programme *Salmo the Leaper*. By twelve-thirty we had finished work and the film-crew had gone to lunch. I stayed behind on Polchrain talking to Arthur, and Eric Robb the gillie. The river was rising and no one thought much of the fishing chances. So far that day nothing had been caught.

At ten to one, Eric went to his lunch. Arthur was taking pictures with his stills camera. To fill in time until he was ready to go, I sauntered down to the pool and started fishing.

After making half-a-dozen casts I felt a sudden impulse to renew my fly-leader. It might, I thought, have got roughed-up during the filming. But why bother? The time was five minutes to one. I had to vacate

the water at one o'clock, besides at any moment Arthur would be ready
to go.

But I still felt impelled to change that leader.

I perched myself on the edge of the bank, fished out spectacles and
scissors and reel of nylon, and started tying knots.

"Aren't you coming to lunch?" Arthur called.

"In a minute", I said. "Hold on. I won't be long."

("I couldn't think what you were doing", said Arthur later. "I saw
you fiddling on the bank. Thought you were sorting out a tangle. It
never occurred to me you would start fishing again.")

In retrospect, what happened had a strange dreamlike quality—as
though I had become detached from myself and was simply watching
what this other self was doing. Having re-tied the fly, vaguely conscious
that the atmosphere had become "alive", I started fishing again. On the
second or third cast the line tightened . . . Again I experienced the same
uncanny feeling of fulfilment.

A picture of that fish, airborne and hurtling downstream, is on the
opposite page.

*   *   *

So there you have two examples of the "feeling". Make of them what
you will. In view of my comments on middle-of-the-day fishing, you
may have noticed the taking times of those fish I caught. But I certainly
wouldn't make much of that. Salmon simply don't behave so predictably.
To rely on catching them at certain times of the day will lead only to
disappointment. Fish at those times by all means, but don't expect too
much from them.

The reliability of the "feeling", however, is altogether another matter.
On those occasions when it has seized the mind, I have never known
it fail.

"That's as maybe", I hear the sceptical reader remark. "But if your
so-called 'feeling' is as strong as that, how come you haven't shared it,
by telling someone beforehand when you were going to catch a fish?"

Well, as a matter of fact I have, and the last time it happened was
only a very short while ago.

The place was Deeside in the spring of 1982. A chilly morning with
the threat of heavy rain, the river low. A few fresh fish had found their
way into the beat, but although the other rods had been out since first
light, so far that day nothing had been caught.

Billy the gillie looked at the river and the sky and said he thought
chances were none too bright. There was, however, a piece of water

"Again I experienced the same uncanny feeling of fulfilment . . ." Photographed by Arthur Oglesby seconds after being hooked, the salmon has "taken off" and is running downstream, tail to camera. Line, leader and fish all clear of the water! (He weighed 13 lb.)

I hadn't fished before where, he suggested, I might as well fill in time until the storm broke. So off we went.

I liked that stretch the moment I saw it. There wasn't a lot of it, but what there was looked promising. About forty yards of fastish stony shallows full of swirl and eddy, ending in a long streamy glide.

I went to the top of the pool and started work. Billy, whose heart wasn't in it, sat on the bank about halfway down.

Well, I had fished about a third of the water when, with what I can only describe as a strange tingling sensation, the notion began to steal upon me that not only was I heading for a taking fish but that I was going to catch him!

Billy was on the point of moving further downstream.

"Stay where you are", I called. "There's a taking fish down there and you're standing against the skyline."

Billy shrugged his shoulders and sat down again.

"I tell you there's a fish there, Billy, and I'm going to catch him."

He said nothing. Just looked at me.

What he thought about it was all too plain. But I didn't care. I was too tense with anticipation to worry about Billy. Anyway, he had a surprise coming to him.

Wading deep, I was casting a long line right across the current; then, by shooting extra line, making a huge mend; so that, before it started to swing across, the fly hung for a moment between current and slack on the far side of the stream. (The classic way of fishing the greased line in that sort of water, according to A. H. E. Wood, See p. 233).

Just as well I took the trouble. That was where the fish turned out to be lying.

I saw him swirl as he took the fly. Then I raised the rod and felt his weight, and sensed again that dreamlike feeling of elation: of fulfilment ... As I started to back-in towards an astounded Billy, a flash of lightning brought the first big drops of rain.

* * *

As I say, that incident happened only a short time ago, so every detail is still vivid in my mind; the sense of magic undiminished. I have quoted it because it illustrates the practical value of this curious "feeling" I experience from time to time. If I am right, it is a part of the shrivelled instinct-to-hunt that I think lies deep inside all of us and is therefore potentially available to every angler.

Some of my readers, resisting the idea of a "hunting instinct", may think it an outrageous notion that sophisticated modern man remains subject to the dictates of an instinctive animal urge. Well—each to his own philosophy. I recommend others to keep their options open, and by concentration—by becoming as one with their angling environment—to allow the "feeling" I describe a chance of making itself felt.

Elsewhere I have suggested that what brings it about is a combination of water-sense and some weird subconscious, computer-like assessment of our angling chances in relation to the ever-changing conditions at the riverside. After all, the experienced angler is always on the look-out for change. The sea trout night fly-fisherman is quick to note a cloud-bank that slides across the moon; or the softening of a bright, starlit sky, with its probable accompanying rise in temperature. The salmon fisherman welcomes a gleam of sunshine on a cold spring day; a breath of wind in June; the first hint of rising water. But there are changes that although less noticeable are no less important. And I think that when our senses are attuned to draw an inference from these changes, we find ourselves acting on the "information received", although hardly aware of why we are doing so.

If, as I believe, this in-built computer really is a survival from our dim and distant past, and common to each of us, it represents an important asset that every angler can develop with advantage. After all, if I am right, what is known as the "hunting instinct" is no mere figure of speech. Dissipated by centuries of urban living it may be; but it must still be lurking there deep inside us and ready, if given the opportunity, to assert itself in the development of our water-sense and stealth.

This affinity with nature—with what is going on around us—will never help in casting a lure farther or more accurately. But eventually it may help us to decide *what* to cast and *why*. This is because if we train ourselves to notice what is happening on and beside the water, we may begin to notice and, which is more, to understand what is going on *in* the water.

So—far from distracting our attention from fishing, nature detective work will ultimately help us to catch fish. By reading simple stories of the countryside on our way to the river we have had to use our eyes and our brains. And use them moreover, in a new way: the way of our ancestral hunters.

In doing so, we too become hunters—even before we start to hunt.

*　　　*　　　*

Before we can land a salmon, however, he must be hooked. To achieve this, our lure must be fishing attractively. This in turn depends on presentation. And since on many rivers successful presentation demands deep wading, it seems sensible to include some notes on wading technique and angling safety.

Wading in the water is not only an agreeable thing in itself, but absolutely necessary in some rivers in the North that are destitute of boats . . . If you are not much of a triton, you may use fisherman's boots, and keep yourself dry; it is all a matter of taste . . . Avoid standing upon rocking stones, for obvious reasons; and never go into the water deeper than the fifth button of your waistcoat; even this does not always agree with tender constitutions in frosty weather. As you are likely not to take a just estimate of the cold in the excitement of the sport, should you be of a delicate temperament, and be wading in the month of February, when it may chance to freeze very hard, pull down your stockings, and examine your legs. Should they be black, or even purple, it might, perhaps, be as well to get on dry land; but if they are only rubicund, you may continue to enjoy the water, if it so pleases you.

William Scrope, *Days and Nights of Salmon-Fishing*, 1843

VII
The Approach

PART FOUR: WADING AND ANGLING SAFETY

Apart from an ability to cast a long and accurate line, it is on wading skill that in many pools successful salmon fishing depends. Learning to throw a long line is an early task confronting the novice, and most people with "hands" and any sense of timing learn to do this quite quickly. But long casting, although important, is not in itself enough. The reason why we need to wade is seldom because we cannot cover the fish, it is because in streamy water unless the angle between rod and fish is reduced we cannot cover them *effectively*.

For most of our fishing, simply to cast a lure over salmon is pointless unless its speed and depth can be controlled. To achieve this control in the strong current of a big river we must narrow the casting-angle between the rod and the lies we want to cover. Throwing a long line is one way of doing this. Deep wading is another. On a big, strong-running river like the Spey, these two skills must be married at peak performance. Failure to understand this and to attain high enough standards in both is the reason why many newcomers catch relatively few fish on that famous salmon fly river.

Broadly speaking, the stronger the current the more difficult the control of our lure becomes, and the deeper we need to wade. And since wading becomes progressively more difficult as current and depth increase, *skilful* wading—gaining those extra inches in depth, but safely—is more than a useful adjunct to success, it is essential.

In order to decide where and how deep we should wade, we need to know where the salmon are lying. This is when a good gillie becomes so important. Irrespective of the height of the water, he should be able to tell you the exact position of the lies, as well as something about the underwater contours of the pool. On many fisheries, however, you will not have the services of a gillie. In which case this vital information will depend on either a knowledgeable companion or your own water sense.

Unless we have a very shrewd idea of where our fish are lying we cannot decide where or how deep we should wade; or, indeed, whether we need to wade at all. Just how important this is becomes very apparent on some of the bigger rivers where one often sees anglers fishing where they should be wading, or wading where they should be fishing.

Frequently, wading is unnecessary. Some pools can be fished in a pair of shoes, and well back from the water's edge at that lest we disturb the lies. In others, no more than token wading is advisable. This is particularly the case in the glassy water of long, smooth glides. To wade incautiously down one of those stretches sends every fish ghosting away into deeper water. Depending on the depth, strength of current, and nature of the water surface, each stretch of river must be treated on its own. Often enough on some pools we need to keep well back from the water's edge when starting to fish; moving into the water and wading deep as we fish through the centre, and then moving out on the bank again as we come to the tail. In another pool this process may be reversed.

Knowing what lure to use, and where and how to present it, is the essence of successful salmon fishing—and, indeed, what practically the whole of this book is about. But presentation of our lure depends largely on the position from which we cast it, and in many pools only by wading can we get ourselves into that position. So, an ability to read a river—to determine when and where to wade—is an indispensable element of water-sense.

Having made that point, however, I must stress the importance of stealth and concealment. Either ashore or in the water we are wise to move with the deliberation of the heron, that most stealthy of waders. Underwater noise—the rattle of nailed boots or a metal-shod wading-stick on stone, a rumble of shingle dislodged on the bank—does nothing to advance our cause. Nor does it help us if the fish become aware of our presence. It is vastly more sensible to move and cast against a background of foliage or a steep bank, rather than from the top of a bank silhouetted against the skyline. Similarly, provided the water is rippled and we avoid treading on the fish, we increase our chances of concealment the deeper we wade.

It may seem contradictory that to wade deep, and therefore nearer the fish, should help *conceal* us, but the less of us there is sticking out of the water the less of us the fish can see from his "window"—that circular patch of surface just above his head through which he can watch the outside world. Strangely, fish seem to ignore the movement of those long green or black legs that stretch from the surface to the bottom. As I have been fascinated to observe on many occasions, no matter how clear the water, provided the surface is rippled one can wade very close to fish.

Just how close, sometimes, was illustrated by a dramatic incident when Arthur Oglesby and I were struggling to complete a film. Pressed for time (as always) and desperate to hook a fish for the camera, we were fly-fishing in tandem waist-deep. I was in front with a floating line; Arthur about thirty yards astern fishing sunk line, his fly just missing me at the end of its swing. Intent on watching my line, I nearly jumped out of my waders when a salmon suddenly took Arthur's fly and leaped from the water with a violent splash not three feet away, drenching me as it did so.

Something very similar had happened a few years before when that famous American angling writer, Ed Zern, had hooked a fish when following Arthur down the same pool. "The salmon took right alongside me", Arthur said later. "If he'd missed it, the fly would have hooked me in the waist!"

It is significant that in both cases there was a good ripple on the water.

Surface ripple, caused either by current or wind, has considerable influence on our fishing chances. Although anything of a wind removes much of the pleasure in fly-fishing, a slight breeze—enough to wrinkle the surface—is very welcome. When the water is rippled, the fish's window is disrupted and the movements of angler and rod become blurred. When wading in low water, surface disturbance is something we are usually careful to avoid making. Nevertheless, on some pools in smaller rivers, when wind-ripple is absent, a worthwhile ploy is to *create it*.

Simulated wind-ripple is contrived by waggling the knees, or by a circular movement of the hips—sufficient to send a series of tiny waves rolling across the surface, thus breaking up the clarity of the fish's window. It is a useful trick to use on the glassy tails of shallow salmon pools during late evening fishing in summer. I have also used it successfully on sea trout pools in low water when fishing on clear moonlit nights.

Rivers vary enormously. Some, with firm gravel bottoms, are easy wading; others are treacherous, with tumbled boulders, shifting banks of shingle, or jutting strata of rock from which a single false step may pitch you straight into the deeps. An experienced angler who knows his water can tell at a glance where he can wade in safety; but even the expert can make a misjudgement. A stretch safe to wade when the river is, say, a foot above summer level, may be impossible after a further rise of two inches. In a lake a two-inch rise means that the wading depth is increased by exactly that amount. In the river two extra inches mean not only two added inches of depth but a stronger current. This increased pressure raises the water level against your back. Also, in order to keep your footing, you must brace yourself at a greater angle against this faster-flowing current, thus further reducing your safety margin. The combination of these factors shows a "rise" of considerably more than two inches.

Remember, even when you are standing still in a river, the current is always piled higher against your back than your front (looking down-stream), so that always you have a smaller margin of safety than you may think. As soon as you start to wade upstream against that current, which in order to regain the bank may at times be obligatory (see p. 142), the water will pile up higher still—not only from the added pressure of the current, but the greater angle at which you have to lean. In these circumstances even though you may escape a swim, it is very easy to get wet. River bottoms seldom maintain a perfect level. A sudden lurch forward into a bit of a hole and water slops over into your waders. The icy trickle filling up round your feet on a cold spring day can be very disenchanting, and I add here a most important note: *always* carry a spare change of clothing in your car boot. This is an essential piece of salmon-fishing tackle. Never drive to the river without it.

Some anglers are disdainful of the wading-stick, seeming to think its use beneath their dignity. I urge my reader not to be so silly. As a strut and water-gauge as we move step by step, a wading-stick is a blessing in any river; additionally, as a probe for rocks and sudden holes in a strange river, it is indispensable. A stick has saved me from many a wetting.

But do use an efficient stick—i.e., heavy enough in the butt. Such a stick is described on p. 175, together with notes on its use.

So that you may wade silently, your wading-stick should be tipped with rubber; your boots with felt. Felt-soled waders are much safer than nails, by far the best on slimy rock. They are slippery on wet grass, but nailed heels take care of that—if you avoid walking on your toes.

Whatever the type of wader soles you are wearing, don't stand on top of rocks, whether submerged or dry. It is easy enough to get up, but in a current very difficult to get down again without losing your footing.

With water foaming round his buttocks the author Spey-casts across a very strong current, against which he can just keep his footing. His wading-stick, well weighted in
the butt, stands like a strut instantly ready-to-hand. (Note difference in water-height
fore and aft.)

The salmon lies his fly will cover are on the left of the patch of foam. They could
be covered from the bank, but only by wading can they be covered *effectively*. Wading,
therefore, helps us to increase our *effective casting range*.

Note: ECR is described on pp. 225–230.

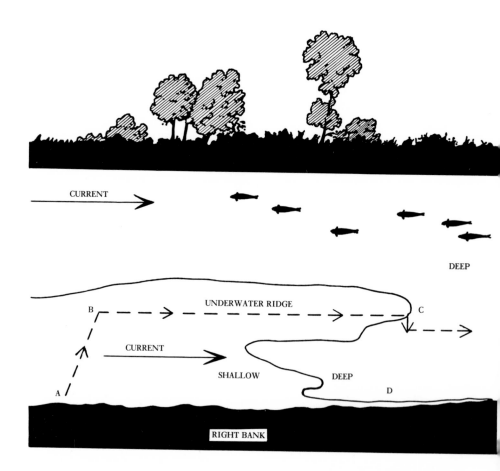

CURRENT

DEEP

B — — — → UNDERWATER RIDGE — — — — — → C

CURRENT

SHALLOW DEEP

A D

RIGHT BANK

When wading, watch for signs of a rising river: water welling up round dry stones; leaves and straws starting to float down on the current. And always be sure of the depth of water between you and the bank. Your path may lead you along an underwater ridge with deep water on either side. In which case the only possible line of retreat is straight back upstream. Wading against even a weak current is much more difficult than wading with it.

In the diagram above, an angler wades out from A to B in order to cover salmon lying under the opposite bank. He fishes his way along a submerged spit to point C. There he comes to deeper water and finds he can wade no farther downstream. Owing to the strength of the current he is unable to retrace his steps. Not realizing his position he tries to wade straight in towards the bank along the line CD. Almost at once he steps into deep water and is swept away downstream.

And talking of current, always be sure of the depth between yourself and the bank. When wading downstream your path may run along an underwater ridge ending in deep water. Before you can head in towards the bank from such a position you will have to retrace some of your steps upstream. Wading against even a weak current is a good deal more difficult than wading with it. Rather than turning round and facing the current, you will find it easier to wade back sideways, like a crab.

Don't be in a hurry. Always take your time. Whether on the bank or in the river, haste is the biggest time-loser of all. Wade carefully and deliberately, making sure that one foot is safely placed before moving the other. Never forget the tragic case of that youngster long ago who got his foot jammed between rocks, and drowned in a rapidly rising river.

Keep an eye on the water-height. It may seem unlikely that rivers can rise rapidly enough to catch a wading angler on the hop. But some can. And occasionally do!

But no matter how careful we may be, wading in wide, fast rivers is always something of an adventure. However experienced, anyone can make a mistake and get carried off heavily clothed and booted into deep water. Each year suffers its toll of fatalities, made all the more unfortunate because few wading accidents should result in anything more serious than a drenching. Unhappily, many people have no affinity with water and are easily frightened, especially by *deep* water, which they seem to regard with feelings akin to supernatural awe. I remember an old Scottish angler, when I was a boy, urging me to avoid a certain dark, cliff-girt pool. It was, he assured me, thirty feet deep. "Horrible, dangerous place", he would mutter in sepulchral tones. "Great black rocks the size of tombstones. Why, if you fell in there, you'd never get out alive. It would suck you down."

I was very curious about this. Quite why the pool should be any more threatening than water half its depth, and whence came its strange powers of suction, I couldn't elicit. The old man would simply shake his head and mutter. But so terrified was he of the pool that had he ever tumbled into it he would, I feel sure, have drowned at once.

One day when he wasn't with me, I decided to put his suction theory to the test and amused myself by diving in. When someone told him of this he got very upset. "You shouldn't have done that", he said sorrowfully. And then, pointing sternly: "Doing such a stupid thing! You'll come to a bad end."

Well, that could happen yet. But not, I trust, through ignorance of water.

It is often said, and unfortunately a lot of people believe it, that if you fall into deep water wearing waders your boots will drag you down.

It is *not* true. If you fall into deep water wearing thigh boots and *keep your head*, you will *not* go down like a stone. To swim in long waders is a perfectly simple matter and, provided you don't panic, there is no immediate danger. Although waders don't make swimming any easier they certainly don't make it impossible. Indeed, the air trapped in your boots and clothing will help you to stay afloat—if you give yourself half a chance, and don't panic.

It is panic that drowns most people. When, for whatever reason, they suddenly find themselves out of their depth, they throw up their arms in fright and shout for help.

Two involuntary actions, both fatal.

Mouth open, water rushes in. Arms up, the body sinks—"like a stone" indeed. And if they keep their arms up they will probably stay sunk. But is is not the fault of their boots. If they lower their arms they will soon bob up again.

Swept off his feet by the current, Blyth Oxley kept his head (and his rod) and allowed his feet to come to the surface. Despite the cold water of early May, he soon struggled out unharmed.

Panic in such a situation can be fatal.

Panic stems from fear. Paralysed by panic, you do not even need to be out of your depth to drown, you can die in water only a few feet deep. What can happen, and how quickly, is described by a medical friend of mine, Dr Roger Burns:

While fishing the Tauranga Taupa River in the North Island of New Zealand, I was casting opposite a man who lost his footing and fell in. The river was fast and deep at this point, but quickly shallowed and widened out. Terror-stricken and shouting for help, he was rapidly swept downstream, and although soon in only about three feet of water, he was still floundering blindly with his head going under, when I ran along the opposite bank, waded in and shouted to him to roll over and stand up! I'm sure that if I hadn't done this he would have drowned. It was an example of sheer panic, which I wouldn't have believed if I hadn't seen it.

*   *   *

But if thigh waders have had a bad press, what of those that enclose the body?

It is probable that breast-waders are involved in many wading accidents simply because the higher his waders the deeper an angler is tempted to go; until, sooner or later, a step too many is taken. When this happens the water is not up to his knees or thighs, but to his chest, and in all likelihood he is swept off his feet by the current.

If some of the literature is to be believed, his chance of survival in breast-waders is even slimmer than in thigh-boots, especially if they are fastened round the waist. In that event, according to legend, his feet are brought to the surface by air trapped in the legs and his head is pushed under. A recent publication contained the following pronouncement:

Because all waders, even in deep water, do contain a certain amount of air in them in spite of the pressure of the water, the type that fastens round the waist, either with a running cord or a belt, can be dangerous. The fisherman who falls in even in shallow water wearing waders so fastened, can very easily be drowned because water cannot get into the waders to displace the air, and in consequence his legs are liable to float, and his head go down.

The author of that passage, echoing the popular fallacy, cannot possibly have written from experience. Had he ever tried swimming with breast-waders so fastened, he would have found how much easier it was to keep himself afloat. The position he describes: legs floating with head well back, is the very position the angler should adopt in this sort of emergency.

I assure you that no matter what type of waders you are wearing or how they are fastened, when the worst happens and you find the water closing over you, *there is no immediate danger*. But you must not throw up your arms and shout. If you do you will sink, swallowing water as you go down. Pay no attention to those stories of drowning men coming up three times. If you ship enough water first time down you won't come up at all. But if you keep your mouth shut and your arms at your sides, you will soon re-surface.

Remember: when vertical the body sinks. When horizontal it tends to float. So—lie on your back, arms stretched at right angles, legs on the surface, head right back in the water. This is the "crucifix", the classic safe floating position. Once in this attitude you can start shouting for help.

The "crucifix", classic safe floating position. Arms stretched out, legs up near the surface, head well back in the water.

It is easy enough to swim while holding a rod. But if you find this impossible you will have to let it go. After all, its loss is nothing compared with your life. With line out, however, there should be a good chance of finding it later.

Don't try to swim against the current. Drift with it, feet first. Then it is your boots that may strike a rock, and not your head. Kick with your legs, paddle with your hands and gradually edge in towards the bank.

Don't keep feeling for the bottom with your feet. As your legs go down, so will your body. Keep your legs kicking away up near the surface until you reach the bank, or go aground at the tail of the pool.

Don't try to pull yourself out of the water up a steep-to bank. Waterlogged waders and clothes will exhaust you. Float downstream until you find somewhere more suitable.

Don't stand up at once on reaching shallow water. Tired and suffering from shock, you may stumble and hurt yourself. Better to turn over and crawl out on hands and knees.

Don't kick your waders off too soon, you may cut your feet on rock or gravel. Lie on your back and let the water run out before attempting to walk.

*   *   *

Inexperienced anglers would be well advised to treat rocky, fast-running rivers with caution. When wading an unfamiliar beat, the experience of a knowledgeable local angler, or gillie, should always be sought in advance. It is silly to be wise only when you are wet.

And on the subject of gillies and what they may be expected to do, perhaps a word or two here will not be out of place.

Out we went again with two flies, nor had we made many turns when my beautiful rod got a drag, that made every loop in it sing, and I had firm a most enormous spring fish . . . away he went down and across for a considerable distance then doubled against the stream . . . I wheeled up very quickly, until the weight came on my "Multiplier", and then one yard I could not get up. At this time, a malignant grin passed over the stern phiz of Kean. I made another effort to wheel up, with all the force I could employ, when smash went the multiplying machinery . . . the line would not run; it twisted up, my rod snapped in the butt, about a foot and a half from the wheel, and my brute got off, taking about forty yards of line. He was one of the largest salmon I ever saw. "I knew", said Kean, "what the multiplying wheel would do."

O'Gorman, *The Practice of Angling* (Vol.1), 1845

VIII
The Approach

PART FIVE: THE GILLIE

If there is just one gillie on the beat you are fishing, should you be fortunate enough to have one at all, you will of course have to share him with the other rods. But if he is a personal helper, *your* gillie, there are certain services you should expect.

In the old days, in order to assist my income as a writer, I did all sorts of odd jobs. Gillying was one of them. So, these notes are being written, as it were, from both sides of the fence.

Perhaps I took it all rather too seriously, but when gillying I would have been ashamed to turn up in a pair of hob-nailed boots carrying only my lunch. Any gillie worth the name, I felt (and still feel), should have his waders handy, and be prepared to wade at his rod's elbow if requested to do so. And the inexperienced rod, if he is sensible, will certainly request it. As I soon learned from the number of anglers I saved from a wetting, some people are not at their best in body waders with the current swirling round their bottoms.

An elderly angler, trying to cast with a double-handed rod while struggling to keep his footing in some fast, deep, boulder-strewn reach, is unlikely to be fishing the water to much advantage. To have someone competent beside him with a ready hand in case of emergency, advising him of the nature of the stream and the river bottom ahead and ensuring he doesn't wade in all the wrong places, is a great comfort. The additional confidence he derives from this will enable him to concentrate on his casting and undoubtedly help him to catch fish. Besides, some rivers are brutes to wade and, for the inexperienced rod, downright dangerous. It is silly to take risks. Accidents do not happen often, but once may be too often.

Good gillying made light of what was nearly a fatal accident on

Speyside recently. A girl, wading deep in a very strong draw, staggered and lost her balance when hit by a sudden freak gust of wind. It happened just as she had removed her fly from the rod-ring preparatory to casting, and in that fateful second the wind-blown rod dragged the big fly hook deep into the ball of her right thumb. A moment later, and the current would have swept her into deep water. But the gillie, who by great good fortune was wading alongside, braced himself against her, seized the rod with one hand and snipped the leader with the other; took her arm and step by step helped her to the bank. There, he extracted the hook, before driving her to the local hospital for anti-tetanus jabs and first-aid. After which he whisked her back to the fishing lodge for tea and brandy.

She had guts, that girl. Later, sore-fingered but undaunted, she was fishing again.

Her narrowest of escapes emphasizes the importance of being on the alert for danger. No one is ever entirely safe on a river. Had that gillie not been wading beside her, with scissors slung ready for instant use, what chance would she have had? Floundering out of her depth, suffering the agony of a hook sunk deep in her finger and unable to free it as the swirling Spey current swept her rod downstream and pulled her after it, she would quickly have added another name to the long list of fishing fatalities.

But she didn't panic. She didn't even scream. She kept her head and made it as easy as possible for the gillie to help her.

What a girl! What a gillie!

The true worth of a gillie, however, does not lie simply in his willingness to shoulder the bag, row the boat, or even wade beside you—important though this is. It is the ability to give good advice: the advice of an expert professional who knows his water and something of the fish it holds. The first-class gillie provides the water-sense you lack.

In addition to a thorough knowledge of the river bottom, such a paragon will understand the way of the river itself, with its swirls and eddies, and the effect of the ever varying current on the behaviour of your lure. Above all else, he will know the exact position of the main taking lies— the all-important piece of knowledge when it comes to catching fish. It is this expert advice that, hopefully, you pay for when you employ him. And if he really does know his stuff, you should pay him well.

Payment, incidentally, does not include filling him with whisky in the middle of the day. This advice is based on no teetotal inclinations but on plain commonsense. The time to open a bottle is not when we may shortly be stumbling about among the rocks and wading some difficult water, it is when the rods have been put away and the day is done.

You may not often meet a *very* good gillie. There is no particular reason why you should. The gillie's job is no holier than any other trade. But it is more demanding than most, and only the naive angler would assume that the engagement of a gillie is an automatic key to success.

Gillies on some of the big beats today are invested by absentee fishery owners with an authority that not all are able to exercise without insolence. It is, I suppose, symptomatic of the times. But if some of the modern gillies fail to measure up to the standards of their predecessors, so, it must be said do some of the anglers.

The gillie is often in a position of sole charge. He has no easy job, having to protect his beat not only from the depredations of professional poachers, who seem to proliferate, but from parties of modern "sportsmen" who take every opportunity to fish illegally. Small wonder that at times he is responsible for restrictions being imposed on the hours these gentlemen may fish the water!

When you do meet a really good gillie, grapple him to your heart with hoops of gold and treasure what he says, for it is all too seldom heard. Such men are usually more than good anglers, they are good countrymen, too, with a deep feeling for the river and its surroundings.

One such as this is my friend Eric Robb, whose advice many anglers could note to their advantage:

Always treat salmon fishing as a relaxation. Never fish for personal gain, or rush around as though being chased by a swarm of bees. This will only spoil the pleasure the sport can provide.

Fish the fly whenever possible, and have in mind that other anglers may be fishing down after you are finished. Ensure that by your treatment of the water, they have the same chance of catching fish.

Should you fish on a strange river or pool, especially with fly, try and get expert knowledge from someone who really knows the water. I always maintain that the longer you fish the same stretch the more salmon you'll catch.

Although I have gillied a beat on the Spey for many years, I am still learning something new about salmon lies and lures during the river's many different moods. Even so, experience has made me aware that during the course of a season there are only about fourteen or fifteen perfect fishing days.

The essence of such a day? Well, the salmon most likely to take are those that are fresh-run. Salmon that have been in the river for some time, say from two to four months, are much harder to catch.

So—the first essential is a stock of fresh-run fish.

Then the river must be at a good height, with a water temperature around 50°F. And since dull days are better than bright days, we want a dull, warm day with high cloud ceiling.

Generally speaking, river conditions are good when:

1. The water temperature is rising steadily between 40°–56°, or dropping when above 57°.

2. When the water height holds steady for a good length of time.

3. When the water is starting to rise (for the first six inches) after a drought.

4. When the water is dropping after a spate.

Fishing is poor when:

1. Mist is coming off the water ("harr"). Usually in the early morning or evening.

2. The air temperature is much colder than the water temperature: say a difference of 15°F.

3. A very bright sun is shining straight downstream into the salmon's eyes.

4. A strong gusty wind is blowing in squalls, with rapidly changing light. Very few fish are caught in these conditions, no matter whether the wind is blowing up or down the river. (The only good wind for salmon fishing is the one that doesn't blow! Although I do like a light, balmy, steady breeze when fishing a smooth glide.)

5. The river is in full spate, with weed, grass, logs etc. coming downstream. This is worst of all and usually hopeless for fishing; a chance to go sight-seeing, or to overhaul your tackle.

To improve his chances of catching fish, the novice should try to get proper tuition and advice. Here are some suggestions:

1. Fish with properly balanced tackle, and make sure that rod, reel, line, leader and hook are always in perfect order.

2. Cast a straight line with as little disturbance as possible.

3. Always try to cast first time, especially with a double-handed rod.

4. Keep on the move; taking one pace after every cast, while the fly is below you.

5. Always fish facing the light. Hence, some pools fish better from one bank in the morning and the other during the afternoon.

6. Never strike when a salmon takes the fly.

7. Having hooked a fish, keep the rod well up, at 2 o'clock, and keep a little downstream of the fish.

152

8. Never let the line go slack.
9. Never try and hold the fish should it "take off".
10. Always take your time when playing a fish; and, when it is ready, beach it and land it by hand. *Never ever* use a gaff on a fish unless it weighs 25 lb plus, and then gaff it through the back of the head or underneath the bottom jaw. An angler who sticks a gaff into the middle of a beautiful salmon I wouldn't trust with his granny's purse!

But however experienced your gillie may be, always try to do as much for yourself as possible. Especially when it comes to choosing lures. No matter how well they know their beats, some gillies are inclined to be conservative regarding lures and tend to be dogmatic. Whatever the pressures, always feel emboldened sooner or later to try your own fancies. The reason why certain lures have acquired the reputation of being indispensable on certain beats is usually because for years on that water little else has been used.

As I well remember from the days when my big Sunk Lures and Surface Lures were treated with scorn, this conservatism is as prevalent among sea trout men as those who fish for salmon.

Contrary to common belief, it is not really the gillie's job to set up your tackle and tie on your lure. A knot is a very personal matter. To lose a fish because a knot slips is a grisly business. If it is going to slip it is better that *you* should have tied it. If in doubt, get someone to show you the best knots to use, and then always tie them yourself.

And on the subject of doing things yourself, you will be well advised always to set up your own tackle. Only then will you be sure that the reel is firmly attached; the line correctly threaded; the leader securely fastened. Similarly, you should seldom allow anyone else to land a fish for you. Unless in difficulties, or he is a very big fish, always do it yourself. Too frequently one sees some willing helper, with gaff extended, craning eagerly forward at the water's edge ready to swipe at the first opportunity!

A good gillie can of course perform all of these elementary tasks just as well as any of us, and better than most. But in fairness to him as well as yourself you should be responsible for putting your tackle together and, whenever possible, for landing your own fish. Then, if a knot slips, or the reel drops off in the heat of action, or a hasty gaff stroke breaks the leader . . . you have only yourself to blame.

It is better that way.

The Spey fishermen, who I think are the finest underhand casters in the world, use rods made especially for the purpose. The upper portion, instead of being straight, is made in a curve, and, when fishing, the curve faces the stream, which gives a rod made in this fashion a greater lifting power than an ordinary one, but I have always found I could make as good a cast with the latter.

Major John P. Traherne, *Salmon-Fishing with the Fly*. included in "*Fishing*" by H. Cholmondeley-Pennell, 1887

IX
Fly Fishing

PART ONE: TACKLE

Check-List

Those of my readers living in the shadow of a defective memory will be sensible to compile an angling check-list. To arrive on some far-off water minus one's reel, and have to trudge back for it, is ageing and dulls the spirit. As I have learned, miserably, this unhappy experience can repeat itself—unless we take the precaution of writing down everything we need.

It is difficult to overstress the importance of this. Not everyone believes that they, too, have their share of human fallibility. There are those among my friends who regard check-lists as a sign of senility and in consequence turn up to fish without their waders, or flies, or waterproofs—sometimes even their rods. If they do remember to bring everything with them they invariably leave something behind on departure. Equally irritating, when it comes to returning the stuff.

So, in case it may be helpful, I have jotted down various items of tackle and clothing from the check-lists I use myself (if I remember to).

When away from base a few of these live in the car or with my luggage, but most are kept in the tackle-bag—although a bag is something I seldom lug about on the river bank. It is a pleasant angling contradiction that the bigger the fish the fewer the demands upon our tackle requirements. By comparison with the trout fisherman, the salmon fly-fisher's wants are few. So simple, indeed, that everything he needs can be carried comfortably on his person.

Consider.

Apart from *rod*, *reel*, *line*, *leader* and *fly*, which are assembled ready to use, I carry the following:

Fly case.
Spare nylon. These are stowed in my breast pockets. I have six of these repositories: two in my shirt; two in my waistcoat; two in my fishing coat or wading jacket.

Scissors.
Spectacles. These live on loops around my neck. Carried thus they are instantly ready to hand, and will not fall into the river and get swept away if dropped.

Polaroids. I wear these nearly all the time, either on or off the water. This is partly to help me see what is going on under the surface; partly to shield the eyes from water glare, and partly to protect them from the fly if it gets blown off course by a rogue gust of wind.

Priest. This is carried either in the front pocket of my breast waders or, if I am fishing in thigh boots, looped round my belt. Some anglers disdain to carry a priest, relying on the river bank to provide a substitute. But I *always* carry one, having once lost a big fish through being without the means of despatching him.

Strictly speaking, these items together with a *handkerchief* are all that we need for much of our salmon fly-fishing. But, depending on the type of water, a *wading-stick*, and very occasionally a *net* may be required. So, we add these to our check-list. In addition, for personal comfort, I carry the following:

Insect repellent. Essential. It is kept permanently in one of my side pockets. Keeping it company are a simple:

Fish carrier. And a small roll of:

Lavatory paper.

And finally, for emergencies less acute, one of my trouser pockets always holds a stout *penknife* and a twist of *string*. They often prove useful.

If you think you can get along without any of these, just cross them off your list. On the other hand you may well wish to add to them: a *hip-flask*, for instance; *tobacco* and *matches*; some *sweeties*. Why not? You have plenty of pocket space.

Next, the tackle-bag.

This is simply a hold-all for ancillary equipment and spares. It is not intended to be carried about while we are fishing, but stays with our transport or in the fishing hut. *Note*: My own tackle reserve is stored in a Bell's dozen-bottle whisky carton. This is both inexpensive and convenient: it stands upright in the car boot and is much easier to delve into than the traditional bag. But in deference to those readers who sport the real thing, "tackle-bag" it shall be called.

When on active service it contains the following:

Spare reels and lines. From floating; sink-tip; sinking.

Spare reel spring. Not often needed. But doesn't take up much space.

Spare nylon. According to size of lure, for sunk-line fishing I use 20 lb–25 lb b.s. For floating-line: 18 lb down to 6 lb b.s. Most of this spare nylon is carried on:

Nylon dispensers. Very handy little gadgets.

Spare flies. Whether setting out to fish large flies or small flies, always take a few of the other sort with you. I have caught salmon on sunk-line and big fly in high summer, and on small fly and floating line in early spring. This would not have been possible had I not been prepared. (Such "out-of-season" success is only very occasional, but absurdly pleasing.)

Lead wire. A twist of thin lead wire is handy for weighting tubes on the spot when faced with a stretch of deeper or faster water than the rest of the beat, and so will sometimes provide a fish that might otherwise not have been hooked.

Split-shot. A small split shot does for the small fly what lead wire does for the big fly. You will very seldom need it, but when you do—as described in Chapter XIII—it may catch you a fish.

Darning needle. This lives permanently inside my fly case. Useful for needle-knotting a new leader by the waterside.

Wader repair kit. A small roll of rubberoid or whatever, with a tube of sticky, saves much discomfort following an encounter with barbed wire.

Adhesive tape. For taping rod joints and reel fastenings. Useful for on-the-spot-repairs to all sorts of things.

Spring balance. Saves much argument.

Artery forceps. For removing deeply embedded hooks.

Thermometer. It is interesting and instructive to check air and water temperatures. Especially the latter.

Spare elastic bands. Handy things to have; both for slipping round fly cases and as preventers on the HF River Spey Wading Stick (see p. 176).

Nylon bagging. For wrapping fish to be deep-frozen.

Basses. For carrying fish.

Skin cream. Etiolated anglers coming to the river straight from office desks will be wise to add a pot of skin-cream to their list. Face and hands get easily chapped when exposed to unaccustomed wet and cold.

Although living very much of an outdoor life myself, I have had all the joints of my fingers crack open after a few days' hard fishing in early spring.

Band-Aid plasters.

Candle stub.   For waxing carbon-rod ferrules.

Carborundum.   For sharpening your penknife—and removing the sticky sharpness of fly-hooks.

Pipe cleaners.   See illustration: "Pipe-cleaner safety-catch".

Nail varnish.   For touching-up the whippings on flies.

Flask.   For personal comfort.

And lastly, in addition to *flashlamp* and *hand-towel, don't* forget that hold-all with a spare change of clothes. In emergency this will save you from losing a day's fishing. Mine holds: *trousers*; *underclothes*; *shirt*; *sweater*; *stockings*; *handkerchief.*

An angler's clothing is very much a personal matter. But here are a few reminders:

Thermal underwear.

Fishing coat.

Wading jacket.

Long legs. ⎱   waterproof
Dry bums. ⎰   pull-ons

Neck towel.

Mittens.   Two pairs.

Wader inserts.   Two pairs.

Waders.   Breast; thigh; wellies.

Pipe-cleaner
safety-catch

Now, a closer look at the more important tackle items. And since an appreciation of the present is heightened by some understanding of the past, a brief glance at angling history.

The Rod

Tackle development through the ages was painfully slow. It took nearly 4,000 years to advance from a tight line—that is, a line tied to the rod top—to a loose line, which slipped through a rod-ring or rings.

The rod it seems originated in ancient Egypt; since when, for century after century until little more than 300 years ago, the angler's outfit remained a stick with a horsehair line tied to the end of it. If a large fish was hooked and demanded line the angler simply hung on, or threw his rod into the water and hoped to recover it later when the fish had tired itself out. Not until the mid 17th century, with the introduction of rod rings and reel, did salmon fishing become much of a proposition.

In his book *The Pleasures of Princes*, 1614, Gervase Markham considered the salmon:

> Unfit for your travaile, both because he is too huge and cumbersome, as also in that he naturally delighteth to lie in the bottomes of the great depe Rivers, and as neare as may bee in the middst of the Channel.

Many of Markham's contemporaries shared his view, although salmon *were* occasionally being caught on rod and line as, indeed, they were at least two centuries earlier. Salmon fishing is mentioned in *A Treatyse of Fysshynge wyth an Angle*, the first angling book to be printed in English, attributed to Dame Juliana Berners, Prioress of Sopwell Priory, probably written c. 1425; hand-copied by monks c. 1450, and published in the *Boke of St Albans* in 1496:

> The Samon is the moost stately fyssh that ony man maye angle to in fresshe water . . . ye may take hym . . . with a dubbe at suche tyme as when he lepith in lyke forme and manere as ye doo take a troughte or a gryalynge.

So, even in medieval times, although undoubtedly in quite small numbers, salmon were being caught not only with rod and line but with the fly.

We know exactly what an "angle rod" of that time was like, the *Treatyse* gives a detailed description. A wand of hazel, willow or mountain ash, as thick as one's arm and nine feet in length, formed the bottom section of the rod, which overall was in two pieces. This was hollowed out in a tapering hole by means of red-hot irons. The top joint, which fitted into this bottom piece for ease of transport, was a yard of hazel with about six feet of blackthorn, crab, medlar or juniper whipped to it. The whole two-piece "harnays", when mounted for action, measured about eighteen feet in length and had a horsehair line fastened to the top.

Other rod materials listed during the following centuries included ground-witchen, sallow, beech, poplar and whale-bone. By the mid 19th century, ash, cane, greenheart, hickory and lancewood were the most popular. Thomas Tod Stoddart wrote of lancewood:

> For top-pieces it is reckoned invaluable, possessing a spring and consistency, together with a capability of being highly polished, not found in any other wood.

There is no doubt that those eighteen and twenty foot Victorian salmon rods could do their job well enough, but they were monstrous tools. According to Lord Walter Gordon-Lennox:

> The true Spey rod is glued, spliced and whipped throughout, never taken to pieces. With ash butt, hickory centre-piece, and lancewood top, the whole is welded into a weapon of most responsive play to the hand.

One could imagine that such a "weapon" would Spey-cast splendidly—while one still had strength to wield it!

Lancewood, even heavier than hickory, gradually fell out of favour. So, too, did hickory—although it was still used until quite recently for the handles of big-game rods. Greenheart and cane remained popular. Strong and elastic, unaffected by water, greenheart was a highly suitable rodmaking material.

Cane rods were being made early in the last century and came into vogue during late Victorian times; although greenheart still held its market, especially for salmon rods on the big rivers. In 1895, Alexander Grant cast 56 yards with his 20 foot greenheart "Grant Vibration".

Since 1945 rodmaking development has been spectacular. First glass then carbon fibre* began to oust both greenheart and built cane. Now, natural fibrous materials have been almost totally eclipsed and it is likely that, with very few exceptions, man-made materials will continue to replace all others in rod manufacture.

Like the big cane salmon rods, the splendid old spliced greenhearts of yesteryear, excellent for Spey-casting and impervious to the weather, have almost disappeared. Sad in a way. But, as with cane, when comparisons are made with modern carbon—which will do all that greenheart could do, and at a fraction of the weight—few anglers will mourn its loss.

*   *   *

Irrespective of its construction the salmon fly-rod—like any other fly-rod a spring when we are casting a line, a lever when we are playing a fish—is simply an extension of our arms. Its chief function is to help us present a fly. Second in importance, since it *is* longer than our arms, is the help it gives in keeping the line clear of the water and so free from obstructions and the drag of the current while a fish is being played. Any relationship between the rod's size and strength and the size of the salmon it lands is coincidental.

* Carbon fibre rods are excellent conductors of electricity! *Beware of overhead power-lines.*

It is on the accurate placing of the line, which presents our fly where it may attract a fish, that successful salmon fly-fishing depends.

The weight of the line is impelled by the spring of the rod, and this must be powerful enough to do it. Whatever type of fly you intend to use, make sure your rod will enable you to cast it with the minimum of effort. It may be anything from a tiny size 14 summer fly, fished on floating-line, up to a four-inch weighted tube-fly fished on sunk-line in early spring. But whatever the fly's size and weight, your rod must enable you to present it effectively in all conditions of weather and water—*with no false casting.*

False-casting becomes a habit that wastes time and effort. Reducing the number of times the line flashes to and fro above the fish avoids disturbance. It also helps you to keep the fly out of trouble, and lessens the danger of hooking yourself.

Provided our reserve of line is adequate, and line and leader are of suitable breaking-strain, the biggest salmon can be landed on the smallest rod. For low-water fishing with very small flies nothing more than a trout rod is needed on some of the small rivers. The reason why single-handed rods are not used all the time for salmon is *convenience.* The longer and stronger the rod, the more easily a long line can be cast with one action, without false-casting; the more efficiently the fly can be controlled when we are fishing it across the river, and the better our command of the fish when we hook him.

We can cast, using only an arm as a rod, hook a fish and play and land him from a hand-held reel. It has been done—by the famous American salmon angler Lee Wulff, among others. But as a method of fishing, it is neither comfortable nor efficient. Obviously, the use of a rod is much more convenient. The rod's primary function, however, is not to play and land the fish, it is to project the lure into a position where the fish may take it.

What dictates the choice of rod is not the size of the fish; it is the method of fishing, the type of lure and the distance it has to be cast, bearing in mind that the object is to do so as easily as possible. A salmon fly-fisherman casting a four-inch leaded tube on high-density line in early spring or late autumn needs a powerful fifteen or sixteen-foot rod to present and control it. He can fish the same water for salmon in June or July with a three-quarter-inch tube on floating line using a ten-foot single-handed trout rod, and probably will. Using a shooting-head line with monofilament backing, we can cover most rivers with a single-handed reservoir trout rod. But salmon fishing a river with such tackle proves irksome. Spey-casting with a long double-handed rod is so much easier, both when it comes to presenting and controlling the fly and, later, when it comes to controlling the fish, for the rod's extra length helps to prevent the line from being drowned in the current.

A technique that has received much undue publicity is the American cult of salmon fishing with a very short single-handed rod. I advise the novice to avoid this. It is an affectation and offers no advantage whatever. The shortness of the rod is a decided handicap while a fish is being played since, on big rivers, from other than a high bank, it is difficult to prevent the line from being drowned, which increases the chance of getting broken. Far from being commendable, therefore, the use of such a rod must be considered unsporting.

In practice, the ultra-short rod has another disadvantage. I have noticed that, good fly-casters though they are, American anglers using such tackle on a big river need to make five or six false casts in order to extend a fishable length of line—a distance that any competent angler using, say, a fifteen-foot carbon double-hander, can Spey-cast with ease. As mentioned before, flashing the line about does nothing to help us catch salmon.

As a general principle, wherever you are fishing and whatever you are fishing for, use a rod of sensible length. In any but exceptional circumstances a short rod incurs unnecessary handicaps. For most river salmon fly-fishing, with either floating or sinking line, a fifteen or sixteen-foot carbon double-hander is the tool. Irrespective of your age or physique, the lightness of carbon removes any physical hardship from using a rod of this length.

For stillwater fishing from a boat, there is a twelve-foot carbon single-handed rod on the market that I have found ideal for fishing a light line and tripping a bob-fly along the trough of a wave well out from the boat. Again, the lightness of the material makes it possible to fish a single-handed rod of this length without undue tiredness.

The third fly-rod I recommend is the carbon "Salmon and Sea Trout" ten-foot-six single-hander. I have found it excellent for summer salmon dry-fly fishing and all forms of sea trout night fly-fishing with either sunk or floating line.

Like the glint of gun barrels, rod flash can be seen a long way off. At times, this *must* disturb fish. I wish rod-makers would turn out a matt finish.*

* As this book goes to press I discover to my astonishment that although some rod makers are able and indeed anxious to provide a matt finish, the great majority of rod buyers reject it!

The Reel

The fishing reel seems to have originated in China, where illustrations depicting a kind of "winch" were printed several centuries before its first mention in English literature. Its arrival in Europe was very slow. Dame Juliana's *Treatyse* made no mention either of reel or rod-ring, and although salmon were certainly being taken on rod and line during the Wars of the Roses, not for another two hundred years did the reel and all its advantages become available to British anglers. Before that time—and doubtless for most anglers many years afterwards—the playing of a fish was hopelessly restricted, the casting-line being fastened directly to the rod-top with no reserve to offer a running fish.

Even as late as 1614, in *The Pleasures of Princes*, Gervase Markham says nothing about a reel, or even a rod-ring. He fished with a line tied to his rod and described how the angler should carry line and spares when not in use:

> Then he shall have some fine smooth board of some curious wood for show sake, being as big as a trencher, and cut battlement-wise at each end; on which he shall fold his severall lines.

The first unequivocal reference to a reel is Thomas Barker's in *The Art of Angling*, 1651. He also mentioned a line that could be drawn in or let out through a ring at the rod-top.*

> The manner of his Trouling was, with a Hazell Rod of twelve foot long, with a Ring of Wyre in the top of his Rod, for his line to runne thorow: within two foot of the bottome of the Rod there was a hole made, for to put in a winde, to turne with a barrell, to gather up his Line, and loose at his pleasure.

---

*In *The Arte of Angling*, William Samuel, 1577, there is a very interesting remark. Piscator says: "My master that taught me to angle could not abide to catch a ruffe; for if he took one, either he would remove or *wind up* and home for that time." (My italics). Now, what did Piscator mean by that? Did his master wind the line up round the rod, or on a line-winder? Or was this a reference to an early "winde" or reel? If so, it is certainly the first in English literature. According to the Shorter Oxford English Dictionary, the first recorded use of "wind up" referred to the hoisting of sails, c. 1205. It is subsequently used in the figurative sense: "to sum up or conclude". One finds: "to winde up all in a short conclusion" in 1583—which is close to the publication date of *The Arte of Angling*. Probably, Piscator simply meant that his master would "pack up and go home". If not, if the author really referred to a winde or reel, he had scooped Barker by seventy-four years!

Incidentally, in Barker's time "trouling" (or trolling, as we spell it now) did not have its modern meaning of dragging a lure about behind a boat. It meant fishing in the style known today as "sink-and-draw"—a method made easier for Thomas Barker by his having the line running through a ring at the rod top.

How simple it seems, the idea of a Ring of Wyre to let the line run through from a "barrell". And yet, since the dawn of time no one had thought of it—at least, not in Europe, whatever was going on in China.

Whoever he was, that unknown angler who for the first time used rod-ring and reel in British waters was responsible for the greatest break-through in our angling history. From then on the playing of a big fish became feasible, and salmon fishing assumed a new dimension.

A reel similar to the one Barker described can be seen on the title-page of *The Experienc'd Angler, or Angling Improved*, 1662, by the Cromwellian soldier, Colonel Robert Venables. "The salmon taketh the artificial flie very well", he wrote.

His title page, however, caused much confusion. The rod on the left has a knob on the butt resembling the modern screw-in rubber button. But the rod on the right is fashioned with what looks like a gun-butt. At least, so it seemed to generations of anglers. In fact, it is a bait-horn—standing in front of the rod. Another bait-horn can be seen on the shelf, top-left. The picture also contains the first illustration of a fishing reel or "winde". See enlargement opposite.

Early reels were kept in place by means of a pin that went through a hole in the rod handle and was fastened with a wing-nut. This reel, enlarged from that shown on the previous page is our earliest illustrated example.

An example of an early fishing reel.

A heavy 18th century salmon reel, brass with iron handle. Some of these reels weighed as much as two pounds. The needle holes in the reel seating are for the leather padding.

A fly-reel is simply a revolving drum big enough to hold casting-line and backing; but, as we soon appreciate when a big salmon sets off at speed, only the best reel is good enough. Of the many cheap reels on the market some are cunning foreign imitations of top British makes. Avoid them. As I know, having tried them, they are unreliable. Sooner or later they will let you down and cause the loss of a fish. In simple terms of cash value, that fish will probably outweigh the cost of a good reel. So get a good one to start with.

The top-class modern fly-reel has come a long way since the days of Thomas Barker's "winde". In my opinion British makes are still the best. I use the following:

Hardy Marquis Salmon No. 2 (for the carbon 15′ double-handed rod).
Hardy Marquis No. 10 (for the carbon 10′6″ single-handed rod).

Also in service are:

Hardy St Andrew 4″ salmon.
Hardy Perfect $3\frac{7}{8}″$ salmon and sea trout.

> *Note*: To prevent over-run, but at the same time avoid excessive jerk when a fish is running on a light leader, a change of check-setting may be necessary. So—whatever reel you buy, make sure it has an efficient check-adjuster.

The Line

Writing 1,900 years ago on the choice of rod and line, Plutarch advised:

> Choose a rod which is slim, for fear lest if it cast a broad shadow it might move the doubt and suspicion that is naturally in fishes . . . Take order that the hairs which reach to the hook should seem as white as possible, for the whiter they be the less they are seen in the water for their conformity with it.

So much for Plutarch on the subject of horsehair lines. He has his detractors today; those who denigrate the modern white Air-cell casting line.

Does it really make any difference? I confess I don't know. I do most of my fly-fishing with a white line because when I wanted a new size 11 double-tapered floater in a hurry, white was all I could get. Frankly, I have a sneaking preference for brown or green, but cannot give any *reason* for this. The under-plumage of plunge-diving sea-birds is white and, in theory, this should be the best colour for a fly-line. In practice, I am not so sure. Certainly I prefer a darker line for loch fishing. This is because when friends and I have been casting with lines of white and brown, the white has seemed to get fewer offers. Needless to say, this could have been coincidence.

Taken all in all, what I think matters more than colour is the way the line is fished. If false-casting is eliminated (something I am always preaching), white is probably as good as anything.

Whatever its colour, a fly-line should be smoothly-tapered and shoot with minimum friction through the rod-rings. Consult a reputable dealer and get the best you can.

Don't economise on fishing tackle. It is not the number of fish you catch that really matters; it is the time you spend fishing. Did you enjoy casting your line? That is what counts at the end of the day, because fly-casting is a joy and can be enormously satisfying, however few fish you hook. It is fun just to visit the river and spend an hour or so going through one's repertoire of overhead-casts, roll-casts, single Spey-casts, double Spey-casts; enjoying the excitement of trying to throw the near-perfect line; seeing the leader shoot out above the water and settle like gossamer thirty yards away. There is so much more to fishing than catching fish.

So—use the best tackle you can get.

I use the following lines myself:

Air cel double-tapered No. 11 floater
Air cel double-tapered No. 11 floater with sink-tip
Wet cel double-tapered No. 11 fast sinker
For the Walker 15′ carbon salmon rod

Air cel double-tapered No. 7 floater
Air cel double-tapered No. 7 floater with sink-tip
Wet cel double-tapered No. 7 fast sinker
For the Bruce and Walker 10′ 6″ salmon and sea trout rod

It is important for river fishing that the rod and line should be in balance. As a guide, the rod manufacturers usually print the recommended line size, in the shape of an AFTM number, just above the rod-handle. Once you have found which AFTM number suits a rod, whatever kind of line you want—floater, floater with sink-tip, slow or fast sinker—you can ask for it by that number in the tackle-shop and be sure of getting a suitable line for the rod in question.

The key to the AFTM system is as follows:

DT: Double-tapered.
WF: Weight forward (or forward-tapered).
F: Floating.
S: Sinking.

FS: Floater with sink-tip.

ST: Shooting taper, or shooting-head.

   3–12: Line size.

   Thus: a line marked DT 11 F is a double-tapered No. 11 floater.

   Note: A weight forward (WF) line is useful for distance casting if an overhead cast is used, but *not* for roll or Spey casts. For these we need the thickest (heaviest) part of the line close to the rod, as provided by the double-taper. As we shall see, Spey-casting plays a very big part in our salmon fly presentation, for which a double-tapered line is obligatory. (There is an urgent need for special Spey-casting lines, both floating and sinking. Manufacturers please note.)

The Backing

Backing is an extension of the casting-line; a reserve available for playing a lively fish. It is advisable to have a hundred to a hundred-and-fifty yards, and it needs to be of sensible strength: say 30 lb b.s. Plaited nylon or nylon monofilament makes good backing, being rot-proof and offering strength with thinness.

Nylon is slippery stuff. When fastening the backing to the reel-drum, use the knot shown in the diagram, and tie a safety knot in the end (at A.). Also shown is the knot for fastening backing to casting-line, (p. 173).

The Leader

The leader is simply a slender nylon link between casting-line and fly. In my opinion there is no need to err on the side of lightness. The first responsibility of any angling sportsman is to avoid being broken, and since during all the time I have watched salmon they have shown no signs of being unduly "gut-shy", I think it sensible (and sporting) to use the strongest link compatible with the size of fly we happen to be using.

Tapered leaders are available from tackle dealers, but unnecessary. Although it is true that a tapered leader will turn over slightly better at the completion of a cast, a length of level nylon off the spool will serve perfectly well. Anyone who feels so disposed, however, can easily make up tapered leaders by joining several nylon lengths of differing thickness, using a Water Knot or a Double-Grinner.

A time when the leader automatically becomes tapered is when we change down in size of fly. A small fly will not "work" attractively on nylon that is too thick. So, when we go down in fly size we change our leader-point in sympathy. For this reason several thicknesses of nylon need to be carried.

168

SUNK LINE FLIES

PLATE 6

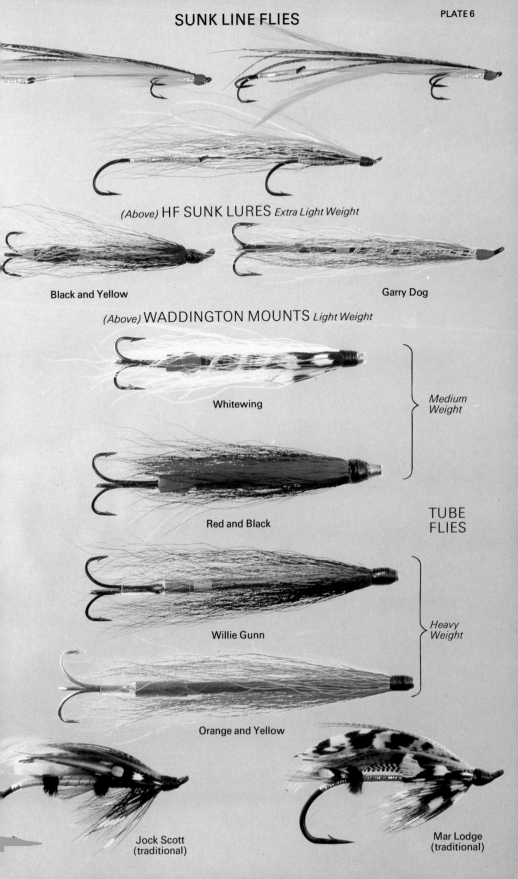

(Above) HF SUNK LURES *Extra Light Weight*

Black and Yellow

Garry Dog

(Above) WADDINGTON MOUNTS *Light Weight*

Whitewing

Medium Weight

Red and Black

TUBE FLIES

Willie Gunn

Heavy Weight

Orange and Yellow

Jock Scott (traditional)

Mar Lodge (traditional)

PLATE 7

FLOATING LINE WET FLIES

Blue Charm

March Brown

(Above) A.H.E. WOOD LOW WATER

Thunder and Lightning

Silver Blue

Jock Scott

Hairy Mary

Munro's Killer

Falkus Fancy

Garry Dog

Willie Gunn

Silver Doctor

Stoat's Tail

Naver Brown and Gold

Dame Juliana's
August Fly

Surface Riffler

MODERN HAIRWINGS (excluding August Fly)

PLATE 8

FLOATING LINE WET FLIES

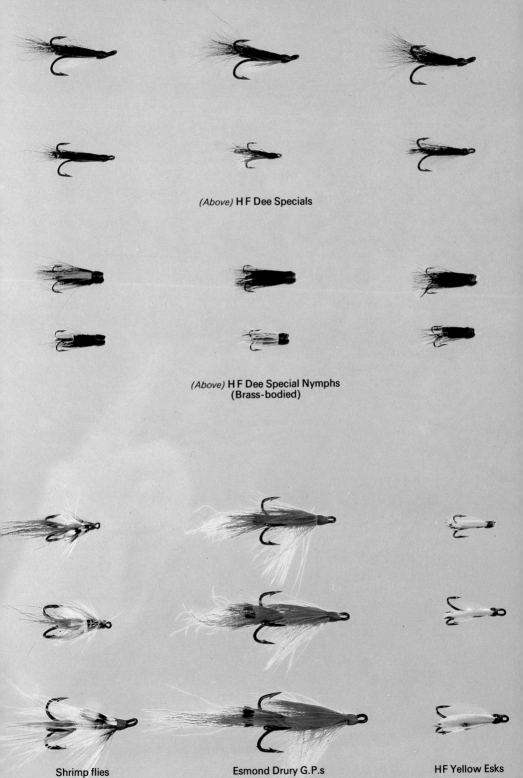

(Above) H F Dee Specials

(Above) H F Dee Special Nymphs
(Brass-bodied)

Shrimp flies   Esmond Drury G.P.s   HF Yellow Esks

PLATE 9

DRY FLIES AND LOCH FLIES

Muddler Dollies

Yellow Dollies

Black Buzz

| Black Maria | Claret | Black Fairy |

| Black Pennell | Dunkeld | Zulu |

| Connemara Black | Muddler | Ian Wood |

Buzz-Buzz

Stored in my tackle-bag are spools of 6, 8, 10, 12, 14, 16, 18, 20, 22 and 25 lb b.s. From this range, leaders—or leader-points—can be fitted to suit any size and weight of lure, from heavy four-inch brass tubes down to tiny three-eighths-of-an-inch dry-flies.

The best nylon? A matter of opinion. Of the many different "brands" most are the same make, since nylon is produced by only a few large chemical combines.

There are several ways of joining line and leader. I employ them all from time to time.

The neatest is to attach the leader direct with a needle knot.

Perhaps the most convenient is to Needle-Knot a couple of feet of heavier nylon to the line, tie a Blood-Bight Loop in this and in the end of the leader, and join them loop to loop. The advantage of this method is the speed with which a leader can be changed, especially in poor light.

Otherwise there is nothing wrong with the old fashioned method of tying the line to a Blood-Bight Loop in the leader with a Figure-of-Eight Knot. But it is slightly more bulky. (See knots section, pp. 173–5).

Care of Nylon

Scientific friends confirm that light-coloured nylon loses its elasticity and becomes more brittle when exposed to sunlight. Dark-coloured nylon is more resistant, and it is significant that the modern roller-reefing headsails made of synthetic fabrics used on small yachts are given leech and foot strips of dark blue to help protect these permanently exposed bands of sail from sunlight. So perhaps it would be safer if we used monofilament of darker hues.

Provided we use it sensibly, regard monofilament as being expendable and try not to get too much work out of it, what we use today will serve us well enough. But it is wise to keep our spare spools covered up.

> *Note.* Nylon monofilament can be lethal! Each season I find hundreds of yards of it strewn on river banks. This is disgraceful, for it gets caught up with bodies, legs and wings of wild creatures causing mutilation or death. When you throw nylon away, wind it round two fingers in a tight coil, then cut the coil with your scissors. This reduces it to a bundle of tiny ends that are harmless.

The Hook

Pretty well everything I have to say about hooks will be found in my book *Sea Trout Fishing*. It is not much. But then, not being a metallurgist, I don't know much about hook-making. All I know is that good hooks are hard to find.

A famous hook manufacturer once sent me a packet of fly-hooks for approval. They looked fine. But I straightened out every one in my fingers against a thumbnail.

What I like in a hook is a short point; a wide gape; a round bend; a short shank. Not too brittle in the temper, but strong enough to withstand all the pressure one is likely to apply when playing a fish—without straightening. I used to like a fine wire, but now I am not so sure. When fished on a strong leader early in the season, fine-wire trebles seem to *pull through* a seemingly good hold.

For fly-hooks I prefer doubles and trebles to singles. These days most of my flies are tubes, or dressed trebles. Yes, I know about the supposed advantages of singles, But I still prefer doubles and trebles. If it gets a good hold, a flat single is as good as anything. But before it gets that hold it can slide sideways out of a salmon's mouth, and I am sure that sometimes it does. A single with offset point is surely more efficient.

I think small hooks are preferable to big hooks—provided they are doubles or trebles—they usually get a better hold. So often a tiny double or treble embedded in the gristle of a salmon's mouth needs to be cut out, so strong a grip does it have. (See picture of the size 16 treble embedded in the cock salmon's "scissors" on p. 320.)

I have long thought that the perfect summer fly hook should have two rings—as shown in the drawing—so that the leader could be tied to the second ring and still allow the hook full play irrespective of nylon thickness. It would avoid the use of very light leaders when we fish tiny hooks in hot weather. The fly would waggle about attractively no matter what strength of leader it was fished on.

I tried out this idea with a biggish hook and the smallest split-ring I could find, and it worked a treat. Alas, despite repeated attempts to get one of the manufacturers to produce such a hook, nothing has been

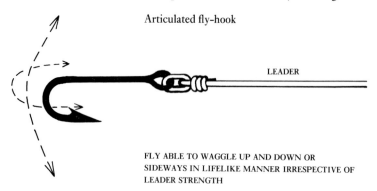

Articulated fly-hook

LEADER

FLY ABLE TO WAGGLE UP AND DOWN OR
SIDEWAYS IN LIFELIKE MANNER IRRESPECTIVE OF
LEADER STRENGTH

forthcoming. So, I pass on the notion with my compliments, as usual, to any reader who cares to experiment. I feel sure that something of this sort would be possible. If so, it would make fishing with tiny flies much safer, since a leader of, say, 14 or 15 lb b.s. could be used with a size 14 or 16 fly. This is the size of fly a salmon often prefers on a sweltering midsummer evening.*

Then again, it seems to me that a hook shaped *not* with a round section near the barb, but flattened on the inside of the bend, like the fluke of an old fashioned anchor, would get a better grip in the flesh of a fresh-run fish. But hook-makers seem to be very conservative. It is not without significance that there has been no substantial change in hook design for hundreds of years. Indeed, the bronze-age hook found at Grays, Essex, c. 500 B.C., is almost identical to the single hook in use today.†

It may be argued that my flattened-section "anchor" hook would not penetrate flesh so easily as a rounded section. Maybe. But surely this is only a question of how hard we pull once the fly has been taken. As I say, from fish hooked and lost, I feel certain that small, fine-wired, rounded hooks sometimes drag through the flesh of fresh-run spring salmon, although having, in theory, a perfectly good hold.

Hook point

This is given a section to itself because for some anglers hook-sharpening is almost a fetish. They test the point of a hook by drawing it across the thumbnail. If it sticks in the nail, all well and good. If not, it is honed until it does stick. The assumption being that the sharpest hook provides the best hold.

In my opinion the reverse is often the case.

Whereas a very sharp point will undoubtedly help to hook leathery-mouthed fish such as carp, it is not likely to do so with bony-mouthed fish such as salmon and sea trout. For fish such as these the hook should have a sound point; but it should not, I think, be honed to razor sharpness. Too sharp a hook will stick in the first piece of bone it strikes, giving only a very brief hold. It should be sharp enough to penetrate gristle easily, but *blunt enough to slide across a bony surface until it comes to the gristle*. This happens in a fraction of a second. But it is what happens in that instant, I think, that makes the difference, sometimes, between a fish that stays on and a fish that doesn't!

*In fact, as Mr Paul Windle-Taylor has kindly pointed out, the Grinner Knot, loosely tied, will do just as well. "As the Grinner is a noose/lasso type of knot it will not undo, and any tension will cause it to tighten. Meanwhile it has the effect of your articulated hook."

† Messrs Partridge of Redditch are now working on a broad-sectioned "anchor" hook of the type suggested.

Every book that I have read recommends a game fisherman to carry a carborundum stone to touch up his hook points from time to time. In my view they are all wrong. I think it is a false practice. Unless a hook has lost its point altogether, the carborundum should be used to take some of the sharpness *off*, rather than put it on. And I am not trying to be iconoclastic. This is how I fish myself.

It is interesting that a very early angling writer, John Dennys, was aware of this principle. In *The Secrets of Angling*, 1613, he writes of a hook:

His Shank should neither be too short nor long,
His point not over sharpe, nor yet too dull . . .

An excellent piece of advice, in my opinion. But it was not appreciated. William Lauson, who edited a later edition of *The Secrets of Angling*, with his own notes, c. 1620, criticized Dennys's line about the hook:

He means the hook may be too weak at the point, it cannot be too sharpe, if the metall be of good steele.

There are plenty of places in a salmon's mouth where an over-sharp hook can catch—momentarily.

But Lauson was wrong. Like all the angling writers who have echoed him ever since, he had missed the point (no pun intended) of what Dennys had written. A hook *can* be too sharp—and often is.

If my reader disagrees, let him do what I have done many times: open the mouth of a dead salmon and proggle about with hooks of varying sharpness. He will find that it takes very little pull to drive a point into gristle, but also how easy it is for an over-sharp hook to catch on a bone.

I am not suggesting that the point should be *blunt*. Simply that it should not be *too* sharp. Next time you hook a salmon that gives you a strong pull and jumps just before the line goes slack, take a good long look at your hook. Then test its point. And think.

KNOTS

Note. 1. To help overcome friction and "set" a knot, always lubricate nylon by moistening in your mouth before drawing it tight.

2. When tying knots in nylon don't economize. Give yourself plenty of loose ends to play with.

Overhand Knots: for joining nylon backing to reel. Note safety knot at A.

A

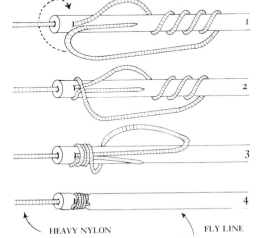

Needle Knot: for joining backing and leader to fly-line. The nylon does not *have* to go through a hole in the end of the fly-line. It can simply lie alongside; a method I use myself. An alternative method of attaching fly-line and leader is to tie a *Blood-Bight Loop* in the leader and fasten line with a *Figure-of-Eight Knot*.

1

2

3

4

HEAVY NYLON   FLY LINE

173

Blood-Bight Loop: The loop for a level nylon fly leader.

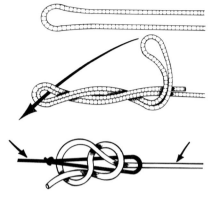

Figure-of-Eight Knot: For joining line to loop in leader.

Loop to Loop: Another simple method of joining line and leader is to *Needle-Knot* a "leader-base" (two or three feet of heavier nylon) to the line, tie a *Blood-Bight Loop* in leader-base and leader, and join loop to loop, as shown.

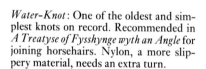

Grinner Knot: For attaching fly-hook, bait-hook or swivel to nylon leader. This is the old *Fisherman's Knot* with four turns. It is neat, safe and strong.

Water-Knot: One of the oldest and simplest knots on record. Recommended in *A Treatyse of Fysshynge wyth an Angle* for joining horsehairs. Nylon, a more slippery material, needs an extra turn.

Double-Grinner Knot: Just as good as, if not better than the *Water Knot* for joining nylon, and slightly less bulky. It looks complicated, but is really very simple.
1. Tie one end and pull it fairly tight.
2. Turn the knot over and tie the other end.
3. Pull the two knots together and snug down.
Note: Both *Water Knot* and *Double-Grinner* can be used for tying droppers. In each case, fasten the fly to the stalk running *away* from the rod. The other stalk stands out better from the leader, but is weaker.

Bowline: A knot every angler should know. Apart from being the best method of tying a boat's painter to a ring-bolt, the loop formed by a bowline should *always* be tied at the end of a rope thrown to a person in difficulties. Once the loop has been slipped over head and shoulders, anyone in danger of drowning can be drawn to safety, even though in the meantime they may have lost consciousness.

The Wading-Stick

For any angler fishing *any* salmon river, big or small, that he needs to wade, a wading-stick is his most important item of subsidiary tackle. Sooner or later it will save him from a wetting. It may even save his life. But its use demands almost as much skill as the use of a fly rod.

Whenever I hear an angler complain that he finds a wading-stick an encumbrance—because it tends to get between his legs and trip him up, or catches loose line while he is casting—I know at once that no one has ever shown him how to handle one. It is also likely that the sticks he has been saddled with have been hopelessly inadequate.

If a wading-stick is long enough, with sufficient weight at the butt, it is a blessing. If not, it is a curse. Without exception, every commercial wading-stick I have ever used has been a curse.

A bad wading-stick is too light in the base. As a result, it floats on the surface in anything of a current—which is just when we want it to stay upright with the butt firmly on the bottom. A good wading-stick forms a strut, heavy enough at the base to stand beside you, even in a strong draw, ready-to-hand. It should be tipped with rubber to reduce underwater noise, and slung so that the handle is always just the right distance from your grasp. Its overall length should enable the handle to stick out of the water when you are waist deep—otherwise your hand goes under and you get a wet sleeve. Very cold in early spring.

The Gaff

Referring to salmon in the River Thames, Thomas Barker wrote:

Close to the bottom in the midst of the water
I fished for a Salmon, and there I caught her.
My plummet twelve inshes from the large hook,
The lob-worms hang'd equall, which she never forsook.
I wound up my tackle to guide him to shoar;
The landing hook helpt much, the cooker more.*

*Barker's "landing hook" is probably the first mention in English literature of a gaff. His "I wound up my tackle" the first personal reference to using a reel. (See also, p. 163).

The H. F. River Spey Wading-Stick. Long enough in the shank to be grasped in the deepest wadable water without wetting one's sleeve, the stick is sensibly weighted at the butt and will stand up in the strongest draw. A rubber-shod butt reduces underwater noise.

When a fish is hooked and the angler has backed in to the bank, the quick-release clip, seen in close-up opposite, enables the stick to be dropped at once, without the harness being taken over the angler's head and knocking off his hat (when worn).

It is made to my own specifications by J. S. Sharpe (Engineering) Ltd., Seaforth Road, Aberdeen. Since I use no other myself, I can thoroughly recommend it. If you have not already done so, go and buy one at once. You will bless me for this advice!

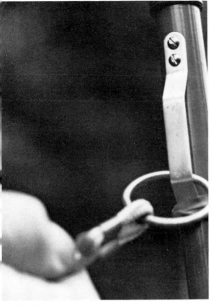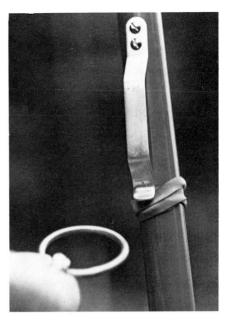

Quick-release clip. A sharp tug frees the stick from the harness ring. The elastic band acts as a "preventer"—that is, it prevents the clip from releasing the ring too easily.

The cry "Lost at the gaff!" has become an angling cliché, and not without good reason. The barbless steel hook is an uncertain instrument, and many fish have been lost by its inexpert use. Unless you are a very experienced angler (in which case you probably won't want to) *don't* carry a gaff, you will not then be tempted to use it.

A gaff is seldom needed. It is of value only when conditions make the beaching of a fish impossible, or where a strong back-eddy and a high bank make tailing difficult; when fishing from a boat; or when the line is caught on some obstruction and the fish, although beaten, cannot be brought closer to hand. Nearly always a large net is preferable.

Why violate a creature so beautiful as an Atlantic salmon by sticking a meat hook into him? Why run the risk of losing such a prize by trying to land him in this uncivilized and dubious manner? The time to approach a played-out salmon and take him from the water is when he is lying on his side, exhausted. If a gaff is to be used, that is the time to use it—and even then, not by pulling it into his flank, but whenever possible by slipping it in under his chin and *drawing* him ashore.

But if the fish *is* played-out and beaten, the gaff is superfluous. Nature has equipped the salmon with a tail by which he can be lifted.

Landing a salmon "First push the fish forward up the bank clear of the water . . ."

". . . then in the same movement, pick him up."
Hugh Blakeney, hand–tails a Spey salmon in nice style.

To land a fish by hand is in every way more satisfactory. The fish is undamaged, and any danger of a broken leader or the fish being knocked off the hook by a hasty gaff-stroke is avoided.

But of course there is more to it than that. The use of your hand demands that a salmon is lying on his side, beaten and therefore ready to land. So often, the possession of a gaff lures the angler, or his gillie, into the error of trying to land the fish too soon. Frequently, some misguided helper will rush forward and slash at a fish that has come within reach quite early on in the fight. This has one of three results:

1. He misses the fish but breaks the leader.

2. He misses the fish, which sees him and rushes off in terror—thus prolonging the fight and giving itself more time to get rid of the hook.

3. He gaffs the fish and drags it ashore.

The last, perhaps, is worst of all, for it leaves a novice with an entirely wrong impression of how a fish should be played out and landed. Understandably delighted by the sight of his fish on the bank, and in such quick time, he is emboldened to repeat this unhappy trick. Sooner or later it will end in tears.

For a fish to swing into the side shortly after being hooked is commonplace. But such an incautious act as trying to gaff it out will result in many more losses than gains. It is something that should be tried only in emergency: for instance, when a fish, tired and unable to swim up against the current, is being carried downstream and in danger of being swept out of the pool (as described in Chapter XI). In such a situation, the angler has everything to gain and nothing to lose by trying to gaff the fish out. This is just about the only occasion when I think the use of a gaff can be justified for landing any but a very big fish.

There are two golden rules when playing a salmon—or, for that matter, any other fish: never to let the fish see you, and never to force him. If he swings into the side early on in the fight the chances are that he has no idea of what is happening. Far from lunging at him with a gaff, both you and your gillie should take care to *keep out of sight*. Nothing frightens a fish more than human beings moving on the bank. Once a salmon is frightened he will resist to the limit of his strength. There are exceptions, but a scared fish will fight far longer than the fish that never sees the fisherman. If I had to put a figure on it I would say that, on average, it adds five minutes to the playing time.

Salmon that have not been frightened in this way often give up quite quickly—especially if they have been treated to a "walking" session up or down the pool (see p. 245).

Wherever there is a place convenient for beaching a salmon no landing tackle of any sort is necessary. The best spots for this will have been (or *should* have been) selected before you started fishing. When the fish is beaten he is drawn ashore at one of these places, not by reeling in but by walking backwards. Once he is lying on his side with his head aground the fight is over and you can relax. He will not move again. To close matters, approach him from downstream, reeling in as you go. Then, keeping sufficient line out by holding the rod at arm's length inshore, take the wrist of the tail firmly with thumb and forefinger, the back of the hand uppermost and pointing towards the fish's head. First push the fish forward up the bank clear of the water then, in the same movement, pick him up. It is a very simple operation.

The Tailer
This is a running noose of wire, rather like a fox snare, that slips over the wrist of a salmon's tail and enables the angler to lift the fish out of the water. It is rather a fiddly instrument, but has one great merit: it cannot be used, at least not effectively, unless the salmon is played out and lying on his side—unlike the gaff, which is commonly called into service far too soon, often with disastrous results.

The Landing Net
There is no doubt that the landing net, as we know it, has been used in Britain for many centuries. Its first mention in English literature was probably by William Samuel author of *The Arte of Angling*, 1577, our second-oldest angling book, printed at the Sign of the Falcon in Fleet Street by Henry Middleton and sold at his shop in St Dunstan's churchyard.

Only one copy of *The Arte of Angling* has been discovered. In this book which, almost certainly, was parroted by Izaak Walton, the experienced angler, Piscator, is teaching the "arte" to his pupil, Viator. After helping his master to land a large perch by hand Viator, aglow with satisfaction, not unnaturally asks:

What would you have done if I had not been here?

Piscator replies:

I left one of my tooles at home for hast, whiche if I had brought I could have landed him without your help.

Of course there is no absolute proof that Piscator referred to a net. A piece of tackle used in the sixteenth century for snatching pike (which evolved into the modern salmon fish-tailer) may have been implied:

> He will be haltered, and some men use that way very oft to kill him, for hee will lie glaring upon you, as the hare or larke, until you put the line with a snittle over his head, and so with a good stiff pole you may throw him to land.

But not long after publication of *The Arte of Angling*, Gervase Markham in *The Pleasures of Princes*, 1614, wrote:

> Lastly, you shall have a little fine wanded Pebbe to hand by your side, in which you shall put the Fish which you catch, and a small round net fastened to a poales end, wherewith you may land a Pike or other great Fish.

So, almost certainly our angling ancestors were using landing nets in Shakespeare's time—and perhaps very much earlier, since according to A. Courtney Williams's *Angling Diversions*, 1945, the first record of a landing net can be seen on one of the Leptic Magna mosaics of the first or second century, discovered in Tripoli:

> The picture depicts two Roman anglers, one baiting his hook, the other in the act of landing a fish; he is holding his 7 ft rod high above his shoulder in his left hand, whilst with the other he guides the fish towards his net.

The triangular type of net, Courtney Williams writes, was no modern invention, but was first described by Frère François Fortin in *Les Ruses Innocentes*, 1660.

*   *   *

Except when boat fishing we seldom use a net for landing salmon. But when we need one, we need it badly. So, its choice is worth some thought.

The most important point to remember when choosing a net is that a small net will accommodate only a small fish. As Richard Walker once wrote in one of his many excellent articles:

> I've seen plenty of fish lost because the net was too small but never because the net was too big . . . Anglers grudge paying a good price for a first class landing net before they've lost the fish of a lifetime because the net proved inadequate. Afterwards they express different opinions.

Don't economize. Get yourself a good big net to start with. And if you value your sanity *don't* buy a folding net. In *Sea Trout Fishing* I said:

> Having uneasy doubts about all folding gadgetry . . . I prefer a solid outfit. My idea of a landing net is something simple and strong, with a great big wide mouth. Do-it-yourself enthusiasts can construct a net frame with laughable ease from a length of thick fencing wire and a stout ash stick.

And so they can. But now, I am pleased to inform them, it is unnecessary to do so. The "Salmon and Sea Trout Net", made to my specifications, is produced by Sharpes Engineering of Aberdeen, the firm that makes the HF River Spey Wading-Stick (p. 176).

The solid frame construction with extension handle is utterly foolproof, and will offer comfortable accommodation to any salmon (or sea trout) most anglers are ever likely to catch. When fishing steep-to banks or from a boat, this is the net. Photographs on the next page show details of the "quick release" and extension handle.

To bring the net into action is simple. While one hand holds the rod with played-out fish, the other hand pulls the "rip-cord". Instantly, the slip-knot becomes undone—and the net slides round the angler's shoulder into his hand. A method used by the author for over fifty years.

For use further afield, out comes the strong extension handle. Note: when an angler is alone, rod in hand, with a fish ready to net but out of reach, the extension handle can be drawn out one-handed by dropping the net-head to the ground (or river bed) and putting a foot on it.

184

Note. Many supposedly experienced anglers are surprisingly inexpert in the use of a landing net. It is not used to dig the fish out of the water. It is a trap; and, as with all traps, should be concealed. When the hooked fish is exhausted, *and not before*, he is drawn over the waiting net—which is completely submerged, except for the handle. As the fish comes overhead the net is raised to encompass him.

Once the fish is safely inside the net, your rod can be put aside, so that you have both hands free. The fish is *not* lifted straight up out of the water (unless you are fishing from a boat) but, with the net rim held just above the surface, drawn gently in to the bank. If the fish *is* to be lifted out, shorten your grip on the handle to give the net frame extra support.

To prevent the belly of the net bulging up when immersed in water, toss a pebble into it to keep it down and out of sight. A bulging net frightens a fish, and so prolongs the fight.

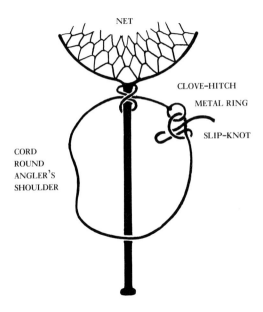

Clove-Hitch and *Slip-Knot* used for holding and fastening the landing-net (see p. 183). Both knots have been left loose for sake of clarity.

The landing net completes the list of tackle requirements for most of our salmon fly-fishing. That is, apart from the fly itself, and how to cast it. But all this demands its own chapter.

Audacious your odyssey,
Salmo the Leaper:

You were so near your redd,
Your shrunken gut
Forbade all feeding,
Urged you to ripen;

But you came to my lure,
Betrayed yourself
For a feather.

Tom Rawling, *Ghosts at my Back*, 1982

X
Fly Fishing

PART TWO: THE FLY AND FLY CASTING

THE FLY

As we know today, their loss of appetite on return from sea discourages salmon from seeking food in fresh water. It is necessary that this should be so, since most rivers would be unable to support large numbers of hungry salmon. Nevertheless, although it happens only occasionally, salmon do sometimes interest themselves in food items, including a rise of fly; behaviour noticed by anglers of olden days who understandably assumed the fish to be feeding in the usual manner. Robert Howlett in *The Angler's Sure Guide*, 1706, was simply voicing current opinion when he wrote of the salmon's "extraordinary excessive feeding all the summer in fresh rivers".

So—believing that salmon fed avidly on flies, just like trout did, those bygone anglers tied lures like big trout flies to catch them on.

And catch them they did. Even if fished partly for the wrong reasons, those early flies caught salmon—just as they would if fished today. For instance, the August Fly, described in Dame Juliana's *A Treatyse of Fysshynge wyth an Angle*, drab, straggly and dark (see plates of flies) would catch a fish in any summer river.

The occasional success of the mediaeval salmon fisherman is not surprising. What *is* surprising is that the sport of salmon fly-fishing should have started as early as it did, considering the primitive tackle of the time. As stated in *A Treatyse of Fysshynge wyth an Angle*, salmon, albeit in very small numbers, were undoubtedly being taken on artificial flies early in the 15th century, and perhaps even earlier. At that date, however, the salmon fly *per se* was unknown. None of the twelve flies listed in the *Treatyse* was specifically intended for salmon. And it was not for another two hundred years that fly-tying became more sophisticated and the salmon fly started to assume its own identity.

This happened in the mid-sixteen hundreds and coincided with the introduction of the fishing reel. Before that, in *The Pleasures of Princes*, Markham had mentioned flies for salmon fishing as for trout; but Markham was a notorious parrot, and it is probable that he cribbed most of his book from Leonard Mascall's *A Booke of Fishing with Hooke and Line*, 1590, which says much the same thing. Mascall, for his part, had leaned heavily on Dame Juliana's *Treatyse*; some of his comments on salmon fishing being copied almost word for word.

Izaak Walton, in *The Compleat Angler*, 1653, referred to fly-fishing for salmon when he mentioned them being caught "as the Trout is, with a worm, a minnow which some call a Penke, or with a fly". But Izaak, for all the charm he conjured up, was not a salmon fisherman.

His contemporary Thomas Barker, however, undoubtedly was. With his "Ring of Wyre" at the rod top, and "a Winde to turne with a barrel, to gather up his Line, and loose at his pleasure" Barker was equipped for dealing with a big fish. In the second edition of his important book: *The Art of Angling*, he claimed to have caught a salmon in the Thames. This he could well have done, since the Thames was a noted salmon river at the time and he worked as a cook in London for many years— although if it was the fish he wrote a poem about, it was caught on lob-worm not on fly.*

In those days, incidentally, no distinction was made between salmon and sea trout, so it is likely that some of the "salmon" referred to by the early writers were in fact migratory trout. In *The Experienc'd Angler*, 1662, Robert Venables referred to "young salmons under a quarter of a yard long." These fish, he said, had tender mouths, and for catching them he advised the use of a double hook. They were undoubtedly young sea trout, or "herling".

In his *Northern Memoirs*, (written in 1658 although, strangely, not published until 1694), Richard Franck—like Venables a soldier in Cromwell's army—described the tying of salmon flies in considerable detail. Among other materials, he listed:

> Silks of all kinds, threads, thrums, moccado ends and cruels of all size and variety of colours; dogs and bears heir; besides twisted fine threads of gold and silver: with feathers from the capon, partig, peacock, pheasant, mallard, teal, snipe, parrot, heron-shaw, paraketta, bittern, hobby, phlimingo, and Indian flush; but the mockaw, with exception, gives flames to the hackle.

*See p. 175.

The "dapple feathers of a teal" were also recommended. And there is little doubt that by the latter part of the 17th century, salmon fly-fishing was beginning to settle in. Venables, who like his fellow Cromwellian, Franck, seems to have been a widely travelled and experienced angler, observed that "the Salmon taketh the artificial flie very well; his flies must be much larger than you use for other Fish; the wings very long . . . with very long tayls . . . He delights in the most gaudy and Orient colours you can choose."

James Chetham, in *The Anglers Vade Mecum, 1681*, suggested that salmon took the same flies that "trout generally doth, whether natural or artificial." He also recommended "Silver-twist" and "Gold-twist" as being "good to use in dubbing the bodies." His *Horseleech Fly* is said to be the first example of a named salmon fly.

Salmon fly-fishing seems to have been fairly widespread during the 18th century, certainly in Scotland. A fifty-four pounder was caught on fly near Aberfeldy on the River Tay in 1765—no mean feat considering the indifferent tackle of the time.

Richard Bowlker in *The Art of Angling Improved in all its Parts*, 1747, discussed one or two named salmon flies—as did Richard Brookes in *The Art of Angling*, 1766 (incidentally, the first author I believe to mention the use of prawn). But it was not until the 19th century was well under way that tackle improvements began to bring salmon fly-fishing more into line with the sport as we know it today. From being whipped direct to the horsehair casting-line, later to a length of gut, the hook became gut-eyed, *c.* 1835. Now, for the first time, the fly could be detached from the leader, or "cast" as it was known—a term extending to the present-day from the trout angler's "cast of flies". Later still, the metal-eyed hook replaced the gut eye, and towards the end of the century the salmon fly reached its peak with the elaborate, gaudy and highly complicated dressings recorded by Francis Francis and George Kelson.

The eighteen hundreds had been ushered in by a small spate of angling writers, chief among them: George Bainbridge with his *Fly-Fisher's Guide*, 1816, which gives detailed instructions in fly-tying, and includes his "invisible" knot for finishing-off a dressing. But although the 19th century produced some very good anglers and writers, only one or two of the more perceptive suspected the returning salmon's indifference to food.

Foremost among these was Sir Humphry Davy (*Salmonia*, 1828) who noticed that salmon stomachs when opened were invariably empty, and suggested it was the salmon's memory of feeding in parr-hood that caused it to take a fly. Very advanced thinking for the time. But he was in a tiny minority. Most people still believed that salmon continued to feed in freshwater and, since it was presumed that taking fish must be feeling peckish, flies were designed to assuage their hunger. These were of two varieties:

1. Dull-looking, sober flies, intended as vague imitations of natural creatures—the March Brown, for instance, which, wrote John Younger of Kelso in his book *River Angling for Salmon and Trout*, 1840, "the fish feed on in low water exactly as the trout does."

2. Bright, gaudy, attractor flies of glittering tinsel, with wings and hackles in strong, contrasting colours. During the second half of the 19th century, these new, vividly-hued patterns, which had originated in Ireland some years earlier, started to push the duller, more simple flies into the background.

This invasion of gaudy Irish patterns did not occur without some local resistance, notably on Tweedside where the salmon fishers—according to a contemporary writer—not only held what was called "the Irish fly" in ridicule, but actually forbade the use of it on those parts of the river they individually rented. This was not because they thought it too deadly for everyday use, but solely because it was considered: "a kind of bugbear to the fish, scaring them from their accustomed haunts and resting spots."

This had little or no effect. The popularity of the imported Irish salmon flies increased apace—much to the disgust of that stalwart traditionalist of the time, Thomas Tod Stoddart who, in *The Angler's Companion to the Rivers and Lochs of Scotland*, 2nd edition, 1853, noted acidly:

Not absolutely discarding the old standard and local lures, modern anglers have introduced into their stock at least a thousand-and-one other varieties, all dignified with the name of killers ... For every season and month, for all hours of the day, for all changes of weather, for waters low, flooded, or in mid state, sunned or clouded, deep or shallow, streamy, wind-ruffled or still, icy-cold or at blood heat, black or clear, leaf-strewn or otherwise, they have a peculiar and favourite lure: nay, were it possible, by some adaptation of phosphorus to cause hooks to reveal their trimmings in the dark, no doubt a nocturnal assortment would become added, possessed, as became it, of all the powers of *diablerie* and witchcraft.

It was no good. Once started, the new fashion in salmon flies quickly climbed to unprecedented heights of fancy. Whatever their effect on the fish, these new lures certainly hooked the fishermen. And so started the Victorian era of slavish attention to detail. Every fibre of every exotic feather, every twist of silk, every turn of tinsel had to be exact. In vain did Stoddart write with sturdy commonsense:

> There is, I cannot help thinking, a great deal of prejudice, self-conceit, and humbug exhibited by salmon-fishers generally, with respect to their flies—a monstrous mass of nonsense hoarded up by the best of them, and opinions held, quite at variance with reason . . . Is the fish, too, so capricious, that a single fibre wanting in the lure, a misplaced wing, a wrongly assorted hue, will discompose and annoy it?

But nobody paid much attention to Stoddart. They had already entered the great age of salmon-fly dressing—equalled as an angling cult only by the chalk-stream dry-fly, which flourished at the end of the century. At its peak, the fully-dressed salmon fly was a work of art, demanding as much skill in its construction as any minor artifact of Victorian society. Consider the intricate dressing of the *Jock Scott*:

Tag:	Silver wire and yellow floss.
Tail:	Golden pheasant topping and Indian crow.
Butt:	Black ostrich herl or black chenille.
Body:	In two equal halves: (1) Yellow floss-silk veiled with six orange toucan breast-feathers and ribbed with fine oval silver tinsel, followed by a butt of a black herl. (2) Black floss-silk, ribbed with broader silver tinsel in front of a black hackle. In large sizes of fly the hackle is guarded from the flat tinsel by a thin ribbing of silver twist or thread. In small sizes, the second ribbing is of medium oval silver tinsel.
Wings:	A pair of brown turkey-tail strips with white tips: outside these a sheath of mixed wings, married strands of peahen secondary, or dyed swan, yellow, scarlet and blue, of bustard, florican and golden-pheasant tail, two strands of peacock sword-feather tied in to lie along the upper edge; narrow strips of teal and barred summer duck, married before being put on; brown mallard strips as a top to the wings.
Throat:	Speckled gallina.
Sides:	Jungle-cock neck-feathers.
Cheeks:	Blue chatterer.

Topping: Golden pheasant.
Horns: Macaw tail, blue and yellow.

The eponymous inventor of this fly—which first caught a salmon in 1845—was fisherman to Lord John Scott on Tweed, and later a fly-tyer at Kelso, birthplace of many famous flies. Francis Francis included some of them among the two hundred-and-thirty-five patterns listed in his *Book on Angling*, 1867. And many more patterns were on the way. There was no shortage of fertile minds. The Limerick influence had taken root, and on this side of the Irish Sea gillies and anglers alike were out to make a name with new creations. Far-ranging in their demands for exotic materials, salmon flies came pouring forth, meticulous in detail. George Kelson, High Priest of the cult during late Victorian times, recorded no fewer than two-hundred-and-fifty patterns in *The Salmon Fly*, 1895. And these were only a selection from the number available.

Kelson had considerable influence in angling circles of the time, and it is amusing to learn that although his list of fly patterns was enormous he used comparatively few of them himself. This, however, was not common knowledge, and his many disciples with infinite patience and attention to detail painstakingly tied the Master's complicated dressings for themselves. Nobody understood what it was they were trying to tie, since nobody knew what these creations were supposed to represent. But they all caught fish.

Modern flies, too, will catch fish. They are different from those intricate over-dressed and brilliantly-coloured examples of Victorian imagination, tending to be dressed once more with sparse simplicity. But as to what they represent—we are no wiser than those fanciful fly-tyers of a century ago.

What part did the exotic materials of Victorian fly-patterns play in attracting salmon? They were certainly successful. The *Jock Scott*, best known of all flies, must have caught a great many fish. And some anglers still use it. Among many notable salmon it has accounted for was General Home's fifty-one-and-a-half pounder on Tweed in 1921. But most of those traditional patterns are seldom fished today. And not only because of the difficulty in obtaining their supposedly vital components. It seems certain now that they succeeded in spite of rather than because of their dressings—which says more about the salmon than the flies themselves, a point of no small importance to today's fly-dresser and easily proved by the success of such simple patterns as a plain *Stoat's Tail*.

The more salmon lying in a pool, the more chance of finding a poop in the group. And with the huge runs of fish that filled our rivers in Victorian times, there were plenty of potential poops. As we know today, at times salmon will take almost anything they can grab. And from the great number of fish in their rivers, those anglers of yesterday found no trouble in attracting sufficient takers to the contemporary flies in use. To be successful today, however, with far fewer fish at our disposal, we need to be more discriminating in our offerings. There can be little doubt that the modern fly is successful not in spite of but because of its comparative plainness and sparsity of dressing.

A. H. E. Wood, of greased-line fishing fame (see also p. 230), showed that salmon would take flies far more lightly-dressed than anything used hitherto; indeed, that they would even take hooks with no dressing at all. He also proved that they would take flies fished almost on the surface; and, moreover, move several yards to do so.

Much has been written about salmon flies with the idea of making them more conspicuous in varying conditions of light and water. But this approach is surely wrong. Whatever its colour, if a fly is to appear natural, to seem like a living member of some small prey species, it should be *inconspicuous*. For their safety, prey creatures are usually well camouflaged in ways that tend to make them as unobtrusive as possible. So, our best chance, it might seem, of stimulating the predatory instincts of the salmon is to offer him something shady and tantalizing. Not the representation of, say, a little fish, but the *impression* of a little fish. For this reason (no matter what it is supposed to represent) a rather drab-looking, tenuous, lightly-dressed fly that flickers across the pool is likely to be more attractive than something solid and neat and "over-stuffed". And the success of the straggly, lightly-tied hair-wing fly bears this out. There is nothing new, of course, in the use of hair in salmon flies: Richard Franck included "dogs and bears heir" in his list of fly dressings over three hundred years ago. But hair "wings", which flicker so enticingly in the water, have certainly come back into prominence during recent years, and with great success.

There is another point. When looking upwards, a salmon can see through the surface only at an angle of $41\frac{1}{2}°$ from the vertical. Outside this, the surface acts as a mirror, so that beyond the fish's surface circle or "window" he can see through, a fly approaching near to the surface is seen against a reflection of the river bottom. If we think that the tonal values of a fly are important in relation to that reflected river bottom, the fly we select should appear *not* in contrast to that bottom but in sympathy with it: a fly designed not to stand out from it, but *to blend with it*, for that is how a salmon would expect a prey creature to appear.

Whether the salmon can detect such a fly against that background is the least of our worries. The vision of a salmon is extremely acute. Not only will he see the movement of a dark fly against a dark background but, as I have proved many times, he will do so even in very coloured spate water.

Of all hair-wing salmon flies for late spring and summer fishing with floating line, the simple *Stoat's Tail* is one of the best we have. It does not of course have to be made of stoat's tail, any dark hair of sufficient flexibility will do. Modern fly-tying is essentially very easy. Wrap some black hairs from your Labrador round the bare shank of a single, double or treble hook, and you have a fly that will catch salmon. You can, needless to say, make it as intricate as you please by adding various body-silks and tinsels together with hackles and butts and tails and anything else fancy dictates in the shape of dyed hair and feathers and other multi-coloured materials. Such flies provide so much pleasure in their tying that eventually, I suppose, one's fly finishes up among the ranks of the traditionals. But it is all great fun, and the more skilled your fingers the more beautiful and exciting these creations become—and for some people, fly-tying is an art form, an end in itself. But to be practical, the first plain fly you tied will hook you fish. Probably more than any other.

Not everyone is content with such spartan simplicity, however. A recent authority, perceiving greatness in the future, considers the "greased-line fly" to be "in a state of evolution . . . perhaps a relatively early stage", and submits a "tonal and functional list" of "silhouettes, translucent illusions, normal images and flashing illusions." As well as a mixture of these for good measure.

Perhaps equally surprising, J. Arthur Hutton in an age of "flashing illusions" seventy years ago, was moving in the opposite direction:

> One thing I am quite sure about, and that is that there is no necessity for the enormous number of patterns there are in existence, and I also doubt very much whether the salmon care one brass farthing about all the little fads adopted by fly-dressers . . . I believe myself that simply-dressed flies made of comparatively few materials would kill just as well as some of these complicated patterns which involve the use of feathers from half-a-dozen birds, in addition to several various coloured silks and two or three different sorts of tinsel . . .

I do not think that the pattern is of great importance ... I daresay I should kill as many fish as I do now if I never fished with anything but a Thunder and Lightning, varying the size to suit the water.

And so say many of us, I fancy, in the light of modern experience. Compare the complications of, say a *Jock Scott*, *Mar Lodge*, or *Akroyd* with the *Dee Special* shown on plate 8. This plain little fly, tied in a few seconds, is no more than a bare size 10 treble with a few black hairs wrapped round it together with a hint of blue (or orange) and touched off at the head with nail varnish. It boasts no body-dressing, no silks or tinsels. No cheeks, horns, topping, tail, throat, butt, tag or hackle. But during a couple of days recently on the Dee, it caught me nine salmon in a row.

Fish can be caught on hooks with no dressing whatever, and there is no doubt that the hook itself should always be taken into account as part of a fly. The movement of a hook shank swimming across the current is utterly different from and much more lifelike than any river debris floating downstream, and bare hooks have accounted for both salmon and sea trout. But dressing of one sort or another makes a hook look more attractive.

That salmon can be taken consistently on a plain black fly has been amply demonstrated by many anglers. Indeed, of all colours, black is by far the most successful. So—does this mean we should abandon the use of other colours altogether?

No. Why should we?

Whatever the success of a sable dressing, most people (quite apart from those with an instinctive dislike of Puritan conformity) relish a touch of colour in a fly. And so do I. I don't think it will very often make much difference, but I like it. Whatever its effect on the fish, it pleases me. Anyway, it probably does no harm and, who knows, may even be helpful at times—if only through the tonal values which, if cunningly intermingled, will render the fly less conspicuous. A result that may make it slightly more "shadowy" and illusory, and therefore, more real, and so more attractive to a salmon.

Besides, whatever the success of a plain black fly, unless it is proved that salmon become colour-blind on their return from sea—which (for reasons mentioned in Chapter I) appears unlikely, it is silly to suggest that fly pattern can *never* play a part. Who can say that at some time or other a flash of junglecock cheek or a gleam of gold ribbing on a fly has not *induced* a fish to seize it? And what, indeed, of the prawn-like and highly productive G.P.!

In addition, we should not forget that successful presentation is helped by what we *think* about our fly. Without confidence in it, we will never fish with sustained endeavour. If your confidence is renewed or increased by changing the fly pattern, *then for heaven's sake change it!* Apart from any therapeutic value, changing the colours of the day adds to the fun, and fun, above all, is what salmon fishing should be.

There is, however, an important proviso: fly-changing should never become a fetish, for this results in "fly-twitch"—a disease whose consequences, although unsuspected, are none the less unfortunate. Sooner or later an angler suffering from this miserable affliction—never content for long with any pattern he chooses, and constantly wading ashore to fiddle with his scissors and fly-case—*will miss the chance of a taking fish.* This particular salmon, resting briefly on its way up-river, has moved on again by the time our hero has completed yet another change of fly and returned to the fray.

This book is being written from my own experience, and although the attraction of a black fly has been proved many times to my satisfaction, there have been occasions when colour in a lure has seemed to make a difference. Apart from experiments with variously coloured prawns, described in Chapter XVI, there is The Curious Case of the Orange Fly. I have told the story before (in *Sea Trout Fishing*), but it is worth re-telling because it perfectly illustrates my axiom that nearly every statement made about salmon fishing needs qualifying.

Many years ago, when fishing a salmon and sea trout lough of the far West, a friend and I struck oil with a vivid orange lure originally tied for reservoir fishing. The fish would take no other fly we offered them. It was uncanny.

As it happened, we had only one of these lures which, since we had no fly-tying stuff with us, we shared, fishing the thing in turns. At length, when being extracted from the gristle of a salmon's jaw, this precious fly got broken—after which, we caught nothing more. We tried every pattern we had, using flies that seemed identical in shape and size to our orange original, but of different colours. Useless. The fish might sometimes boil at them, but *would not take.* Not another fish did we hook—until, eventually, we drove all the way to Rogan's and got some similar orange flies tied up. After this, we both caught fish again—but only on that particular pattern.

Had I been fishing alone I might have ascribed the failure of the other flies to my incompetence. But I was not alone. My companion, who fished with equal frustration, was my former co-author Fred Buller, experienced all-round angler. His efforts exactly reflected my own.

From time to time since then I have tried a similar pattern of fly in many different locations, but never with such dramatic success. Nevertheless, you will understand why I do not altogether discount the importance of fly pattern—although never again have I known the "colour of the day" to be pinpointed so precisely as it was during that extraordinary week in Ireland years ago.

Often, by fishing all season through with different sizes of just one fly pattern, anglers have caught their share of fish. I have done so myself, having on three successive seasons used only a Blue Charm the first year, a Thunder and Lightning the second, and a plain Stoat's Tail the third. Compared with other catches on the same water I did very well, and at no time felt deprived. But does this really prove anything? Would I have done even better if I had widened my choice of patterns? After all, unless the incident of the orange fly was sheer coincidence, which I don't believe, there may well be times when a fly's colour or colour combination plays a part in attracting salmon.

So, although I remain convinced that black is the most attractive colour for a salmon fly, and although nowadays I tend to regard the old traditional patterns as little more than beautiful curiosities, I still like to experiment and to "ring the changes".

Most salmon flies have been designed as coloured "attractors". Few represent known living creatures. Exceptions are lures such as Elver and Sand-eel, the March Brown, sundry Nymphs, the Silver Blue—surely intended to simulate a little fish, as are my own Medicine and Sunk Lure. And, of course, the G.P., devised by that excellent salmon angler Esmond Drury.

The story of this fly is highly entertaining. Here it is, as told me by Esmond himself:

I originally designed the G.P. for use on a small pool on the River Test, just upstream of Romsey and immediately below Great Bridge. This pool—which had silted up last time I saw it—was only a few yards long. Because of rhododendrons on the near bank and an overhanging willow on the far bank, with the bridge just above, it was virtually impossible to fish downstream with fly—and the beat rule was fly only.

The pool often held a fish or two; they could be seen in the gin-clear water. But an orthodox fly lobbed upstream under the willow and allowed to drift down was regularly ignored. As I had learned in Ireland, a prawn cast upstream at about forty-five degrees from one bank and allowed to drift down, can prove attractive to reluctant salmon and this knowledge led me to tie a "fly" that could be fished in the Rhododendron Pool like a drifting prawn. The result was the G.P.— and it worked like a charm.

The first time I fished it upstream in the Rhododendron Pool I had two salmon on it, and another one from a pool lower down where I fished it in the usual way. Since then it has proved effective in many rivers of the United Kingdom, Iceland and Norway.

Originally, I made the fly approximately the same size as a medium prawn, and dressed it only on size 2 hooks. Later, however, I found that in conditions of low, warm, water, smaller sizes could be very effective.

I christened the fly "G.P." because most of the ingredients are golden pheasant. But I later changed this to "General Practitioner" because it proved so deadly!

Esmond also found that his G.P. had a similar effect to the natural prawn when fished with a sink-and-draw technique.

Provided one can get into the river above the lies, the trick is to let a size 2 fly down to the fish on a sinking line. This should be done very slowly—a yard or less at a time, with frequent pauses when the fly is allowed to swing in the current. To get it to do this, the rod should be swung slowly from side to side, to make sure the lies are covered.

This technique is similar to the method of fishing a pool neck described in the picture caption on p. 290, when of course a G.P. can be used.

Sometimes a fish will take the fly firmly, in which case he will hook himself. But sometimes fish can be felt "pecking" at the fly—just as they will at a natural prawn from time to time. In this case, no action should be taken. The fish may well come again. If not, or if "pecking" continues, a smaller G.P. fished down in the same way may do the trick.

*   *   *

Like every other facet of this enchanting and challenging sport, no definitive statement can be made about the salmon fly. For all our fine theories we simply do not know what the salmon thinks he sees, or how he sees it, and we are foolish to restrict ourselves to any particular colour or shape. However unlikely the importance of pattern may be we are, surely, silly to close our minds and pronounce that it never matters.

With its infinitely varied behaviour, the salmon is for ever surprising us and making nonsense of dogmatic statements. A vivid reminder of which comes from none other than George Kelson. Modern writers, counting only his fly patterns, are sometimes unkind to George. But he was nobody's fool. For all the meticulous care lavished on the fly dressings of his day, the old sage knew his quarry. In *The Salmon Fly*, 1895, he wrote:

At times salmon will take anything, at times nothing. In a fever of excitement the King of Fish will exercise his royal jaw upon a thing it were an outrage to call a salmon fly . . . Nay, this same whimsical despot has been known to bring destruction upon himself and discomforture on all theory and calculation by fixing his momentary affections upon a single Jay or Jungle feather tied anyhow on a bare hook! Only a few years since, I believe in '83, a well-known fisherman, passing from pool to pool at Ringwood, and dangling his end fly in the stream as he hurried along, hooked, in eighteen inches of water, and successfully landed, a forty-two pound fresh-run fish. "Hi-Regan" tells me of another, caught in the upper Moy with a field daisy impaled on a small hook . . . Fishing the Earn one sultry day in '87, I saw within six feet of me a salmon working up a gravelled shallow. Several flies had previously been tried in vain. The last, made by a novice, having just lost its Mandarin drake wings, was lying on the bed of the river, for the purpose of keeping the gut in order, whilst I whipped up another like it. On nearing the rude hook—it was but little else—the salmon came about a yard out of his way, picked it up and made off down stream at a flying pace. I soon got in command of him, and went home carrying 11 lbs more than I started with.

Putting aside bare hooks and daisies, I feel sure that if you select any popular fly and fish it in varying sizes and degrees of dressing the season through, you will do as well as you would with a host of patterns to choose from. Indeed, it could be argued that you might even do better—since you will not suffer the agonies of indecision and waste time wondering which pattern to choose, or whether what you have on at any moment is really providing the best chance of hooking a salmon! Even so, although restriction of pattern may not reduce your catch it may, I suggest, reduce your pleasure. There is more at stake than the hooking of a fish. Conjecture offers its own excitement. Deny ourselves the delight and fascination of those fly-cases crammed with patterns of such richly differing colour and design, and for many of us salmon fishing would lose much of its present charm.

FLY CASTING

Now that we are equipped with tackle and fly, the next step is to present our fly to a fish. For this we have the choice of several methods, the most common of which is the straightforward overhead cast at which most anglers are reasonably skilful. Sooner or later, however, obstructions behind the rod—trees, bushes, a steep bank—make overhead casting difficult, if not impossible, and some form of switch cast becomes essential. Unhappily this branch of fly-casting seems to be woefully neglected. (I use the term "switch" in a loose sense to cover roll and Spey casting.)

In view of the casting demonstrations by experts at game fairs and country shows all over Britain, and the amount of good tuition available, this general inability to switch cast is unaccountable. Nevertheless the lack of casting versatility I come across on my travels is very striking. As an example, there was this chap fishing opposite me on Tweed below Melrose.

He was casting—or, I should say, trying to cast—from the left bank which, at that part of the river is steep-to and thickly wooded. He was a competent overhead caster, judging by the lift of his backstroke, but that was as far as it went. His forward stroke was seldom completed—his fly invariably being caught up in branches on the slope behind.

It seemed incredible. The expense of tackle and fishing rent must have set him back several hundred pounds, yet here he was on this lovely stretch of river with no idea of how to put a Spey cast together. During the time I was on that pool, his fly couldn't have been in the water for longer than five or ten minutes at the most. That he hadn't spent just half-an-hour learning the rudiments of switch casting before committing himself to such a beat is hard to understand. But there it was. The poor chap had no distance to cast, most of the fish were lying on his side of the river. Five minutes' instruction would have sufficed to teach him a workable method of putting out a line, but there was no one to show him. When I left the pool he was scrambling up the bank for the ninety-ninth time, groping for his fly.

You may think this an extreme example, but it isn't. Most of the anglers I watch can make a fist of the overhead cast, but are completely foxed when insufficient space behind them precludes it. As a result, many good lies are seldom fished. There are, for instance, pools that fish better from one bank when the river is well up, but from the other bank when the water has fallen and *vice versa*. If this other bank is wooded, as it often is, the angler tied to the overhead cast is at a considerable disadvantage. On most rivers a fly fisherman unable to Spey cast can never realize anything like his full potential.

It is a waste to equip yourself with expensive tackle and rent a costly beat if you haven't the technique to take full advantage of it. An ability to switch cast—that is to make roll, single-Spey and double-Spey casts— is essential to every salmon fisherman. And not only because of its value in covering what is otherwise difficult or impossible water; there is another quite separate advantage. When we are switch casting *the hook can never get into trouble.* Its position is always in view, well clear of the bank and never out of sight behind us.

There are few if any salmon fishermen who have not at some time lost fish because of a broken hook. It can happen so easily, especially with a fluky wind blowing. The angler executes what seems to be a perfectly good overhead cast, except that, caught perhaps by a slant of wind, his leader dips behind him and flicks the fly against a rock. Unaware that such an appalling disaster has happened, he fishes blissfully on down the pool—only to hook and lose what may be his only salmon of the day.

This miserable business, which leaves us with thoughts of suicide, is not likely to happen when we are roll or Spey casting. *We know exactly where the fly is during every moment of the cast.*

Many anglers start their fly-fishing on the reservoirs. They are usually highly competent overhead casters and often expert at double-hauling, but with no idea of Spey casting. If my reader falls into this category I urge him to remember that reservoir trout fly-fishing and salmon fly-fishing are poles apart—not because double-hauling has no place on a salmon river, it has, but because Spey casting is rarely seen on a reservoir, and to a salmon fisherman the Spey cast is indispensable. For my own part, I seldom use any other.

*　　　*　　　*

It is not likely that anyone can learn to cast solely by reading about it, however good the description. And Spey casting is certainly not easy to describe. A few authors have made the attempt, and variously dubbed it: "Hardly possible"; "An incredibly difficult thing to put down accurately"; "Of all casts the most difficult to describe on paper"; "By far the most difficult cast to describe", and so on. And I agree with them. The following notes—which should be studied in conjunction with the photographic sequences—are included simply in the hope that they may assist the novice, while he is learning and practising his casting, by refreshing his memory about what he is trying to accomplish. They also include one or two points I have not encountered in the literature. First, a few observations on the overhead cast.

Overhead Cast

Stance: contrary to most of the casting diagrams I have seen, the weight is best taken on the leg under the shoulder you are casting from. When casting off the right shoulder, have the right foot forward, lean slightly on the left leg during the back cast and bring the weight on the right leg again as the forward stroke is made.

This stance will be found less tiring than casting off the other leg, and holds good for all casts—except when tournament salmon-distance-casting and single-handed double-hauling, in both of which the caster is frequently looking back over his shoulder, and so requires an open stance.

The most common fault in making the overhead cast is circling with the rod top, which results in loss of distance and a poor finish to the cast. A lot of anglers do this because they think that if they don't the fly will foul the line during the forward stroke. It is *not* necessary. The line should come straight back over the rod point and back down again on the water. It should be thrown back well up in the air with a *not-too-tight loop*. If this is done, the fly will not foul the line or leader as the cast is completed.

Here is a tip for making a big change in casting angle.

When a cast has been fished out, bring the rod round horizontally upstream and point it in the direction you wish the next cast to go. Then, keeping the rod at that angle, make your cast. The line will go out at this new angle straight as a spear.

Generally speaking, *don't* look back over your shoulder at the line as it goes behind you. This usually results in a crooked cast. Other faults to avoid are:

Waving and pushing the rod—instead of using it as a spring and propelling the fly at the completion of the forward stroke with a strong flick of the forearms and wrists. *Pushing dissipates power.*

Breaking the wrists too much during the back cast and letting the rod go too far past the vertical. This allows the line and leader to dip, and so endangers the hook—which may lose its point if it flicks a rock. This is a very common occurrence, responsible for losing a lot of fish. Indeed, a broken hook is probably the most common of all avoidable ways of failing to land salmon. It happens time after time, season after season. It will not happen if you perfect your roll and Spey casting.

Casting too tight a loop. This causes a fly to catch the line on the forward stroke.

Starting the forward stroke too soon. If this is done too violently the line will crack like a whip. When this happens, examine your leader at once. You will be lucky to find the fly still with you.

Starting the forward stroke too late, so that the fly drops during the back cast. This is another way of suffering a broken hook.

Starting the back cast too soon; that is, before the line has been brought to the surface (see p. 211). This can easily happen when you are fishing a sunk line. Drag a sunken line up out of the water and the chances are it will come hurtling back—straight at your face.

Study in expertise.
A common mistake when using very light rods is to put too much effort into casting; to try and force the line out, instead of letting the action of the rod operate properly. Less effort leads to better casting.

Relaxed, with right foot slightly forward, casting hand and arm perfectly postioned, the Connecticut angler seen above effortlessly throws a long line across the river.

However questionable their use of ultra-short rods for salmon, most American game-fishermen are superb fly-casters.

Roll Cast

Roll casting is the prelude to single and double Spey casting. If you are unable to perform these casts, remember the plight of that unfortunate angler at Melrose—and learn how to make them forthwith.

I urge you to visit a good casting instructor. Like learning to shoot, fly-casting is vastly easier to learn when you have an expert to teach you. Besides, once acquired, bad casting habits are difficult to eradicate. (To the good casting instructor, the faults in technique of most self-taught fly casters are all too obvious.)

Most of the books that discuss the matter will tell you that Spey casting is difficult, the cast of the expert, an arcane rite denied to all but a gifted few. This is utter nonsense. Spey casting is really very easy to learn. Much easier than the overhead cast—if only you will start at the beginning, and that is with the roll cast. Roll casting is the basis of Spey casting. If you have the patience to master that first, Spey casting will seem laughably simple. And it does not demand *much* patience. Indeed, of all casts the roll cast is undoubtedly the simplest. The reason why anglers find switch casting difficult is because they try to teach themselves, and in forty-nine cases out of fifty they get it wrong.

The roll cast starts with the rod horizontal and the line extended in a straight line across the water.

The rod is brought slowly upwards and back, the arms being raised meanwhile so that the reel comes about level with the chin. This brings the fly feathering towards the rod for a short distance along the surface, and a loop of drawn-in line forms *in front of the rod*. As the rod reaches its top position just backwards of the vertical, the forward stroke is made with a strong, snappy flick of the wrists. (Try to break the rod!) This punch of the wrists sends the loop of line rolling out dead straight *above* the surface. As the line unrolls it picks up the fly, which curls over and plops quietly into the water as the leader straightens out. The cast is made with one unhurried but continuous movement.

> *Note.* The action of forearms and wrists in the roll cast is exactly the same as that used in the Spey casts. It is like driving a spike into a wall with a double-handed hammer. That is to say, we do it with a *strong snap of the wrists*. One does not *push* a hammer forwards. Nor does one push the rod. It is the flexing of the rod, which acts as a spring, that impels the fly-line. And this is done in the roll cast—as it is done in *all* casts—with crisp forearm and wrist action only. Above all, do not attempt to roll the line by pushing the arms out and rolling the shoulder. *Keep your shoulder down.* If you have trouble doing this, get a friend to hold your shoulders firmly from behind while you practise the cast.

Whether with double-handed or single-handed rod, the roll cast is useful whenever a high bank or trees at an angler's back inhibit overhead casting.

The forward stroke of the roll cast seen from the side. This cast, performed with a strong flick of the wrists, is the basis of Spey casting—essential to every would-be salmon fly-fisherman. Note how the line rolls out *above* the water, not along the surface.

205

Forward stroke of the roll cast seen from behind. The common mistake in making this cast is *pushing* the rod and rolling arm and shoulder to make the line curl out, instead of flexing the wrists and using the rod as a spring.

Spey Casting

An angler's choice of fishing single-Spey cast or double-Spey cast depends mainly on wind strength and direction. The single-Spey is used when a strong wind is blowing upstream; the double-Spey in a strong downstream wind. The ability to cast off either shoulder is essential.

Spey casting is sometimes condemned for causing excessive disturbance. In practice, on most of the water we fish, the splash-down of the single-Spey and line-riffle of the double-Spey (see illustrations) are harmless, since they occur close to the angler. Moreover, if the casts are properly executed the line does *not* roll out along the surface, but shoots out *above* the water and settles with no more fuss than the conclusion of a good overhead cast.

There are times, however, when line-splash or riffle may scare close-lying fish in glassy glides or smooth, shallow pool tails. On such water an overhead cast is preferable. If bankside obstructions prevent an overhead cast being used, there remains the ever-useful roll cast—aimed upwards.

Note: the roll cast can be made off the right shoulder only from the right-hand bank; the left shoulder from the left bank. If these are reversed the fly will foul the line on the forward stroke.

Single Spey Cast

Once the essential wrist action of the roll cast has been mastered Spey casting becomes simple and straightforward. All we have to do is to bring the fly from where it finished up, downstream, at the end of the previous cast, and place it two or three yards, out and just upstream of the rod. By doing this we form a big loop of line, which we can punch out at whatever angle we wish using the same action that we used in the roll cast. (See illustrations on p. 205.)

It is essential that we place the fly upstream of the rod; i.e. *above the angle at which we wish to make the forward stroke*, otherwise it will invariably snag the line when we cast forwards.

When trying for distance, start by stripping in the back taper of the line through the rod-rings. This stripped line is easily shot if the forward stroke is aimed upwards.

1. The angler's intention is to retrieve the fly from its position downstream, where it finished up after fishing out the previous cast, and place it in the water just upstream of his right shoulder; then (in the same continuous movement) form a loop of line that with a strong flick of the wrists will carry the fly out towards the camera.

To do this, the rod is swung slightly inshore and raised, all in one movement.

2. Now the angler swings the rod round upstream in front of him, bringing the line and fly up off the water. As the rod moves round, it curves downwards almost to the horizontal so that it *guides the line and fly* towards the splash-down position just beyond his right shoulder. (Note downward curve of line near the rod).

3. "Now the great thing in this cast, the pure essential part upon which it entirely depends, is to compel the line to strike the water after lifting it out instead of sending it back in the air."

Geo. M. Kelson, *The Salmon Fly*, 1895.

4. The splash-down. The fly, together with leader and the last few yards of line, has been placed just upstream in the intended position. From here it can be cast at the required new angle without its fouling the line as it shoots out.

The moment the fly hits the water, the angler forms a loop of line by swinging the rod round and bringing it up just backwards of the vertical, raising his arms slightly as he does so to bring the reel level with his face. (Note stance: right leg slightly forward).

5. The forward stroke is made, the angler's weight being taken on his right leg as the loop of the line followed by leader and fly starts to curl out across the water.

Double Spey Cast

In the double Spey cast, to ensure that it never fouls the line, the fly must be left *downstream* of the rod—*below* the angle at which we wish to make the forward stroke. The cast consists of four movements:

1. The rod is raised to help bring the fly to the surface.

2. Swung at right-angles across the angler's body through nearly 180°—to bring the fly a certain distance upstream and provide enough line for a big loop (as in the single-Spey).

3. Swung back downstream to form this loop of line.

4. Flexed in the forward stroke to punch the loop out over the water in the predetermined direction.

Success in achieving this depends on split-second timing of the forward stroke. Start it too late, and the loop of line has collapsed. Start it too soon, and the loop is not fully formed. Both result in a mangled cast.

Apropos of which, here is a useful tip:

Out of the corner of your eye watch the tiny riffle of surface spray as the line is brought back downstream with the third rod movement. When the riffle stops, the maximum loop of line will have formed. So, *it is at this precise moment that the forward stroke is made.*

Writing recently in the angling press, an author brushed the double-Spey aside as being "merely a fancy cast". But I urge the reader to reject this. Properly performed the double Spey is a cast of great practical value, and not only on an obstructed bank in a strong downstream wind. Of all casts, it is the *safest*—especially when a big tube-fly is being fished on high-density line, since the lure is brought only a comparatively short distance upstream and never comes anywhere near the angler's face.*

Injury caused by a heavy lure is a very real danger when the forward stroke of an overhead cast is mistimed, or the back stroke started before the lure has been brought near enough to the surface.

In making the double-Spey cast the beginner, having raised the rod. may find it helpful to use the rhythm of waltz-time, saying to himself:

"One-two-three" (rod upstream, line brought up along the surface towards him).

"One-two-three" (rod swung back downstream, line riffling down across the surface to form the loop).

"Wham!" (The moment the riffling stops, the forward stroke is made and the line goes shooting out across the river, uncurling *above* the surface to complete the cast in exactly the same manner as the single-Spey.)

*See p. 53.

1. When making his first cast, the angler strips off a fishable length of line and lets the current take it downstream. To ensure that his fly is on the surface he raises his rod slightly . . .

2. . . . then swings it round in front of him upstream through nearly 180°—which brings the fly feathering along the surface towards him.

Note. When starting the double-Spey it is essential to leave the fly *below* the direction in which the forward stroke is to be made.

212

3. The angler then swings the rod back downstream. As he does so a loop of line follows leaving a little riffle of spray on the surface.

4. As the rod (having been swung round downstream through the position shown in Fig. 1) is brought up towards the vertical beside his right shoulder, the angler starts to raise his arms . . .

213

5. . . . bringing the reel level with his face. Then, just as the surface riffle comes to an end (with the rod slightly past the vertical, and a big loop of line formed beside him), the angler makes the final stroke with the same flick of the wrists used in roll and single Spey casting.

6. Aimed slightly upwards, the loop of line shoots out above the water, taking with it the fly leader . . .

7. and 8. . . . which curls over and straightens out to complete the cast.

SPEY-CASTING CHART

FRESH OR STRONG UPSTREAM WIND

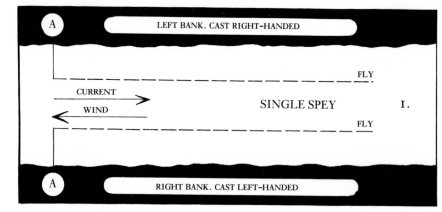

FRESH OR STRONG DOWNSTREAM WIND

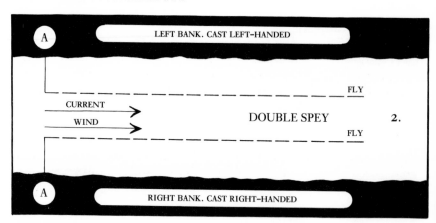

A = Angler—whether on the bank or in the water is immaterial.
Dotted lines show position of casting line and fly at start of cast.

Summary

When switch casting in a fresh or strong *upstream* wind, use:

 The single-Spey (fig. 1).
 From right bank cast from left shoulder.
 From left bank cast from right shoulder.

If there is a fresh or strong wind blowing *downstream*, use:

 The double-Spey (fig. 2)

From right bank cast from right shoulder.
 From left bank cast from left shoulder.

Note. The ability to cast from either shoulder is a great asset. Stance and grip can be adjusted to suit the wind direction and whichever bank is being fished.

A word of advice. Rain or shine, get in the habit of wearing polarized sun-glasses most of the time you are fishing—and always when you practise casting. Besides enabling you to see through the surface glare and spot fish movements, and shielding your eyes from water-flash, they will protect you from getting hooked in the eye if a gust of wind blows the leader across you face.

Tailpiece

There is nothing esoteric about fly-fishing for salmon. If you are a beginner, don't allow its supposed mystique to affect your confidence. If you do, you will lose most of the enjoyment it has on offer. Concentrate on your Spey-casting. When you can make a fist of that—which with good instruction won't take you long—your pleasure will soar, for irrespective of bank obstructions you will be confident to tackle any stretch of water.

You will, furthermore, have learned a great truth: that most of the fun in this wonderful sport comes not from what you can catch but how you catch it.

*   *   *

Now that we have considered our approach to salmon fishing, acquired some fly tackle and learned how to cast, we can start to think about putting it all into practice.

As soon as rain is in the offing, the salmon in the pools become restless and often will not look at a fly. Conversely, this persistent refusal to rise is frequently taken as a sign of the coming of rain.

Eric Taverner, *Salmon Fishing*, 1931

XI
Fly Fishing

PART THREE: STRATEGY

General Principles

No form of angling is basically so simple as the often exasperating but altogether delightful sport of fly-fishing for salmon. No matter whether floating or sinking line is used, so little is needed in the way of tackle. To burden yourself with a heavy bag is quite unnecessary. A rod, reel, line, leader, fly and, if the river demands it, a wading-stick; these are the essentials. All spare tackle can be carried on your person. A case of flies; a nylon-dispenser; scissors and, if needed, spectacles for knot-tying; a priest. What else? Since on most pools a salmon can be beached and tailed by hand, a gaff, net or tailer is usually superfluous. It is true that a length of cord or a simple fish-carrier can live with advantage in your pocket, but a bag is needed only for carrying lunch.

If for the time being we ignore such rites as dry-fly fishing, dapping and dibbling, there are two ways of fishing fly for salmon:

1. With the big fly—length two to four inches—fished close to the bottom on a sinking line.

2. With the small fly—length about half-an-inch to one-and-a-half inches, and sometimes longer, fished close to the surface on a floating line: once called the "greased-line" method, in the days when silk fly lines were smeared with floatant to keep them on the surface.

Nowadays, silk lines are seldom used and it is no longer necessary to grease or ungrease a line in order to make it float or sink. As discussed in the tackle section, there is a comprehensive range of floating, sink-tip and sinking lines that serve for most types of water. Each pool or run on each river has its own characteristics, and the angler can choose the line or lines that will suit the particular water he is going to fish.

On a shallow pool in low water during early spring on, say, the River

Tweed, a sink-tip floating line will sometimes fish the big fly better than a quick-sinking line: there is less chance of the hook getting snagged on the bottom. In high water during summer on many fast-running spate rivers, the sink-tip is often better than the all-floating line for fishing the small fly—the couple of yards or so of quick-sinking tip carries leader and fly under the surface and prevents them from skidding round on top.

Like other aspects of this intriguing sport, the little we know about salmon fly-fishing has been learned mostly by trial and error. Bit by bit it has been discovered that in early spring or late autumn we may fail to catch fish because our fly is too small. In summer we may fail because our fly is too big. Whether sunk line or floating line methods are fished depends, it seems, mainly on the water temperature.

As a rough guide, the big fly fished on sunk line is in operation when the temperature is under 45°–50°F. That is, until about mid-April. The small fly on floating line is fished from then until the water temperature again falls below 45°—usually late autumn. During the period when temperatures fluctuate between 45° and 50°, either method may be successful—depending on the duration of any particular cold or warm spell of weather.

Not surprisingly, in view of the salmon's complex character, there are some exceptions to this.

In cold water when salmon usually tend to take large flies sunk deep, they will sometimes take small flies fished at similar depth; and sometimes they will follow the big lure and take it almost at the surface. And in the warmer weather, when they are mostly taking small flies fished near the surface, they will occasionally take *large* flies fished in this way. I have caught salmon on the 2½–3 inch sea trout Sunk Lure fished just under the surface in the middle of the day in mid-summer. And sometimes fish after fish has shown an interest in a tiny fly sunk deep on the hottest day.

These are, however, mainly exceptions and are mentioned as reminders that *Salmo* is a wonderfully perverse creature, always avoiding any form of neat tabulation. There are times, for instance, when he can be caught on small flies fished near the surface in early spring, and on large lures sunk deep during the heat of summer.

But notwithstanding all these contradictions, salmon *are* creatures of definite tendencies. Irrespective of location, there are these two distinctly different ways of fly-fishing to which the fish generally respond.

The big fly sunk deep in cold water.

The small fly fished near the surface when the water has warmed up.

And it is around this change of behaviour that our salmon fly-fishing philosophy is formed.

The point at which the change occurs is not clearly defined. Claims have been made that salmon switch their attention from the big fly to the small fly at the mystic figure of 48°F. But this is an over-simplification. As experience proves, the salmon is not so precise. The small fly will sometimes succeed when the temperature is in the low forties. The big fly may catch fish when the temperature is up in the middle fifties, or even higher.

Not long ago on the last (very cold) day of the River Tweed's trout season, three experienced salmon anglers tried floating line, sunk line and spinner without an offer. Three others, on the opposite bank, who fished themselves into a state of near exhaustion, also registered a blank. The only salmon of the day, these six worthies learned later, had been hooked before their arrival by an early-rising trout angler at a quarter-to-eight that morning on a size 16 Greenwell's Glory!

The other side of the coin turned up neatly one blazing June day on the River Spey. The water was dead low, the pools full of "potted" fish, the water temperature in the high sixties. Everyone was using tiny flies on floating lines—and catching nothing. Exasperated by the sight of so many salmon sloshing about, my cunning old mate Arthur Oglesby, ever ready to experiment, put on a sinking line with a heavy two-inch tube. Fishing it right down near the bottom of a deepish pool he landed five salmon in quick succession. This was no fluke. A companion who followed suit caught a thirty-six pounder, his biggest salmon ever.

Exceptions they may be, but examples such as these emphasize the foolishness of being dogmatic. It is the angler who remains open-minded; who can recognize and take advantage of these departures from what experience has taught us to regard as "normal" behaviour, who succeeds when others fail.

So strange and varied is the salmon's taking behaviour according to location, water conditions and time of year, that often it seems one might be fishing for an entirely different species. Nor does this variation always depend on change of river or season. A salmon's taking reactions can differ dramatically within minutes, or even seconds, although the fish is offered the same lure in, so far as we can tell, precisely the same way.

What can one say about such recondite behaviour? Of all the species of fish I have pursued during a long lifetime's angling, only that of the sea trout can be compared to it.

I suggest that the nearest we can come to a definitive statement is to say that salmon *tend* to react to large flies sunk deep at temperatures below 45°, and to small flies near the surface at temperatures above 50°; and that changes in taking behaviour coincide with changes in water temperature, happening *gradually* as the temperature moves between the mid-forties and the fifties.

During early April when water temperatures often seem to be in a state of flux, dodging up and down between forty-five and fifty, the fish may accept either big or small flies. Because of this, many anglers tend to change to the small fly too soon. This is understandable: the floating line is so much easier to fish than the sunk line.

It is a mistake, though.

Undoubtedly in these fluctuating conditions some fish will be caught on the small fly, but until the water temperature has been settled for several days on a figure close to 50°, there is likely to be a better chance of catching salmon on the big fly.

At this time of year, anticipating no sudden change in behaviour, I find it often pays to try both methods: to set up two rods, so that either sunk or floating line can be tried without having to strip down the tackle and change reels. Sometimes as an experiment I take three rods to the waterside. The same chilly spring morning has seen fish hooked on a size 6 fly fished on floating line; a $2\frac{1}{2}$ inch tube-fly on sunk line, and a 4 inch Toby spoon on the spinning rod. I did this by concentrating solely on one known resting-lie for running fish, trying each of the three methods in turn. It was great fun.

An axiom quoted by many writers states that there is always a better chance of catching salmon on the small fly when the air temperature is higher than the water temperature; that when the air is colder than the water the fish are more reluctant to come to the surface. Hence the dislike of "noyous" north and east winds which, usually, are colder than winds from the south and west.

Well, there is probably some truth in this. After all, when the air is cold, and so cooling the water, it means a lowering in the temperature of the fish themselves, with a consequent slowing-up of their metabolism. The dissipation of energy in rising to grab lures is, therefore, something one might think the fish would avoid. As one writer has put it:

When the air is cooler than the water is, we must accept the fact of as poor a condition for greased line fishing as it is possible to have. But it is equally poor for any other form of legitimate fishing.

This was the fish that took the Toby!

Nevertheless, logical though this seems and although for years without thinking about it much I tended to accept it as Gospel, I don't take much notice of it nowadays. Whatever the reactions of other fish species to cold winds, experience continues to teach me that the salmon is a law unto himself. I prefer to fish in a warm wind rather than a cold wind if only because it is kinder to the fingers; but if the water temperature has been on or close to 50° for several days on end, and I think there are fresh salmon in the water, I will fish the small fly hard and with confidence irrespective of the wind direction. I have caught salmon with floating line and small fly on too many cold days, and failed to catch them on too many warm days, to worry unduly about air temperatures—unless the difference is very great, say ten degrees or over.

Recently, during nearly a fortnight on the river, my companions and I had our best day's fishing with floating line in a bitter east wind. The water temperature was 49°, and the air temperature never higher than 43°. The following day, although the wind had changed and the air temperature was in the fifties, we caught nothing. Yesterday's fish had moved on, and none had run up into our pools to replace them.

When it comes to catching salmon, the presence of fresh fish in the beat is much more important than warm air. As mentioned in Chapter I, runs of salmon may occur quite irrespective of the air temperature.

FLY PRESENTATION
SPRING/AUTUMN and SUMMER

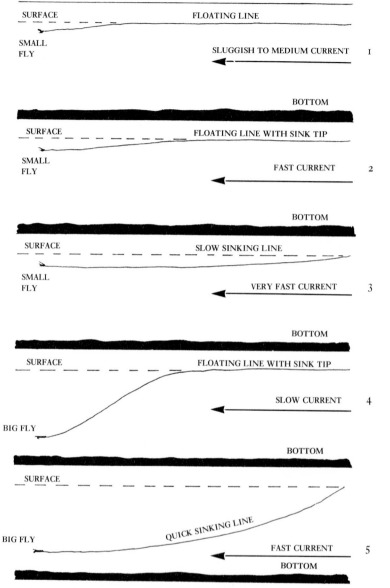

1–3: Summer fishing with small fly. In each case the fly fishes at required depth (approximately four inches) irrespective of current strength.

4, 5: Spring and autumn fishing with big fly sunk deep. Sink-tip or quick-sinking line used according to depth of water and strength of current.

Effective Casting Range

But however many fresh salmon may have arrived in our water, we are unlikely to catch any unless the fly is presented in a way that will attract them. This seems so obvious that I cannot imagine anybody disagreeing with it. From what I see each season, however, some anglers seem either unwilling or unable to put it into practice.

Whether fished on sinking or floating line, the fly must approach a salmon at a controlled speed and depth: near the bottom in the case of the former; near the surface, the latter. And it is important that whatever its depth, its speed should approximate that at which a living creature of similar size could reasonably be swimming: say, between $1\frac{1}{2}$ and 3 m.p.h.

Since we never know at any moment how many from any given number of salmon in a pool are "takers", it follows that the more fish our fly covers attractively, the more chance we have of hooking one. It must, therefore, travel at a controlled speed and depth across every place a salmon may be lying. And it is precisely because the expert angler can make his fly do this, through his water-sense and casting skill, that he catches so many fish. As I have already suggested, there is much more than mere luck in successful salmon fishing.

But no one can tell when the magic moment will come. So, each cast, from first to last, deserves equal thought and care. A river current seldom runs steady and true. The surface of most pools is twisted into numbers of little swirls and eddies where the stream changes direction, or is bent by the ever-changing contours of the river bottom. A fly that swings untended from a fast stream into slack water, or into the turbulence of a back-eddy, will suddenly lose all semblance of life and start to sink. The behaviour of this fly is quite different from the overhead "plopper", which sometimes induces a "crunch" take. Although a salmon may move towards a faltering fly he seldom takes it.

Of course, in high water most salmon are lying close to the side and are easily covered with a comparatively short line. But in lowish water with fish spread out across the pool, the number of lies our fly will cover attractively depends on our effective casting range.

The ability to cast a long and accurate line should be the aim of every angler. But *effective* casting range is not the overall distance cast— however far that may be. *It is the distance from our rod to an imaginary line drawn down the river parallel to our own bank, inside which our fly is working at the depth and speed likely to attract a fish.*

On our understanding of this hangs our success as salmon fly fishermen. Merely to cast across a strong current and leave the fly to swing round is pointless. As soon as the line touches down, the current starts to drag it round in a huge bow. So that, like the tail skater at the end of a "snake" twisting on an ice-rink, the fly comes whipping round at excessive speed, often skidding across the surface when on a floating line, and swimming far too close to the surface when on a sinker. In neither case is it likely to hook a salmon—although it may ultimately have covered every fish in the pool. We may have been casting thirty yards across the river, but nearly all of this distance has been wasted, for the fly was not working effectively until slowed to an acceptable speed—by which time it was hanging almost straight downstream from the rod. Not until the fly had reached that point would a salmon have been likely to take it.

Measured across the river, our effective range during each cast was nothing like thirty yards. It was, indeed, little over the length of our rod—if held out over the water at right-angles to the bank. A distance of no more than six or eight yards!

So, any fish lying further out than that are not going to be hooked by us. The fly may have passed over them, but at too great a speed. *And it is for this reason more than any other that so many inexperienced anglers fail to catch salmon.*

Assuming we are throwing as long a line as we can, our effective casting range can be increased in two ways: by line-mending, and by deep wading.

Mending is done with a circular movement of the rod almost immediately a cast has been completed. The belly formed in the line by the current is switched over, so that the *downstream* curve becomes an *upstream* curve. This has the effect of slowing down the fly and causing it to move across the river in a lifelike manner.

To maintain this semblance of life in a strong draw, several more upstream mends may be necessary as the fly swings round. But these can be made only with a floating line. When casting a quick-sinking line we need to throw a big upstream curve the moment the line starts to touch down. To form this curve we shoot extra line. How to do this is described in the chapter on sunk line fishing (see page 267).

It is true that sometimes in fast water a fly cast at forty-five degrees or more upstream, and stripped back over the salmon, will be grabbed. But for all the times I have tried this it hasn't worked very often. And when it has, the fish has seldom been well hooked.

In a moderate current no mending is necessary. The fly will fish round perfectly well if we cast at whatever angle we choose, leave it alone, and let the current work it round over the lies. This angle of cast is very important, but we shall go into more details at the riverside in the next two chapters.

When the current is more sluggish still we go into reverse. That is, cast more squarely across the river and mend *downstream*—shooting extra line as we do so. Here we purposely form a big downstream curve for the current to "bite" and help swing the fly across the stream.

Remember: mending should be done only on rippled water, *not* on flat, glassy surfaces where it may cause disturbance. And on no account across those smooth, shallowing pool tails which, in summer, are often good taking places. When the river is low these tails are better left unfished until dusk.

A stretch similar to that referred to on p. 220. Salmon take just off the current, which is flecked with foam. At this height of the spate, ideal for fly-fishing, the current is too strong to allow the small fly to sink to a fishable depth on floating line. A sink-tip line—which takes the fly three or four inches under the surface—is obligatory.

Almost the whole of salmon fly-fishing strategy lies within the compass of the diagram opposite.

In fig. 1., an angler at A1 casts to B1. Caught by the current, his line is swept round the "S"–shaped curve B1–C. On its way towards the bank, the fly passes two salmon lying at Y. Owing to its excessive speed, however, caused by line drag, the fly will not be fishing attractively until it reaches the horizontal dotted line R1. So—although he may have cast perhaps thirty yards to B1, the angler's *effective* casting distance extends no further across the river than the line R1, and if he continues to fish in this manner any salmon outside that line will remain uncatchable.

In fig. 2., the angler casts again to B1. This time, however, he mends his line from rod top down to somewhere near the join between line and leader. This upstream curve irons out much of the current drag and slows down the speed of the fly. A considerable advantage is gained, since his fly will now effectively cover the two salmon at Y. His *effective casting range* has increased as far as the line R2.

In fig. 3., the angler has waded into the river as far as A2, and cast again, this time to B2. Again he mends his line correctly, and the fly can now cover the two salmon at Z—hitherto out of reach. His *effective casting range* is now at its maximum: the line R3.

By fishing this piece of water from the two positions A1 and A2, and judicious mending of the line, he can effectively cover all four fish.

Note. If he starts by wading to A2 and casting to B2, he will over-cast the fish at Y. To wade into a pool and start off by casting as far as possible across the river is a very common mistake. *The nearer water should always be fished first.* As shown in fig. 2.

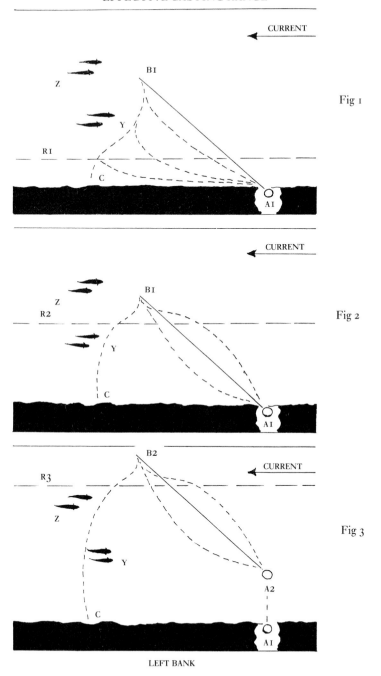

CURRENT

B1

Z

Y

R1

C

A1

Fig 1

CURRENT

Z

R2

B1

Y

C

A1

Fig 2

B2

CURRENT

R3

Z

Y

C

A2

A1

Fig 3

LEFT BANK

R 1, 2 and 3 represent the limits of effective casting range inside which the angler's fly is working at an appropriate speed and depth.

229

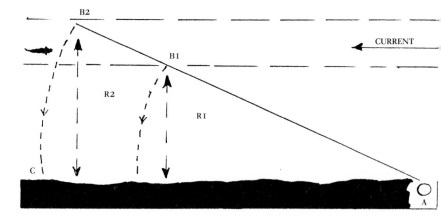

When we are faced with unrippled water where line mending is likely to cause disturbance, the only way to reduce line drag and cast *effectively* is to reduce the casting angle BAC.

The advantage of being able to cast a really long line (A–B2) rather than a line of average distance (A–B1) is obvious.

*   *   *

At this point, in deference to the memory of A. H. E. Wood, the "father" of greased line fishing, there is a snake I should like to scotch. Wood's concept of fishing a fly near the surface was not original—it was being done hundreds of years ago—but the "greased line" method he devised was a brilliant innovation, and every salmon fisherman who sets out today with small fly and floating line is in his debt. Unfortunately, for years he has been the butt of criticism by people who have failed to understand him, and it is time the record was put straight.

Briefly, the complaint has been that because Wood wrote of avoiding "drag" he must have intended his fly to drift downstream, inert, with no sideways movement.

Did he really intend this? No, of course he didn't! Wood was no fool. Fishing an inert fly was no more likely to prove successful in his time than it is today. And Wood was very successful. Careful reading of what he wrote makes it abundantly clear that fishing with inert flies had no place in his technique of wet-fly salmon fishing. So, what was he up to? This is what he wrote:

230

My experience of greased line fishing has shown me that a salmon is more ready to take a fly on or just under the surface than at any other level, except very near to the bottom. I therefore aim at keeping the fly at the surface, or sink it right down to the stones; and I have entirely forsaken the ordinary practice, which causes the fly to swim in mid-water . . . Fishing in the usual way, you lose control of the fly, more or less, once it is under water, and hardly know where it is or what it is doing. With the greased line, you are able to control the position and angle of the fly in the water and also, to a very great extent *the speed at which it travels* . . . (My italics).

I cast rather more upstream than the orthodox cast of a salmon fisherman, then lift my line off the water and, without moving the fly, turn over a loop of line upstream and *across* to prevent any drag on the fly.

Great nonsense has been made of this passage during the past forty years by writers who have failed to grasp the simple truth it contains. Wood did not rely on words alone to convey his meaning, he drew several diagrams*. As they make clear, he did *not* advocate casting *upstream of the rod* so that his fly drifted down inert. He meant exactly what he wrote: that he cast at more of an upstream angle than other people did. He had discovered what every experienced salmon fisherman must surely know today, that *effective* casting range can sometimes be increased by throwing more squarely across the river and putting a big mend in the line. This was something that Wood's contemporaries could not do, for hitherto they had neither greased their lines nor understood how to "mend" them.

It was Wood who was responsible for this technique. But in trying to pass on the message, the poor chap has suffered the fate of most prophets and been hacked to pieces.

As we have already considered earlier in this chapter, when thrown across a current a line is dragged into a big bow, so that if left alone the fly comes whipping round at speed. By preventing "drag", Wood meant he was preventing this line-belly from dragging his fly round too fast. And, as he wrote, he did this by turning over a loop of line—or "mending" as we call it:

The lifting-over of a line is done to correct a fault, namely, to take the downsteam belly out of a line and thus relieve the pull or pressure of the current on the line, which is communicated to the fly and exhibits itself as *drag* . . . Always have some reason for doing it: to

*See drawings in *Salmon Fishing* by Eric Taverner and others (1931).

231

prevent drag or, more often, *to control the speed of the fly across the river*. (My italics).

Controlling the speed of the fly across the river is exactly what we try to do today. It is the essence of all our wet-fly fishing. There is nothing *lifeless* about the fly Wood describes. Indeed, how can there be? A fly that maintains its depth in a current of water can never be lifeless. Even when hanging motionless at the end of a straight line, the fly is swimming at the speed of the current. If the current is flowing at 3 m.p.h., the fly will be swimming at that speed. The only way it can become lifeless is when it loses this water-speed, in which case it will start to sink. And if this happens, Wood is very clear about what to do:

> If the fly hardly moves and begins to sink, draw in line with your fingers very slowly and keep the fly as near the surface as you can . . . If the fly floats and skims when the line is fully extended down the pool, straighten the line on the surface and give it a sharp jerk, which should put the fly under; then fish it round to the bank at whatever speed you like.

What is lifeless about that?

There cannot be the slightest doubt that what Wood meant by "drag" was excessive belly in the line formed by the current, which makes the fly behave unnaturally for a supposedly living creature of that size. As he wrote:

> If you swim across the river, you have to swim at an angle to the stream and make use of all the eddies. Let the fly do the same and act in a natural manner, not as if it were attached to a cart-rope.

What better advice can be given on fishing the small fly? It is precisely because we want the fly to appear alive and to "act in a natural manner, not as if it were attached to a cart-rope" that we change our leader thickness to suit the size of the fly in use!

And to let Wood conclude in fitting style:

> The greased line, if fished properly (and this is by no means so every time) has no drag and often is all slack and crooked; but nevertheless you are controlling the speed of the fly and the angle at which it crosses the stream. Unless you have lost control of the line, you can at any time lift the line off the water and place it where it should be; you can then put the fly where you want and make it *swim* properly.

With all of which I concur. Indeed, one could not have a better exposition of what we aim at today when fishing the small fly on floating line. And yet, for so long, by so many, Wood's golden precepts have been almost totally misunderstood.

No longer, I hope. Henceforth, let them be accorded the honour they are due.

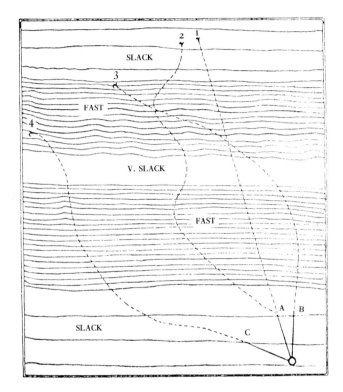

Cast to 1. Never let the line get into position 2 and keep on mending it so that it is in position 3 most of the time. When you get to 4 hold rod at C, and let the fast water pull the fly over the slack water.

One of Wood's diagrams with original caption. It emphasizes that fishing an inert fly had no place in his repertoire.

Extract from A.H.E. Wood's fishing diary at Cairnton, Aberdeenshire Dee, for May 19, 1931.

Salmon caught: 23 (6¼–20¼lb). Mr Wood 12; Mr Menzies 6; Mr Moss 5. All save two taken on Blue Charms sizes 3–8. (2 fish caught on No. 3; 8 on No. 4; 10 on No. 6; 2 on No. 7; 1 on No. 8.) River height 2′ 2″; water temp: 48°; wind: N.E.

The total catch at Cairnton for 1931: 838 salmon, all on fly. Those were the days!

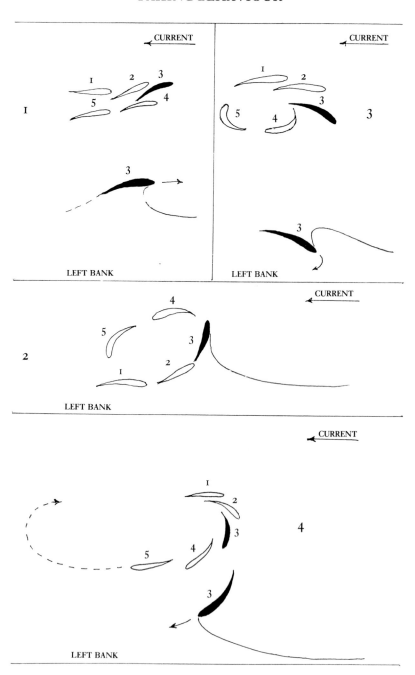

Variations in Taking Behaviour

A salmon takes a fly in one of at least six different ways. See figures 1–6—in which the angler is casting from the left bank. (For an angler on the right back, everything will be in mirror image.)

> *Note.* The right and left banks of a river are on our right-hand and left-hand when we face downstream.

Superimposed on the salmon movements shown in the diagrams is the behaviour caused by the varying motivation suggested in Chapter II. This, I think, is most likely to occur as follows:

Fig. 1. Feeding response. Crunch. Curiosity. Playfulness.
Fig. 2. Feeding response. Crunch.
Fig. 3. Feeding response. Crunch.
Fig. 4. Irritation.
Fig. 5. Inducement.
Fig. 6. Inducement.

1 The fish moves forwards and upwards, according to the position of the fly, to make an interception. He takes the fly in his mouth, continues forward a foot or two, then without turning sinks back with the current into his lie. (See also fig. 7).

If he closes his mouth on the fly (*Feeding response?*), this fish is usually well-hooked. But often the fish holds the fly in a partly-opened mouth as he moves forward. Either way, the best hooking method is to provide slack line.

I think this is the take when all one feels is a tiny nudge (if that), occurring when the fish moves upstream with the fly in half-open mouth and then blows it out again, or simply "chins" it with closed mouth (*Curiosity?*).

Occasionally the fish will drift backwards with the fly "on his nose", or half suck it in and then immediately puff it out again (*Playfulness?*), in the manner described on pp. 240–1.

This fish will sometimes rise rapidly at a steep angle to grab a fly that falls directly overhead (*Crunch*). This form of take usually results in a well-hooked fish.

2. The fish moves forward to intercept the fly, turns against the direction in which the fly is travelling, describes a circle and returns to his lie.

Like the fish in fig. 1., this chap is invariably hooked in the right-hand side of the mouth, when caught from the left bank, and *vice-versa*.

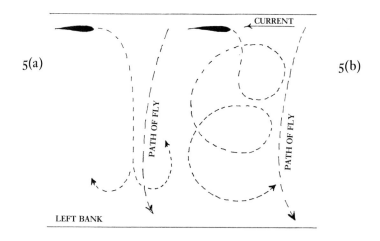

5(a)

5(b)

CURRENT

PATH OF FLY

PATH OF FLY

LEFT BANK

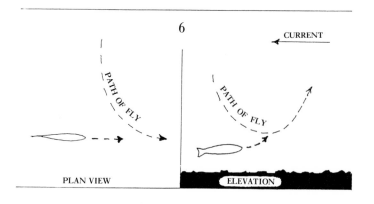

6

CURRENT

PATH OF FLY

PATH OF FLY

PLAN VIEW

ELEVATION

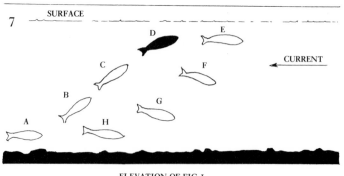

7

SURFACE

D

E

C

F

B

G

A

H

CURRENT

ELEVATION OF FIG I

3. This fish takes the fly after it has passed him, turns in the same direction as that of the fly, and continues in a fairly tight circle back to his lie. Unlike the fish in figs. 1 and 2, he has the fly in the left-hand side of the mouth, and the chances are that he is less well hooked.

4. This fish takes in a manner similar to that in fig. 3., but continues on course downstream for perhaps six or seven yards, before swinging round and returning to his lie. He is nearly always poorly hooked.

I think this is the "take" when an angler feels his line drawn out and then go slack—probably because the fish sucks the fly-in and blows it out again. I have seen parr taken in this way, and immediately spat out. (*Irritation?*).

I think that if we could only see what was happening, we could hook this fish by quick-striking—pulling the line back smartly with the non-casting hand, the rod held low and pointing at the fish. But of course we seldom can see.

I also think that this is the fly-slapping fish; the one that hits it with his tail and is sometimes foul-hooked. (Irritation again?)

5(a). This fish chases after the fly, sometimes for many yards before turning away—sometimes with the fly, but usually without it. Occasionally the fish will "bump" the fly with closed mouth: like the "tail-slapper", responsible for some of those infuriating little nudges an angler feels from time to time.

On several occasions I have seen a fish travel half the width of a pool, right up to the dangle, circling round after a fly as shown in fig. 5(b). The few fish I have caught like this have been well-hooked.

Why a fish should twiddle round in this way after a fly I have no idea. But it happens. These following fish sometimes take at the very last moment, just as the fly is being drawn away from them. (*Inducement?*).

6. A *Hamlet* fish (see p. 303), or one lying doggo in hot summer weather, can sometimes be induced to take by fishing a weighted fly with a nymph-like action. (See Dee Special Nymph, p. 307).

7. Figure 1 in elevation. Salmon rises to intercept and take the fly at position D. The fish continues to move forward to E, then sinks back with the current to his lie.

In figs. 2 and 3., the fish takes at D on the turn, and circles back to the lie. There is no forward movement upstream after taking.

*   *   *

Once the knack of controlling the fly has been mastered we shall automatically increase our effective casting range if, where conditions permit, we wade into the river. On some stretches where fish lie close in, wading may be counter-productive and we need to keep our feet dry. But on many pools, provided we don't scare the fish, the deeper we wade the greater our chances. Long casting is an essential part of the fly-fisherman's technique, but equally important is the ability to wade deep, since on many beats it represents the difference between failure and success.

The importance of sensible wading has been mentioned earlier. But I make no apology for repeating this advice. Some aspects of salmon fishing need emphasizing. And if, in consequence, so crucial a point is remembered and helps someone to catch his first fish, as I hope it may, repetition is justified. One so frequently sees an angler walking through the lies his fly should be fishing, or working his way down a long pool, his fly fishing where he should have been walking. Later, he may bewail the absence of salmon, or ruefully deplore his lack of skill, unaware that however well he had cast and however many fish there may have been, he had given himself virtually no chance of hooking one.

And talking of hooking salmon: what, you may have been wondering, should you do when the miracle happens and a salmon does take the fly?

238

This raises the hoary old question of the "strike"—than which nothing in the sport of salmon fishing is so controversial. And since the answer concerns both sunk line and floating line methods of fishing, it seems appropriate to deal with it in this chapter.

*　　　*　　　*

Hooking a Salmon

Bemused by the huge amount of conflicting literature that surrounds the subject of hooking salmon, the reader studying first one account and then another and finding nothing but contradictions, justifiably throws up his hands in despair. "What", he demands, "is this all about? One chap says I should give a fish loose line when it takes. Another tells me this is nonsense and recommends fishing with a tight line. This fellow points his rod at the fish and strikes off the reel. Whereas that fellow says I should *never* strike—simply hold the rod well up and wait till I feel the fish pull. And so on. They are all supposed to be experts. But which of them is right?

The answer is that *each* of them is right—*sometimes*. But none of them is right all the time.

What an angler should do on any particular occasion depends on *how the salmon takes the fly*. And there can be no single answer to this question because by no means does a salmon always take in the same way. To assume that salmon taking behaviour is forever identical is the mistake so many fishing authors have made. It isn't! As my observations—some of which are described on pp. 235–237—have proved, salmon take in a variety of ways, and *no single method of dealing with them can be totally effective*.

If we always knew exactly what a fish was up to we could react in the way most likely to hook him, and occasionally we can do this; but for most of our fishing time we *don't* know. The salmon is hidden, and remains hidden.

So, of what use are my observations?

Well, they have convinced me that no matter what we do—fish from the reel; hold the rod high, or down on the water; strike; pull the line with our non-casting hand; give the fish some slack—we will hook some of the fish that take, and we will miss out on others.

Edward Hamilton makes an amusing but telling comment on hooking salmon in his *Recollections of Fly-Fishing* . . .

The only place where I ever strike a salmon is in Tumbledown Pool on the Spean, a deep, silent pool, where you see the great fish come after your fly and just seize it like a trout, and if you do not strike, they spit it out again, but this is not always the case, as I have seen salmon come up in the usual way and take your fly and turn down again after hooking themselves.

Salmon behaviour can vary dramatically on different days of the same week, or in different pools and at different times of the same day. We can never predict exactly what they are going to do or how they are going to do it. However experienced an angler, salmon will always find some new way of surprising him—as they did Arthur Oglesby a little while back.

Fishing sunk-line on Tweed in early November with a fresh run of fish coming through, Arthur enjoyed some excellent sport, but discovered that the fish were taking in an unusual way. He got few offers as the fly was swinging round. But salmon after salmon took as he was retrieving at the end of a cast. *Not* when he had pulled in just a yard or two of line, but after he had stripped-in *eight or ten yards as fast as he could* preparatory to casting again. Then, right up near the surface, as he was on the point of pulling-out and making his back-stroke, a fish would take—with a bang!

He was fishing with a fifteen-foot carbon rod, a twelve-yard shooting-head of fast-sinking line, and a large heavily-weighted yellow and orange tube. As he told me:

> The shooting-head assisted me in making long casts, and the heavy line and fly enabled me to feel confident that my lure was well down and quite visible to the fish. But they happened to want it as it was being dragged up fast towards the surface. I was pulling in hard, so there was no question of fishing with any slack line. But they took fiercely and were firmly hooked.

Of course, if Arthur hadn't tumbled to what was happening he would almost certainly have landed far fewer fish than he did. He recognized what was going on, and took advantage of it. It is what any angler can do on occasion, if he suspects that salmon are behaving rather oddly and can change his technique in sympathy.

An example of strange taking behaviour is well described in this account given me by a friend. He was having lunch one day beside his own beat of a Highland river:

I was sitting at the head of a long, deep pool. The river at this point is very narrow, the water approximately eighteen feet deep, with a huge boulder about ten feet down, just below me. I have caught numerous salmon from the lies behind this boulder. It was a warm day. We had not had any rain for several weeks, and the river was low and clear.

Suddenly, I noticed a salmon of about 12 lb rise as though taking a submerged fly. A short time later it happened again. But over the next half-hour or so I noticed that there were *two* fish, rising occasionally to take what looked like stone-flies. Intrigued, I lay on the bank and watched. It seemed that when a fly was coming downstream one of the salmon, swimming forwards and up, would intercept the fly—and then back downstream with the fly more or less balanced on the tip of its nose.

After drifting backwards for three feet or so, it would suck in the fly; then, moving about eighteen inches forwards, blow it out again. You could see bits and pieces of the insect come shooting out a couple of feet or more.

It seemed to me that something similar to this must happen from time to time while we are fly-fishing.

He was quite right. It *does* happen, as I have seen on several occasions. Incidentally, how similar the behaviour he describes to that of the "performing seal" in Chapter II, the fish that drifted back with the worm "glued to her nose"!

Such incidents are reminders of what salmon get up to. Most important of all that, if we cannot see the fish, no single hooking method can possibly be a hundred percent successful.

So—when we are fishing "blind" and a salmon takes our fly, what are we to do?

In his thoughtful book: *Fly Fishing for Salmon*, 1951, Richard Waddington writes:

We are now back to the old, old argument, "to strike or not to strike". There is, in my opinion, no possible doubt whatever as to the correct answer. Given the proper hooks there is only one way in which you can fail to hook a fish, and that is by *any form of striking* . . . Immediately you become aware of a fish, drop the point of the rod, let go any loose line in your hand, pull more line off the reel, step forward—do in short, anything that will help to create a good big belly in the line well downstream of the fish. When all this is done you may now strike or not as fancy pleases you. It will make no difference, for by now the fish is hooked.

And for river fishing, when almost invariably our fly is swinging round in a current—no matter whether we are using sunk or floating line—I agree with him. (In stillwater it is a different matter, but we will come to that.)

Having experimented with every conceivable method of coping with a taking salmon in running water, I have found that my highest success rate comes from *doing nothing*.

If a fish is determined to have the fly, sucks it in, closes his mouth on it and turns away, I don't think it matters *what* we do. Provided we don't pull the fly away from the fish just as he is going to take it, we can give him line, or strike, as we please. It will make no difference. But as described in Chapter II and elsewhere, I know from observations that many takes are far from being so positive and, on balance, I feel we have a better chance of hooking a fish if we avoid tightening the line too soon: if we let the speed of the water set the hook for us.

So—you can chalk me up as one of the loose-liners.

Whether fishing with sunk or floating line, I keep a yard of slack line trapped in the crook of my rod-hand forefinger. This is held so lightly that the slightest nudge, even a floating leaf, will draw the line away.

If the fly stops, for whatever reason, I do nothing. There is no conscious releasing of the line-loop, it is dragged out the instant the fly is stopped on its swing round. Frequently, *it is the current not the salmon* that straightens the line.

As I have seen, a salmon will often take a bait or lure and hold it for a short time on a "cushion" of water inside his partly opened mouth. If this is our fly, any action on our part can only pull it away. Far better to take no action at all. The current will instantly belly the line, and drag the fly backwards into the side of the jaw, or the "scissors", automatically hooking the fish. Naturally, the fish is not *always* hooked. But hooking is vastly more likely to happen if we leave the fly alone, for if we pull it the chances are it will come straight out of the fish's mouth.

If you doubt any of this, take your rod to the river with a friend and a fly with no point on it. Then, with your companion standing in the current downstream ready to play the part of a taking salmon, cast out and fish the fly round, keeping the rod low and holding a loop of line as I suggest. See what happens to the line the moment your friend stops the fly. Then change places and test for yourself the backward drag on the fly as you check its swing and the line suddenly bellies.

If this doesn't convince you, nothing will.

It is strange how heated some anglers get when discussing their own particular method of hooking a fish; often, it seems, without having thought the matter through. A somewhat dogmatic angling author of not long ago devoted pages of ridicule to the notion of giving a taking salmon slack line—and at the end of it all blandly offered the following advice:

> The rod point should be held fairly high off the water. This is to let the line hang in a curve, instead of a straight line, from the point to the water. The time taken to straighten this curve, when a fish takes hold, is all that is required to hook it properly.

If this isn't giving a fish slack line, I don't know what is!

Anglers who follow that advice and fish with their rods in the air are merely exchanging one sort of loop for another. They are doing *in effect* precisely what the angler does who fishes with a loop of line held by his finger—only they are not doing it quite so well.

Fishing with a line-loop has three advantages:

1. It prevents an angler giving the line an involuntary jerk (all too easily done) when a fish takes.

2. It allows us to hold the rod low down on the water. This prevents a gusty wind snatching at the line as the fly swings round.

3. It enables the rod to be pushed down underwater to help get the line well sunk—when this is needed.

Pushing the rod-point under is a trick I use sometimes when fishing sunk-line for sea trout on a cold night. Oddly, I have never seen anybody fishing like this. And yet plunging the rod underwater to help get the fly down deep is the obvious thing to do.

The "Droop": rod held low and pointing at the fish. Loop of line held ready to slip out the instant anything stops the fly.
Note: In a strong current the rod should always be held well up during the first third of the fly's swing round, to keep as much line as possible clear of the water.

243

There are times of course when no slack line is given to a fish. These include nymph fishing, dry-fly fishing and fishing in stillwater—methods that will surface later in their respective sections.

Another time when no slack line need, or indeed can be given, is when we are handlining the fly towards us at the completion of a cast.

A salmon that grabs such an "escaping" lure, after however short a chase, usually takes it firmly—that is, he sucks it in and turns away with a closed mouth. In this situation there is no point in offering the fish slack line. He is already hooked. But as suggested above, many fish do *not* take like this. They intercept the fly on its swing round in one of a number of different ways. And on balance, since we can seldom see what is happening, our best chance, in my opinion, is to fish with a loop of slack.

*   *   *

Playing a Salmon

And what happens when a salmon takes? Well, there is usually just a tiny pluck, and away goes the loop of line. We raise the rod, feel the slow tug of a fish, give him some stick for a moment to make sure the hook is set (if he is going to get off, it is better now than later); then, holding the rod well up to keep as much line as possible clear of the water, we wade ashore.

Well—we don't *always* wade ashore quite so quickly. There are exceptions even to this! On hooking a fish it sometimes pays to stay out there where we are in the river. More especially when fishing a quick-sinking line. If a big salmon takes off, it is easy for the line to get drowned, with disastrous consequences. Much depends on the type of bottom and how easily we can move about after our fish, but if movement is possible and he is running to the far side of a wide river we are wiser to stay for a time as close to the fish as possible. To have thirty yards of sunk line washing about out there in the current is likely to dent our chances. When we have the fish under some sort of control, it will be time to think about getting ashore and well up on the bank.

This applies to boat fishing as well as wading. Don't go ashore until you feel you are in control.

Once ashore and up on high ground it is just a question of keeping the line out of trouble. Ninety percent of playing a fish consists of just that. Only, don't wander down towards the water. Until the fish turns on his side, stay where you are. Furthermore, enjoin any spectators to stand well back, too; preferably behind you, so that at no time will the fish see them, either.

Except in emergency no one should be encouraged to approach the river until the fish is ready to land. A hooked fish that sees someone peering at him from the water's edge will take fright and add minutes to the playing time. These are precious minutes during which a weakened strip of skin may break and the hook come loose. Get a fish ashore as fast as you reasonably can. This is best done by staying out of sight.

If he is a big fish try to walk him up and down a short stretch of the pool. This helps to shorten the fight. "Walking" a fish seems to dishearten him, and besides keeping him away from the pool tail enables you to do battle in water of *your* choosing.

When you walk a fish, hold the rod steady and at right angles to the river with the butt set firmly against the body. The fish is not towed up the pool, and no attempt is made to *pull* him along—you are indulging not in a trial of strength, but the art of gentle persuasion. Usually, so long as a steady but unhurried progress is maintained upstream, the fish will follow quietly. He will often, in fact, gain ground, so that by the time your stopping place is reached he is somewhere out in the middle of the river and conveniently opposite the rod. This is now some distance from the pool tail and the best place for bringing matters to a conclusion.

Sometimes a fish allows himself to be brought close to the bank very early on. This apparent submission is quite common and may be described as the danger time. At this moment, far from lunging at him with gaff or net, *keep well back* so that he cannot see you. As soon as he feels the water shallowing he will turn and set off again into the middle of the river. Do nothing to stop him. You have plenty of line on the reel and complete confidence in your tackle, for everything was checked earlier. This is no time to discover a faulty rod-ring, or have the reel fall off, or the line foul up.

When a big salmon sets off on an irresistible run you will feel very thankful you took the trouble to re-wind the line before fishing started (as recommended on p. 248).

Again you bring the fish in, trying always to keep him on the move so that he cannot rest and recover his strength. And again he turns and makes a rush for deeper water. He will make several more runs probably, but now each is likely to be shorter than the last.

After this it will not be long before you see the flash of a silver flank as he half rolls in the current. He is nearly ready to land. Nearly, but not quite! This is the crucial period. *Don't* try to haul him in too soon.

When he feels the stones under his belly he will flap violently and may throw the hook. Wait until he turns on his side.

Wherever there is a place convenient for beaching a salmon no landing tackle of any sort is necessary—unless you are dealing with a very large fish. Draw him ashore at the place you have chosen, and when he is lying on his side with his head aground the fight is over. He will not move again. All you have to do is to approach preferably from downstream reeling in as you go, grip the wrist of the tail firmly with forefinger and thumb (as shown in the pictures on pp. 178 and 179), push him on to dry ground and then pick him up.*

This is how most hooked salmon behave. But the tactics described do not always work so neatly, especially if one is using unsuitable tackle.

When younger and sillier I once hooked a thirty pounder on a very light leader. I had not expected to hook anything as big as that and was fishing fine because the water was low and clear. I couldn't do anything with him. He got down beside a rock near the head of the pool where the current bore down on top of him and held him in position. There he stayed, and refused to budge. Attempts to dislodge him with stones and "walk" him proved unavailing. I was determined not to be broken, but after an hour of stalemate began to feel desperate.

Eventually, tired of throwing stones, I resolved to try sterner measures. To shift him from his lie and keep him moving, I swam over him across the pool—fully clothed and taking my rod with me. Six times I had to cross the pool, three times each way, making him rush about each time, before that fish started to tire. This was in March with ice fringing the river, and snow showers. But I landed the fish.

Looking back on it after thirty years I still have a faint feeling of pride that he didn't break me. But I wouldn't attempt it now, and it is not a method I recommend. Nor should such a drastic measure be needed. After all, it was entirely my own fault. I should have been using tackle of sensible breaking strain.

So—be warned. And always be prepared.

It is worth noting that if, soon after being hooked, a big fish runs downstream to a spot where bank obstructions prevent your following him, you can often coax him back—after he stops—by stripping line

---

*To help with landing a fish, here is a tip culled from *The Tale of a Wye Fisherman* by H. A. Gilbert. He is referring to that great angler, Robert Pashley.

Pashley gaffed his own fish, taking them into a backwater where he stamped about, raising clouds of mud. When the fish was brought to the gaff, it was blinded by the mud and did not sheer off.

off the reel. The pressure from the belly of line that forms in the current behind him urges him to swim back upstream towards his original lie. *But remember*: the danger of losing a big fish is greatest when he is very tired, because then he is unable to resist being carried off tail-first by the current. In this case no amount of line hanging below him will have the slightest effect, for he is exhausted. It is an easy matter to bring a big fish *downstream* to a landing place. Quite another to bring him up. Unable to swim against the stream he will gradually be swept away downriver and, if you cannot follow him, will almost certainly be lost. The last unhappy glimpse many an angler has had of a big fish is when

Landing a salmon. How to do it.
By walking backwards, Roy Hayhurst has just beached his salmon in exemplary style. Lying on its side half aground, the fish will not move again. At his leisure, Roy can walk down, reeling in as he goes, and tail it out by hand.

247

it vanished from sight, rolling over and over, down the rapids at a pool tail—just before the leader broke!

* * *

Preparation

Now that we have an idea of what we are trying to do, and have the means of doing it, we may as well fit some of our tackle together. This will avoid digression in the next two chapters, where everything is put into practice.

As already suggested, you should never let anyone tackle-up for you, however skilled and willing they may be. Only by doing it yourself, and checking it all while you do so, will you be certain that everything is faultless. And faultless it must be. A big salmon is a powerful fish and quickly exploits any tackle weakness. The successful landing of salmon, as indeed of any other species, depends largely on *attention to detail*. Failure to observe this simple rule has filled the literature with tales of woe.

To wade into position and start casting, only to discover you have a turn of line wrapped round the rod between rings is, to put it mildly, irksome. To have the reel slip off while a fish is running curdles the blood. To leave in a fish the fly some helpful friend has just tied on, and find a curl of nylon at the leader point, induces thoughts of homicide. So, as you tackle-up, test everything.

A salmon is difficult enough to hook. Don't throw it away through carelessness.

For example, when you have assembled rod, reel and line, strip all the line off the reel, together with some of the backing, and re-wind it firmly and evenly.

Re-winding the line should always be done before fishing starts and *after a fish has been landed*. During a fight some slack coils may form down near the backing. Later, while a fish is running, a turn of line pulled hard down into these loose coils underneath may cause the reel to jam. This results almost invariably in a smash. It has cost some very big fish.

And now, on goes the leader—the monofilament nylon link between line and lure. During early spring and late autumn when we fish with sinking lines and big lures, we need only a short link. Five or six feet is ample.

For summer fishing with floating line and small flies, a longer leader is needed so that the fly can swim at the required depth of a few inches.

Nine or ten feet is the customary length, its thickness governed by the size of fly and diminishing as the size decreases.

Observation indicates that there is no reason to suppose salmon to be particularly shy of nylon leaders. So, within the limits of good sense, always "err" on the side of strength.

Never forget: to be broken by a fish is always a disgrace. Reasons there will be for such a disaster. But excuses, none.

When it comes to fitting a leader, treat the idiot who declares proudly that he fishes fine "to give the fish a chance" with the contempt he deserves. No valid definition of sportsmanship can include giving a fish the chance to swim away with a hook in his mouth and trailing a length of nylon.

The reason why we need to vary the leader thickness is because casting heavy lures on thin nylon is weakening; whereas small flies tied to thick nylon do not swim attractively. As a rough indication of what to use, I suggest the following:

For flies of 4″ down to 2″...................... 25 lb–20 lb b.s.
For fly sizes 2. and 4. .... 18 lb–16 lb
For fly sizes 6. and 8. .... 16 lb–14 lb
For fly sizes 10. and 12......................... 14 lb–12 lb
For fly sizes 14. and 16......................... 10 lb– 8 lb
For dry-fly fishing .... 8 lb– 6 lb

*   *   *

Having given some thought to the principles of salmon fly-fishing and discovered that our strategy changes with the seasons to accommodate the changing habits of the fish, we are now in a position to start fishing.

Since it seems sensible to do this in some sort of chronological order, we may as well start at the beginning—with a sunk line.

When the water is very bright and clear in the pools many a fish may be hooked and landed by allowing the fly to sink as deep as you can, and then slowly sink and draw, never bringing the fly near the surface. You see a movement in the water—a swirl and a twist, and your line tightens. You might fish all day in such times, with the fly near the surface, and never move a fish.

Edward Hamilton M.D., *Recollections of Fly-Fishing for Salmon, Trout and Grayling*, 1891

XII
Fly Fishing

PART FOUR: THE SUNK LINE

Objectives

As described in the previous chapter, fly-fishing for salmon falls into two categories: floating line and sunk line. These two contrasting methods reflect the salmon's change of taking behaviour as the river gradually warms during late spring and summer, and cools again in late autumn and winter. During the former, salmon will rise and take a small fly fished close to the surface. During the latter they will not—at least, not often. Although it is true that even in a low water temperature salmon can sometimes be caught on the surface, they are far more inclined to take a lure fished deep.

Fish appear to be very sensitive to changes in water warmth. Being cold-blooded, their functional rate of metabolism alters appreciably with temperature. The rate at which chemical reactions proceed usually decreases rapidly with a drop in temperature, and there is little doubt that for the same reason fish can take in and burn oxygen less quickly in cold water than in warm water with similar oxygen content. It is thus on temperature that the rate at which fish can generate energy largely depends. Lying in a pool in the cold water of early spring, salmon probably find conditions restful and soporific, and have no urge to rush about.

And so, in these conditions—salmon metabolism being what it is—to give the fish an easy chance of taking our fly, we must get it down to where they are lying.

This means that from January until about mid-April, in those rivers that have early runs of salmon, and again from about mid-October until the end of November, or into December where the season extends so late, a sinking line is the order of the day.

Experience has shown that our best chance of hooking a salmon in cold water is to fish a big lure deep and slow. Thus, the use of flies ranging in length from two to four inches overall, tied for convenience mainly on tubes. And to help these big flies get down to the fish in varying currents we use a range of sinking lines, from high-density to a floater with sink-tip.

I have purposely repeated the principles of sunk line fishing because judging by questions I am sometimes asked, there seems to be confusion about what our objectives really are.

In essence, they are plain enough. A large lure made of feathers or hair, preferably the latter, is drifted slowly round in front of a fish, ideally just above the height of his nose. One writer, however has sought to discredit this idea; his theory being that the depth of the fly was unimportant, and that salmon would always rise to it even though it was being fished in cold water.

Well, they will certainly do so in late spring and summer. And occasionally, as the last chapter described, in autumn before the water gets too cold. But although salmon *will* take from the surface in early spring, even when the water temperature is under 40°F., it is not common, and anyone following that advice will miss many opportunities of catching them. Fishing at depth offers far more chance of success.

Apropos of this, as I mentioned in the Preface, some very misleading statements have been made about salmon behaviour, a few of which are quoted in these pages. I know only too well the long, hard labour involved in writing books, and have no wish to berate or belittle my fellow travellers (which is one reason why my name is never found on book reviews), but I should be shirking the responsibilities implicit in writing this book if I failed to criticize—albeit cloaked in anonymity—certain relevant passages that I know to be false.

The following assertion is a case in point. Anyone might be forgiven for thinking it another reason why he should try to *prevent* his fly from fishing at depth!

The first thing to understand is that no salmon ever takes anything which is actually on the bottom and below his own level.

This extraordinary statement was written by an accepted authority. And yet, as anyone who has ledgered a natural bait such as worm or prawn will know, it is untrue. Salmon frequently take creatures that are moving beneath them, or lying motionless on the bottom. They will even pick up stationary artificial flies.

Kelson's account of a River Earn salmon taking a static fly is quoted on p. 199. And something precisely similar happened to me on the Erriff River in County Mayo. I had just cast into a small pool when, seeing a friend approaching and having cast only a short distance, I put the rod down to offer him a drink from my flask. In the fairly clear, slackish water, the fly came to rest on a rock just below us. I could see it lying there. To our astonishment, as we sat sipping our drinks, a fresh-run cock fish swam lazily upstream, sucked in the fly and made off with it . . . He weighed fourteen pounds.

Observation makes nonsense of so many hasty statements about salmon, and the absurdity of declaring that they ignore objects moving or lying beneath them is an example. As I have seen many times, they will suck things up from the bottom as skilfully as any tench. And there is no doubt that in the icy water of early spring when they are reluctant to move far or fast, deep and slow is the best way of presenting our fly.

Note. But as a reminder that salmon can turn every angling statement about them topsy-turvy, here is a droll experience I had recently on Tweed. A timely warning of the "minefield" threatening any author who pontificates on salmon behaviour, it is reminiscent of Arthur Oglesby's recent experience quoted on p. 240, except that the water was some six or seven degrees colder than when he was fishing.

On a bitter afternoon in February, 1983, with the air temperature 38°F, and the water temperature 37°F, I caught my only salmon of the day on a fast-moving fly *right up on the surface*. Wading deep, I had completed a cast (across water fished down half-an-hour before), drawn in several yards of quick-sinking line, raised my rod and brought the fly—a four-inch black and red tube—to the top. Then, just as I was quickening into my back-cast, bringing the fly riffling towards me along the surface with the first movement of the double-Spey, this fish came with a swirl and a splash and grabbed that fly—like a big sea trout seizing a Surface Lure on a summer night!

He turned out to be a fresh-run ten-pounder, and the hook was halfway down his throat.

As mentioned earlier, the salmon is an animal of definite tendencies. In conditions of low temperature he seldom moves far or fast, and there is no doubt that to fish deep and slow in cold water offers the best chance; it will certainly be more successful than fishing a floating line. But as I have just described, even in water as cold as 37°F, salmon *will* sometimes rise to a fly on or near the surface.

As for taking advantage of such incidents, I can only repeat the advice already given. Never fish with a closed mind. Be prepared for anything to happen, no matter how much it contradicts the text books. And when salmon are hard to catch, try all the tricks you know, however crazy they may seem—for you are trying to catch a crazy fish.

*   *   *

When we are fishing one of the big salmon rivers from a boat in February, with the water very low and sluggish and the fish concentrated in the deepest part of a pool, it sometimes pays to anchor upstream of the main lie and fish cast after cast very deliberately. The line is given plenty of time and encouragement to sink, and then stripped in from the dangle an inch or two at a time. A salmon may not by any means take straight away. But after a while, the inch-by-inch movement of the lure seems to tantalize a fish and goad it into taking.

I knew a woman years ago who used to fish like this in a deep, slow pool of the River Tay. She would sit there in the boat for hours, seemingly motionless, chucking out a big weighted lure and slowly pulling it in towards her bit by bit. And every so often her rod would arc into a fish. Not a very exciting method of fishing, perhaps, but successful. It illustrated the truth of the old axiom: "deep and slow". In fact, a boat is not always necessary. I have known places where salmon could be caught with a similar technique in low water by wading deep.

In view of my earlier remarks on the subject of over-fishing a lie, the reaction of these salmon to this continued casting is highly significant, for it supports my contention that provided we angle with care and skill a salmon lie cannot be over-fished.

Catching salmon during the first few months of the year is rather laughably called "spring" fishing, but on most early rivers between January and April there isn't much spring in the air. Trying to cast a line on a grey February day, with the river funnelling a north-easter like a frozen wind-tunnel, can be bitter and frustrating. And I am not ashamed to confess that there have been times when, on hooking a fish, I have waggled fingers like stalks of ice and prayed that I hadn't hooked a whopper, so quickly did I need to land him before losing contact with my hands. Notwithstanding the temperature, however, an angler to whom the challenge of fishing means more than the fish he kills, will whenever the water permits always fish the fly in preference to spinner.

My plea for the use of fly tackle has nothing whatever to do with its being more *sporting*. I am merely trying to convey something of the enduring satisfaction of fishing fly, demanding as it does accurate casting, deep wading and skilful line control. Handling a high-density line and heavy lure in a strong draw, with a winter wind whining in the willows, is as difficult and daunting as anything any branch of angling has to offer. Compared with this, throwing out a spinner is schoolboy's stuff.

But in addition to its aesthetic appeal, the fly rod has material rewards. Anyone who perseveres and takes the trouble to master the technique of sunk-line fishing will derive satisfaction not only from its application but from its success. The reason is that in water of suitable depth the fly can be presented more attractively than spinner. It can sometimes, for instance, be hung over a lie—a feat impossible with the spinner in most pools, if fished other than from a boat.

It is generally thought that in high water, spinning is a more worthwhile method than fly. This is a common fallacy. Once fly casting techniques with sinking line have been mastered, salmon are more readily taken on fly than on spinner. And the higher the water, the more pronounced this advantage. As I have proved time and time again, in spring when the water is up, the correct fly well presented will frequently beat the spinner.

By "correct" fly, I mean the correct length and, in particular, *weight*. Weight is crucial. As we shall see, the height and speed at which the fly approaches a fish is of paramount importance. And the reason why a skilled fly-angler will often out-fish his spinning companions is because, by the very nature of his tackle, his lure will usually be under better control.

An illustration of this occurred recently on Deeside in early March. During a week when the river height varied between four and six feet above normal level, with water temperature 36°–38°F., and air temperature much the same, a single fly-fisherman caught the same number of salmon in the same beat as the total catch of four other rods, each of whom was spinning! Most of those fly-caught fish were hooked little more than a rod's length from the bank; sometimes within only a yard or two.

I mention this to encourage the keen fly-fisher. Take your spinning rod with you by all means. But if you are looking for success in addition to angling pleasure, use the spinner only when gale-force winds make fly-fishing a misery.

Boat fishing, although it makes fly casting easy, has little place in this chapter, and very little in this book. In the absence of a bridge, boats are useful for crossing the river, and occasionally necessary in wide, deep pools to help cover lies that otherwise could not be fished. But catching

Alan Shipman fishing the Lower Bridge Pool on Lower Crathes, Aberdeenshire Dee. Water five feet above normal. At this height the Taking-Strip is no more than a rod's length from the bank. Here, Alan controls the speed of the fly on its approach to the Taking-Strip by keeping his rod at right angles to the bank.

Now the fly is led slowly across the lie. A fish will take only a yard or so out . . .

As this one has.

Eventually, almost ready to land, the fish swirls in the very spot where he took the fly—his nearness showing the importance of stealth when walking the bank prior to fishing.

The fish comes to the net a yard or two further downstream . . .

A fourteen-pounder, straight from sea. Evidence of his freshness is the female sea louse above the anal fin.

salmon from a boat makes very small demands upon angling expertise. Most of the skill is in the head and hands of the boatman. Knowing the lies, he can place the angler in such a position that casting is negligible. No water sense is needed except by the man behind the oars—or at the end of the rope, if he is "letting you down" the pool.

Boat fishing reaches its nadir in "harling". This consists of trailing lures at depth astern with (usually) two rods set out abeam like mackerel spreaders, while the gillie works the boat slowly from side to side, swinging the lures, mainly spinners and plugs, to and fro across the lies. It is a method much favoured by anglers on the River Tay.

Oh well, each to his own taste. And after all whether he is caught on fly or spinner makes no difference to the salmon.

Nevertheless, it is a pity that the spinning rod holds such sway, especially on shallow rivers that are much better fished with fly and where its use so often results in the mishaps described in Chapter IV.

But, as also explained in that chapter, some salmon water is *not* suitable for fly-fishing. Those deep, slabsided, chasm-like dubs on parts of the River Eden are an example. To fish a bait deeply and slowly enough to attract salmon in such difficult stretches presents its own challenge—in addition to expert yard-by-yard knowledge of the water. And spinning, often from a boat, is the only feasible method of achieving it. Fishing such water entails not only a heavy bait but a considerable amount of lead. Use of the fly rod is pointless.

There is a perfectly proper time and place for spinning, as there is for every legitimate method, and it is a part of the sensible angler's understanding of the sport that he knows exactly when and where to use each one. The fly fits into this pattern. If used skilfully in suitable water its chances of catching fish are as good as, if not better than anything else. *But* it must be given a proper opportunity to show its worth. To get it down to the fish is imperative. And the difficulty of doing this effectively in strong, deep water, is the reason why the use of heavily-leaded spinning tackle pays higher dividends.

*   *   *

Reconnaissance

It can be said, I think, of sunk-line fishing more than of any other method, that we catch our fish before putting a fly in the water. And we achieve this, first of all, by knowing the depth of the lies we are going to fish. Secondly, by ensuring that our tackle is adjusted as near perfectly as possible to fishing those lies at the required depth and speed.

This demands a clear picture of the pool's underwater contours.

There is not the slightest doubt that over a period the better we know our water the more salmon we will catch. And yet I would hazard a bet that if asked whether they knew the depth of water they were fishing, few anglers would come up with more than a very rough guess.

Knowing the water is important in all forms of salmon fishing. In sunk line fishing during early spring it is essential, for only this can guide our choice of line and lure. Not *pattern* of lure, but *weight*.

Many anglers approach the river only when they go to fish. This is perhaps their greatest mistake. *Time spent in reconnaissance is never wasted.* Never was this truer than in preparation for spring fishing. On most beats the best time to do your recce is when the river is at its worst for fishing—that is, dead low. Don't miss the opportunity when it comes. For people living hundreds of miles from the water they propose to fish, such visits are impracticable. But those living close enough to spend a few hours on the river studying the pools will reap their reward.

In his highly readable book *Torridge Fishery*, 1957, L. R. N. Gray, a friend of long ago, describes catching a salmon when fishing sunk fly one March on the little Devonshire River Mole: a minor triumph made possible in precisely this way.

Arriving at a small pool he finds it being fished by several other anglers, and so goes to the only piece of water available—a fast, shallow run-in at the head of the pool. As he starts to cast, one of the others remarks that he is wasting his time fishing there, as the water is only a foot or so deep. But Gray, who had done his recce long before, remembers:

> . . . a small depression behind a stone no bigger than your head . . .
> I saw a fish bulge at my fly as he was speaking . . . A moment later
> the fish was hooked and racing down the run!

It is from such little scraps of knowledge gleaned from observation that success in salmon fishing so often derives. To the outsider, such a catch seems entirely fortuitous—as it did to the other anglers on the occasion recounted by Gray. But of course it was not chance alone that caught him his fish.

Like Gray, the successful salmon fisherman realizes the importance of attention to detail. He takes the trouble to find out where his fish is likely to be lying. He discovers enough about that lie—its swirls and eddies, and in particular its depth—to enable him to adjust his tackle and present his fly attractively. He catches the fish it holds even before stripping line off his reel to make a cast.

The Big Fly: Size and Weight

During early spring when the water is still very cold, fish tend to lie in the deepest parts of a pool, mostly in the slackish water. As the water warms, running fish move into other lies and may then be found in the shallower, faster water. But some fish will have been using the fast water much earlier—which sometimes surprises people. Anyone taking account of the salmon's metabolism in cold water and expecting him to conserve his energy, would be right. But fish can lie in the fastest water with the minimum of exertion, and often do. How they manage this is obvious from the raw patches often found under the chins and stomachs of fresh-run fish. These show where fish have been resting on rock or gravel in some depression where the current can press down and hold them in position, thus allowing them to keep station with the minimum of effort. This is quite the opposite of what one might suppose when, from the river bank, one views the speed of current where the fish are lying.

A knowledge of such lies is of the greatest value. It sometimes enables the thoughtful and prepared angler to catch fish when everyone else fails—as it did L. R. N. Gray that time he went to fish the River Mole.

But often enough you will be far from home and with no intimate knowledge of the water you have come to fish. In which case you are thrown entirely on your own devices—unless, of course, you enjoy the luxury of a gillie. If you do, he will know the variations in depth that are all-important to your preparation, or he *should*. Sometimes, however, he doesn't. Either way, before setting up your tackle, take a good long look at the river and read what you can of it for yourself. If you do have a knowledgeable man with you it is pleasant to have your prognostications confirmed. If you haven't, it is on your own water-sense that you will have to rely.

Anyway, however good your gillie, don't leave everything to him and just follow his instructions like an obedient dummy. Try to do as much as you can for yourself. Take his advice about the water by all means; it is this knowledge that, optimistically, you pay for when you engage his services. So use it! But don't let him squash your initiative, especially when it comes to choice of lure. After all, *you* are going to fish the thing.

Some gillies sulk if their "rods" show independence of spirit and prefer their own fancies. Let them. They usually recover quickly enough if you hook a fish. If you don't, never blame them for your failure, and never let failure influence their financial reward. It is sometimes the custom to tip so much per fish caught. A poor tradition. I have never thought much of it.

One word of advice, however. If you are a stranger to the water and your gillie expresses strong views on choice of fly in relation to the conditions, you will be sensible to give his ideas a try first.

Whatever our personal skill as anglers, if we haven't a thorough understanding of our beat we can seldom do ourselves justice. To coin an aphorism: salmon fishing success on any particular water is directly proportionate to our experience of that water. And experience comes only with time. Knowing the water is important in any form of salmon fishing. In sunk line fishing it is of *paramount* importance.

Next in importance to knowing the water is the ability to adjust our tackle to fish that water to its best advantage. This means overcoming the speed of the current and fishing our lure deep and slow wherever the salmon are lying. This is not to imply that all spring flies should be heavily weighted. Far from it. Some should be made as light as possible.

Generally speaking, the lighter a lure the more life-like it will appear as it swings round with the current. In a fairly shallow stream a lightly dressed and slender-bodied hair-wing fly may work perfectly on a high-density line; the line being heavy enough to sink the fly and allow it to flicker attractively across the lies. Whereas, a heavier fly even though fished on a more buoyant line may drag the bottom, so that in order to avoid snagging we have to keep hurrying it along by drawing in line— thus fishing it too quickly. On the other hand, if we fish too light a lure in fast water it will undoubtedly swim too high across the lies. To appear life-like, our fly should swim as a direct continuation of our line, but *at the right depth*.

Sunk-line tackle adjustment, considerably more difficult than that of floating-line, depends on skilful combination of line density and weight of fly. Where a strong current and deep water demand it, a heavily-weighted fly we *must* use—in addition to a high-density line—if we are to sink it deep enough to have a chance of attracting fish. So, we need a comprehensive range of lines, in addition to a set of flies that vary in weight as well as length. First of all: flies.

A certain confusion reigns over the sizes of sunk-line flies in use today. These are usually tubes, and a tube is classed by its own measurement minus the treble-hook. But if we are to assess the length of a fly accurately, the hook itself must be taken into account. Obviously, since salmon can be caught on bare hooks, a tube-fly's hook has to be considered part of the "fly".

This means that roughly one inch can be added to the overall length of a tube-fly when armed. So that a two-inch tube plus treble becomes three-inch. A two-and-a-half-inch tube becomes three-and-a-half-inch. And a three-inch tube (usually the longest) becomes a four-inch. I mention this so that we don't kid ourselves that a salmon has taken, say, a "three-inch" lure when, in fact, what we are fishing with really measures four inches. For most of our early fishing we use flies that, so far as the salmon is concerned, are from three to four inches in length.

Sunk line on the Lune in April. The author, careful to wade in no further than ankle-deep, is fishing a 3″ Sunk Lure very slowly across the stream. The fish lie along the edge of the current, which is clearly defined parallel to and just above the length of the rod.

A yard or so of slack line is held loosely in the author's left hand, ready to let go at the first touch of a fish. To minimize snatch when this happens the rod is held low, pointing straight at the fly.

Seconds after this picture was taken a salmon seized the lure—and was duly landed. It was followed almost immediately by another. The time was twelve-thirty, the fish fresh -run.

Note: A bag is seldom needed when we are fly fishing, since most spare tackle can easily be carried in our pockets. The small bag in the picture contained an alternative reel and line. The ability to make a quick change of method—from floating to sinking line, or *vice versa*—sometimes results in fish that might otherwise not have been caught. As it did on this occasion.

We shall not go far wrong if we equip ourselves with the following:

Three sizes of fly:

Big	Medium	Small
4″	3″	2″

Three weights for each of the above sizes:

Heavy	Medium	Light

And for fishing them, three lines:

Fast-sinker	Medium-sinker	Slow-sinker, or floater with sink-tip

Permutations from these flies and lines should enable us to cope satisfactorily with most waters we are likely to fish during early spring, and late autumn.

*　　　*　　　*

"Fine", says a newcomer, having acquired an appropriate rod, together with sinking lines of varying density and an assortment of heavy, medium and light flies. "I have got all the recommended tackle, and found out everything I can about the water I propose to cover. You tell me I must fish my fly deep, and I now know roughly how deep that should be. *But how do I know how deep my fly is fishing?*"

A very good question.

It is, however, one that with suitable preparation he can answer easily enough for himself, if he will only take the trouble. It will be well worth his while to do so, for the results will revolutionize his sunk-line fishing.

Together with an observant and willing companion, on a day set aside for the purpose, he should take his tackle to some clear-water stream that offers stretches of slackish, medium-fast and fast-running water on which he has permission to experiment, and in each location, using his different lines, fish flies of differing size and weight. If he cannot see what is happening to them himself, his companion can. Or his companion can do the casting so that *he* can observe their behaviour. He will soon gain a good idea of how deep each type of lure is fishing on whatever line, in water of whatever strength.

From this information it is a simple matter to decide what tackle to use on any stretch of river he is faced with in the future.

If it is to be done thoroughly, all this will take some hours of research. But it is time exceedingly well spent, for the priceless data that accrue will benefit him for the rest of his angling life.

Something similar was carried out often enough on my own stretch of fishing by various friends—not only in preparation for salmon fishing but for sea trout sunk-line fishing at night. They found the results highly rewarding. But either through indolence or ignorance, few anglers I meet on my travels have ever bothered to experiment in this way. In consequence, they claim little more than the vaguest notion at any time of how their lures are behaving.

Small wonder we are so frequently told that successful salmon fishing is nothing but pure luck!

The angler armed with this knowledge born of experiment and observation will approach the river with new-found confidence, for now he has something more tangible than mere hope on which to base his fishing. He has been taught what he should be trying to do when using sunk line, and now, for the first time, knows how to go about doing it. His strategy is no longer one of simple chuck-and-chance-it, but a commonsense plan based on computation of his various lines and lures.

It is this kind of approach that helps the intelligent angler to make the pursuit of salmon slightly less of a lottery. And as a result, quite irrespective of his catch, he will derive vastly more pleasure from his fishing.

*   *   *

The Big Fly: Appearance
So far although we have considered the size and weight of our sunk-line flies, nothing has been said about their appearance. A great deal has been written on the subject of big salmon flies and how the various writers think the fish see them in differing conditions of water and light. All of it is interesting and some of it plausible. But not surprisingly since no one *knows* what any fly looks like to a salmon or what indeed he thinks it is, the views expressed are somewhat contradictory. And as this book is essentially practical we shall disregard most of it, anyway. Nevertheless we must start off with some idea of what to offer the fish, call it what we may. So—what pattern should we use? Is colour important? And if so, what should it be and when should we use it?

According to one expert:

> Salmon have a definite preference for certain shades of various colours. They prefer a deep orange-yellow to a pale yellow and their favourite blue is kingfisher blue.

On the rivers he fished perhaps they did. But how the author arrived at these conclusions is not explained. And after all, is it true? The yellow-belly, one of the most popular of modern spinning lures is nothing if not pale yellow.

Some writers have advised selecting colours according to the light, and the clarity of the river:

> You must have a light-toned silver-bodied fly for fairly bright days and one with plenty of yellow and orange for coloured water,

suggested one of yesterday's elders. But another was of the opinion that colour selection depended more on the run of fish:

> I have proved to my own satisfaction that one particular *run of salmon* requires one colour of fly or lure, while *another run* may require lures of a different colour.

Perhaps the most famous advice came from the old Victorian angler who prescribed:

> A bright fly on a bright day, and a dark fly on a dark day.

Although according to the experience of a contemporary:

> A small sad-coloured fly is to be preferred in a bright and shallow water; a large and gaudy one in discoloured or very deep rapid water or on a blustering day. The salmon, like the grayling, lies at the bottom even when prepared to rise; in stormy weather therefore, or in dis-coloured water, he cannot see a small, dull, unobtrusive fly. In such cases, large and gaudy is your only chance.

Another pundit, sweeping this aside, stated firmly if rather vaguely:

> It may be laid down as an unwritten law of successful angling that the flies should be changed if salmon do not rise to them. A large sized hook may be substituted for a smaller, or vice versa, and a darker colour for a lighter. I have known stubborn fish to be moved to activity by this plan.

This was similar advice to that of another famous old salmon-killer who also recommended frequent changes, but to a "reddish" fly which, he claimed, caught him fish in autumn "that had refused all other flies". Why he didn't start off with his "reddish" fly if it was that good remains a mystery. Nor did he explain how he *knew* those fish had refused his other flies. Of course (as with those of the previous example) they *may* have done. But when seeking answers to salmon fishing problems it is so easy to look in the wrong cupboard. For example, we may fish down a pool once, perhaps twice, without an offer, then change our fly to one of similar size but different pattern and, on the next turn down, hook a fish. In itself this is nothing unusual. But we must be sure of our facts before claiming that success was due to the change of pattern. I am not saying it *wasn't*. Simply that we must not jump to conclusions, for there are other possibilities. Our fish may only just have come up into that particular lie from the pool below, or the pool tail, or from some other lie. Or perhaps he was a fish that in the inscrutable way of salmon had just "come on the take"—and might have accepted the original fly had it been fished down yet again.

I write with a certain degree of scepticism because at some time or other, in water low and clear enough to observe salmon reaction to various lures fished by friends, I have seen all sorts of strange things happen: salmon fleeing from a lure as though in terror; salmon following a lure and nibbling or knocking it; a salmon refusing the same lure several times, and then taking it; a salmon that had just moved into the pool being fished, first refusing a lure and then, perhaps half-an-hour later, being caught on it; and much else besides. Had these fish not been *seen* to act as they did, their behaviour might have been interpreted very differently, for the anglers concerned had no notion of what was happening.

But very seldom are we in a position to be so sure of what is going on beneath the surface. As I have just pointed out, there are many variables to be considered before we can pronounce on the effect of different fly patterns. The salmon is constantly confounding our theories, and whoever hurries his conclusions hurries into error.

As explained earlier, I don't altogether reject the importance of colour in a salmon fly. Weight of opinion seems to favour the idea that, tonal values apart, colour may occasionally influence salmon—although I cannot begin to guess how, when or with what this might happen. In Chapter XVI I describe experiments with prawns of various hues when I tried to take this business of colour a stage further. But no dramatic claims can be made, and I may as well say now that however attractive to salmon the prawn may be, and whatever its colour, this bait often fails to stimulate the slightest interest.

So, with regard to choice of fly colour for any particular conditions I cannot be very helpful. The truth is that I simply don't know how big a part colour really plays in a salmon lure, let alone when it is likely to be effective.

Unless I am in a position to watch a salmon as a lure approaches, and see a positive reaction as this "intruder" comes near to his territorial boundary—the quivering pectoral fins; the more pronounced undulation of the body—I can neither predict whether that fish is going to take, nor even hazard a guess at what lure is going to attract him. Furthermore, for all their fine theories concerning the salmon's vision on light days and dark days; in coloured water or in clear; response to flash, and the rest of it, I don't believe anyone else can either.

For a final quote from the salmon-fishing sages let us consult John Ashley-Cooper, one of the most experienced of our modern exponents. This is what he says about fly colour in *The Great Salmon Rivers of Scotland*, 1980:

> It does not seem to make a great difference. Black, yellow or orange, or a mixture of these, are as good as any. There is nothing better than jet black in clear water.

In the absence of further evidence this is as near the truth as we are likely to get and I will certainly go along with what he says, for nothing in my experience contradicts it.

Nowadays for all my sunk-line fishing I use a tube fly of black hair mixed with red/orange and a touch of gold. Mind you there is probably no need for the red/orange and gold. But the fly looks good. It pleases me, and it seems to please the fish. At any rate, they take it. So naturally, it is fished with confidence. And not surprisingly, since I use little else, this is the fly that catches me most of my sunk-line salmon.

If offers are not forthcoming I sometimes change to a yellow fly, and perhaps to a Whitewing at dusk. Not because I think the change is all that important, but because, when salmon are hard to catch, fishing something different lifts the flagging spirit and offers fresh hope; one casts with renewed vigour—just to see whether this new offering has some special magic. And sometimes it seems that it may have—if it produces a fish. But although I try to keep an open mind, there is seldom any real conviction that I wouldn't have caught that fish on my original fly, had I persevered with it longer.

I am sure that what matters far more than the fly's colour is its size. And that what matters most of all is how we present it to the fish.

Presentation
Sunk-line fishing in high water is simple enough. The Taking-Strip is usually very close to the bank, and a long line is seldom if ever needed.

In low water, however, the Taking-Strip has probably extended across most of the river. Now, our lure must be presented over as wide an arc as possible; so that success hinges on our achieving not only maximum casting range, but maximum *effective* casting range—a very different proposition (see text and diagrams on pp. 225–230).

As the diagrams illustrate: in a strong current, line and fly are helped to sink and to travel more slowly if the line can be given an upstream curve. But a quick-sinking line starts to go under as soon as it hits the water, so that there is usually only one chance of giving it such a curve. Furthermore, this chance must be seized very quickly—before the line starts to sink.

To achieve this, we don't wait until the line has touched down and started to swing round; we do it *just as the line is coming down on the water*.

The instant dipping-under of a sinking-line also means that, as we shall not be getting a second chance, when we *do* make our upstream curve it must be as big a curve as possible. So, when fishing a quick-sinking line we don't try to "mend" a downstream curve formed by the current—as we do sometimes when fishing a floating-line—we *create* an upstream curve by shooting some extra slack line as the cast is completed.

Usually, when a cast has been fished out, we strip in a few yards of line preparatory to casting again, this stripped-in line being shot when we make the next cast.

The length of line we use for making our upstream curve is, of course, a reserve of slack *additional* to what has already been stripped-in.

When we make our next cast we shoot the normal amount of stripped-in line. And then, just as it is starting to settle on the water, we form its upstream curve by rolling the rod over and, with a strong flick of the wrists, shooting this reserve of slack.

It is important to appreciate that this extra line *must* be drawn off the reel beforehand. There is no time to do it once we start to cast.

Here is a trick of my own for providing and controlling the line that, with a little practice, works well.

When your first cast of the day has been fished out and the usual amount of line has been stripped-in ready to be shot with the following cast, pull an additional two or three yards of line from the reel and throw them hard down on the surface beside you. Now, make your second cast. As usual, the stripped-in line will shoot as the cast goes out across the river—but only up to these coils of extra line lying in the water.

These, having sunk slightly, will stay where they are. Then, as you switch your rod over and make the upstream flick, these few coils of reserve line will lift off the water, follow the rod and form the curve.

Obviously, once you have pulled this length of extra "curve-line" off the reel and flung it down on the surface preparatory to your first cast, it is available all the time you are fishing. After this, at the completion of each cast, you simply throw the first few yards of stripped line into the water beside you; then strip in the length you are going to shoot with the next cast—and carry on. As you make the cast, you shoot the last few yards you stripped in, then "mend" the "extra" as before.

This is not nearly as difficult as it sounds. In fact, after a cast or two it all becomes so simple that you find yourself doing it automatically.

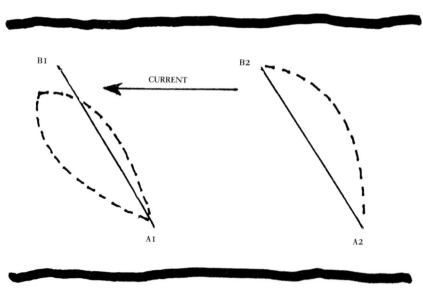

LEFT BANK

Angler at A1 casts to B1. When the line is dragged into a curve by the current it can be switched over ("mended") to help control the speed and depth of the fly. But this is only possible with a floating line. By now, a sinking line will have gone under.

Angler at A2 casts to B2 with a sinking line. As the line comes down on the water *before it has time to start sinking* he rolls his rod over and creates an upstream curve by shooting extra line.

This is the technique for all sunk-line fishing when strength of current makes mending obligatory. It can of course be used with floating line as well, and often is.

268

One further point: to assist line and fly to sink, *don't* move downstream straightaway after completing a cast, but *make your next cast from the same position.* Move your usual two or three paces downstream *after* you have cast and made your upstream curve in the line. This enables line and fly to drift down for a short distance, sinking as they go, before starting their swing round.

Clearly, when it comes to making this big upstream curve, the longer the rod we use the easier it is.

Of course, the angle at which we cast downstream and the amount of curve thrown upstream depends on the strength of current. In a quiet stretch of river having only a gentle flow, no upstream "mend" may be necessary. In which case, all we need to do is cast at an appropriate angle and allow the river to swing the fly slowly round across the lies. In more placid water still, we may even need to throw a *downstream* curve after casting, to give what current there is the chance to belly the line and work the fly across. And sometimes we may simply work the fly by hand.

There are of course exceptions, but generally speaking when you are wading, wade as deep as possible. Then, at the end of fishing out a cast, as the fly completes its swing round lead it across the dangle by moving the rod inshore ahead of it. And as you do so, draw in a yard or two of line with the non-casting hand. Follow this by drawing in another couple of yards slightly faster than the first. What you have drawn in is the stripped-line you will shoot with your next cast; but its pulling-in has altogether another function: attracting a fish that may have followed the fly towards the dangle.

Sometimes, when you draw in the line, a fish that has been following will seize the fly just as it starts to move away upstream, especially when it starts to accelerate slightly—as it does when you draw in the second arm's length.

That the salmon taking in this way just when a fly seems to be "escaping" is sometimes a fish that has *followed* the fly, I can affirm—for I have seen it happen.

Sunk-line fishing is a difficult method not so much because of the fly's size and weight, but of the line itself and its casting problems. Your drawing-in of those four or five yards at the completion of the previous cast automatically brings the line a little nearer the surface. But if it had been sunk really deep, pulling in this amount is not likely to raise it sufficiently to let you make the next cast. So, bring the rod to the vertical. This lifts the line higher and positions the rod for a roll-cast.

Next, roll the fly straight downstream, aiming slightly upwards. Then, as the line loops out, and before it has time to sink, go into your back cast.

At the end of fishing out a cast, draw in a yard or two of line with the non-casting hand ... a fish that has been following the fly may seize it just as it starts to move away upstream.

For fishing sunk-line, Spey casting is undoubtedly the best technique. Preferably the double-Spey. For one thing it is less dangerous than the overhead cast—for which line and fly are brought straight back towards you. If the line is not near enough to the surface and the fly hangs as you make the overhead back cast, it is likely to spring from the water and hurtle straight at your eyes. A three-inch tube in the face gives the day a poor start.

The double-Spey cast, which keeps the fly well downstream and nowhere near the angler, is much safer. It is also more powerful, better for switching direction in one go, and made with no false casts. Swishing the line to and fro, common enough with overhead casting, squanders time and energy, besides frightening the fish—especially if the fly keeps hitting the water, which a weighted tube frequently does.

Some people find it impossible to mend a sinking line when Spey casting. This is because they *roll* the line out along the surface. By the time the line has straightened, part of it—the length nearest the rod—has already dipped underwater, frustrating any hope of throwing a good upstream curve. As described in Chapter X, this is not the way the cast should be completed. As the forward stroke is made, the line is aimed upwards, so that it straightens in the air. It should touch down as it does at the finish of an overhead cast.

However skilful an overhead caster you may be, don't forget what I have said about the double-Spey cast being safer. And if you haven't already done so, I urge you to master it at once. The sight of an angler staggering from the river with a hook in his ear and blood streaming down his neck lives in my memory.

*   *   *

And when is fishing not worthwhile? Never. Even if the river is in high spate a very occasional fish can be caught. So, if free to fish, then fish, for you will catch nothing if you don't. However hopeless the conditions may seem, if the beat is booked and paid for you might as well keep your fly in the water.

Anyone can catch a salmon when river conditions are good and the pools full of fresh-run fish. It isn't often that salmon are "mad for the fly", but it happens. When it does—as someone once said: "You can throw your hat at them and they'll take it!" The measure of a good fisherman, however, is not the number of fish he catches when they are coming eagerly to the fly, but what he achieves when they are not. If he can hook fish when other anglers haven't even bothered to put up their rods he is, indeed, an expert.

It happened like that once on Tweed. I had gone up to Kelso to join my friends Arthur Oglesby and the late Eric Horsfall Turner at the famous old Ednam House Hotel. Arriving at dusk preparatory to fishing the following day, I met them coming off the river with three fish. Now, to anyone who remembers the glories of early Tweed spring fishing twenty-five years ago, three fish won't seem much of a catch. But the river was in roaring flood; as high and dirty as I have seen it, the chocolate-brown spate water swirling down and bringing every kind of rubbish with it. Eric and Arthur took those fish in a tiny lay-by off the main stream where running salmon must have swung in to rest. The last fishing tenant of the beat had taken thirty fish the previous week, but those three represented an incomparably better feat of angling.

I asked around that evening for news of the other beats. Not another rod had been out.

So—you never know with salmon. Those creaking old apothegms: "It pays to persist", and "You don't catch a fish unless your hook's in the water", are shiny with use—but still true! I could give other examples of fish caught in "impossible" conditions, but the point has been made.

As stressed earlier, although the weather is pretty cheerless when you are fishing sunk-line, the time of year being what it is, never make the mistake of packing-up too soon. However shivering the day, always fish on into the darkening. Both during early spring and late autumn I have hooked salmon in the dusk when daylight was nearly done.

The best hour of the day. Whatever the month, always fish well on into the darkening.

As the world spins and winter turns to spring, the water temperature rises and salmon tend to move about more freely. Our fly is still fished on sinking line, but need be neither so large nor sunk so deep.

And then, some time during the middle of April or thereabouts, salmon start to take a smaller fly fished higher in the water. This form of fishing is much easier than the technique we have been using hitherto and comprises about ninety percent of our sport with the fly-rod. It is, in fact, what most anglers usually mean when they refer to salmon "fly-fishing".

Henceforth, until late autumn, we put aside our sinking-lines and big tubes. From now on we shall catch most of our salmon with small to tiny flies fished no more than a few inches below the surface, and presented on a floating line.

272

The River Tweed at Sprouston, once the home of H. Wright the famous mid-Victorian fly-tyer. Fred Buller (left) and J. Bruce-Gardyne display their morning catch taken on the big sunk fly, 6th November, 1981. Note the net marks on the biggest fish.

273

I should advise you not to pay over much attention to the maxims current among salmon fishers as to what fly you should use or what you should do in this event or that. Such maxims may be good working rules, but one thing you may be sure of about a salmon, you can never tell either what he will do or when he will do it, and if the fish doesn't come when invited in what you consider the orthodox manner, don't give him up, but try him in the most unorthodox way that you can think of, and I should suggest, to begin with, an absurdly small fly.

A. H. Chaytor, *Letters to a Salmon Fisher's Sons*, 1910

XIII
Fly Fishing

PART FIVE: THE FLOATING LINE

Choice of Fly

In the whole world-wide range of angling there can be no mystery more baffling than *Salmo*'s acceptance of tiny flies fished on or near the surface. Even if salmon were feeding, and the lures were alive, the amount of nourishment contained in creatures so minuscule, taken in isolation, would scarcely repay the expenditure of energy involved in rising to them.

As it is, irregular though it may be, such behaviour is astonishing in a fish that, during his return to the river is fasting and steadily losing weight, and to whom energy conservation must be of considerable importance.

One can understand the taking of a three-inch or four-inch lure in early spring or late autumn on sunk line; a lure that passes close to the fish's nose and can be taken with the minimum of effort. But for a twenty or thirty-pound salmon to swim up through five or six feet of water and take a fly no bigger than size 8 or 10, or even smaller, seems utterly absurd.

Nevertheless, this is typical of *Salmo* during late spring and summer, and great good fortune for the fisherman—for the salmon's take on floating line and small fly provides the very peak of angling excitement.

As I know from experience, having at some time or other caught pretty well every species of fish in Britain, both salt water and fresh, each form of fishing has its own excitement relative to its particular skills. A dry-fly disappearing into the dimpled surface of a chalk-stream; the flash of a specimen roach; a sea trout's slashing rise in the darkness; the swirl of a big bass, or a mullet at daybreak; the first tiny tremble of a pike-float; the bow-wave of a big carp cruising past sun-flecked lily-pads towards a floating crust . . . they are all electrifying. But the miracle that happens when a salmon takes the small fly on or just below the surface cannot be surpassed by any other sporting climax on earth.

It is this magic that as salmon fly fishermen we are privileged to enjoy. But first we must select a likely fly, and consider how best to fish it.

You have, we will imagine, arrived on a stretch of good salmon fly-fishing in May. The air temperature is 58°F, the water, 51°. Occasional snow-melt from the distant hills is keeping an average height of river for the time of year, the current running steady but not too fast. The sunlight is softened by high cloud, which has spread across the sky throwing the sparkling, tree-lined water into avenues of shadow. Without being strong enough to injure fly-casting, the warm southerly breeze is poppling the surface of those long, glassy pool-tails that at this time of year are starting to hold fish. Conditions are near-perfect for catching salmon on the small fly. A fresh-run fish shows briefly in the broken water downstream. Further up, another fish leaps forward in a flashing cascade of silver. *Pace* a sea trout pool in the half-light of a myrtle-scented summer dusk, if there is a more exciting place for a game-fisherman to find himself I do not know it.

The water temperature and comparative shallowness of the pools you will be fishing have banished any thoughts of a sinking or sink-tip line and big flies. Automatically, therefore, you have set up your rod with a floater. But so far without a leader, because leader depends on the size of fly, and this has not yet been decided.

Now comes the rub. What fly do you choose, and how do you choose it?

Over the years, not surprisingly, many attempts have been made to answer this question. In a sport so unlikely as salmon fishing, which consists of offering food to an animal that has no appetite, the angler obviously needs to bolster his confidence with some sort of theory. In consequence, a vast amount of mumbo-jumbo has been amassed—few writers being as frank as old George Kelson a hundred years ago:

> It is impossible to lay down any hard and fast rule for selecting a fly. The art of doing so is only acquired by long experience, and the best of us are often at our wits' end to know what fly to select.

Despite the advancement of science since Kelson's time, we are not much wiser today. All the same, we *must* have confidence in our fly because if we haven't we shall not fish it hard enough or with sufficient concentration, and at the end of a season it is the most persistent angler who, given reasonable skill, is more often than not the most successful.

In *Torridge Fishery*, L. R. N. Gray, who was no fool with a fly-rod, wrote:

> I know of no greater help to a salmon fisherman than confidence . . .
> We do not know what we do when in a hopeful frame of mind that
> is in any way different from our actions when we are in despair of
> ever getting a pull, but at least we ourselves are trying, and presumably
> our lure is trying instead of merely going through the motions.

A form of "pathetic fallacy"? Maybe. But I believe it works. Gray thought so, too. He continues:

> A way of ensuring that a guest gets a fish is to catch one yourself
> on a fly of your own tying, and then give him the fly and advice on
> where and when to fish it to be sure of getting a fish. The mere fact
> that the fly is a proved killer on that day, that it is somewhat different
> from a standard pattern and therefore probably some special "medi-
> cine" for the river, is quite sufficient to imbue it with the magic of
> confidence which results in a fish.

As Gray wrote years ago, confidence counts for much in salmon fish-ing; our success very largely depends on it. But if we are to fish on and on, cast after cast, hour after hour without an offer, and have any chance of hooking a fish, we *must* tie on a fly we believe in. And how can we believe in a fly that has not been chosen for some particular reason—be it fact or fancy?

But what reason? Size? Shape? Colour?

For summer flies, as for those of early spring, various colours are sometimes recommended on the grounds that in certain conditions they enable a fish to *see* the fly better and that, when these conditions obtain, the use of brightly-coloured flies will automatically result in more offers.

As already suggested, this is very doubtful. Salmon have excellent vision. They may refuse a fly for any number of reasons, but an inability to see it well enough—even in dark spate water—is not likely to be among them. I have consistently caught fish with small flies, no bigger than eights and tens, on floating line in water the colour of oak when other anglers were spinning.

As for choice of colour . . . Although, as already mentioned, I think it possible that salmon do sometimes react to colour, can anyone say what colour is likely to stimulate them at any given moment?

In an attempt to be helpful I can only repeat the advice offered earlier:

that if I had to choose *one* pattern of fly to use at any time in any river for the rest of my life, it would be something like my Dee Special: a tenuous dressing of plain black hair with a hint of orange or blue tied on a slimline black body—ribbed with silver or gold just to make it look nice. I would fish quite happily with this simple pattern, tied in various lengths and amounts of dressing on different sizes and weights of hooks. (And most of the time nowadays this is all I do fish with.) Nevertheless, remembering the salutary experience of that long-ago streak of Irish orange, I willingly concede the possibility that on occasion some more colourful pattern might do better.

So, to return to our imaginary river bank where we left you engaged in the salmon fisherman's daily wriggle-and-writhe—in other words, choice of fly—in answer to your query: "What pattern?" I reply: Anything you fancy, for whatever reason.

Anything? you exclaim. But what about the light?

What about the light?

Well—light and colour. A bright fly on a bright day, a dull fly on a dull day, and so on. Don't you think it makes any difference?

Frankly, no. However plausible some of the theories I have read, nothing in practice has convinced me that it makes a scrap of difference.

But never mind what I think. If you believe in the bright-light, bright-fly; dull-light, dull-fly theory, or what-have-you, why not make things as easy for yourself as possible and do all your fishing with just two patterns: a bright pattern and a dark pattern, say a Silver Blue and a Thunder and Lightning? Two splendid, well-proved salmon flies. Carry them in a comprehensive size-range: 2, 4, 6, 8, 10, 12, 14, with varying amounts and lengths of dressing, tied on double-hooks and trebles—and, if you fancy them, on tubes, too. And a few on single hooks as well; there's nothing like being prepared.

Will this do you?

No, you object. It certainly will not! You have no wish to be restricted to two patterns. In fact restrictions are out. Like every other salmon angler, you already own several cases crammed with small flies of every shape and colour. What you want is a simple method of choosing one.

Very well. Give them all numbers and get your wife to call one. Nearly as good as any other method.

No? Not scientific enough?

Oh, well, perhaps you are right. Let us examine it in greater detail.

First of all, leaving colour aside, I suggest that the most important point to consider when choosing a fly is *the depth you want it to swim.*

The simplicity of salmon fly-fishing at its best. Speyside in early May—a salmon fisherman's dream. Felt-soled waders, a carbon fifteen-foot rod with floating line. Priest. Flycase. Nylon. Scissors. One needs to carry little else. The author's wading-stick has been left at the bottom of the bank—where the fish was tailed by hand.

A salmon may take a fly that is swimming at a certain depth, but refuse the same fly if it is swimming higher or lower. Hypotheses abound. But although many thousands of words have been written about it, no one *knows* the reason for this curious behaviour. And with regard to the depth at which a fly should swim, most writers are very cagey. Nevertheless, a great deal seems to hinge on it, and the answer I offer is: from three to five inches. In other than special circumstances, the ideal depth for fishing the small fly is about four inches.

"Special circumstances"? They may not occur often. But from time to time there are one or two little tricks we can play on salmon when attempting to *induce* a take. We shall come to them in due course.

Four inches, then, is the depth at which I try to fish the fly on floating line. *But*—and it is a very important "but"—there are times during the warmth of summer and early autumn when salmon relish a long, thin-bodied fly fished very close to the top, even riffling in the surface film; a much longer fly than the customary "greased-line" lure used at that time of year. This lure is a slender, long-tailed, hair-wing creation, one-and-a-half to two inches in length and sparsely dressed. It may consist of a few dark hairs, badger or deer perhaps, on a short very thin tube armoured with a size 12 or 14 treble. Or, it can be dressed on a small single or double or treble hook, its tail projecting an inch-and-a-half or so behind. But whatever its make-up, lightness is all, since its purpose is to riffle in the surface film.

Casting back in angling history, we realize there is nothing original in this. Robert Venables and Richard Franck probably knew about it over three hundred years ago. "The salmon taketh the artificial flie very well", wrote Venables. "The wings very long, with very long tayls."

"Dibble but lightly on the surface", instructed Richard Franck.

Put the advice of those two Cromwellian salmon-fishing soldiers together, and there you have it!

But this we shall leave for the time being, and concentrate on our choice of the more customary type of small salmon fly that is fished on floating line during the latter stages of the late spring and early summer run.

When appraising a fly, the first point we notice, apart from the overall colour scheme, is its manner of dressing. The dressing is important for several reasons, but of primary importance, I suggest, is neither the colours nor the materials, it is the *quantity*, for it is this that plays a big part in controlling the depth at which the fly will swim. A slender, lightly-dressed fly will sink more readily than a bushy dressing on a similar hook. And since weight usually decreases as the hook size diminishes, a lightly-dressed size 8 may fish at the same depth as, say, a more heavily-dressed size 6, on the same length of leader fished on the same type of fly line in the same strength of current. So, if the current is congenial, both these flies may fish let us say at our prescribed depth of about four inches. *But* these two flies are of different sizes. How should we make a choice? In other words, which *size* should we choose.

Experience has shown that size of fly is determined by two factors: the height and temperature of the water. First of all, temperature. Here as a very rough guide is a Size/Temperature table:

Temp. °F.	Size
45–50	2–6
51–55	6–8
56–60	8–10
61–65	10–12
66+	12–16

As we can see, from the big sunk fly of early spring, when the water temperature is in the thirties and low forties, the fly size steadily decreases from a size 2, the biggest we shall be using on a floating line, to a size 12 and even smaller. In conditions of summer heat, with the river low and the water very warm, we shall probably be using flies as small as sizes 12 or 14. Indeed, late on hot July or August evenings we may be wise to fish a size 16. It is not by some miracle that the trout angler so often hooks a salmon on his tiny fly. This is the size of fly a salmon is most likely to accept in these conditions, and the sensible salmon angler takes advantage of it.

(This "Midsummer Fly" is best tied on a tiny double or treble hook rather than a single. And since we need to fish fine, a trout rod is advisable—hence the carbon ten-and-a-half footer recommended in Chapter IX.)

The required fly size, then, seems to diminish with water temperature. And although as a guide this is only rough-and-ready (small flies will kill on sunk lines in spring and autumn; big flies will do so on floating lines in summer) experience shows that the basic methods of big and deep, small and high, give us the best chance. As for hook size, this again is only a peg to hang our hat on. Many different lengths of dressing may be tied on any one size of hook, giving very different appearances. What will differ, too, is the depth at which they swim in a given current. And if anything has any importance at all in this irrational sport of salmon fly-fishing, I think it is that.

There seems to be no connection between fly-size and depth of water. This is very odd. One would think there would be. But if there *is*, I don't know about it.

Recently I was fishing a pool that runs through a big, slack "pot" over twenty feet in depth. I have never heard of anyone hooking a salmon in that pot other than on bait. It is seldom if ever fished with fly.

While I was taking my turn down the pool, my companion went to this dark, deep, patch of still water to practise his casting. He stood at the edge, chucking out his size 8 fly, retrieving it and chucking it out again. After ten minutes of this, to his astonishment, and the gillie's, and mine, a fifteen-pounder took the fly.

What does this prove? Only what I have said again and again in this book—that we mustn't make unqualified statements. If anyone *has* tried to establish a relationship between depth of water and size of fly, there must be plenty of exceptions to it—as there are to every man-made "rule" about salmon.

Another factor that determines size of fly (which is commonly measured by size of hook) is the water height. Generally speaking, the higher the water the stronger the current, the bigger the hook the larger the fly. Conversely, the lower the river the slacker the current, the lighter the hook and the smaller the fly. But of course there is no need necessarily to increase the size of fly just because there is more water. Within limits,. we can simply use a heavier hook of the same size. We can also, of course, if we wish, adjust the overall amount and length of fly dressing irrespective of the hook.

It is often suggested that the condition of the river is important; that a larger fly should be used in coloured water on the grounds that a smaller fly cannot be seen. But not believing this, I pay no attention to it. Nothing in my experience leads me to think that a salmon cannot see the smallest fly in the darkest water.

This opinion of the salmon's visual acuity is nicely supported by the experience of a friend, years ago, on a beat I often used to fish. Whiling away a summer evening dibbling a tiny fly for trout in a coloured backwater of the flooded River Eden, he was astonished to hook an eighteen-and-a-half pound salmon. On his light trout tackle he fought the great fish up and down the pool, and eventually after a protracted struggle succeeded in beaching it. Exhausted, but still without his trout, he returned to the backwater—and hooked another eighteen pounder!

I know that backwater, he showed me the spot. When I asked him what the water was like, he said it was "the colour of teak."

So far as I am concerned, when fly-fishing for salmon in summer, the vital part of the equation is not the colour of the water; it is the depth at which the fly is swimming: i.e. about four inches.

But returning to the task in hand. You know the water temperature is 51°F. And since you must start with *something*, you consult your Fly-Size/Water Temperature Table and decide to kick off with a size 6. So, after a glance at the pool, you begin by selecting those flies in your box whose dressings you think will enable them to swim at the required depth in the current you are about to fish. Already your choice has been considerably narrowed.

Next, the *pattern*.

Take a look at the sky. Is the light hard or soft? Now, another look at the pool. What sort of bottom has it got? Is the water clear or peaty? If you seek guidance from such gnomic wisdom as "A bright fly for a bright sky; a dark fly for a dark lie", or *vice versa*—or from some other homespun maxim stitched in runes—select only those patterns that seem to fit your particular bill. This reduces the ultimate choice still further.

Now, from the flies you have picked out so far, choose only those whose hairs or feathers are soft and flexible; which when they move through the water will flicker and seem alive. We can be positive in thinking that a straggly, tenuous, chewed-looking fly is more attractive than something stiffish and neat and "over-stuffed".

You have now short-listed perhaps three or four possibles. Tip these into your hat, close your eyes and pick one out.

Good. You have now chosen a fly. And what have you come up with? A rather battered, double-hooked, size 6 Blue Charm. And a very good fly, too.

In fact, while you are at it and have your fly-case out, you will be wise to select two or three other flies of different sizes: say, 4, 8, 10, and have them handy, stuck in the fly-pad on your fishing coat. We shall come to the whys and wherefores of this shortly.

*   *   *

Choice of fly boils down to what was written a century ago. There is no magic substitute for experience. Experience merely reduces the number of flies you tip into your hat. When you are very experienced you may not need to tip in any at all.

It is only an imaginary hat, of course. But all the same, you could save yourself the agonies of choice if your fly-case offered nothing but replicas of just one or two simple patterns.

Never mind. One thing is certain: whatever fly you attach to your leader, its success—like that of the sunk-line fly—will depend very much on how you fish it.

FISHING "ROUND-THE-CLOCK"

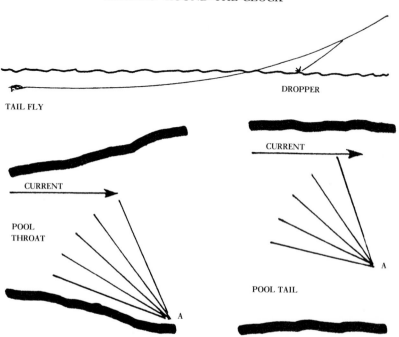

An exciting method of using a dropper both for salmon and sea trout, particularly on warm summer evenings, is "round-the-clock" fishing.

With a water-knot or a double-grinner, make up a 10-foot leader. Place the dropper about six feet from the point. Tie a size 8 or 10 greased dry-fly on the dropper and a small wet-fly, say 12 or 14 on the point.

Wade carefully to a position from which fish lying opposite and upstream can be covered with a fairly short line. Cast up and across; each time putting the flies in a different place. Work the flies so that the tail fly fishes just below the surface, with the dropper dragging across the top leaving a tiny wake.

Don't let the flies slow down or stop, but recover with the same smooth action. If a fish rises but refuses, don't cast over him again too soon. Leave him for a short time and make several casts round-the-clock in other directions first.

The single-handed, carbon, twelve-foot "Bob-Fly" rod is ideal for this form of fishing. Use the lightest line you can conveniently cast. Your loch tackle should do admirably.

Fish well into the darkness.

284

Presentation

Your approach to fishing a floating line is much the same as you made earlier in the season. The more intimately you know the beat, the more likely your chance of catching fish. To rush up to a river and start casting is always a mistake. Far better to sit down, take another look at the water, and do some thinking.

The first question to be decided is whether you intend to fish a dropper. This is by no means a regular practice. It varies from river to river. Some people swear by it and use a dropper for nearly all their greased-line fishing; their theory being that it doubles the chance of catching a fish.

Well—maybe. All the same, a dropper can be a curse. In my opinion the only sensible time to use one is when we are loch fishing; or for a dry-fly in conjunction with a wet fly on the point, fished "round-the-clock" on summer evenings. And in both these situations we are fishing mainly for small salmon or grilse. Speaking for myself I always feel happier fishing with a single fly—certainly if there is the slightest chance of hooking a big fish. For all the salmon that droppers may have caught, angling history is studded with sad stories of fish they have lost.

Years ago at the spot where I am fishing in the picture on p. 21, I watched a visiting angler playing a ten or twelve pound salmon. It was the first salmon he had ever hooked and, unfortunately, he was using two flies. The fish was hooked on the tail fly. He played it most carefully; but as it weakened and he drew it in towards the bank his dropper hooked itself firmly into a reed stem, and the fish would come no further. There it lay, half on its side, a tantalizing yard or so out of reach.

"Oh, hell!" he said helplessly. "Whatever shall I do?"

"Pray", I suggested. And perhaps he did. But however fervent his supplication, no divine help was forthcoming. Almost at once the salmon gave a final wriggle, and dived. The reed stem disappeared abruptly underwater—then the leader broke at the dropper.

"Oh dear", said the V.A. "Oh dear, oh dear."

That was all he said, and I marvelled at his restraint. But he seemed close to tears, and the scene was tinged with an inexpressible sadness. As the dusk closed about us he wound up his line and walked slowly away, shaking his head.

He had a fishing ticket for the week, but I never saw him again.

I don't know what Major the Honourable John Ashley-Cooper said on that disastrous day at Delfur when the big salmon broke him. He doesn't tell us. But the rest of the unhappy incident is recounted in his book *The Great Salmon Rivers of Scotland*:

> The biggest fish which so far as I know I ever myself hooked in the Spey was in the tail of the Two Stones at Delfur, one May. This fish took a No. 6 double-hooked tail fly (I was using two flies), and he played deep and strong for some time, though without any fireworks. Eventually we saw the length of his back above the surface, and it took one's breath away. He was huge. I played him from the left bank for about three-quarters of an hour, when he dropped down the rapids into the next pool below, called Beaufort. All went well, and after an hour he was getting tired and was in the tail of Beaufort nearly half a mile below where I hooked him. Several times he came to the surface and thrashed, though he never jumped out. At last he came almost to within gaffing range, and Allan my ghillie saw him clearly in the water and let out an appropriate expletive. Then he made one last run across the pool and was coming back tamely, so we counted our chickens as hatched. All at once while he was still in midriver there was a sudden nasty pluck, and the loose line came flying back to me with the gut broken at the top of the cast. Simultaneously a small fish of about 10 lb made two unbalanced jumps in midstream, while I stood on the bank helplessly. It did not take long to realize what had happened; as my big fellow was easing back across the pool, this second small fish had either taken or been foul-hooked by the dropper, and for a second or two both fish had been tied together after my cast had broken. So I lost two fish and two flies, when if I had not been using a dropper the chances of landing the big one were by that stage most promising. I put this big fish at over 40 lb. Allan later said it was over 50 lb, but I hope this was going too far.

So, next time you feel emboldened to fish two flies, remember the moral of this dreadful story—and have second thoughts. For myself, I have never hooked a salmon as big as John Ashley-Cooper's; it is not likely I ever shall; but, if I do, it will not be lost because of a dropper!

Nevertheless, pushing my prejudice aside, there is an aspect of this that should not be ignored. The use of a dropper does allow us to offer a fish *two sizes* of fly. At times this may well result in our tempting a fish which otherwise might have refused. Esmond Drury makes this point in a letter to me:

Lt. Colonel Esmond Drury D.S.O., M.C. Begetter of the famous "General Practitioner".

Size of fly does seem to *be* a factor. In all but exceptional summer conditions—when a small (size 12 or 14) Stoat's tail seems to be as effective as anything, and more so than most—I usually hedge my bets and fish a size 10 fly on the point and a size 8 fly of a different pattern on the dropper. I mostly start the day with a Tosh or Stoat's tail on the point, with a General Practitioner or a Shrimp fly on the dropper—simply because I have confidence in this combination.

Over the years I have taken approximately the same number of fish on point and dropper.

Other combinations may well have proved more or less effective. How can one know?

When I use a dropper I tie it about four feet up from the tail fly.

This is because I move downstream about four feet between casts. This means that every fish covered is covered twice. I think that the first fly over a fish may sometimes set it up to take the next one.

When fishing bad, rocky pools, I remove the dropper.

So, there you have it. Although I seldom employ one myself, *judicious* use of a dropper may well increase your chance of an offer. But have a good look at the water first. If it has rocky outcrop, or weed beds (or reeds!), or there is a gusty wind blowing in your face—think again.

*   *   *

Now, to return to where we left you, sitting on the river bank. You are naturally eager to start fishing. Before making a move, however, check your tackle: leader; knots; hook-point. And make sure you have re-wound the line.

Don't let this repetitious insistence on tackle inspection slide too smoothly over the mind. I know the advice is obvious and rather boring, but it is all-important. And often ignored—with subsequent regret. Too many salmon are lost through haste; through failure to check details, and check them regularly. Usually, while we are fishing, it is the hook—straightened in a fish, perhaps, or broken against stones on the back-cast. But faulty knot-tying; wind-knots in the leader; line or dirt jamming the reel, quite apart from untested nylon, also claim their share of disasters.

Now, having made sure of your tackle, take a look down the river. As discussed in the previous chapter, it is reasonable to suppose that the size of fly and the speed at which it should be fished are directly related, and that when presented to salmon the fly should move no faster than the speed at which a living creature of that size—perhaps a shrimp or a tiny fish—could move. Yes, there *are* exceptions. I have seen a salmon with its back half out of the water chase after a fly that was skidding round a pool tail at what seemed a ridiculous speed—and take it! But I haven't known such a thing happen very often. It is rather odd that although—as discussed later in this chapter—I have caught salmon on dry-flies skidded across the surface, I have seldom done so when a conventional "greased-line" fly has come to the top and behaved in a similar way. Often I have lost control of my fly and had it skid round—but not with a salmon in pursuit. Presumably because it was moving too fast.

The skidding dry-fly we will deal with later. For the time being we shall stick to the customary "greased-line" method of fishing a small fly a few inches below the surface. As already mentioned, experience indicates that correct presentation demands careful control of speed and depth—the latter being, if one has to put a figure on it, about four inches.

In order to achieve this marriage of speed and depth all the way down the pool, a careful examination of the river is advisable before you start fishing.

So, having set up and checked your tackle, put your water-sense to work. Observe and memorize the position of all likely salmon lies. A sunken rock often forms a lie. But the surface swirl and eddy that usually betrays it may affect the behaviour of your fly. This is easily corrected, provided you know in advance where it is likely to happen. Note the strength of the current and where it changes in speed and direction. See where the surface is glassy smooth, and where it is rippled. Line-tip, leader and fly go under more readily in a ripple than in a flat glide.

Most important, note that narrow strip of water between current and slack on the inside of a bend. Almost invariably such places hold taking lies for salmon. But remember that the fly's speed and height must be maintained as it swings from the current into slacker water, otherwise it will falter at the very place where a running salmon may be resting; indeed, where you can *expect* him to be.

Bearing in mind that the fly is to be fished at a depth of about four inches, it soon becomes evident as you read the water, how often, if at all, you will need to change the weight (or size) of fly in sympathy with the changing current. The river flow almost certainly varies from a fast run-in at the head of the pool, through a slacker middle, down to a streamy tail. To fish it all properly, that is to give yourself the best chance of hooking a fish at every cast all the way down, you may need to make a change of fly; possibly two or three changes.

To fish the very fast run-in at the pool neck, you may decide to start not with your chosen size 6, but a size 4, changing to the size 6 for fishing the first third of the pool itself. Then, perhaps, a size 8 for the middle of the pool, before changing back again to the size 6 for the draw of the tail. In the patch of slackish water where the current goes rather dead about half-way down, it may be worth trying a few casts with a size 10.

If you believe that the darker bottom you may find in this part of the pool deserves a duller fly than the one you are starting with higher up, where the bottom is scoured by the current, then select an appropriate fly in the size you want and have it ready with the others you have chosen.

To be able to change flies safely and quickly when you are wading deep is essential. To keep trudging ashore each time is disruptive and irksome. With practice it is very simple. Stuff the rod butt down inside your breast waders, or tuck it under your arm, so that you have both hands free. The stripped-in line can belly downstream with the current; drag on the leader being prevented by holding some of the line in your teeth. You can, if you wish, wind the line in, but I never bother to do this myself.

What I do is to decide in advance, when making the reconnaissance, what extra flies are going to be needed and have them stuck in the fly-pad on my wading jacket, which is also ready to receive each fly I cut off. A fly-pad is a much better way of carrying spare flies than sticking them in your hat, from which they can be difficult to extricate. Being slung

Before starting work on a pool, it is sometimes worthwhile to wade well out and hang a biggish fly in the rapids at the pool neck. Fish often lie in no more than two feet or so of water. The fly is worked by moving the rod slightly from side to side, the line slowly being drawn in with the non-casting hand for a yard or two. It is then released so that it drops back downstream close to the water's edge well clear of the fish, before again being worked slowly to and fro across the lies.

Experiment soon shows which pools are suited to it. With experience, a glance is sufficient to tell whether a pool neck has potential holding water. Anglers skilled at low-water upstream worm fishing for salmon and sea trout will recognize such water immediately.

on loops round my neck, spectacles and scissors are equally handy, and of course safe from being dropped in the river. An elastic band round my head from the two wings of my polaroids keeps them from going overboard when pushed up on my forehead to make room for the reading spectacles—without which I can no longer see to tie a knot. The rest is simple. One's fly-case is never in danger of being lost, for it is never in use.

To make allowance for shortening the leader when changing flies, I add a couple of feet when tackling-up, and start with eleven feet of nylon instead of nine. This, incidentally, is no bad thing. The current where you start fishing is almost certainly stronger than it is elsewhere, and the extra leader length at that spot helps the fly to find its depth and therefore fish better. Only a tiny point, certainly, but worth noting. And, while on the subject of leaders, always regard nylon as being expendable. *Never economize*. Fit a new leader each morning and afternoon. And of course whenever you think that abrasion or excessive strain has weakened it. Only a fool hoards monofilament—with the safe landing of a salmon at stake!

Some anglers may scoff at various of the minutiae I am discussing. They may for instance think that these changes of fly are unnecessary. Having decided on a size and pattern, some are content to fish it down a stretch irrespective of water changes. If that is your pleasure you will probably do the same. But I assure you that although for much of your fishing such fly changes *are* unnecessary, sooner or later if you ignore the possibility of a change being needed you will undoubtedly miss the chance of a fish.

Over the distance, attention to details—wader soles and wading technique, knots, loops on spectacles, extra nylon lengths, fly-pads, reserve flies and fly-changing drill—will help us to catch salmon. Particularly the latter. As we shall examine shortly, there are times when a salmon will move to a fly but refuse it. Such a fish will sometimes take properly if offered a larger or smaller fly. And as we shall see, to have some different sizes and patterns already selected and handy to tie on, is a great saving of time and fiddle.

There is a further point. Keeping alert and working at our sport in this way adds to the interest. We are not just fishing automatons, but thinking all the time of how our fly is working and whether its behaviour is likely to attract a salmon. In other words, we are hunting with purpose. And whether or not we succeed in hooking a fish, we shall certainly enjoy a deeper sense of fulfilment from our fishing.

However wide the river, just because we are wearing breast waders and using a big rod doesn't mean we should start by wading as deep as possible and casting thirty yards of line. There are many places where to start with we shouldn't even wet our feet. And some where we should keep right back from the bank and make our first couple of casts across-country. A running salmon will sometimes swing-in to the side and rest in very shallow water. Surprisingly shallow. So, remember when you approach the river, there could be a fish—and a taking fish at that—lying no more than a yard or two from your own bank: from the very spot indeed where you propose to start fishing.

Approach the bank unstealthily and that fish will ghost away into deeper water. And with him will go any chance of your catching him. A chance so often missed, because it is so often unsuspected.

Always start by fishing the nearer water. And when you do, don't waggle the rod about lengthening line straight out over the river, as beginners invariably do, sometimes letting the fly settle while more line is stripped off and then dragging it out again until arriving at the maximum amount of line you can cast. By the time you start fishing you will probably be covering empty water.

There is almost as good a chance of hooking a salmon with your first cast as with any other. Don't waste it. Imagine there is a fish lying close to the bank and put a cast or two over that piece of water first. Having done that, approach the water's edge, or wade in a short distance and take up whatever position you intend. Then, to lengthen line, strip some off the reel and allow the current to take it downstream in the shallows beside your bank. When you have a workable length out, make your first cast in one movement with no false casting. Fish that cast out. Then, without moving your position, strip off more line and cast again. And so on, fishing each cast with equal care until you have your optimum length of line extended.

Now you can start to fish down the pool, taking a couple of long paces between each cast, remembering the importance of *effective* casting range (see p. 225), and trying to control the fly's speed over as wide an arc as possible.

Fishing the floating line is so much easier than fishing sunk line that many anglers, exulting in the use of their rods, become fascinated by casting and stand where they are in rapt delight. Taking too much time over fishing down a pool is a common fault. And it *is* a fault. Far better to fish a stretch of water twice quickly, than once very slowly. By this I don't mean that the *fly* should be fished quickly, simply that the *angler* should keep on the move downstream between casts and not cover the same place time after time.

Particularly should you be conscious of keeping on the move when someone is following you down the pool or waiting to start. Nothing is more frustrating than fishing behind some hesitant snail who makes eight or ten casts in the same spot, before shuffling another half-pace downstream.

In case what I have written earlier, in the Introduction and elsewhere, has been forgotten, I must make it clear that your avoidance of covering lies repeatedly has nothing to do with the possibility of overfishing them. Until the rivers drop in summer, salmon are likely to be on the move. The more water you cover when you start fishing, the better your chance of getting an offer.

So, fish all the lies before any salmon they hold have run on upstream.

Later, if you know of some prime resting lies and have them to your-self, you can concentrate on them for as long as you wish. Even if they hold fish that ignore the fly, continual casting will not diminish your chances. The widely-believed falsehood that salmon tire of seeing lures pass over them has saved the lives of many fish. So long as taking lies are occupied the fish remain catchable. And if you learn nothing more from this book—remember that.

*   *   *

As you fish on down the pool have a shrewd look at each new piece of water your fly will cover and read what you can of it. Crafty mending of the upper part of the line one way or the other will enable you to guide the fly at an acceptable speed and depth through the various swirls and eddies, before you lead it across the dangle.

This leading of the fly is important. The "dangle"—that spot straight downstream of the rod, where the fly is often allowed to finish up—is a notoriously bad place for hooking a fish, but where a fish will often take. There is a better chance of hooking him securely if you fish the fly *across* that negative patch, by moving the rod round in advance (see picture sequence overpage). Having done that, always strip in a yard or two of line before you retrieve and cast again. A fish could be following the fly, but undecided. Drawing the fly away upstream may induce the fish to grab it.

293

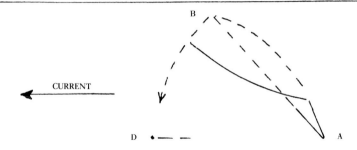

Angler at A has cast to B. The line has been mended but the rod is kept nearly at right angles to the stream to help control the speed of the fly during the early stage of its swing round in the faster water.

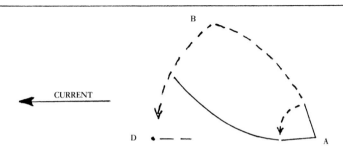

Before the fly reaches the dangle (D) straight downstream of the angler, the rod is moved round ahead of it . . .

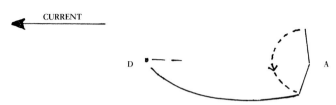

. . . and leads it across. Now, if a fish takes the fly straight down below the angler there is a better chance of hooking him securely.

"Two-Way" Fly Control

As emphasized throughout this book, it is my contention that provided the occupant has not been scared out of it, a salmon lie cannot be over-fished. A fly brought fruitlessly across a salmon in one direction may sometimes be taken when fished in the opposite direction—and except in the case of very distant lies or too strong a current, this can nearly always be done.

Even though one is unable to cross over to cast from the other bank—for reasons of single-bank fishing perhaps, or the absence of a bridge – the lie can still be covered in reverse by "Two-Way" fishing. This is a method I have devised for working a fly both ways without taking it from the water. A rather droll but very handy trick to have up one's sleeve, it has caught me salmon I would *not otherwise have hooked.*

"Two-Way" fishing is made possible by perfectly balanced tackle, accurate roll casting, and the grip of surface tension on the line. Thus, when a big upstream loop of line is thrown so that the fly hangs so to speak from the far side of a "Wheel", the line when gently drawn in will move around this wheel and bring the fly upstream against the cur-rent. (While this is happening it is, of course, necessary to continue throwing loops of line upstream to prevent the wheel's downstream drift.) There are some fascinating variations on this theme.

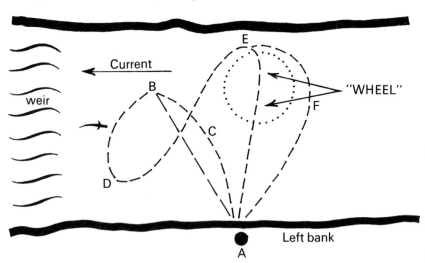

The diagram depicts a salmon in a known lie above a weir. To cover the fish in a conventional manner, the angler (A) casts to B, mending his line if necessary (C) to control its speed as it swings round past the fish to D.

At this point, however (the salmon having refused), a big loop of extra line is roll cast upstream and across to E, a position well beyond the fish. This extra line was drawn off the reel before fishing started—somewhat in the manner described on p. 267—and cast *without moving the fly* at D.

By skilful mending, drawing in line and repeatedly shooting more line further upstream (F), the angler can make the fly swing back across the lie, or hang stationary for a short time. He can also move it upstream *away* from the fish—a ploy that sometimes induces a take.

This fly movement backwards and forwards and upstream can be kept going for a considerable time if the current is not too strong. A fish may sometimes be hooked after half-an-hour or more of such "goading".

*   *   *

As you continue downstream, a shaft of bright sunlight shines from a split in the clouds as a bend in the river brings the sun directly behind you. If possible I should leave this next stretch for a while, and fish elsewhere until the earth has spun far enough for the sun to shine more obliquely across the river.

The reason I suggest this is not because the fish are looking towards the sun, and that our fly passes across its beams. Observation of salmon taking-behaviour leads me to think that the dazzling effect of sunlight, as we experience it, is nothing like the same handicap to the fish. In my opinion, the disadvantage of casting with a bright sun behind the rod, especially in late afternoon when the angle of light begins to lengthen appreciably, is that the shadow of our fly and tackle crosses the lies in advance of the fly itself.

This is worst of all when the long, red light of sunset shines straight down a pool.

Salmon are wary of shadows that move other than with the flow of the stream. Those of, say, driftwood or other flotsam, are accepted, but the shadows of humans or of rod and line, and even of the fly itself moving across the current, can frighten them. I have seen it many times.

Occasionally as you fish down a pool, particularly in low water, a fish that, presumably, was covered only a short time before, may move on the surface behind you. A good ploy is to back-up to him at once, casting as you go. Backing-up is also worthwhile when known-lies have failed to produce an offer. Like sea trout, salmon will sometimes take a lure when water that has just been fished down is fished in reverse. And the same lure, at that.

There are three possible reasons for this:

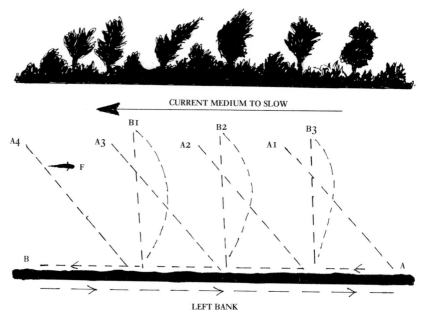

CURRENT MEDIUM TO SLOW

LEFT BANK

The object of backing-up a pool is to approach fish from *behind*. The fly makes a sudden appearance, instead of coming nearer and nearer, cast by cast, as it did when the pool was fished down.

The pool above has been fished down by an angler starting at A and casting to A1, A2 and so on to B. On his return journey, fishing back up the pool from B to A, he can if he wishes vary the fly's behaviour by casting more squarely across to B1, B2, etc., making big mends in the line by shooting extra slack.

Backing-up will quite often produce a salmon that refused the fly on its way down. As indeed will a sea trout at night, when I have found backing-up to be a very good ploy. The sudden appearance of the fly seens to *induce* a fish to take.

The practicability of backing-up depends largely on the type of ground; easy on a gravel or otherwise level bottom, but difficult and sometimes hazardous when it is rocky and uneven.

The *effectiveness* of backing-up depends on the nature of the water and position of the lies. Prior to casting, it is essential that the angler can back-up past the fish without disturbance. As for example in the diagram: backing-up from B, he must pass the fish at F before covering it by casting to B1.

1. The fly hasn't covered the fish properly on the way down.

2. Some fish may show delayed reactions.

3. Not having been watched by the fish as it approached yard by yard down-river, the sudden appearance of the fly inside the fish's territory may *induce* a take. I think the dry-fly or the nymph, fished up and across as we work our way upstream, sometimes succeeds for the same reason.

Whatever the reasons for its success, backing-up is well worth a go whenever conditions allow. One can of course *start* by backing-up a pool, although for my part I prefer to fish down first. It depends on the water. Often, the nature of the bank or the river bottom, or the close-in position of the lies, makes backing-up impracticable or imprudent.

But whatever our approach and however attractive our fly and the manner of its presentation, the take of a salmon is not always the positive suck-in-and-back-to-his-lie response resulting in a well-hooked fish.

As your fly swings across the pool, perhaps after several hours of fruitless fishing and just when your attention is wandering, you feel a sudden twitch at the rod tip. A foot or so of line is drawn out—and then goes limp. The jolt to the nervous system is electrifying.

So near to hooking a fish—and still so far away! What did you do wrong?

Nothing. So let there be no flood of self-recrimination. That fish was one of the "twitchers" described in Chapter II. There is no way you could have hooked him, for it is next to certainty that the fly was never properly inside his mouth.

But although there was nothing you could have done to hook that fish, there is certainly something you can do to help you hook one in the future. Memorize the spot. Mark it carefully with some feature on the bank. This fish is not likely to come again immediately—though by all means give him another cast or two to make sure. But you may catch him later on, if he is still in residence—or perhaps a salmon that has taken his place. For although you are still fishless, you know a spot where a fish has *offered*. You have found a lie.

Add it to the list of taking-places you already know. As you learn your beat of fishing, most of these lies will be remembered by the names you or other anglers have given them. The Ash Tree. The Fence End. The Bushes. The Rocks. The Rhododendron. The Big Stone, and so on. (All names of lies I know well.) These places you will fish with extra interest—and care. Many chances are missed because of a casual cast, bankside elephantics or clumsy wading. Yes, I know about fish being caught by dreadful casts and splashing anglers. Forget it. Always err on the side of stealth. Ultimately, good hunting will pay dividends.

When the known-lies fail you and salmon are hard to catch, try the "ridiculous". However low the water and high the temperature, fish a big lure on sunk line. If that doesn't work, try fishing a weighted size 10, 12, or 14 right down near the bottom.

If you haven't a sinking line or a weighted fly handy in your tackle-bag, pinch a split-shot on the leader a foot or so from the fly.

You haven't any split-shot, either? Well, you should have. They are listed on p. 157. A split-shot is a useful little tool. You seldom need it, but when you do it may turn an empty day into a golden occasion.

Failing that, try the fly with the "long tayl"—the $2-2\frac{1}{2}''$ summer lure that riffles in the surface film.

If all these attempts fail, it will be time to think about trying nymph or the dry-fly. A description of these methods is coming soon.

By the way, in other than very low water, whether you take a pool downstream or back it up, always fish the tail right out. An occasional salmon has a habit of lying well back in the streamy outflow. When you think you have finished fishing a pool, have three more casts—taking a pace between each. Further, having made the third cast, strip off some line, shoulder your rod and leave the fly to its own devices while you wade ashore. Over the years I have bagged quite a lot of salmon in this way.

It is true that the fish caught in these tail-ends are usually small—I can't remember ever hooking a whopper down there in the shallows—but small fish are sweet.

Talking of whoppers, it is said that the size of salmon one hooks is a matter of chance. And mostly it is. But not *always*. A few lies tend to hold bigger fish at times. Find such a lie, fish it hard and often, and sooner or later you will hit lucky. It will take a long time—or the services of a very knowledgeable gillie—to learn the water well enough for such a planned catch, but the hope is not entirely unreal.

This applies to sea trout, too. During many years of night fishing, such lies have produced me a number of double-figure fish.

Why is this so? What makes one lie more attractive than another? Why are some lies better *taking* lies than others?

I confess I don't know. Naturally, one assumes that *all* resting fish choose to lie in a steady well-oxygenated current, where they can breathe comfortably and maintain station with the minimum use of their precious energy.

But having, in periods of drought, examined a number of these good taking places where fish lie in higher water, I have found little in the way of clues. Sometimes there is a single rock, or a ledge of rock; or a cluster of small rocks or stones; sometimes a slight depression in a hard gravel bottom. More often, so far as I can judge, there is just a plain stretch of river bed, with nothing that makes one particular lie seem more congenial than any other.

Observation of *Salmo* continues to teach me how little I understand about him.

300

No one is happy to lose a fish, whatever its species. But the salmon is something special, he can project an angler into purgatory. There is something about him (and to hell with the cynic who talks of cash) that excites our deepest predatory instincts. Of all fish lost, no other inflicts so deep a wound.

A thought worthy of brief discussion.

*　　　*　　　*

Fish Lost—and Hooked

Piscator:　Oh me! he has broken all; there's half a line and a good hook lost.

Venator:　Aye, and a good trout, too.

Piscator:　Nay, the trout is not lost, for take notice, no man can lose what he never had.*

Having just bid a salmon goodbye, there are few anglers I fancy who will not accuse Piscator of sophistry. Venator, with robust commonsense, goes straight to the point. And I may as well take this opportunity of warning you—if you are not already miserably aware of it—that sooner or later you are going to lose fish. In fact, you are going to lose quite a lot of fish.

This has nothing whatever to do with faulty tackle or technique. It is simply that from time to time runs of misfortune occur that are unaccountable—except by witchcraft. They happen to most anglers in the end, like runs of bad scores happen to test cricketers. Do what you like, the fish will not stay on. It is well you should be prepared for this, so that when it comes up you can accept it philosophically. Salmon are difficult enough to hook, and such fortitude is not easily achieved. But at least, when misfortune hits you try not to take it too much to heart. Some people regard losing salmon as personality failure. They get upset about it.

Don't. You alone have not been singled out for fate's icy finger. It happens to all of us. Hell! It happened to me. There was that dreadful day just after the war, when I pricked eleven salmon in a row.

I had been away since 1940, with nothing but dreams of fishing. Now this! I could have wept.

As the terrible day went by I became quite desperate. It was like a nightmare. I tried every trick I knew. No good. Those fish just would not stay on. They came off early, they came off late; some right at the bank. Eleven of them!

* Izaak Walton, *The Compleat Angler*, 1653.

I went out the next morning full of fresh hope—and lost two more.

Not long after that I turned up on Speyside in response to an invitation. When I arrived, my host, a famous general, was playing a thirty-pounder.

"Ah, Falkus", he said, in high spirits. "Come to fish?"

"Yes, sir", I said, standing to attention. "Here I am."

"Well, hang on a minute, there's a good fellow. While I get this chap in."

"He seems a good fish", I volunteered.

"Yes", said my host. "He is. He's a big 'un."

"Has the fishing been good, sir?"

"Marvellous", he chortled. "Haven't lost a fish all week. Landed every one. This is my twenty-first."

As a matter of fact, it wasn't. It was twenty-one unlucky. As he drew it in to beach it, the hook flew out of its mouth.

"Bugger!" said the great man, succinctly. "That's the best fish I've hooked." He sat down, mopping his brow. "Funny how things go."

It was. He lost five more that afternoon.

So there you are, dear reader. Let disaster not find you mentally unprepared.*

But we mustn't end this on a note of frustration. Before a salmon can be lost he must first be hooked. And that in itself is the most exciting experience any angler can ever have. One of these days, if you keep your pecker up and fish like a hero, usually when least expected, a salmon will take your fly.

It is seldom dramatic. The take of a salmon can be as gentle as a kiss. Suddenly, you feel a little pluck and the loop of line slides out—as though the fly has touched a leaf, or been taken by a tiny trout. Indeed, you are sure it has been. Then you lift the rod and the line goes taut, and you feel the slow tug-tug of a fish. And in that blinding split-second you realize the impossible has happened; that lugging on the end of your line is *Salmo* the leaper, the Atlantic salmon, the most wonderful creature in the world.

Whether he stays with you hangs largely on chance. But that is in the future. Come what may, he has taken your fly—and nothing in the gamut of human emotion can equal the magic of that moment.

*A unique example of angling triumph and disaster, almost certainly caused by variation in taking behaviour, is Lord Home's experience on Tweed: "One morning I hooked and played for a short time 11 spring salmon and lost the lot. After luncheon I hooked 11 more and landed the lot. Salmon are strange tantalising beasts—that morning they must have been 'nipping' with devilish skill."

A restful method of fishing out a cast. The rod is held just below the point of balance and supported by the forearm.

The Hamlet *Fish*

But when presented with a fly, not every salmon is so positive. Sooner or later you will undoubtedly be faced with the problem of the *Hamlet* fish. Like Shakespeare's vacillating Prince of Denmark, this is the fish that cannot make up his mind.

You are working down a beat in the usual manner, everything quite normal, when quietly and without fuss, up comes this fish, looks at the fly—and refuses it. There is a bulge on the surface, perhaps a glint of silver, but that is all. Down he goes again.

Now, if the reason for this refusal was sudden suspicion; that on closer examination the fly turned out to be different from what the fish had thought it was (whatever that could have been) his behaviour is understandable. It is what we should expect. But a fish will sometimes continue to rise to and refuse the same fly time after time.

That the salmon should rise to such a tiny morsel as a "greased-line" fly—is surprising. But to rise and refuse, and *continue* to rise and refuse, is ludicrous. As an example, there was the salmon my friend Jimmy Skene rose on the River Thurso.

303

So far as I remember there were no exceptional features in the weather or conditions. I was fishing down one of the beats with "greased-line" when I saw a fish come at my size 8 low-water fly with a deliberate swinging rush. It made no connection. So, employing the usual tactics of remaining where I was with the same length of line out, I cast again—only to achieve the same result. It was rather uncanny. The fish seemed to behave precisely as it did before. Thereafter, no matter what pattern or size of fly I changed to, the fish continued to rise. But still it refused to take. Eventually, despite several changes of fly, I counted up to eleven rises in exactly the same place from what I firmly believe to have been the same fish. The comedy ended with the fish still in the water, myself in a mixture of exasperation and amusement.

Eccentric behaviour, one might think. Certainly inexplicable. But sometimes the *Hamlet* salmon reaches into the realms of fantasy. On the River Derwent, early one summer morning, I watched a big fish rise and nudge my fly by cradling it with his body. Curved like a crescent moon, he hung broadside to the current, dorsal fin breaking the surface, and let the fly slide slowly along his flank. I was in no doubt that he intended it to do this. His every movement was plainly visible. Having just started to fish, I was casting only a short line, and the light was at the right angle for me to see what was happening.

Standing as still as a heron, I covered that fish repeatedly. He was lying in four or five feet of water and rose on another three occasions, brushing the fly each time, before going down for good. During the day I returned to that spot and tried for him many times. But I never saw him again.

If you think that my earlier references to a salmon's sense of "playfulness" were far-fetched, how do you account for this behaviour? If the "cradling" or cossetting of that fly wasn't a form of play, what could have inspired such an extraordinary response? I know of nothing remotely similar in the repertoire of a fish's hunting behaviour.

However, this is all rather discursive. Let us shift from theory to practice. In whatever way he does so, the fish that moves to our fly but refuses, is obviously a possible taker and merits our attention.

After all, the fly has elicited a response which, even if negative, is probably more than we have had from any other salmon in the pool. So, is there a chance we might get this fish to take properly? And if so, how do we do it?

Provided the fish remains in his lie, unfrightened, there is a *chance* of catching him, certainly. But before deciding what to do, let's be clear about how good this chance is. And since eye-witness accounts of salmon behaviour are so much more valuable than anything we *think* may happen, here is a short story from Esmond Drury, who took the trouble to observe some fish while his companions covered them.

> There were thirty or forty salmon lying in this pool, which was fished first by a skilled angler. He got two of them. As far as I could see, two other fish, and only two, moved towards the fly, but thought better of it.
>
> Ten minutes later, a novice using a similar fly literally splashed his way down the pool—and took two more fish. But neither of the previous movers showed any interest. We know from experience that salmon freshly run into a pool are more likely to take than the old stagers. But even these new arrivals can be very capricious!

So there you are. That gives you some idea of what we can be up against. And knowing what we do about this fish, it comes as no surprise. The salmon is unpredictable, and even a fish that has moved to a fly may henceforth ignore it.

All the same, however negative the fish, if we are to give ourselves any chance of success we must at least have a go. And in the case of the *Hamlet* fish there are various options open to us.

What I usually do myself is to stay exactly where I am and try for him again straightaway.

Without altering the length of line I make another cast or two with the same fly. If that fails, I retreat a few yards and fish down again with the same fly—but this time getting it to work in a different way. To achieve this, I strip off some line, cast more squarely across the current, make a big mend, and then another—shooting extra line each time (as described on p. 267) to encourage the fly to sink—after which as the line swings round I strip in a yard or two; so that, when the fly covers the fish it is swimming like a rising nymph towards the surface. I have had occasional success with this little ploy which, I think, *induces* the fish to take.

> *Note.* If we decide to spend some time on this fish and are prepared to make some tackle adjustments, there is a better way of fishing a "rising nymph". We shall return to this theme shortly.

If the fish makes no response I retreat once more and try another fly. And it is now that the ability to make an adroit change of flies when standing deep in the river is so useful. This is made easier if we have some reserve flies sticking ready in the fly-pad, and our scissors slung as suggested.

First I try a big fly: size 4 or 2. If this is refused I try a smaller fly—say, size 10, 12 or 14.

If this fails, I usually give the fish best and carry on down the pool. This decision depends on circumstances. If there are very few salmon about and offers are scarce I will concentrate on that particular fish for half-an-hour or so, perhaps much longer. But if I know there are fresh fish in the water, and prospects seem good, I will give this chap just a couple of casts and leave him. Remember, he can always be tried again later on, after the rest of the available water has been covered.

Whether on our return to such a lie the fish is still there, is another matter. The chance of his remaining for long in that lie depends largely on the water conditions and time of year. If the river is in good ply and a run of fish is coming up, he may well have moved on upstream. On the other hand, if he has taken up residence or is unable to run further for lack of water, there is certainly a possibility of catching him later.

Edward Hamilton, in *Recollections of Fly-Fishing for Salmon, Trout and Grayling*, 1891, records a classic example of this. Apart from its successful ending, the incident is strangely similar to Jimmy Skene's experience on the Thurso.

> I once on the Spean, at the tail of Fern-a-mór, rose a large salmon eleven times without his touching the fly, and he then left off—no other fly would tempt him. "We'll try him again in the evening when we come down", and sure enough at the first cast, a few yards above his morning position, on our return about six p.m., up he came, and I had him, and after an exciting contest of more than an hour, and a terrific run through some rapids, I landed him in the pool below: $23\frac{1}{2}$ lb. He fought a game battle, and when he gave up it was at the further side of Mac-Kintyre's Pool, and I had to bring the monster across on his side almost a dead weight.

In a clearwater river, I have caught *Hamlet* salmon *several days* after they first showed interest in a lure. That these were indeed the same fish is in no doubt, for they could be easily observed and, by their markings, recognized.

I have also caught *Hamlet* fish by crossing the river and covering their lies from the other bank. Apart from differences of light—which at the times referred to seemed unimportant—why salmon should refuse a fly that is moving one way, but accept it when it is moving in the opposite direction, I don't know. But sometimes they do. As sometimes do salmon that have shown *no* prior interest at all. And I urge you to remember that, provided you are entitled to do so, *to fish a pool from both banks is always well worthwhile*. It is surprising how often this results in a salmon.

To conclude. Over the years I have hooked *Hamlet* fish with each of the ploys suggested above. But in my view the best chance of success is to offer them A. H. Chaytor's "absurdly small fly". The offer of a bigger fly than the one the fish refused will work occasionally, but experience indicates that the odds are two to one in favour of something much smaller.

The odds are even better if this tiny fly is designed to fish like a nymph, and presented accordingly. This, however, is a fascinating angling method in its own right, and it shall have a little section to itself.

* * *

The Dee Special Nymph

If our change to a smaller fly presented at the usual depth of a few inches fails to entice a *Hamlet* fish, it is worth trying a small *quick-sinking* fly fished deep. This is a ploy that sometimes takes the pot when all seems hopeless. So, always to have something of this sort handy makes good sense, for on it may hang the hooking of a salmon.

The fly can be dressed either on a short brass tube $\frac{1}{4}''$–$\frac{1}{2}''$ in length, or direct on a weighted treble-hook (see Dee Special Nymphs, plate 8), and my advice is to carry several of these flies in sizes 10–14, or on the $\frac{1}{4}''$ to $\frac{1}{2}''$ tubes, if you prefer them.

When sunk deep and fished with a nymph-like action—a technique familiar to most trout anglers—this little fly seems to *induce* salmon to have a go, and although my experience of using it is not great it has caught me a number of fish I would not otherwise have hooked. It has done so, moreover, in difficult conditions of high summer, with the river low and fish lying doggo in the pools.

I claim no credit for this method. L. R. N. Gray put me on to it thirty years back when he still lived in Devon. He referred to it in his book *Torridge Fishery*:

For several years past I have had much better results with salmon just before dusk on summer evenings by fishing for them, exactly as if they were large trout, with weighted nymphs. Sawyer's Pheasant Tail and Ivens' Green Nymph, tied on sea-trout hooks, have been successful instead of normal salmon and sea-trout flies fished down and across in the ordinary way. When our salmon have been trapped in a long, slow pool by several weeks of summer drought, they become hard to approach unless the surface is rippled, and unless you want to descend to a minnow on monofilament line, cast up and across and spun down, an upstream nymph is sometimes the only chance.

You may of course prefer flies tied as Gray suggests. But what success I have had has been on tiny black flies such as my Dee Special, mostly in the evening—as Gray did—but occasionally during the day as well.

Fished on a single-handed rod with an 8 lb leader, it is a delicate and delightful method. And of course we don't have to wait for a vacillating *Hamlet* fish before trying it. Its purpose is to provoke a reaction from an otherwise disinterested salmon. And I think that one reason why sometimes it does so is because it makes a sudden appearance, by dropping down inside the salmon's territory, or very close by; it doesn't approach gradually from many yards upstream.

As fine a floating line as our rod will cast should be used, and the last few yards well greased to keep them from dipping under. This allows the line-tip to act as a sort of indicator or float. Also greased is the first foot or two of the leader; its ungreased length being just shorter than the depth of water where fish are lying.

As usual, a close knowledge of the pool's underwater contours and the main salmon lies, gained either from the gillie or your own experience, is of the greatest service. It is important to know exactly where fish are lying and in what depth of water.

So that you may throw as short a line as possible, wade with great stealth to a spot slightly downstream of the fish. Then, cast the fly at an angle across and upstream of the lies. This angle, like the position you are casting from, depending on the strength of current.

Allow the fly to sink until you reckon it has almost reached the bottom—watching the line-tip very carefully, for a fish may take the fly as it sinks. Then draw in line with the non-casting hand and start the fly on its upward path as it comes downstream over the fish. This action can be varied cast by cast. Sometimes the fly should be fished with little jerks, by movement of the rod. Sometimes with a sink-and-draw action. Sometimes bring it straight up towards the surface with one continuous draw.

Hold the rod point low with the line running straight from reel to leader. Watch the line-tip intently and raise the rod the moment it slides away. With the tiny trebles in use, this raising of the rod is all that is needed to hook a fish.

Sometimes, when the angle of the light permits, you may see a gleam of white as the fly is taken. If you do, tighten instantly. The time lapse between seeing this signal and raising the rod—caused by the comparative slowness of our reaction is usually just right for hooking a fish. But you don't see it often. When you do it will probably be from a fish lying opposite you, although I have seen a fish turn from upstream and follow the fly for several yards, seemingly taking it, and then blowing it out. At any rate, I failed to hook him.

Absolute concentration is essential. Let nothing, but *nothing* distract you. So gentle is the take sometimes that it is almost imperceptible. You may feel only the slightest touch, or see but a twitch of the line-tip. If on raising the rod you find you have missed the fish, try tightening by drawing line back smartly with the non-casting hand as the rod is raised. But be careful. Most of my fish have been only small salmon and grilse, but you never know when you might hit a big chap, and it is so easy to break on a salmon when striking in this way—especially if the big double-handed rod is in use, as it probably will be if you are casting to a *Hamlet* fish.

For low water fishing a ten-foot or ten-foot-six single-hander is the best tool for the job.

A weighted fly tends to land in the water with a bit of a plop. But this is not a bad thing. It can produce the effect of "overhead fishing" suggested on p. 58 and results in a "crunch" take. On the rare occasions when this happens, a fish grabs the fly almost as it hits the water. There is surely nothing in the sport of angling more dramatic.

Wherever we may be fishing, if this method fails to hook a fish it is sensible to try a floating lure. After all, nothing could be easier. The single-handed rod we are using is ideal and, apart from a change of lure, our tackle is set up ready for fishing dry. A method we shall deal with next.

Dry-Fly Fishing

I must straightaway confess that my experience of catching salmon on the dry-fly has been very limited. From what I gleaned from the books years ago it was a method that worked well enough on the other side of the Atlantic, but not in Britain. Several of the top American anglers had written about it, notably the famous G. M. L. La Branche and E. R. Hewitt, and La Branche had even come over to fish it in British rivers, but without success. And indeed right up to the present time, apart from a few articles in the sporting press, there is little in the literature to guide an angler wishing to fish dry for salmon in British waters.

Many of my acquaintances had tried it from time to time, but like me without much luck. It was something that one might fish very occasionally in the summer when the water was low and salmon showed no interest in conventional flies.

It is true that now and then one of my friends would report an unexpected success when fishing dry-fly for trout, mainly on southern chalk streams; the flies taken being mayfly and sedge. And, as related in Chapter I, I had read of salmon being caught on the dry-fly in Ireland when the mayfly hatch happened to coincide with the end of the spring salmon run. But all this was regarded as being exceptional. And it is, I think, largely because such fish were considered rarities that, like myself, few anglers had persisted with this method. Even when conditions might have been propitious for fishing dry, anglers preferred to catch their salmon in an easier and more orthodox way.

Over the years, inspired by the American writers, I caught a few fish, mostly grilse, on greased, fuzzy, American-type lures when fishing small Highland rivers; in particular the Avon—chief tributary of the Spey. This beautiful, fast-flowing little river, with its crystal-clear water, has enabled me to observe much salmon behaviour. Of all rivers I have ever known, the Avon in low-water is the most suitable and exciting for fishing the upstream worm (see Chapter XV), but it is also the river that provided most of my modest success with the dry-fly.

My favourite spot was a small, fairly fast-flowing pool, deep but clear, in which I could follow nearly every movement of the salmon. This was made possible by a convenient ledge of rock on the deep side of the pool shaped rather like a shallow grouse butt. With trees and bushes behind, I could creep up into this "butt" without disturbing the fish, and see what was happening from the ring-side.

First I tried throwing the fly upstream and letting it drift down. But

as this met with no success, I followed the advice of that long-ago Cromwellian writer Richard Franck, and "dibbled" the fuzzy-wuzzy "but
lightly on the surface", using the breeze and the length of my rod to
hold it in position. This was more encouraging. Even so, although fish
would *rise* to the fly presented in this way, they seldom took it. So,
eventually I tried fishing it *across* the surface on a dropper, with a small
conventional low-water salmon fly trailing astern and a couple of inches
or so underneath.

This approach I soon found worked best when the flies were cast
squarely across the pool, or only slightly upstream, and brought straight
back towards me, so that the tail fly remained just underwater and the
fuzzy-wuzzy dropper skidded across the top leaving a little wake.
Reminiscent of my sea-trout Surface Lure fished at night, it was the wake
rather than the fly itself, it seemed to me, that attracted the fish. Anyway,
although more fish took the tail fly than the dropper, I did catch a few
on the surface—and felt I had done well enough.

All right. You may complain that this is not dry-fly fishing. And strictly speaking I suppose it isn't. But I am not arguing the point. The
definition of salmon "fly" fishing was dealt with on p. 100. So far as
I am concerned, the method described is "fishing dry"—and we will
leave it at that.

I must admit that although this style of fishing was fascinating and
very exciting—since in that clear water one could see it all happening—I
didn't use it a lot. It was a bit of fun; a method to try when all else
failed—which, what with all the fish there were about and the delights
of fishing upstream worm, wasn't often. Then again, for every take I
got on the fuzzy-wuzzy there would be many rises. And in those far-off
days, fearful of overfishing the lies, I would leave the water and move
on, thinking that the fish would be disturbed if I went on and on casting.
Some years were still to elapse before I realized the impossibility of over-
fishing a lie, and the need to persist. Looking back and remembering
the great number of salmon lying in the rivers of that time, I feel certain
that had I known then what I have since discovered, results might have
been very different.

Then again, there was this business of the fly itself. Following the
lead of those American masters, large fuzzy-wuzzies were the sort of
flies I used. And, like a few other anglers who persisted with similar
flies, I enjoyed some small success with them. But only on certain rivers,
and very occasionally at that. And it never occurred to me to take salmon
dry-fly fishing very seriously until I made the acquaintance of that fine

all-round sportsman Derek Knowles. He, far more than anyone I had ever met, was enjoying regular success with the dry-fly—or, to be more precise, with a special fly of his own invention: the "Yellow Dolly".

Hitherto, like fishing dry-fly for sea trout, which I had found worked well enough on some rivers but little or not at all on others, my varied success with salmon on the different rivers I fished did not surprise me. Migratory fishes return chiefly to the rivers of their birth, and so almost certainly follow slightly separate lines of evolution. On different waters I expected them to display some difference in characteristics. And perhaps they do. But their differing reaction to the type of fly I offered them seems to me now to have been due more to my jellied thinking than lack of potential response on the part of the fish!

As the owner of a large and remote sporting estate in the northern Highlands, which includes an excellent beat of salmon fishing, Derek Knowles has had splendid opportunities for experimenting with dry-fly. And as the remainder of this chapter illustrates, he has done so very successfully. Now, having fished with him and put his methods into practice I am alive to various points not previously considered. For one thing, notwithstanding their occasional success, it seems clear to me that the fuzzy-wuzzy flies I was using were altogether too big and coarse. Derek ties his Yellow Dolly in several sizes, but catches most of his fish on one no bigger than three-eighths of an inch, with a size 18 treble hook!

But enough of the third person. To describe the Yellow Dolly there is no one better than the inventor himself. In some letters to me, Derek has written a very clear outline of his methods. And here it is.

Fishing the greased Yellow Dolly

The fly is the unique part of the method, and named *Yellow Dolly* because it looks like a little doll. It is tied on a thin red tube from $\frac{1}{4}''$ to $\frac{5}{8}''$ long and dressed with a skirt of stiff yellow hair, tied in at the tail over a collar of thread, which flares the hair outwards like a ballerina's skirt. The same is done at the head of the tube with stiff black hair, using half or a third the amount of hair used in the skirt. The fly is trimmed as shown in the drawing on page 320.

The overall size of the fly varies from $\frac{3}{8}''$ to $\frac{3}{4}''$ in length. A smaller fly can be dressed on a tiny piece of tube, just a skirt of yellow hair $\frac{1}{4}''$ long, and fished with a size 20 treble.

I use a 9′ rod and a W.F.7 white floating line, with 10′–12′ of 6 lb–8 lb b.s. nylon. The object is to keep the fly on the surface, even in broken water, so the last 6′ of line, the leader, the fly and the treble are all greased.

My favourite time for fishing the greased Yellow Dolly is when a spate has run off and the conventional salmon fly is only catching the odd fish. On my river, this means 6″ or less on the gauge. With a rising glass and a good breeze, conditions are perfect.

I fish in the same manner as with dry fly for brown trout, casting mainly upstream. But, being an idle fisherman, the wind is the main dictator of which way I fish any particular lie. Although I catch a lot of fish by casting upstream, I like to fish downstream as well.

I fish a long line, casting across and down, and make the fly come along the top of the water across the flow. It is very similar to a miniature version of your Surface Lure for sea trout. I try a $\frac{3}{4}$″ Yellow Dolly first. Usually, this either moves the fish to show an interest or frightens him out of his lie, in which case he often throws himself out of the water some 20 yards down the pool. If this happens I leave him and try for him again on my way back up the river.

Fishing both downstream and upstream gives a lot more fishing. When fishing upstream I cast and recover the line quickly to keep pace with the current, casting further upstream with each cast, but never false casting.

Fishing upstream in rough water, there is always drag on a fly no matter how carefully you fish it. I think that a movement of the fly contrary to the flow indicates to the salmon that it's a living creature and not a leaf or piece of general debris. I called at Pitlochry once to watch the flow of water through the viewing chamber and was amazed at the amount of debris in what one would have said was clean water. Watching this debris swirling around in the water, it became obvious to me that a loose fly swirling with it would never be taken by a fish. But attach that fly to a length of nylon, and its movement is retarded. No matter how you mend or slip the line, the fly behaves differently from the surrounding matter, and thereby seems to be alive. This, I think, is the key to the successful fishing of the Yellow Dolly (or any other lure for that matter).

When the little fly, twitching on top of the water, suddenly appears over the salmon's lie, the fish may come up and try to drown it by flopping his chin on it, or follows it and *then* tries to drown it, or else swirls short of it. Very seldom does he take it first time, and until he does you can watch a marvellous display of his behaviour. If he hasn't seen you when he first came to the surface you have a 90%

chance of catching him. I try him three times with the same fly. If I haven't hooked him by then, I stop fishing, change to a smaller fly, grease it and start again. Very often he takes it at once and I have him with the first cast.

With odd fish you occasionally need to go down even smaller; sometimes, larger—but that's generally when fishing downstream. I vividly remember one fish, noted in the game book, which I moved with a Yellow Dolly in the run-in to the Rock Pool (where you, too, have caught fish). I had stalked the lie and was crouching down in a gully slightly upstream and only about seven yards from the fish. He came up the first time the fly covered him—at 11.30 in the morning. I kept on changing flies, and the fish rose to the fly first cast every time a different fly was put on. I went up and down in size. The fish came up and looked at the fly, and sometimes turned and followed it. But he wouldn't take. No matter what I did, that fish would not open his mouth.

At 1.30, after I had crouched in that little rocky gully for *two hours*, I gave him best. He was still rising. But I was suffering agonies from cramp. I stood up, wished him "good-day", and left him in peace.

Anyone who thinks I have exaggerated the unlikelihood of over-fishing a salmon lie, and the time spent covering that fish mentioned in the Introduction, may care to digest Derek's account of two hours' casting to that still-responsive *Hamlet* fish in his "Rock" pool—a lie I know well and have fished with Derek (see pictures opposite). Who knows whether this salmon might have taken if he had been covered for yet another hour or so?

But, as Derek describes in the following anecdote, such extreme persistence is not often necessary:

I'll tell you an amusing little story. I was staying in Caithness a few years ago for the grouse shooting. The hill was as dry as a bone and we had been shooting for about a fortnight. As the dogs were very weary we decided to have a day off from the shooting and I was given the chance to stalk a sika, or go fishing. It was too warm and midgey to go into the woodlands, stalking, so I decided to potter off to the little spate river and catch a few trout to smoke for supper.

The river was very low, but there was a good upstream wind. I started at the tail of the nearest pool, fishing up with a dry fly. Having caught a few trout, I was half-way up the pool when I saw a salmon show in the head. I kept on fishing my way upstream and caught

Derek Knowles fishing the Rock Pool lie mentioned in the text. It was here that for two hours a salmon continued to rise to a greased Yellow Dolly—but refused to take.

Experimenting recently, the author caught a salmon in this pool on a two-inch sunk fly within minutes of Derek catching one on a three-eighths-inch dry fly. A neat example of how salmon continue to turn so much of our angling theory into nonsense.

another trout. As I was taking it off the hook the salmon rose again. I decided I'd try for him. So, I put on a little $\frac{3}{8}''$ Yellow Dolly with a size 18 treble, and greased everything again. Then I stalked the fish. He came up twice, and I hooked him on the second rise.

"Jolly good", I said to myself. "I'll try the next pool, too." Which I did, and got another salmon—again, right in the head of the pool. To cut a long story, I tried seven pools, and caught five salmon. They were all in the streamy water feeding the pools, where the wind was cockling the surface against the flow of the current.

My hostess, when presented with the fish, was so astounded at what had been caught in one afternoon in her little river that she promptly telephoned her factor. In a very serious voice, she summoned him to "come at once and see what Mr Knowles has done!"

He dropped everything and leaped into his car with terrible thoughts going through his mind, the first being that I had put a bullet through the drawing-room window while stalking sika. Arriving at great speed, he dashed into the lodge—to be met by a little smiling lady and a great silver tray bearing five salmon . . .

To finish, I must say that my favourite size of fly is a $\frac{3}{8}''$ YD with a size 18 treble and 6 lb leader (for beginners I advise 8 lb). The heaviest fish I've had on this tackle is $15\frac{1}{2}$ lb—and I recommend changing the leader after every fish.

*　　　*　　　*

When used at the same time in the same water, how does the greased Yellow Dolly compare with the conventional small salmon fly fished wet? Here in another letter, Derek describes what can be done on his water when fishing dry in suitable conditions:

Yesterday (7th August) we got our first spate since the middle of May. I caught four fish on conventional $1''$ tubes fished wet. Tomorrow, Monday, if it stays fine, I shall be fishing the greased dry-fly . . .

Monday was a fine day, and for your benefit I decided to fish conventional flies in the morning, going down the river, and a greased Yellow Dolly coming back upstream in the afternoon. My companion was a school-girl who had never before hooked a salmon and longed to catch one. During the morning she moved one fish. I caught one. And then in the Rock Pool (which you will remember well), the last pool we fished before lunch, I moved another.

316

In the afternoon, starting back upstream in the same pool but this time using a $\frac{3}{4}''$ Yellow Dolly, greased, I hooked and landed a fish the first time that particular lie was covered.

The next fish I cast to also took the Yellow Dolly first time over— but came off. Then, when I was casting directly upstream, a fish rose to the fly as it floated down with the current. Next cast he rose again. On the third cast, he took it. I lifted the rod—but he'd gone!

I inspected the fly and found that a point of the treble was stuck in the tube! However, in the head of the pool a fish rose to the fly and took it first time over.

So—already I had caught two fish, from the pool in which I had moved one with the wet-fly on the way downstream.

The next pool was where the girl had moved her fish that morning. We both fished it down, but did nothing.

The next stretch of holding water (which we fished together you may remember) is that very long pool with a lot of bends. I changed down to a $\frac{3}{8}''$ Yellow Dolly, with a size 18 treble.

The girl fished the lower half of the pool, which can be covered easily right-handed. I who, as you know, am left-handed, took the top half which, when fished upstream, is an easier cast from the left shoulder. Twice a fish rose to my fly. On the third cast he took it, and I landed him.

I tried the next bend, where the wind was catching the water, and was taken at the second attempt. A fine $12\frac{1}{2}$ lb cock fish, which I was lucky to land—since he had half-straightened one of the points of the size 18 treble!

While changing my leader and treble, and greasing everything again, a fish showed. I shouted to the girl (who was also fishing a Yellow Dolly) to come and try for him.

We stalked in as near as we dared and waited for a cloud to shade the sun. Then she cast for him. Three times he rose to her fly, coming up with a closed mouth and "chinning" it each time. Then, fourth time over, he took—and she was into her first salmon, which was duly landed!

Well—after she'd calmed down and spent some time admiring the fish, I said that just before we went home I'd try a cast across the wind to a lie under the far bank. As we crawled into position the sun came out again. "Never mind", I thought. "I'll give him a throw." So I cast, and straightaway a fish rose at the fly. It was marvellous to watch. I continued to cast, and time after time the fish came up and put his nose on the fly—chinning it! With the angle of light we could see it all happening. Eight times the fish rose and nudged the fly! And then, the ninth time he came up he opened his mouth, took the fly and turned with it like a big trout . . .

We finished with seven salmon for the day. One caught on a conventional fly, fished wet; six on the greased Yellow Dolly.

P.S. The young girl who caught her first salmon on the Yellow Dolly was so impressed that she tied a fly for herself, went down the river, caught two salmon and tailed them both by hand!

Derek Knowles and the author fishing the greased Yellow Dolly on a Sutherland river. Here, Derek has just cast to a known lie. A few seconds later, the fish has risen and sucked in the fly. As he turns and goes down with it the rod is raised, and the fish is firmly hooked.

Nearly ready to land, the fish wal-
lows on the surface.

Having been brought in on his side to a gently shelving piece of bank, the fish is tailed
out by hand.

Two points of the tiny treble are embedded in the gristle of the "scissors". Despite the size of hook, there is no way that such a hold can ever work loose. In this instance the fish, although a male, was returned, neither angler wishing to keep red fish. Having been held head to current for a few minutes to recover his strength, the fish swam off—seemingly none the worse for his adventure.

YELLOW DOLLY—TYING INSTRUCTIONS

Overall Sizes: $\frac{3}{4}''$ $\frac{1}{2}''$ $\frac{3}{8}''$

The hairs must be stiff so that the finished fly sits on top of the water, *not* in the surface film.

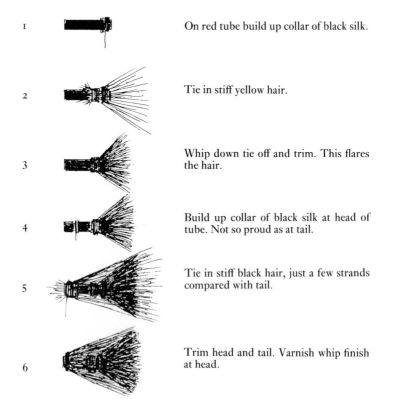

1   On red tube build up collar of black silk.

2   Tie in stiff yellow hair.

3   Whip down tie off and trim. This flares the hair.

4   Build up collar of black silk at head of tube. Not so proud as at tail.

5   Tie in stiff black hair, just a few strands compared with tail.

6   Trim head and tail. Varnish whip finish at head.

320

In a further letter, Derek compared some recent catches:

Here is a quick breakdown of 120 consecutive salmon I've caught in my river:

64 on greased Yellow Dolly, 3 on greased Yellow Badger, 1 on size 12 trout Dry Fly, 27 on 1″ Brass Tube, 10 on 2″ Brass Tube, 7 on $\frac{1}{2}$–$\frac{3}{4}$″ Aluminium Tube, 5 on Yellow Dolly fished wet, 2 on size 8 low-water Blue Charm and 1 on $1\frac{1}{2}$″ Aluminium Tube.

You will see that the greased surface-fly caught 68 fish (57%) compared with 43% on the wet fly. This is not a total of fish caught, I haven't got my fishing diaries with me, but it does give a comparison of the success of different methods, which varies from year to year. 1977, with its small spates and low water, suited the tantalising action of the greased Yellow Dolly and was a good year for it, but not for ordinary low water salmon flies. I never use these now, with the exception of a low water Blue Charm, which I switch to when an interested fish will not take the little Yellow Dolly.

My friends and guests fishing their conventional flies give me an indication of success rates. 1981 was not a good year for Greased Yellow Dolly—too much water, whenever I was on the river.

The earliest I've caught salmon on a greased fly is the 23rd May, and the latest, 30th September. I've used it successfully on the Helmsdale, the North Tyne, the Cumbrian Derwent and rivers in Caithness, Sutherland and Connemara.

Like Derek I have found the greased Yellow Dolly to be successful on a number of rivers, particularly in low water. Recently on a Scottish tour in drought conditions, a companion and I caught fish after fish on tiny Dollies fished dry on trout tackle, after our wet flies, however small, had been consistently refused.

> *Note.* When fishing dry it is essential that the fly sits right up on top of the surface film. Apropos of which I have found a Muddler dressing very satisfactory. The clipped deer-hair head greatly improves the lure's floatability. (See Muddler Dolly, plate 9).

Finally, a word about hooking procedure. When a fish rises, *do nothing until the line moves.* Then simply lift the rod. But do so gently, to avoid any chance of a smash on 8 or 6 lb nylon. The tiny treble sets itself very easily. This is usually in the gristle at the side of the mouth, and there is no need to pull it in.

The Dolly completes our chapter on floating-line techniques. Since river fly fishing can be given no further space, we will press on and consider the use of bait.

All minnow spinning for salmon, whether in lake or river, is in my experience very much a matter of locality. That is to say, in other words, that it is only in certain rivers and lakes in which the spinning bait can be used with any probability of success . . . for example, on the Awe and Lochy, two of the most celebrated salmon rivers of Scotland, it is of no earthly use, and the minnow spinner might, for all practical purposes, as well fling his hat in.

H. Cholmondeley-Pennell, *Fishing*, 1887

XIV
Bait Fishing

PART ONE: THE SPINNER

Spinning Historical

It is possible that, if not a spinner, some sort of *wobbling* lure was in use over eleven-hundred years ago. In *The Angler's England*, 1938, Patrick Chalmers tells the story of Lodbruc, a sporting Danish nobleman who after sea fishing in an easterly gale finished up on the Norfolk coast. There, it seems, he fell in with Edmund, King of East Anglia, who was planning the capture of a huge pike reputedly lying off an island in "Hyckelyngge" Broad. To Edmund's delight, Lodbruc had the monster out at once on a bait of his own contrivance: "a trowling lure of bryte shel".

We know no more about Lodbruc's lure, but its description has a ring of truth. It indicates that the modern Scandinavian pirk fished with a sink-and-draw action may be nothing new.

"Trowling", or "trolling" as it came to be spelt, is obviously ages old. Until little more than a hundred years ago it meant the technique known today as sink-and-draw. "Trolling" as applied to dragging a bait about behind a boat is incorrect. What we mean by "trolling" is really "trailing". John Bickerdyke defines it in *The Book of the All Round Angler*, 1888:

> Spinning baits are either cast out some distance, and drawn back through the water to the angler, or are trailed at the back of a boat. This trailing is often called trolling in Scotland and Ireland, a mis-nomer which has doubtless caused some little confusion in the minds of anglers. Trolling proper is the use of a dead-bait which does not spin, and is worked with a sink-and-draw motion in the water.

323

Quite how this change came about—how trowling, or trolling came to mean trailing—is a mystery. But of course there are many parallels in the language. Over the centuries some words have acquired entirely different meanings: "presently" is an example. As with these words, the proper meaning of trolling has been changed for so long that to plead for its proper use seems pointless, and I mention all this merely in passing. None of it will help you in your quest for fish. I just thought you might be interested.

With regard to a bait that revolved rather than wobbled, it was Thomas Barker, in *The Art of Angling*, 1651, who described a new method of trowling with a minnow. Having given instructions for baiting the hook, Barker recommended that a swivel should be fixed to the line. So far as I know, this is the first intimation of spinning in English literature.

After this, the others got on to it. There is nothing equivocal about its meaning in the fifth edition of Izaak Walton's *The Compleat Angler*, 1676:

> ... and then you are to know, that your minnow must be so put on your hook, that it must run when 'tis drawn against the stream, and that it must turn nimbly ... the minnow shall be almost straight on your hook, this done, try how it will turn by drawing it cross the water or against a stream; and if it do not turn nimbly, then turn the tail a little to the right or left hand, and try again, till it turn quick; for if not, you are in danger to catch nothing; for know, that it is impossible that it should turn too quick.

As we shall see, this was very sound advice, which could be heeded with advantage by many a salmon angler today.

There is, incidentally, a mention of spinning in Izaak's first edition, but not as clear as this.

In his fifth edition of *The Experienc'd Angler*, 1683, Robert Venables had this to say:

> You must have a swivel or turn, placed about a yard or more above your hook; you need no lead on the line, you must continually draw your bait up the stream near to the top of the water.

More good advice for the modern salmon angler. Always keep the weight as light as possible when spinning—except in the very cold water of early spring.

There is no doubt that what these seventeenth-century anglers were

324

up to was *spinning* a bait. Whether they were also "trowling" it—i.e. fishing it sink-and-draw—is of no consequence. In whatever way the bait was fished, it revolved; it *spun*.

When, where and by whom the first salmon was caught on a spinner is not on record, but it must have been a long time ago. Although Barker's reference to spinning with a minnow was specifically for trout, sooner or later someone must have hooked a salmon, by accident if not design.

Spinning increased in popularity during the second half of the last century aided by improved centre-pin Nottingham type spinning reels, multipliers, P. D. Malloch's famous sidecaster, and finally the fixed-spool reel which, for the first time, made light-bait spinning possible. Credit for this reel is usually given to Yorkshire mill-owner Alfred Holden Illingworth, said to have invented it in 1905. But although responsible for its development, he was in fact second to John Ray of Belfast who had already produced a fixed-spool reel c. 1890.

So long as spinning lines were made of plaited silk, the fixed-spool was never widely used. Customs changed dramatically however, when nylon monofilament became available at a low price in the late nineteen forties.

Famous Welsh all-round angler Moc Morgan with a small August salmon taken on a quill minnow—good bait for salmon in summer, on the River Teifi.

Today's tackle has come a long way from Lodbruc's lure of bryte shel. It would astound even those inventive salmon anglers of a century ago. But about the psychology of *Salmo* himself, we are no wiser.

*　　　*　　　*

The Bait

It is likely that a salmon can be caught on any object he can suck into his mouth. Tie a hook to a pencil-sharpener, fish it across the stream and sooner or later a salmon will undoubtedly grab it. Among other drolleries I know to have caught salmon are bits of rubber and plastic tubing, bacon rind, raw carrot, orange peel, melon skin, swivels and strips of red handkerchief. So—if we accept the miracle that the salmon ever takes anything at all—our ability to catch him by dragging fish-like pieces of coloured plastic, tin or wood through the water is not surprising. Although one suspects that the tackle-maker's more bizarre creations are designed primarily to catch anglers, they will nonetheless on occasion all catch salmon.

Some, however, are more successful than others.

The popularity of individual baits tends to ebb and flow. A new design catches fish and receives publicity. For a while everyone is using it, so naturally it catches more than any other—until something new crops up, or one of yesterday's baits is re-discovered. Then off we go again.

The spinning bait I was brought up on was the natural sprat. We fished this almost exclusively and so, of course, it caught me most of my salmon. When casting from the bank, to protect it from getting knocked about, we fished it in a transparent "scarab" jacket. These jackets were made in six sizes to accommodate baits from $1\frac{1}{2}$ in. to $4\frac{1}{2}$ in., and very successful they were. But from a boat, when the bait was payed out and trailed astern, we didn't bother with the jacket.

There were other "naturals", too: loach and eel-tail, for instance. But sprat was the most popular. Usually, it was the *golden* sprat, which nearly always seemed more effective than the natural, undyed silver sprat. I don't know why.

After the war the brown-and-gold wooden Devon came along and swept the market. This had no special alchemy, but was much more robust and convenient to use than the natural bait—and seemed to catch as many fish.

Nowadays, although the golden sprat retains its popularity—notably on Loch Lomond and the middle and lower Tweed beats—there is no

In classic style, Arthur Oglesby lands a 16 lb Lune springer hooked on a 2″ plastic Black and Gold Devon.

need to fiddle about mounting natural baits. The tackle trade has produced a huge range of artificials to choose from. Faced with such a choice, the beginner may well feel somewhat bemused. He needn't. In addition to the golden sprat (which, if he cares to use it, will always serve him well), the following baits should catch him his share of fish.

1. *The Metal Devon Minnow*

Since the introduction of this bait during the latter part of the last century, the total production of its various types must have far exceeded any other spinning bait. In spite of changing fashions, from what tackle dealers tell me, it seems as popular today as ever. It comes in sizes varying from less than an inch to nearly four inches, and in almost every colour or combination of colours. Had I to fish with one only of these, I would choose a black-and-gold which, over the years has proved a steady killer. But many anglers prefer a blue-and-silver during the spring in clear, cold water—and a brown-and-gold in warmer water, especially when the river is coloured.

Do these colour changes really make any difference? One is tempted to think not. And yet it is silly to ignore experience. Three of my friends, all expert anglers, arrived on the River Exe for a couple of days' fishing in early spring. Although during the previous two days a number of salmon had been killed exclusively on blue-and-silver Devons, they caught ten fish with brown-and-gold Devons—after trying the blue-and-silver without success.

Make of that what you will. I suggest that, as with fly-fishing, if one lure fails try another. Provided it doesn't become a fetish, nothing is lost by changing baits.

2. *The Wooden or Plastic Devon*

Of all baits fished today, this is probably the most common, certainly on the big rivers. Like the metal Devon it is made in a range of colours. Black-and-gold, or brown-and-gold are undoubtedly the most widely used. I prefer this bait to the metal Devon, since it tends to swim better in slackish water, whereas the former, although good in a stream, is liable to sag tail-down at low speeds.

3. *The Yellow Belly*

This successful bait was introduced during the early nineteen fifties. It has proved its worth during early spring, and some anglers never use anything else. In the original wooden version, the spinning fins were made from one piece of metal which passed right through the bait ensuring a durability absent from some of the modern imitations.

4. *The Toby Spoon*

This is the best fish attractor I have ever used—and the worst hooker! It can be improved by preventing the treble-hook from wobbling about,

Twenty-nine pound Dee Springer, caught on a Yellow-Belly by Armin Sieger of Herrliberg, Switzerland, March 1983.

either by stiffening the link with tape, or by removing the treble and split-ring from the spoon and using a flying mount. (See p. 422.)

This new mount is made of alasticum wire and held to the tail of the spoon by a few turns of thread or a twist of fuse wire. When a salmon takes, this hold breaks and the spoon itself hangs clear of the fish's mouth.

Although re-fastening the mount is fiddling on the river bank after getting hung up, this is a small discipline compared with the misfortune of hooking and losing a fish.

I was interested to read in Bill McEwan's authoritative book *Angling on Lomond*, 1980, that he has suffered similar trouble—and found a similar solution. He recommends a flying mount made of strong nylon. Why not?

Being frustrated from time to time by fish which have visited the bait without being hooked, I have resorted to much experimentation with the hooking arrangement . . . The basic idea is to retain the bait action but reduce the unusual positions which the free-flying treble as supplied originally can adopt. Although the bait still flutters attractively,

329

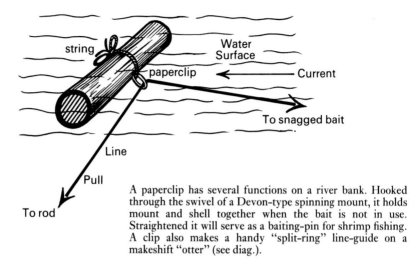

A paperclip has several functions on a river bank. Hooked through the swivel of a Devon-type spinning mount, it holds mount and shell together when the bait is not in use. Straightened it will serve as a baiting-pin for shrimp fishing. A clip also makes a handy "split-ring" line-guide on a makeshift "otter" (see diag.).

It is seldom necessary to carry such a bulky item as an otter about with us while fishing. Most river banks are rich in flotsam. A piece of stick or an empty bottle (plugged) together with a paperclip and piece of string will do the trick. Such an on-the-spot otter has another advantage: a size can be selected suitable for the current strength.

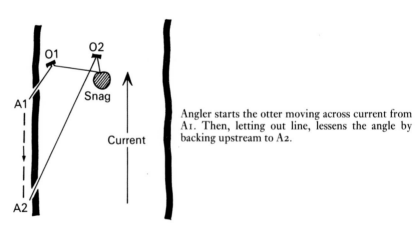

Angler starts the otter moving across current from A1. Then, letting out line, lessens the angle by backing upstream to A2.

The otter is worked out towards the snag by pulling on the line by hand. With luck, when it reaches a point almost directly downstream (o2) a sharp pull will free the bait.

the treble thus secured does not shift about so much, and breaks away when the fish is hooked ... If it seems like too much effort, with little justification, then so be it. It has become absolutely habitual for me to carry out this slight modification.

It is easy to tie up a few spoons and have them ready at the waterside. A mount is simple to prepare, takes no longer than tying a fly and provides a welcome alternative to the television news on a winter evening.

If you are one of those people touched with magic who seldom lose fish on the Toby as supplied, you won't need to bother about any of this.

5. *The Mepps Spoon*

This is an excellent little lure. Made in several sizes it enjoys a well-deserved popularity. The low-friction bearing attachment permits the blade to flutter most attractively when fished at very low speeds—a great advantage.

The Mepps is the best lure I know for upstream fishing when a spate river is dropping and clearing after a rise of water, and particularly good in its small sizes for hooking grilse.

Its weakness lies in its treble-hook, which is inclined to straighten under pressure. At least, it *did*. Some of the recent Mepps I have used had stronger hooks. Make sure yours have, too.

Colours? Anything you fancy. It comes in a considerable range—including red and blue polka dots. My favourite is black-and-gold.

Of course, if the spirit moves you, a spinner can always be touched up with dabs of whatever colour you like. In the old days I always gave the golden sprat "scarab" jackets a dab of red paint at the tail, and do the same with the Toby. The hook-shank of the Mepps gets a dab, too. This all looks very nice in the water. At least, it does to me, and so gives me heart. Whether it really makes any difference, you must decide for yourself.

In addition to prawns and shrimps, which are described in their own chapter, there is a host of other baits not dealt with here: Wagtail baits; artificial dace; natural dace, loach, eel-tail and sand eel; phantoms; gudgeon; wobblers and an army of plugs and spoons. Of the latter, one in particular has served me well:

6. *The Norwegian or Bergen Spoon*

A splendid lure, which I fish at times in spate water on the fly rod. It

331

has a half-scaled silver finish on the outside, gold on the inside.

Cast across the current at an acute angle downstream, this most attractive little spoon swings slowly round over the Taking-Strip on its back, with a most seductive wobble. A profitable and exciting diversion from fishing fly or worm when the beck is falling and starting to clear.

7. *The Blair Spoon*

Although my experience of fishing this bait is very limited, I include it on the insistence of friends. Its outrageous wobble, they assure me, is especially effective in tempting "uncatchable" resident salmon during the falling water of summer spates. The technique, they tell me, is to fish it high in the water slightly upstream and across. It was invented by William Blair of Kincardine O'Neill, and has earned a considerable reputation on Deeside.

As for the rest of the field, I never bother with any of them nowadays. What little spinning I do is with a wooden or plastic Devon or a Mepps or a modified Toby. There are, however, three baits you should know about. They have done me very well in the past, and will doubtless do the same for you in the future. All plugs: the Rapala; the River Runt and the Kynoch Killer. The last shall be first.

8. *The Kynoch Killer*

If you go harling, this is probably your best bait. Like the Blair Spoon, it has a most eccentric and unlikely action. When you first launch the thing and watch it zooming about as it disappears into the depths astern of the boat, you tend to shrug your shoulders. But don't be misled. It is *very effective*.

Occasionally you may find a spot where you can fish it from the bank. This has to be on the deep side of a Soup Spoon pool, preferably with a groyne, well upstream of the lies, from which the bait can be hung over the fish and worked slowly to and fro across the Taking-Strip. Harling from the bank, indeed! But at least there is no boatman doing it all for you.

9. *The Rapala*

Like the Kynoch Killer, this baits darts about. Why salmon are attracted by such erratic behaviour I don't know. But they are.

The Rapala is an easy bait to fish from a boat, and easier than the Kynoch Killer from the bank.

332

10. *River Runt*

As with the Rapala, it is many years since I fished the Runt. This has nothing to do with its effectiveness. It looked after me very well in those occasional pools suited to its technique. Like the Kynoch, it works best when fished from the deep side of a pool with fish lying close to the bank.

At rest, the Runt floats. With pressure, it dives. A summer lure, it is fished at the dangle from a rod's-length out and manoeuvred so that it keeps diving a few inches, and waggling about from side to side. After a few minutes of this it is allowed to come to the surface and drift downstream a yard or two, before renewed pressure starts a repeat performance.

This routine continues down the pool—until either a fish takes, or you get bored with it. Needless to say, a long, stiffish rod is best for this work.

Which brings me, naturally, to the subject of tackle.

Tackle

Time was, and not so long ago at that, when heavy spring baits were cast with revolving-drum reels, and light-bait low-water spinning in summer was unheard of. Improvements to spinning reels and lines during the present century, and particularly during the last thirty or forty years, have changed all that. Nowadays, thanks to monofilament nylon lines and the modern fixed-spool reel, excellent for throwing very light baits, low-water summer spinning with a featherweight single-handed rod of seven feet or thereabouts has become commonplace. Over a season, most spinning is done with light tackle and fixed-spool reels. But on the big rivers in early spring, when big and often heavy baits are in use, the $9\frac{1}{2}$–10 foot rod with multiplying reel is the most effective tool.

What early season spinning I used to do years ago was mainly with a ten-foot fibre-glass Hardy "Carp" Rod, designed by Richard Walker, which may seem a rather idiosyncratic choice, but had certain advantages. For instance, I liked the comfortable cork grip with two sliding rings that let me fit the reel where I wished. And after all, if a rod is well designed, what's in a name?

Its strength was never in doubt. I reasoned that a rod capable of dealing with a forty-pound carp—a very powerful fish—would deal with any salmon I was likely to hook. So it did, in exemplary fashion, in addition to landing me a lot of sea fishes including some big bass and pollack. It also served many years of hard labour at such varied pursuits as stret-pegging for salmon with worm, prawn and shrimp; prawn float-fishing, as well as straightforward ledgering and laying-on, and of course it cast a range of spinners and plugs. But I always used it with a fixed-spool reel, and a fixed-spool is by no means always the best for our purpose. There are times, particularly in early spring on the big rivers, when the multiplier is a better tool. And nowadays, there is a better rod.

The ten-foot Hardy No. 1 "Graphite Salmon Spinning Rod" is made from exactly the same blanks as the old ten-foot fibre-glass "Carp", but superior in that the sliding rings on the handle of my old rod didn't hold a multiplier very securely, whereas the new No. 1 with its screw-grip is much better adapted for spring fishing.

Before acquiring any item of tackle we should ask ourselves the question: what do I want it to do? And more particularly, in the case of a spinning rod, what weight do I want it to cast, and how far?

I mention this because judging by what is happening sometimes on the spring rivers I fish in high water, the average inexperienced angler seems unaware of what it is he should be trying to do. Everyone I pause to watch is striving to throw a heavy bait as far as he can straight across the river, seeming not to understand that the time he needs to throw a long line is not when the water is high, but when it is low—for it is only then that fish are spread out across the river in a wide enough Taking-Strip to merit long casting.

As I shall explain when discussing spinner presentation, for much of our spring fishing a very long line is not necessary. Certainly not in conditions of high water when, far from trying to cast a bait out of sight, our object is to fish it on a comparatively short line with much delicacy over a clearly defined and very narrow Taking-Strip close to the bank. For this we shall use a *big* bait, yes, but not a heavy one.

It is when the river is high that, with his more sensitive tackle, the experienced fly-fisher comes into his own. As we shall see, only by angling with similar understanding and skill can the spinning man hope to equal his success.

*   *   *

For casting efficiency with a fixed-spool reel, the line level on the spool should be fractionally less than one-eighth of an inch below the lip. Over-filling the spool results in tangles when casting. Under-filling reduces the casting range.

Examine the last couple of dozen yards of monofil line very carefully each time you tackle-up. A line usually suffers a lot of knocking-about during the course of a day's fishing, especially in rocky pools when fish are being played, or baits get hung up. Worn or strained nylon is considerably reduced in strength. Never take the slightest chance. A salmon is a magnificent prize—not to be lightly risked. Commit to memory the following couplet:

When in doubt,
Cut it out!

Of course, removal of line lowers the level on the spool. When this gets too low, and casting is affected, the line must be set-up again to the correct level. This is done either by fitting a new line, or adding some backing to what you have left. For a time the latter is acceptable.

To fill the reel, carry out the following drill:

1. Wind backing on top of line until correct level on spool is reached, then cut off.

2. Reverse line and backing, either by running it off across a field, or by winding on another reel and thence to a second reel. (Old centre-pin reels are useful for this job. I use two old sea-fishing "Scarborough" types that have survived from my boyhood.) The end of the backing is now uppermost on the second reel.

3. Tie end of backing to spool with the knot shown on p. 173, and wind on firmly. The line will now finish up on top of the backing and the level at the lip of the spool will be exactly right.

To avoid your line getting kinked while spinning you will need a swivel between line and leader. There are two main types:

1. *Barrel Swivel*
Used as a link between separate parts of a rig, this is a very useful little tool. It is not suitable for spinning, however, since fast-revolving baits tend to overload it.

2. *Ball-bearing Swivel*
This is the spinning swivel I have used for most of my life.

When extra weight on the leader is required to sink the bait you have a choice of four leads. Since they also act as *anti-kink* leads, this is what we will call them. They are:

1. *The Jardine*
Useful as a quick-change lead that can be added to or removed from a leader without the tackle having to be broken down.

335

The Bridge Pool, river Feshie. In clear water pools of this nature much interesting salmon behaviour can be observed.

2. *The Wye*

This too can be removed easily enough if placed between two link barrel swivels. It is more secure than the Jardine, which sometimes comes adrift.

3. *The Half-Moon*

A simple, very useful little lead, especially for light spinning. Easily fitted or removed. Falls off occasionally.

4. *The Hillman*

Another quick-change lead. I seldom use any other myself. It clips into the rod-end of the ball-bearing swivel.

> *Note.* Whether fastened to line or swivel, an anti-kink lead is *always* placed on the rod-side of the swivel.

The length of the leader should be not more than two-and-a-half feet, or less than two feet. It is a good plan to use nylon about 2 lb lighter than the main-line. This should ensure that in the case of breakage when the bait is irretrievably snagged, only the bait itself will be lost. Thus helping to prevent the river becoming festooned with nylon (see pictures on p. 102).

As a rough guide, the line strengths I use are as follows:

Early spring.	Multiplier.	25–20 lb b.s.
	Fixed-spool.	20–16 lb b.s.
General spinning.	Fixed-spool.	15–12 lb b.s.
Low-water summer.	Fixed-spool.	12–10 lb b.s.

336

The percipient reader will have noticed two points about these breaking-strains.

1. That they err on the side of strength. (But nothing wrong with that.)

2. That 20 lb b.s. nylon seems rather heavy to be cast far from a standard fixed-spool reel. So it is. But I find it will cast quite far enough for my purposes. (So, nothing wrong with that, either.)

Preparation

When you have tackled-up but before you start work, to prevent yourself from being too hard or too light on a fish, put the bait-treble in a loop of string tied to a gate-post or some other fixture. Then, standing a dozen or so yards away, tighten the line on your fixed-spool reel and jerk it with the rod as hard as you can.

The object of this is to set the drag adjustment on the spool so that reasonable pressure can be exerted without the clutch slipping and releasing line too easily, and also without the leader snapping however hard you jerk.

When you have made this adjustment, you can play a fish firmly and with confidence, knowing that unless the line is faulty further down on the spool, or gets cottered-up in an obstruction, no matter how hard or suddenly a salmon pulls, he cannot break you.

The Bridge Pool, Lower Crathes, River Dee. Head gillie Leslie George watches Roger Shipman play a 20 lb springer hooked on a Toby spoon. At this height of water the Taking-Strip lies between the ripple of the submerged rock and the bank.

Casting

Although modern reels have made the mechanics of casting very easy, the general standard is surprisingly poor. Most beginners can manage to throw a big bait a fair distance into a wide river with only a few minutes' instruction. But fishing a small summer-bait with the accuracy demanded by an overgrown spate stream is a very different proposition.

Faced with the prospect of fishing such a river, the beginner should practise daily on the lawn or in a field until he can drop a light bait into a two-yard circle fifteen yards away. Then, when he can do that, he should halve his target area. And follow that up by using a saucepan! He should practice not only the overhead cast, but sideways from both sides of the body. Only when he has mastered those casts will he be competent to deal with the obstructions found on many heavily-wooded spate rivers. He will, furthermore, have discovered that there is an artistry in bait-fishing undreamed of by many anglers.

Even so, however accurate the caster, it is one matter to put a bait into the river; quite another to present it attractively to the fish.

*   *   *

Presentation

Our approach to spinning parallels that of fly-fishing: its object for most of the time being to cast a bait across river and bring it round over the lies at a controlled speed and depth.

An exception to this occurs sometimes in very low water when fish are lying packed close together waiting to run. In these conditions a heavy bait is sometimes thrown almost straight upstream and wound back very fast over their heads.

Although it is legal, I deplore this way of fishing. It tends to jag the fish. And they hate it. Besides, it is a favourite method of "fishmongers" whose motive is foul-hooking. A very seedy business. Of all forms of disturbance, jagging is the worst. Although fast upstream spinning will catch salmon in the mouth—occasionally a fish turns and grabs the lure as it flashes past—it is an indifferent way of hooking them. Frequently the hookhold is slight, and many fish are only pricked. Pricked salmon are poor takers. Low-water upstream spinning with heavily weighted baits is a method that fishery managers could watch with advantage.

Note. My criticism of upstream spinning does not apply to fishing the last stages of a rise, when the falling spate stream has lost nearly all its colour, and a small, light Mepps spinner is thrown at an angle up-river and brought quickly back downstream fairly high in the water. This is a perfectly sporting method of hooking grilse. And successful—if you don't tighten on a fish too savagely!

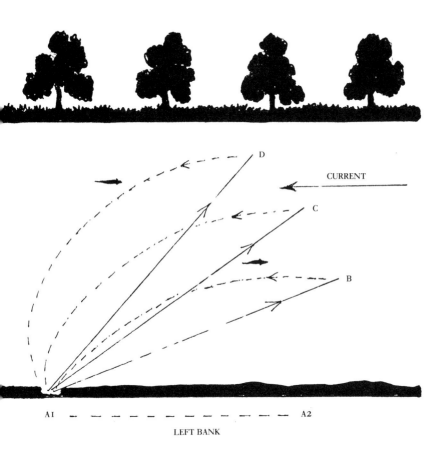

Upstream spinning with Mepps.
Spate stream dropping and clearing after a rise. Fish returning to lies in the centre of the river or on the edges of shingle banks etc.

The bait is cast from A1 upstream to B and brought back downstream slightly faster than the current, so that the Mepps can display its attractive whirling action, but at not too high a ground-speed. Several more casts are made from A1 (to C, D, etc.) before the angler moves upstream to A2 and starts again.

339

But I anticipate. We will start our spinning in springtime, with the river high.

I used to think that to catch salmon in high water a spinning rod was the only practical tool. Time taught me the fallacy in this thinking, and as I gained experience I found myself using the spinner less and less. This was not only because the fly rod gave me more pleasure—it caught me more fish!*

Such a claim may surprise some of my readers, and others may be sceptical. But it is a plain statement of fact. And anyone not already aware of its truth but who cares to follow suit, will undoubtedly reap the same benefit. In these conditions, the Crafty Fly-Fisher will often out-fish the Average Spinning-Man. The reason why is very simple. This is what happens. (See diagram p. 343).

The AS-M (if for the sake of convenience I may be permitted the acronym) arrives on the river in early March and finds it four or five feet above normal. Faced with such a high river and strong current he ties on a heavy bait, with a lot of lead to get it down—for this is what he has been told to do in these circumstances.

So, with a big Toby, or a heavily-weighted Devon, and a heavy anti-kink lead above his swivel, the AS-M sets to work, casting across the river as far as he can with his multiplier reel and twenty-pound breaking-strain line. As the bait swings round he is pleased to feel an occasional bump as it touches a rock. "Fine!" he muses. "The bait's getting right down there and fishing deep. Just where I want it." As the bait comes further round towards the bank and reaches shallowing water he feels a more positive bump—and his heart leaps. But again it is only the bottom. This time, to avoid getting snagged, he raises the rod and starts to wind the reel handle—bringing the bait steadily upstream towards him preparatory to having another fling.

And so, cast after cast, he fishes his way happily down the pool, confident that his bait is swimming deep and getting well down to the fish.

It is certainly getting well down. But the chances are that the fish are nowhere near it. They are not running out there in the torrent. They are making their way upstream through the slacker water close to the bank under which an occasional fish will swing to rest. It is this narrow Taking-Strip, only a yard or two out from his feet, that the AS-M has so far failed to cover. Or, if he has covered it, his bait has been bumping on the bottom, sagging, not swimming attractively.

By lunch time, having touched nothing, he is convinced there are no fish in the water. After all, as he explains to a sympathetic audience,

---

*I write of course only of the rivers I fish. It must be remembered that rivers differ greatly in character. What works best on some will not necessarily do so on others. The Wye, for instance, is a different proposition from, say, the Aberdeenshire Dee.

there was no question of his bait fishing deep enough. He has felt it touch bottom from time to time.

In fact, of course, his morning has been wasted. He has been using too heavy a bait, with too much lead. By the time it got anywhere near the fish it was swimming too deep to cross the Taking-Strip without going aground. Indeed, when the AS-M felt it bump at an angle of about thirty degrees out from the bank, he started to wind it in. Although he has done faithfully what the books tell him to do—cast a long line and fish his bait deep—he hasn't fished it anything like far enough round. It has never properly covered the one place where, at that height of water, taking salmon could be expected to lie.

The strip of river where those fish are resting is far more gentle and far shallower than the main stream he has fished so assiduously. To cover it properly he needed a much lighter lure, brought round much higher in the water.

It is on such a simple hinge that success or failure swings. And they say that salmon fishing is all luck!

One thing is sure. So long as the AS-M continues to fish like that he is going to *need* some luck, for without it he is not likely to catch much. Having watched many an AS-M toiling away, it has surprised me to see him catch anything at all. So often, of course, he doesn't.

The CF-F, fishing the same water with his big fly and quick-sinking line, makes a much shorter cast, puts a big mend in it—shooting extra line as he does, so, as described on p. 267—then leaves it alone. There is no lead on his leader. Having spent some time establishing the depth and strength of water in what he recognizes as the Taking-Strip, and gauged to a nicety what weight of fly will swim that particular piece of river attractively, he uses the length of his rod to help control the fly's speed as it swings round, ultimately leading it across the Taking-Strip on an even keel and at just the right pace. (See photographic sequence p. 256).

The fly itself, a hairwing creation, not too heavily dressed, moves slowly and attractively across the front of a salmon's temporary territory, its "wing" flickering in a lifelike and enticing manner. If the fish in that resting lie is a potential taker, the chances are he will grab that fly. It is, after all, so much more *inviting* (or, for that matter, as a territorial intruder, *threatening*) than a sagging, scarcely revolving spinner that bumps from stone to stone and is suddenly whisked away upstream!

As we shall see, in certain pool formations heavy baits and big leads *are* necessary. Places, indeed, where without them not a fish will be

The Mill Pool on Lower Crathes, River Dee. Taking-Strip at five feet above normal.

The Kelpie Pool on Lower Crathes, River Dee. Taking-Strip at five feet above normal.

342

hooked; where only the spinner is in with a chance, and the fly rod can be left in its case. But this is *not* when the river is brimming its banks. Paradoxically, the time when a heavy lead comes into its own is in *low* water, when the Taking Strip we have been considering is high and dry!

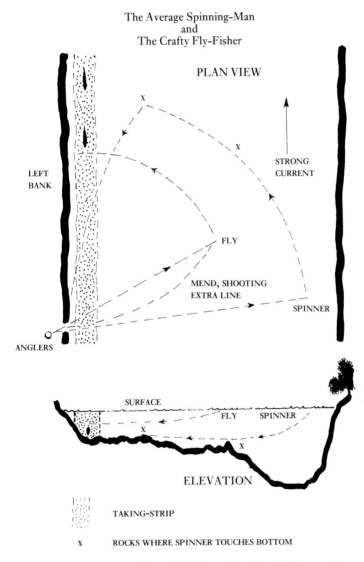

The Average Spinning-Man
and
The Crafty Fly-Fisher

PLAN VIEW

STRONG
CURRENT

LEFT
BANK

FLY

MEND, SHOOTING
EXTRA LINE

SPINNER

ANGLERS

SURFACE

FLY   SPINNER

X

X

ELEVATION

TAKING-STRIP

X   ROCKS WHERE SPINNER TOUCHES BOTTOM

Any angler hitherto unaware of the principles explained in this diagram (see text), will more than double his catch if he cares to apply it to his high-water spinning.

As mentioned in the chapter on sunk-line fly-fishing, weight of lure is crucial. This is equally true of spinning. Just as the fly-fisher needs a range of differently weighted flies, so the spinning-man needs a range of differently weighted spinners. Having these, means that if and when he decides to reduce the weight of his lure to suit a change in depth and current as he fishes down a pool, he is not condemned to a smaller size.

And how often does he carry this range of baits, or think of changing down—or up, for that matter—in *weight* of lure? Very seldom! It is not surprising that the CF-F so often outfishes him.

Even now, although I am expecting it, I am often surprised how close to the bank salmon sometimes take. If a lure is to attract a fish when it reaches that all-important strip of water, it must be swimming at the right depth and speed. To ensure this with the fly is fairly easy, even with a sinking line. A big mend can be thrown initially when the fly is cast. Then, while the fly swings round, as already described, the rod can be held out at right angles to the bank—all fifteen feet of it. Five yards is a considerable distance in these conditions. It ensures that when fish are lying perhaps no more than two or three yards out, the fly can be controlled exactly as one wishes.

This is what you must aim at doing with your spinner. You can seldom put much of a mend in the line—unless the wind is blowing upstream. But you can compensate for that and reduce the bait's speed by throwing a long line at an angle downstream—instead of straight across!

As with fly-fishing, whatever the conditions, whenever the season, wherever you are spinning, direct each cast to an imaginary fish. Work out the position of the Taking-Strip and where in that ribbon of water you think a fish may be lying. After that, devote everything to fishing the bait across that particular spot.

This will not guarantee the reward of a salmon. But you will certainly derive more pleasure from your sport. You are no longer casting like an automaton, and "coffee grinding", but fishing to a plan; fishing with purpose. As already suggested in another context, such an approach arouses your dormant hunting instinct and brings an extra dimension to what hitherto has been merely mechanical. Henceforth you will find yourself fishing with a new excitement.

*　　　　*　　　　*

Sooner or later, and probably sooner rather than later, you are going to get your bait snagged. Owing to the rocky nature of many salmon rivers, this sometimes happens in a series of hang-ups—just when you are approaching the most promising part of a pool. Nothing is more infuriating. It is as though the sense of helpless frustration with which most of us face time's relentless pressure, spills over into what should be one of life's more enjoyable and relaxing pastimes.

When this happens; when, on its path across the pool, the bait suddenly stops, *don't pull*. Having determined that it *is* a snag and not a fish, don't start jerking the rod. This may only make matters worse. Do quite the reverse. Slacken the line and let the current strip it off downstream. When thirty or forty yards have bellied below the bait, check it, then give it a hard jerk. This pull against the pressure of the current results in a downstream pull from the line belly and often releases the bait. Wind in as quickly as possible.

If this trick doesn't work, and you can't free the bait by walking downstream and pulling hard from that direction, you will be reduced to using an otter,* or breaking. You must decide whether your bait is worth the disturbance of freeing it. If you are forced to break, make certain that the line of pull is nowhere near your face, especially if you are using an anti-kink lead. When the leader breaks, as it should, the lead may spring at you from the water like a pistol bullet. This has caused some nasty injuries. What I do myself in this unhappy situation is to wrap the line several times round my arm. Then, holding it well clear of my body, I turn my back on the river and walk away.

Getting hung up is frustrating; leaving the bottom festooned with baits and trailing nylon, unsatisfactory. But it happens to all of us sooner or later. It will not happen so often, however, if we have a better idea of the depth and contours of the pools we fish.

The man who knows his river has a tremendous advantage over the stranger. Tell him the water height and immediately he will picture every pool on his beat. Without seeing the river he will know which pools are likely to fish best, and whereabouts in those pools the Taking-Strips will be. He will know the depth of water in the lies, the strength of the current and what weight of lures to use in each pool. And he will give a very accurate forecast of how all this will alter as the water drops. If you are fishing that beat as a visitor by yourself, you will have to learn as much of this as you can with only your water-sense to guide you.

*See p. 330.

Earlier I suggested the importance of knowing the water when fishing the sunk fly. It is just as important, perhaps even more so, when fishing the spinner.

Most important is the water *depth*. If you don't know it, *find out*—even if the only way of doing so is with plummet and sliding-float. Although it is certainly true that you only catch fish when your bait is swimming, it is also true that sometimes you have a better chance if you spend less time fishing and more in reconnaissance. Five minutes spent fishing a stretch of water correctly may catch you a salmon. A week spent fishing it incorrectly will catch you nothing.

Plotting a pool's underwater contours using plummet and sliding float
(A use for the old bass and pollack floats surviving from one's youth!)

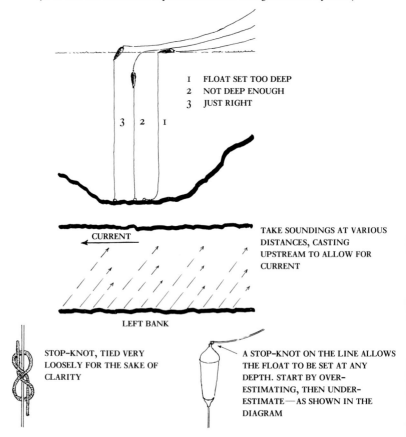

1   FLOAT SET TOO DEEP
2   NOT DEEP ENOUGH
3   JUST RIGHT

CURRENT

TAKE SOUNDINGS AT VARIOUS
DISTANCES, CASTING
UPSTREAM TO ALLOW FOR
CURRENT

LEFT BANK

STOP-KNOT, TIED VERY
LOOSELY FOR THE SAKE OF
CLARITY

A STOP-KNOT ON THE LINE ALLOWS
THE FLOAT TO BE SET AT ANY
DEPTH. START BY OVER-
ESTIMATING, THEN UNDER-
ESTIMATE—AS SHOWN IN THE
DIAGRAM

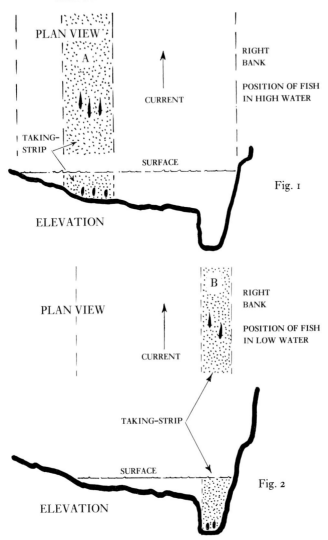

FIG. 1. THE POOL IN HIGH WATER
FIG. 2. THE SAME POOL IN LOW WATER

Years ago I used to fish a pool similar to that shown in the diagram. When the water was up, fish lay in Taking-Strip A. (see fig. 1.), close to the left bank where they were catchable. When the water was low,

347

however, they lay in Taking-Strip B. (see fig. 2.), a deep, narrow gully very close to the steep-to right bank. To catch them in this position with a fly was virtually impossible, and only very rarely could it be done with a spinner. Everyone fished the pool from the left bank, since the right bank was a near vertical cliff, and in low water it had the reputation of being useless. That was until, one day, I had the notion of fishing it one-handed from a narrow ledge on the cliff face.

Clinging on with one hand, I would let a very heavily-weighted sprat straight down almost to the bottom, and then drag it slowly upstream over the fish within a yard or so of the bank. And it worked like magic.

Handling a hooked salmon from such a precarious perch was, to say the least, exciting. He had to be "walked" foot by foot along the ledge until I could scramble off and play him from the bank with both hands. Even then he had to be landed in deep water against a vertical rock. But, being young and agile, I took a lot of salmon from that pool. It was an example of what I suggested earlier: the occasional use of a heavy bait and big lead in very low water.

There are many similar pools that will fish well in low water only if you know the particular trick each one requires. In such places the fly rod is usually put aside, and the spinner comes into its own. A pool of this nature is shown in the next diagram. It explains the curious phenomenon that occurs on salmon rivers from time to time, and which many people find puzzling. We will call it The Case of the Lucky Novice.

Briefly, the story-line runs something like this:

A veritable beginner, who has been taught merely the rudiments of bait-casting, wanders down to the river and chucks in. Immediately, he hooks a fish—confounding the anglers who have been flogging that water fruitlessly for days.

Such a primitive plot forms the basis of innumerable anecdotes heard late at night in the bar of any angling hotel. They are usually recounted by chagrined "experts" in aggrieved tones, the good fortune of this unmentionable novice being ascribed to luck, and adduced as yet another example of the salmon's inexplicable behaviour.

Well—the salmon's behaviour is frequently inexplicable. But not in this case. The reason for the novice's success is simplicity itself—and it provides a valuable lesson.

Examination of the river where such miracles occur usually reveals a deep gully or hole where salmon lurk in low water, and where they were undoubtedly lying when our hero chucked in. Although the Hotel Expert had already fished that water, he had not fished it correctly.

Whereas, albeit quite by accident, the novice had done just the right thing. Releasing the bale-arm of his brand-new fixed-spool reel, he had slung out his spinner. Checked too late, his line had instantly flown into a tangle. But while he was sorting out this bird's nest, his spinner was twinkling down towards the fish . . .

Eventually, having freed his line and started to wind in, the LN was surprised and delighted to find himself fast in a salmon. For the first time that day, or perhaps that week, a bait had been sunk deep enough in that particular place to attract a fish!

The novice was lucky, yes—for he was as ignorant of the water depth as the Hotel Expert. But the latter could have caught that fish by design, not luck, had he taken the trouble to ascertain where salmon were lying, and at what depth.

The sequence of events is shown in the diagram on p. 350.

1. The Hotel Expert, unaware of the pool's underwater contours, cast a long line from A to B.

2. His bait started to sink and swing round with the current to C, where it touched a rock. Immediately, the HE lifted his rod wound in a little line and let his bait continue at the same depth across the pool towards D. This was the most important part of its journey, since it was now covering the fish. It was, however, swimming far too high in the water, and nowhere near them.

3. At D, the bait again touched bottom, confirming the HE's belief that it had been fishing near the bottom all the way across. Again he lifted the rod, and this time wound in his line ready for another cast.

The Lucky Novice, who couldn't cast as far as the Hotel Expert, could only land his bait at E, whereupon his line got cottered up. While he paused to sort it out, the bait was drifting downstream with the current and heading into the deeps where it was promptly taken by a fish at F.

This example illustrates a common problem, especially during early spring when salmon are unlikely to move far in pursuit of a bait, and emphasizes the importance of knowing the depth of water you are fishing.

The diagram is based on a pool I sometimes fish on the River Eden, and is representative of a number of similar stretches on other rivers that have the reputation of being "difficult". The right way to fish the pool in question is shown in the diagram on p. 351.

1. Cast a heavily-weighted bait on a short line only as far as B.

2. Let line continue to run off the reel until the bait has sunk to the required depth at C.

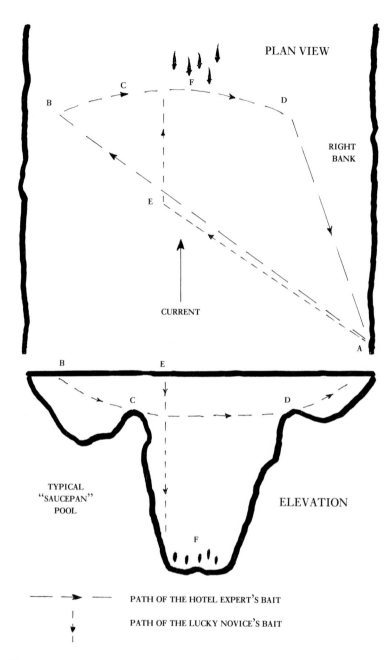

PLAN VIEW

RIGHT
BANK

CURRENT

TYPICAL
"SAUCEPAN"
POOL

ELEVATION

——— ⟶ ——— PATH OF THE HOTEL EXPERT'S BAIT

⋮ PATH OF THE LUCKY NOVICE'S BAIT

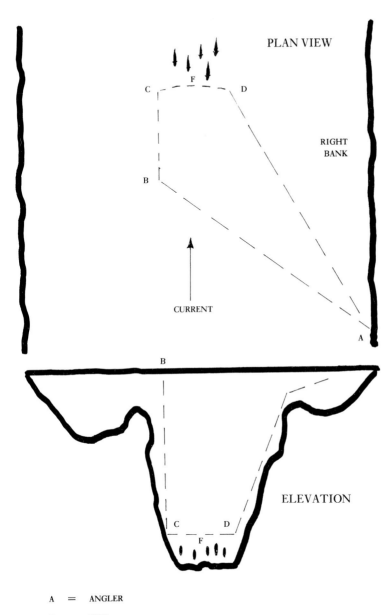

PLAN VIEW

RIGHT
BANK

CURRENT

ELEVATION

A   =   ANGLER

F   =   FISH

— — — PATH OF THE ANGLER'S BAIT

NOTE THE CENTRAL BUT VERY NARROW TAKING-STRIP C–D

3. Check the line and let the bait fish round on the current across the narrow Taking-Strip C, D, then retrieve quickly to avoid snagging on the right-hand side of the gully.

Clearly, the success of this ploy depends on knowing the position of point B, the depth of water at C, and the time taken by a weighted bait to reach that depth. This can be established fairly quickly by:

1. Plotting the pool's underwater contours with plummet and sliding-float.

2. Tying on a hookless bait and adding the amount of lead you think necessary for the bait to sink quickly in that strength of current.

3. Casting to the lie at B; and, by counting as it sinks, noting how long the bait takes to reach the bottom.

4. Adjusting the amount of weight if need be. Then casting again and again until you can judge, by counting, exactly when the bait is about to reach bottom.

By counting out this number when you come to fish the pool in a similar strength of current, you will know exactly when to check the bait in its descent, so that it fishes across the lies at its most effective depth.

Just like sunk-line fly-fishing, spinning success in certain waters depends very largely on practical reconnaissance of this sort. The pool described may seem an extreme example, and perhaps it is. But I know many pools of a similar nature where fish lie too deep to be reached by baits fished in the usual way, and where, in cold water, only by fishing in this manner can one hope to be successful. It is because so few anglers recognize the problems involved in fishing such places that the taking lies are so seldom covered correctly. In consequence, these pools have acquired a reputation for being useless in low water—especially during early spring.

There is another point. Such deep-set "saucepan" type pools are typical of places where bait-fishing is the only sensible approach, and where for once the fly-rod can be left at home.

*　　　　*　　　　*

But spring fishing in pools such as those is not the only time that the fly must take second place to bait. Later in the season when the spate rivers are getting their runs of summer salmon, heavily-wooded and untended banks frequently make long stretches of water awkward if not impossible to fish with anything but spinner or worm.

Many game fishermen indulge their sport only during the annual holidays and on occasional week-ends. But it is on these anglers, in terms of tackle, licences, fishing-permits and accommodation, that a large proportion of today's "angling interest" depends. And seldom are they treated with the consideration they deserve.

Of primary concern to the holiday angler is a run of fish, because that is what dictates his chance of sport. But even when fish are present in a river, the water clean and unpolluted, a visiting angler's pleasure is diminished often enough by the dismal local conditions he has to face.

Naturally, where any angler chooses to go depends on what sort of holiday he is seeking; how much money he wants to spend; what particular method or methods he fancies using. If his holiday is to be built first and foremost round the fishing, he will almost certainly avoid the smaller spate streams with their haphazard rise and fall, and opt for one of the bigger and more stable rivers. But if a *family* holiday is intended, with its inevitable restriction on fishing time, a spate river will probably suit him perfectly. If he is lucky to get a rise of water during his week or fortnight he can enjoy his ration of fishing as the river drops, with every chance of success, and spend the dog-days before and afterwards sight-seeing with the children.

Often, however, unless he is fortunate to fish a stretch of river that happens to be well managed and maintained, he is likely to suffer many disappointments. And these will be the more pronounced if he is hoping to fish the fly.

For instance, although there is very good potential fishing on some of the association waters, their upkeep is sometimes lamentable. Lovely stretches of river, but difficult and in places impossible to fish as one might wish because of untended banks, overhanging branches, snags in the pools.

That any stretch of water holding salmon and sea trout today should be so woefully neglected is hardly believable. Nevertheless, I have come across the most depressing examples.

In some cases, river neglect is due to fishery owners or managers who harbour the curious notion that salmon lies depend on tree cover, and so steadfastly abstain from trimming branches. This results in overgrown water impossible to fish with fly. Indeed, I know stretches impossible to fish with anything—except perhaps a worm, dropped vertically on heavily-leaded ledger tackle in a gap between branches. To be prevented by obstructions from covering a pool containing salmon and sea trout— the most sporting quarries any game angler can aspire to catch—is the

353

Well-kept Association water on the River Usk.

very height of absurdity. And it is extraordinary that such places should exist today. But they do. I have seen them, and tried to fish them: fine stretches of potentially good fly water whose banks are allowed to become wilderness, which increases year by year, simply because of the belief that interference with the leafy, interlacing canopy of branches will drive the fish away.

Never have I found any evidence to support this belief, widely held though it may be. Few of the pools I fish regularly on the big rivers have any shade to speak of, certainly not during the greater part of the day. Some pools on the northern rivers I fish have no trees at all. On some of the best water in western Ireland and Scotland there is scarcely a tree in sight. On the last river I fished in Sutherland I counted three trees in six miles, stunted little things at that, and there were salmon lies under none of them.

There are many pools where salmon do not take advantage of tree cover even when it is available.

This is not to imply that trees are without value on a fishery. Far from it. I know several beats that have benefited from tree planting. Lines of trees, set at a suitable distance back from the water, make excellent wind-breaks, and sometimes, when the light is low, help the angler to avoid throwing long flickering shadows across the water. Trees are invaluable on the south-east side of sea trout pools—by darkening the

354

water on bright moonlit nights. Not that clear moonlight inhibits sea trout from taking, but tree-shadowed water fishes better: it permits us to use a wider range of lures.

Anyway, trees are good to look at, and always interesting—if only for the wildlife they attract. But their true value to the angler is in their *height*. If there is any value in their creation of shade it comes from the foliage of their upper branches. There is no merit in those leafy boughs that spread out like splayed fingers low across the river and make fly-fishing impossible. Salmon do not purposely lie underneath tree branches like hungry trout, waiting for a meal to drop. No harm can be done by removing those obtrusive lower branches, which offer nothing to the fish and serve merely to frustrate the fisherman.

But old myths die hard. Often enough, even in this supposedly enlightened age, the visiting holiday angler finds himself faced with overgrown entanglements. Once again the fly-rod can be put away, and the bait-rod assembled. Not the double-handed ten-footer of early spring with its 20 lb line, but the light, single-handed, seven-footer armed with fixed-spool reel, 10 lb monofil line and a small Devon or Mepps spinner.

As he soon finds, spinning such constricted water calls for casting accuracy of high order. But provided he can fish with sufficient skill, he will enjoy considerable satisfaction from defeating the miserable conditions he has to contend with: casting at all angles; aiming at tiny gaps in branches; putting his bait to within inches of the other bank, and encouraging it to fish down under the leaves towards salmon lurking unseen among the rocks.

It is now that he derives full benefit from those long hours of casting practice into a diminishing target on the lawn. As he soon discovers, there is scant similarity between the hurly-burly of early season fishing on the big spring rivers, and this delicate assault on an overgrown spatestream in the lush growth of summer: its success dependent on an artistry entirely absent from his spinning hitherto.

*   *   *

Fish Hooked and Lost

Runs of misfortune, when more hooked fish are lost than seem reasonable on average, occur with spinner just as they do with fly. Salmon taking-behaviour, as described in Chapter II, applies just as surely with this method as with any other.

Unfortunately I have never kept the figures of fish lost compared with fish hooked, but if I had to make an estimate, looking back over more than fifty seasons, I would say that fewer of my fish have been lost on sunk fly than on spinner. Considerably fewer on floating fly.

There will be exceptions, notably softness of flesh in very fresh-run fish, but certainly many losses must be due to the way in which the lure has been taken. As stated in Chapter II, the theory that fish always take a lure in the same way, I know from observation to be false. And that observation is heightened by what happens on the river bank. I have often noticed that different runs of salmon coming fresh from sea, although perhaps separated by only a day, sometimes seem to display different looks and behavioural characteristics—to the extent, even, of preferring different lures. And, perhaps most significant of all, they tend to *take* differently. About the latter I am in no doubt. And in my experience it applies equally to different runs of sea trout, even though these runs may differ merely by a matter of hours—the time taken by the ebb and flow of a single tide.

This is only an impression: a *notion*. But if it is true it goes some way towards explaining why on occasion there should be such a disparity in our success/failure rate when fish are lost for no apparent reasons.*

As an example. During a week in early spring on the River Dee, I caught five salmon on sunk fly in my first two days. These fish were all much of a size and shape. Typical fresh-run Dee springers, ranging from $7\frac{1}{2}$ lb to 9 lb. Each fish had sucked the fly right into the back of his mouth; the hook so deep in the throat that it had to be recovered with artery forceps.

During the next two days, in addition to having several pulls, I caught two fish but lost three. Those I landed were larger fish than hitherto: 17 lb and 15 lb. They seemed a different stamp of salmon altogether, although just as fresh and with female tide lice on them. Each was *very lightly hooked*, right in the front of the mouth. And remember, three more were hooked but came off.

The following day was virtually unfishable owing to a sudden rise of water and tremendous gale-force winds. I hooked and lost one fish on a spinner.

On my last day I caught three more on the fly, each hooked as firmly as those earlier fish had been, the hook sucked right to the back of the throat so that, again, forceps were needed. And again, these fish were clearly members of a new run, each being 8–9 lb.

This is the sort of pattern I have experienced on many occasions,

* See also footnote p. 302.

356

both with salmon and sea trout, during the times of year when the majority of fish were running. (I may say that, in the example given, all the fish were caught on a $3\frac{1}{2}$ inch fly of exactly the same size and pattern—though of different weights to suit depth and current in the various taking lies.)

Now I don't want to make too much of this. It is all rather tenuous stuff. But it *is* interesting, and I mention it because it may be the reason why on occasion we suffer those irritating runs of misfortune when fish after fish comes off. Also, (although in this case I used the same size and pattern of fly), it helps to explain why certain lures succeed on some days and not on others. Perhaps, most important of all, it encourages us to think that if one lure fails it is worthwhile to try another; that in addition to boosting our confidence, there may really be a chance that this new offering will be preferred.

I will take the matter no further than that—and repeat that it *is* just a notion. Nevertheless, it may offer solace to any unfortunate reader who has suffered an unaccountable and infuriating series of losses, or been puzzled why one fish he lands has the hook at the back of its throat, whereas with another fish, lightly hooked up front, the hook has fallen out on landing.

Note. Apropos of all this, it is interesting that in *A Salmon Fisherman's Notebook*, 1949, that observant Welshman J. Hughes-Parry writes:

> Curiously enough, different runs of salmon seem to prefer different-coloured prawns . . . One can fish right down a pool of salmon using a red prawn, and for the results one gets there might not be a fish in the pool. But if a natural-coloured prawn be put on, or even a light yellow one (I have done this twice in my life, the prawn being dyed with bright yellow Dolly dye) and three or four fish will be landed which must have been there all the time, but had paid no attention to the red prawn at all.*

Lastly, a few general points.

1. Before you start fishing, if you haven't already done so, pay out your line downstream with the current and wind it back with the rod-tip held just beneath the surface. This should get rid of any kinks, and help you to avoid tangles when casting.

A field of wet grass will do the trick, but take care the line doesn't get abrased by stones or grit.

*The response of salmon to prawns of various colours is considered briefly in Chapter XVI.

41 lb fresh-run River Wye maiden spring cock salmon, length 48″, caught on 1½″ Yellow and Green Wooden Devon by Mr Tod Millard in the Old Court beat of the Whitney Court Estate, 27th March 1982. Scale reading showed two years of river life, four years of sea life. "As the fish was gaffed, after approximately 45 minutes of a very hard but generally dour contest, having been walked over 200 yards upstream, the treble hook came away and was found to have only one serviceable point; one point had broken off, one straightened out."

2. Have a good look at the water. Decide on the position and depth of the Taking-Strip—and remember that the purpose of each cast is to fish your bait at the correct speed and depth *over that strip. Everything it does up to then is in preparation for that adventure.*

So—don't start off by casting at ninety degrees straight across the river to the distant bank. In anything of a current you will do better by throwing at an angle downstream, and simply the distance that enables the bait to be swimming at its intended depth and speed as it approaches the fish.

3. Except when fishing slack water; casting upstream and winding back, or purposely varying the speed of the bait, don't keep turning the handle of the reel as the bait swings across the river. If you find yourself doing this to stop the bait running aground, remove some lead or tie on a lighter bait.

4. As a general principle when spinning for salmon, always use as light a bait as possible. If you want to fish deeper, don't put on a heavier bait, but fit a heavier lead at the swivel. A minnow swimming slightly head down and flickering attractively, due to its lightness, is more enticing than a bait that sags tail down as it enters that common Taking-Strip between current and slack. Keep your heavy baits for special occasions.

A light bait, by the way, tends to hook a fish more securely than a heavy bait.

When you need to fish deep down, you must of course use a heavy bait. But usually it is better to spin with too little lead than too much. Except when fishing those chasm-like pools in low water, as described earlier in this chapter, err on the side of lightness.

5. Once you have discovered the right weight for the strength of current and depth of water, chuck out your bait and leave it to swing round as slowly as possible. If you are wading, make sure you fish it right across the dangle. If you are casting from the bank in other than very low water, fish it into the shallows. Salmon sometimes take almost as it hits the side. As with the fly, failure to fish a cast right out with spinner accounts for many missed chances.

6. If the Taking-Strip is some little distance off-shore, with a ribbon of slackish and slack water between there and the bank, don't bring your bait riffling back fast along the surface of this ribbon as you retrieve it, *fish it.* As the bait leaves the current, keep it moving by starting to wind in, and then bring it upstream towards you steadily but not too fast. Salmon will occasionally follow the bait from deeper water and ghost after it, sometimes taking almost at your feet. But they won't if the bait

has faltered and started to sag. Nor if they see you. So—keep your bait moving, and yourself stock-still. This is a time when camouflaged clothing may prove its worth.

7. Try fishing known resting-lies in various ways. Although a salmon has ignored a bait—perhaps several times—he may take it when it suddenly comes at him from a different angle, or passes at a different height or speed.   Wherever possible on small rivers, try fishing the central lies from both banks. It is surprising how often a salmon that has refused a bait cast from one bank will take it when it is cast from the opposite side.

If downstream fishing fails, try a cast or two upstream—especially with the Mepps spinner, which is ideal for this purpose.

8. Unless a strong wind is blowing, hold the rod fairly well up all the time the bait is fishing. The slight curve from rod-tip to surface will help to "cushion" a take.

9. When you get a take and are playing the fish, don't keep turning the reel handle unless line is coming in. Bring a tired fish towards you either by walking backwards, or by a "pumping" action: dropping the rod point as you reel in line, then raising the rod steadily so that you gain a yard or two, which can be wound up as you lower the rod point again.

Some experienced anglers prefer to play a fish with the clutch tight and the handle set at "free". Try both methods for yourself on the lawn. Get a friend to act as a salmon and rush about holding the end of the line, while you practise "playing" him.

10. Be prepared for the occasional fish that, while being played, somehow contrives to get the leader looped round his body—so that the pull is not on his mouth, but on his side somewhere in the region of the pectoral fin. As a result of this he behaves like a tackle-retrieving otter: the harder you pull, the further from you he gets. Even the strength of the current is usually enough to keep him hanging well out in the stream.

I once hooked a fifteen-pounder that got himself ravelled-up like this. At the time I was instructing some beginners in The Art of Angling and, watching intently, not missing a thing, they were being shown how to play a fish.

"Always be firm with a salmon. Don't waste time, just show him who's master", I burbled. "This fish is pretty well played out. Now, watch how easy it is to walk him ashore."

As I walked backwards the fish set off into the deeps, taking out line.

Staggered, I heaved hard on the rod. The fish responded by moving further away.

I couldn't believe it. That fish was beaten, and yet I couldn't pull him in. Silly ass! I didn't realize what had happened. The harder I pulled, the more stubborn the resistance as he crept off into the centre of the river.

And all this time he was drifting steadily further and further downstream—whither, together with my troupe, I was forced to follow. I have never felt quite so stupid.

Eventually, to the huge delight of my audience, the fish floated in to the side belly-up and landed himself . . .

If you ever find yourself in this ridiculous situation, and tumble to what has happened, there is only one thing to do. When the fish is played-out, run downstream very fast and get below him. *Then* pull. The resultant force, aided by the current on his opposite flank, will bring him in towards the bank.

*   *   *

Equipped with a comprehensive range of fly and spinning tackles together with a grasp of the principles involved in fishing them, the salmon angler should now be capable of defeating most of the conditions he will face on most of the water he will fish. There are, however, certain times when extensions to his repertoire will prove both profitable and exciting.

The first of these—a bait whose presentation in all but the rough-and-tumble of spate water demands the acme of finesse—now emerges in a chapter to itself.

The worm.

The lob-worm is a proper bait for salmon. It is to be found in gardens and churchyards by the light of a lanthorn, late on a summer's evening. In a great drought, when they do not appear, pour the juice of walnut-tree leaves, mixed with a little water and salt, into their holes. It will drive them out of the ground.

Richard Brookes, *The Art of Angling*, 1740

XV
Bait Fishing

PART TWO: THE WORM

Fly fishing may be a very pleasant amusement, but angling or float fishing I can only compare to a stick and a string, with a worm at one end and a fool at the other.

The author of this classic aphorism is unknown. In his famous Diary, that great nineteenth-century sportsman, Colonel Peter Hawker, attributes it to Dr Samuel Johnson. And certainly it has a Johnsonian ring, although there is no further evidence to support his authorship. But no matter who uttered it. Is it valid?

Well, no, it isn't. Not because angling hasn't its share of fools, but because Johnson, or whoever it was, chose the wrong bait.

A worm needs someone rather better than a fool on the other end if its merits are to be shown to advantage. Although it is true that a worm can catch fish on a stick even when handled by an idiot, it takes a very good angler to fish that worm on a single-handed fly-rod upstream for salmon in low, clear water. There is indeed much more to worm-fishing than a string attached to a fool.

But the worm is not without its critics. There are anglers who affect a disdain for it; some, most vociferous in their condemnation of its use.

Empty barrels make most noise! It is a fact that I have never yet encountered a single angler critical of salmon worm-fishing who had actually fished this bait or knew anything at all about it. Indeed, when one considers the total ignorance of these so-called "purists", their expostulations sound very like attempts at turning incompetence into moral profit.

Be that as it may. With regard to the sporting ethic of worm-fishing, I can only repeat the proposition of an earlier chapter: that what makes any method unsporting is *the way it is used*. It is never the method that is at fault; always the man. The selfish and thoughtless angler makes *any* method unsporting, fly-fishing included, by his mistreatment of the water and failure to consider the pleasure of others.

Fortunate in having private fishing, and access to other fisheries where I could indulge my fancies, I have been able to pursue the quest for knowledge and experience uninhibited. Indeed, without those hours of bait-fishing and their concomitant opportunities for observation, I would not have seen a fraction of the behaviour that has proved so helpful in my approach to salmon-fishing generally, and fly-fishing in particular.

There are many different ways of angling. Each has its own time and place, with each providing its own interest, excitement and experience. On occasion, in locations similar to that shown on the next page, I have derived much pleasure from the often belittled technique of ledgering: lolling at ease in the sunshine of drowsy summer days, when the river was dead low and fly-fishing only a dream. Thus ensconced among the reeds far from the madding crowd, with only my Labrador and perhaps a sedge-warbler for company, in addition to fish-watching I have scribbled many a note for this book during the long intervals between flurries of activity.

Anyone who restricts his approach to salmon fishing not only denies himself a lot of fun, but deprives himself of much valuable experience. Except insofar as I proselytise and hope to lead him from his narrow ways, it is not for him that this chapter is being written—although, who knows, perhaps something in it may kindle his interest and inspire an urge to try a worm upstream.

We will start at the beginning, with the worm itself.

Of the many species of earthworms in Britain, we need concern ourselves with only two:

1. The Common Lobworm, *Lumbricus terrestris*, also known as dew-worm, rain-worm, twachel, flat-tail, squirrel-tail and night-crawler.

2. The Big Blue-Headed Lobworm, *Allolobophora longa*, also known as round-tail and blue-head.

Other species will catch salmon, but lobworms are best. You can dig them up of course, but a more convenient method is to collect them from the lawn after nightfall. A warm, dark, damp, still night is the most propitious. Worms seldom appear on dry, windy nights, and never when the ground is frozen. They are very sensitive to vibration. So, move with care. For lobworm-stalking you will be well advised to wear rubber-soled shoes or Wellingtons, and creep about. A stealthy approach is essential. Only the frustrated lobworm-hunter who has witnessed it can

Ledgering has a charm of its own. Using a simple running-ledger baited as shown on p. 369, it is a delightful way of spending a few hours in summer sunshine, with the possible bonus of a salmon however low the water. The bait is cast to where fish are known to be lying and left motionless on the bottom with the line slack. Every five minutes or so the line is cautiously tightened and the bait moved a few inches; a ruse that sometimes induces a salmon or sea trout to take.

appreciate the speed at which a frightened worm will vanish down its hole.

Sometimes the whole worm is above ground. In which case, being unable to beat a hasty retreat, it can be picked up. But a worm often anchors itself inside its burrow by its tail, with only its upperworks lying above-ground and visible among the grass-stems. Often it is only this portion of worm that you find when creeping about with your torch and worm-tin.

When you spot what you *think* is a worm, don't prod it to make sure. It will disappear in a flash. Pin it down with thumb and forefinger, or by using the "double-thumb" technique—that is, with a thumb at either end.

Next, transfer your attention to the head. This must be held firmly (but not too firmly, or you kill the worm) until the body is sufficiently attenuated by peristaltic contortion to let you draw it gently from its hole. Anticipate this, and the worm will break in half.

How do you locate the head? By *feel*. On being pressed down, the worm in its attempt to escape undulates toward its burrow. You can feel it doing this, and sense the direction. The head will be at the opposite end. This is the end you now grasp preparatory to coaxing the remainder out of its hole and into your tin.

The literature cites several other ways of collecting lobworms. Jumping up and down on the lawn; driving a fork into the ground and tapping it; pouring mustard down the holes. Perhaps I have not been sufficiently thorough in my research, but frankly the worms I have captured by such methods have never repaid the outlay of effort—and mustard.

Over the years I have found nothing to surpass the late-night stalking expedition. This can be a sport in its own right. (And as performed by some of those after-dinner worm-stalkers lurching round the lawn, not without its hazard and excitement.)

A congenial way of collecting worms is to follow the plough, particularly if you are after the blue-headed lobworm, two of whose favourite haunts are meadow and cow-pasture. Anglers who find themselves short of bait need never despair. A ratch-round in suitable ground should provide them with something to be going on with.

Apropos of this, readers of *Sea Trout Fishing* may remember my experience as a boy, on the hot summer afternoon when I came across that salmon:

> He was lying on the edge of a fast current in about three feet of water, four or five yards out from a large rock. From a crevice in the rock

a small bush was, mysteriously, growing. I crawled up behind the bush. The salmon was now only a few yards away, slightly upstream, and I could see every spot on his flank. I was using an old greenheart single-handed fly rod, but before taking up station behind the bush I had removed the fly from the leader and put on a bare hook. And on the hook—a worm, grubbed up from the bank . . .

I cast the worm upstream and let it float gently down with the current. The fish regarded it without apparent interest. Again I cast, and again. The worm passed first on one side of the salmon, then on the other. Sometimes overhead. The fish took no notice whatsoever, except that when the worm seemed likely to hit him on the nose he moved very slightly to one side . . .

Cast followed cast . . . I decided that while the salmon stayed where he was I would do the same. It had become a most interesting little exercise: how long could I continue without disturbing the fish? I had no genuine hope of catching him. And then, after about fifteen or twenty minutes of this, the salmon suddenly took the worm. There was nothing dramatic about it. He made no avid rush. It was simply that, as the worm floated past for the umpteenth time, he moved an inch or two to one side and very gently took hold of it.

I held my breath and did nothing.

The salmon stayed right where he was, the worm dangling from his mouth almost as though it had drifted there by accident. It seemed to me that any action on my part would accomplish nothing useful—so I waited.

After what seemed a week, but was probably eight or ten seconds, the worm slowly disappeared. As it did so the salmon began to move lazily upstream. I raised the rod and . . . a few minutes later the fish was on the bank.

In an attempt to be helpful I have quoted from that passage for two reasons.

First. To bring to your attention the time-lapse between my starting to cast to the fish, and when he decided to take the worm.

Fifteen to twenty minutes was my estimate. This is a long time to spend casting to the same fish, and I believe it is highly significant—not only with regard to my earlier contention about the impossibility of over-fishing salmon lies—but in an entirely new context that will emerge later in this chapter.

Secondly. With regard to the worm I grubbed-up from the bank.

This was *Allolobophora*, the blue-headed lobworm, a species frequently found in cow pastures. And I mention it in case you ever find yourself, wormless, in a similar situation and confronted with a salmon you would like to attack in a similar way. Excavation of old cow-pats should set you up in business.

But you need never be without worms if you store them properly. Having amassed your treasure, keep it in a big box of damp, torn-up newspaper. Newsprint offers lobworms much better accommodation than moss—which is suitable only for short-time storage. Kept as suggested your worms will live contentedly all summer, and longer if need be. Ensure that the newspaper never gets too dry, by frequently sprinkling it with water.

Keep the box in a cool place, preferably on a stone or concrete floor. A garage or outhouse is ideal. In hot weather reduce the temperature inside the box by having two plastic containers of ice. Keep one in the box on top of the newspaper, the other in the freezer. Exchange them daily.

Don't make the foolish mistake I once made when, in attempting to protect my loot, I painted on the lid: "Worms. Private. Keep out!" This is an open invitation to your friends. In times of summer spate, those worms will be nuggets of gold. Keep them secret. Don't advertise. Tell *no-one* of their existence.

Lumbricus terrestris,
the common garden lobworm.

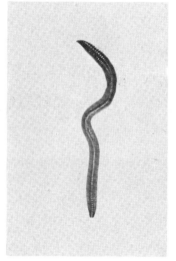

Allolobophora longa,
the blue-headed lobworm.

Ledger tackle, one of the oldest and simplest on record. The "grounde lyne rennynge" or "running line", first described in *A Treatyse of Fysshynge wyth an Angle*.

The bait. *Lumbricus terrestris*. Twice.

When the spate river is brimming its banks and the local worm expert saunters slowly along, pausing here and there to poke his rod through gaps in the bushes and drop a bunch of lobworms into little patches of slack water, he is not fishing at random. He knows from experience that all those places are potential resting lies for running salmon.

If an angler is trying to learn a river from scratch, such knowledge can take years to acquire, for equally important is to know the height of water when each of those lies may be occupied. As a river rises and falls, so the attraction of each particular lie grows and fades. A spot used by a salmon when the river is, say, two feet up, may be tenantless when the water has dropped six inches.

It is this change in water height that foxes so many visiting anglers unfamiliar with the beat they come to fish, and it explains why the longer they visit the same stretch, the more successful they will be—whatever their methods of fishing.

The sort of pattern to be expected is shown in the diagram. Although it is based on a densely-wooded stretch of spate river I fished for many years, the principle can be applied to any pool on any river.

Some of the resting lies that hold fish at some time or other during a spate are easily identified. Farm tracks that lead into the water where cattle come down to drink. Entrances to fords that carry farm vehicles across the river. Steep-to gravelled runs where the bank is undercut. Glides of easy water beneath trailing alder-roots—themselves old-time low-water hods from which the local farmers once "clicked" salmon for their tables, and probably still do. Corners where the river turns sharply, leaving little pockets of slack water over a firm bottom. Always, these high-water lies will be spots tucked-in close to the bank, for it is there in the slack or slackish water that the fish find conditions restful, away from the turbulence and hurly-burly of the main torrent.

Trotting a worm slowly along the edge of the current in such places, before letting it swing in to rest on the bottom for a time, will catch you a salmon sooner or later, for it is there that a running fish will pause. And in my view the worm fisher is harming nobody by catching it. Some of these places are impossible to fish with fly, or spinner either for that matter. Many of our smaller spate rivers are heavily wooded and over-grown. There are often deep spots under those trailing branches that hold salmon in low water—and can never be properly fished with any-thing but worm. It is foolish to judge all angling ethics only by the condi-tions on our big rivers. The spate river is a law unto itself, with its own ethic.

370

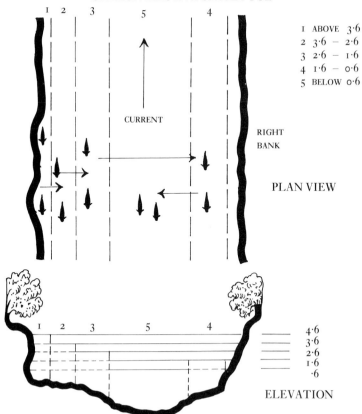

SALMON LIES IN A SPATE POOL

CURRENT

RIGHT
BANK

PLAN VIEW

1 ABOVE 3·6
2 3·6 – 2·6
3 2·6 – 1·6
4 1·6 – 0·6
5 BELOW 0·6

4·6
3·6
2·6
1·6
·6

ELEVATION

The diagrams show how quickly in a spate river the salmon lies can change. Here, the water can drop from above 3ft 6in to below 6in in under twenty-four hours.

When the water is above 3ft 6in salmon lie in Taking-Strip 1. As the water drops below this height they move out into Taking-Strip 2. At 2ft 6in or thereabouts they move out still further into Taking-Strip 3. When the water has dropped to 1ft 6in, they shift across the stream to Taking-Strip 4, close to the opposite bank. After this, when the water has dropped to about six inches, the fish settle in the centre of the river, Taking-Strip 5, where they remain.

This example is based on a pool I fished for many years. But anyone who knows his river could draw diagrams of every pool giving similar information. It shows the importance of knowing one's fishery, and how an angler who is really familiar with his water can tell from a glance exactly where salmon are likely to be lying.

Of course other factors play a part in successful angling. Water-colour for instance. Repeated spates coming close together, with the river rising and falling over several days, clear the water; so that by the time the third rise has come the river is running high but uncoloured. In my experience these repeated rises with the river hopping up and down never provide good fishing for either salmon or sea trout.

But no matter where or how you fish the worm, there are two points — material and moral, and common to all rivers — that are worth making. First, what you should do when a salmon takes your bait. Secondly, your responsibilities both before and after he takes it.

When fishing worm for salmon there is one golden rule entirely without exception. *Never strike.* NEVER. When the worm, on its slow trundle round a pool, suddenly stops, *do nothing.* You may feel very little to start with, perhaps a sort of nudging, a "grating" sensation; perhaps a slight tremor. *Wait.* Hold the line very lightly between thumb and forefinger of the left (or non-casting) hand. If it starts to twitch out, let it go. Always contrive to have some slack available for this contingency.

A salmon seldom gulps a worm straight down. He may toy with it for many seconds. But he will usually end up by sucking it in *if only you give him time.* Try to anticipate this by tightening too soon, and he will immediately blow the worm out.

However long the pause may seem, wait for the salmon to make a move. When eventually he starts to swim off, and the line tightens, you have only to raise the rod and make contact. By now the chances are he has the hook right back in his throat, and a fish that has taken like this will never come off.

Which brings me to the second point.

That salmon is as firmly hooked as any fish can ever be. It is now impossible for you to lose him — unless you allow him to break you. In which case, go home in shame and hang your head. To leave a fish with a hook stuck in his throat is unforgivable.

Always remember this. You are not forced to fish with bait. If you choose to do so, you must accept the disciplines involved. They are:

1. To use tackle of suitable strength. There is no point in fishing fine with worm for salmon. They are different fish from sea trout. I have never known salmon to be "leader shy" — except possibly when shadow is thrown from above. This does not apply to worm fishing.

Test nylon and hook before you start fishing, then you are unlikely to be broken, unless the fish takes you out of the pool and, because of a cliff face or trees or some other obstruction, you cannot follow him. Or, he snags you. This will be avoided by:

2. Making a thorough reconnaissance of the water before you fish it. Satisfy yourself that however big the salmon you may hook, you have a perfectly good chance of landing him. Don't forget, he is likely to have a hook stuck deep in his throat, and if you are doubtful — *don't fish that*

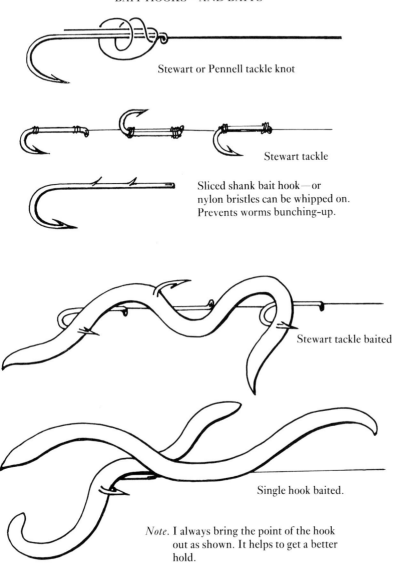

Stewart or Pennell tackle knot

Stewart tackle

Sliced shank bait hook—or
nylon bristles can be whipped on.
Prevents worms bunching-up.

Stewart tackle baited

Single hook baited.

Note. I always bring the point of the hook
out as shown. It helps to get a better
hold.

Note. Successful low-water worm fishing depends largely on knowing the exact amount
of weight to use. Too much, and the bait will continually glue itself to the rocks. Too
little, and it will not fish at the required depth. Weight must be judged to a whisker,
and adjusted if necessary to suit the depth of water and strength of current found at
each new lie—assessment of which will depend on the angler's water-sense and intuition.

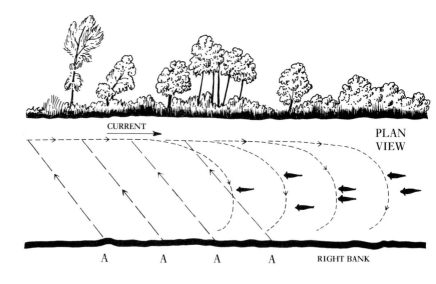

CURRENT

PLAN VIEW

A   A   A   A   RIGHT BANK

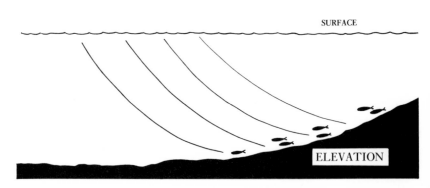

SURFACE

ELEVATION

Fishing the worm in deep water. Cast well upstream with a substantial twist of lead wire on the leader. Let the weight bump round in front of the fish. Can be tried as a change from fly-fishing, provided the bottom is suitable. There is no need to switch to a monofilament nylon mainline as recommended for low-water upstream fishing, a worm can be presented perfectly well on the fly rod with fly line. The leader length should be roughly the depth of water where fish are lying. The floating line will then act as a form of float. Salmon often nudge the worm very gently, and the line will react to every twitch.

I have caught many salmon in this way, when fish have been very dour and obstinately refused every offer of fly—and spinner, too. It sounds a dull method, but is in fact most exciting.

374

stretch of water. Doubts creep in when you see snags in the river, or a long stretch of rapids below the pool, down which for some reason it is impossible to follow a tired fish.

Irrespective of what species he is fishing for, or what tackle he is fishing with, no sportsman should cast to a fish he is not confident of landing.

*   *   *

It seems to be a fairly general belief that if a salmon is going to take a worm he will do so very soon after he first sees it, and that if he refuses several offers, further persistence is pointless. I quote an opinion from the literature:

> The first time a salmon sees a worm is by far the best chance of catching him. After that he shows less and less interest until he shows none at all . . . So you need not persist with a worm for very long unless you have nothing better to do.

With respect to that writer, I don't believe he could have done a lot of worm fishing. He certainly couldn't have spent much time watching salmon. The reverse of what he writes is just as likely to be the case.

As suggested earlier with reference to over-fishing of lies, it is the same with worm as with any other lure, fly included. If you are confident that a particular lie is a good one and likely to be holding fish, don't be in too much of a hurry to leave it—provided, of course, you have the water to yourself.

As indicated elsewhere in this book, the salmon's reactions to worm can be both fascinating and instructive. Besides giving me much pleasure over the years, watching such behaviour has been very helpful when I came to fish with other offerings; and what we observe when fishing for salmon we can see, frequently stands us in good stead when fishing for salmon we *can't* see. This is certainly so in the context of this chapter, when we come to cast a worm upsteam for salmon in low water.

No matter how low and clear the river, broken water with its swirl and eddy rarely permits observation of the fish we are casting to.

In deep or deepish water with an even bottom and fairly slow-moving current, worm fishing is straightforward and not very difficult. It is when the river warms in summer and fish move into those fast, clear, shallow runs of broken water at pool throats and between pools, that worm fishing merits the claim to be angling's most skilful method.

SOME LEDGER AND FLOAT RIGS

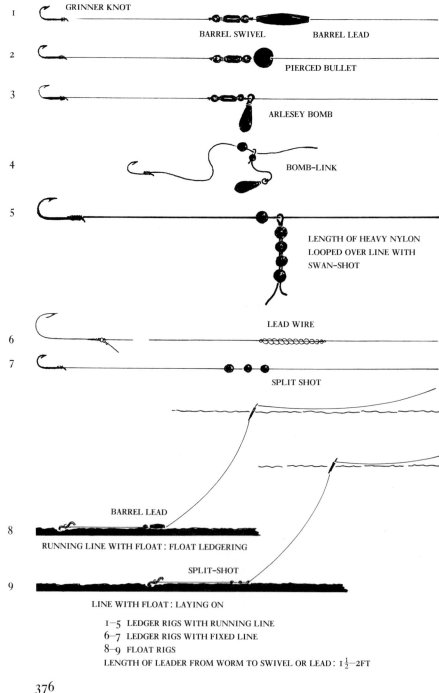

1 GRINNER KNOT

BARREL SWIVEL   BARREL LEAD

2   PIERCED BULLET

3   ARLESEY BOMB

4   BOMB-LINK

5   LENGTH OF HEAVY NYLON LOOPED OVER LINE WITH SWAN-SHOT

LEAD WIRE

6

7   SPLIT SHOT

BARREL LEAD

8 RUNNING LINE WITH FLOAT : FLOAT LEDGERING

SPLIT-SHOT

9 LINE WITH FLOAT : LAYING ON

1—5 LEDGER RIGS WITH RUNNING LINE
6—7 LEDGER RIGS WITH FIXED LINE
8—9 FLOAT RIGS
LENGTH OF LEADER FROM WORM TO SWIVEL OR LEAD : $1\frac{1}{2}$—2FT

Fishing such water, on rivers that have it, is as exciting as anything angling has to offer. It is also rewarding, for fish can be caught in the driest weather when other methods have failed.

Imagine you are faced with a boulder-strewn run dotted with rocks both submerged and awash; a hundred yards of swirl and eddy, laced with broken water and smooth glides sluicing in narrow channels between the rocks. Most of it is under two feet in depth. Nowhere is it more than three feet. That salmon and sea trout should be lying in such water seems hardly believable. But they are. And to take fish from a stretch that many anglers would pass by without a second glance is most gratifying.

Why can we not do so with fly? We can, sometimes. But worm usually causes less disturbance. To present the fly correctly in these conditions— that is, to narrow our casting angle so as to reduce the fly's speed—entails wading which, in such clear, shallow water makes disturbance inevitable. So, if you want to fish such water with fly, always have a go first with the worm.

The technique we use is quite different from upstream worm fishing for brown trout. The trout angler usually wades up-river, casting almost directly upstream. Here, we fish roughly at right angles, casting no more

Exciting water for the upstream worm

377

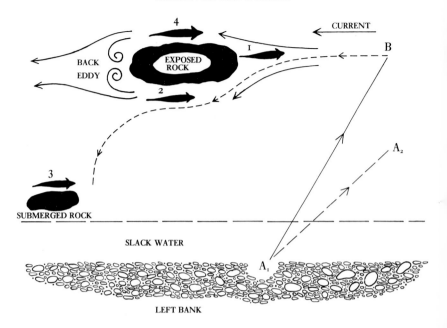

Using fly rod and reel the angler at A_1 strips off line, holds it in big loops and casts to B, a position far enough upstream to allow the worm to achieve a fishable depth on reaching No. 1.

To maintain contact with a worm as it drifts downstream, the angler shortens line by drawing-in with his non-casting hand over the forefinger of the rod-hand.

If fish No. 1 refuses, the worm will go past and, due to water pressure on the big rock, be swung to the left by the set of the current, and the angler must gather more line as it does so.

If fish No. 2 refuses, the gathered line is allowed to slip out as the worm continues downstream.

When it reaches the limit of its range the worm swings round towards the bank and comes on offer to fish No. 3. After which, it reaches the slack water and is retrieved close to the shingle.

Note. Owing to downstream turbulence, fish seldom lie close behind exposed rocks. The usual lies are in front and at the sides—sometimes on top when the rock is well covered.

To avoid disturbing fish Nos. 1 and 2, fish No. 4, which is difficult to cover more than once without the bait getting snagged, is dealt with last of all, and only after the others have been covered a number of times. It may be possible to catch him by wading to A_2, but as with fly-fishing, this should be left until all the straight-forward lies have been thoroughly fished.

Fish No. 3 is lying close to the shingle and could be disturbed by anyone walking past along the water's edge.

378

than forty-five degrees upstream, and keeping out of the water as much as possible. But we can still use the fly rod, and indeed I prefer to do so.

The tackle I use for such water is a single-handed fly rod and fly reel with a nylon monofilament mainline of 20–25 lb b.s. Heavy nylon is advisable, since it can be cast more easily from coils in the hand than anything lighter. On the end of the mainline, a small barrel-swivel on the other side of which, two-feet of leader a pound or two lighter than the mainline.

Using a swivel makes it easy to vary the length and strength of the leader. Having the leader lighter than the mainline ensures that if you get snagged and have to break, only leader and hook are lost. In anticipation of this emergency, it is sensible to carry several spare leaders, with hooks attached, on card "carriers" all ready to tie on at the riverside. This will avoid much fiddle.

Depending on the depth and strength of the water, a twist of lead wire may be needed about eighteen-inches from the hook. But this is never likely to be much.

In quieter waters where salmon have more opportunity to investigate the bait, and hooking is inclined to be surer, I prefer a single hook. But in the rough-and-tumble of fast water, a Pennell or Stewart tackle is probably better. The Stewart, after all, is a sort of snap-tackle and so rather better adapted to the exigencies of the job in hand.

As for the rod itself, the lightness of modern carbon has made everything so much easier. When a boy, I started upstream fishing with a ten-foot single-handed greenheart. Later, I graduated to a ten-foot-six Hardy "Houghton"—which became my favourite sea trout rod. Then, after many years, along came the fibre-glass ten-foot-six B. & W. "New Era". From which it was an easy step to the ten-foot-six carbon "Salmon and Sea Trout". And now? Well, the twelve-foot B. & W. single-handed carbon "Bob Fly" is superb. The extra length is a great blessing when it comes to controlling the line and holding it clear of obstructions.

Now, method. Our object is to present the worm to a salmon as naturally as possible, so that it drifts with the current ahead of leader and line and at roughly the same depth as the fish. Because the salmon is often lying in no more than a foot or so of water, very little extra weight is needed, usually no more than, say, a half-inch twist of lead wire, or a couple of split-shot.

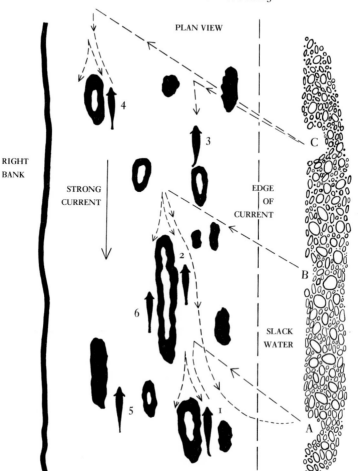

PLAN VIEW

RIGHT
BANK

STRONG
CURRENT

EDGE
OF
CURRENT

LEFT
BANK

SLACK
WATER

SHINGLE

SUBMERGED ROCK

ROCK PARTLY AWASH

SET OF CURRENT PASSING EITHER SIDE OF
EXPOSED ROCK

DIRECTION OF CAST AND SUBSEQUENT PATH
OF WORM

ABC   POSITIONS OF ANGLER

The diagram shows six salmon lying in a short stretch of fast, rocky run, which is being fished from the left bank.

Fish No. 1 is easily covered by casting from position A, but allowance must be made for the set of the current due to water pressure on the front of the rock.

Fish No. 2 is covered next, in a similar manner, from position B.

The angler then moves further upstream and covers fish No. 3 from position C. A straightforward cast, requiring only the normal allowance for strength of current.

After this he can try further afield. By lengthening line he may just reach fish No. 4 which, if he makes due allowance for the set of the current, is not too difficult to cover.

Fish No. 5—very difficult and best left till last because of the rocks and likelihood of getting snagged—may be just catchable from a position between A and B.

No. 6, lying on the far side of the exposed reef, is virtually uncatchable from the left bank. Unless fishing is permitted from the opposite bank, this fish is best left alone.

Note. To avoid disturbing fish that have not yet been covered, always cast to the nearer lies first.

*   *   *

Before starting to fish *always* make a careful examination of the water. Walk the stretch and pinpoint all likely taking-places. Note how the current is setting, and decide how best to cover them. Look for rocks and snags liable to hang you up. But when you make this reconnaissance, don't go too near the water's edge. Fish often lie close in. Frighten them in such shallow water and they will not give you another chance.

Never cast a yard further than you have to, and always start by fishing the nearer lies first. Strip off enough line to cover the first lie, allowing for the distance to be cast above it, and hold this line in large, loose coils in the left hand. (I am assuming you are casting right-handed.) Concentrate on making a smooth, easy throw. Any jerkiness, and the worm is liable to part company with the hook and go sailing off. Cast the bait upstream at an angle of about forty or forty-five degrees, shooting the coils of slack as you do so.

This is quite tricky, and a certain amount of practice is needed to master it. To start with, the coils of line will probably get tangled at the butt ring. The knack is in holding the slack line, using all your fingers, and like other forms of casting you have to work at it. If you simply cannot manage to do it, you will have to revert to fixed-spool tackle.

But a fixed-spool—not nearly so enjoyable to use—is neither so sensitive nor so accurate. A salmon often toys with a bait before taking properly and may have to be covered several times. With the fly reel that amount of line is already stripped off, and the bait can be cast to precisely the same position each time (like that prawn described in the Introduction).

The object in casting upstream is to get the worm swimming at the right depth by the time it reaches the first fish on your immediate list, which should be opposite or very slightly upstream of the rod. The moment the worm starts drifting downstream its distance from the rod tip will be shortening, so maintain contact by drawing in line with the left hand and controlling it under the right forefinger. As the worm passes across in front of you and goes on its way towards the downstream lies (having been refused by the first fish) let this line slide out again. When the line is fully extended, let the worm bump slowly round towards the bank.

All the time the worm is fishing, hold the rod high to keep as much line as possible out of the water. Keep in contact with the bait and *feel* the line with thumb and forefinger of the left hand. Be alert for the slightest touch. A salmon may nudge a worm several times on successive casts before seizing it, so don't expect an immediate take—although of course you *may* get one.

If you feel the bait stop, *do nothing*. Keep the rod up and try to detect what is happening through those two left-hand fingers. It is this direct sense of touch, so much more sensitive than a fixed-spool, that is so valuable in this technique. On no account jerk the line. If it is a fish you will probably pull the bait straight out of his mouth. If the bait is snagged, you may only pull it more securely home. If the bait *is* hung-up you will soon know by the dead drag on the line. If you feel a slight "trembling" sensation, it is probably a salmon, but tighten only when you feel him move away.

Usually, in fast water, this movement is not long in coming. A fish hasn't so long to fiddle with a worm. This is not to say he is going to gulp it straight down. He seldom does. But he is not likely to be so long over it as a fish fooling with a worm in slacker water. Often, as the current bellies the line downstream, the hook is dragged back into the side or corner of his mouth; whereupon, feeling this pull from behind, he will start to move slowly upstream.

Of course, he may be a sea trout; the water will almost certainly be holding these fish as well as salmon. But sea trout usually give a more pronounced pull when they take, and you will often feel two or three distinct "knocks". Besides, they get on the move sooner than salmon.

To hook a fish in such fast, shallow water can be very exciting. If he is a small sea trout you may succeed in bringing matters to a conclusion where you stand. But if he is a big sea trout or a salmon the chances are he will set off fast towards deep water. Usually he will forge ahead upstream for the pool above, but sometimes he will turn and shoot off downstream flat-out towards the pool below—and that downstream rush is galvanizing.

Hold your rod high, at arm's length above your head if necessary, to keep line out of the water and clear of snags, and follow him as best you can. When a big fish goes whizzing off—probably faster, with that current behind him, than anything you have ever hooked before—a mechanically perfect reel and evenly-wound line suddenly assume a new importance. It is now that you need a long rod, plenty of line—and a fair turn of speed!

Mr Gwyfor Jones with two spring salmon from the Tregaron Angling Association water on the upper Teifi.

So far, little has been said about the most important item of all—the worm itself. To avoid throwing worms off the hook when casting, it is obviously important to have them in good training; well scoured and hardened. Freshly-dug worms are too soft to withstand the rigours of continuous casting. But what of the bait's movement: its wriggle? How important is this? Is it true to say that the only worm a salmon will take must be alive and wriggling?

No, it isn't.

Salmon will not only take a dead worm, but a *piece* of dead worm. They will often do so, moreover, even after thay have refused offers of a live worm. I have known them accept parr-nibbled, tailless worms resembling little more than an inch or so of perished rubber.

It makes me wonder whether I have been wrong all these years; whether by an inscrutable twist of Nature, salmon actually *prefer* dead worms to live worms. More than once when ledgering in clear water, I have seen a salmon ignore live worms only to pick up a dead worm that has lain on the bottom for some time.

Why should a fish do that? It seems so unlikely. But then, almost everything about the salmon is unlikely.

Like every other bait-fisher I have ever spoken to or read about, I have always assumed that the worm's movement was part of its attraction; that it was the wriggle that stimulated a salmon's predatory instinct. One writer goes even further and adds scent to its attractiveness:

> I strongly incline to the belief that fish—salmon at all events—often sense or smell a worm in the water long before they actually *see* it, but having sensed its presence are much more inclined to go for those that are alive and active than any that are limp or soggy.

I, too, would have believed that once. It sounds so plausible. But is it *really* true? I don't think so. I incline to the notion that our belief in the importance of wriggle may prove yet another example of false assumption. So often when clear-water trotting, I have watched a salmon refuse the same, fresh, wriggling worm time after time as it drifted past, only to accept it later when it was considerably less active. That salmon I caught as a boy, mentioned in the quotation from *Sea Trout Fishing* on p. 366, is an instance of this, which I could multiply a hundred times. After "fifteen to twenty minutes" of continuous casting, that worm wasn't so vigorous. In fact, it was pretty limp. Was that why the salmon finally took it?

Casting back in memory I can recall fish after fish being caught on worms that had been in use a long time. Is this behaviour coincidental, or does it contain a hidden truth? As every bait-fisher knows, salmon will certainly accept worms that are alive and wriggling. But are moribund worms *more* acceptable?

I don't know. But it seems possible.

Anyway, I have offered you my observations. And I pass on the Dead Worm Hypothesis, with my compliments, to those expert bait-angling readers in Wales. They, if anyone, are qualified to carry out the necessary research.

* * *

On reflection, *is* it so unlikely for salmon to relish a dead worm? After all, they are keen enough to seize a dead prawn or shrimp fished inert on a float, or on the bottom.

But fishing with these little creatures is the subject of our next chapter.

I could see the prawn float across the fish a foot or two above where he was lying and no notice was taken. The next cast brought the prawn within reach and the fish, turning his head quickly, plucked at it, without taking hold, after the fashion of a hen pecking. The angler was ignorant of what had taken place. On being told to repeat the same cast the prawn again came round close to the fish, and this time he took it fairly, just as a pike takes a bait. The inexperienced angler felt nothing and did not respond to my shout to strike until after the salmon had released the prawn and it was too late. I saw the effect of the strike on the prawn, and so did the salmon, for he would not come again.

Henry Nicoll, *Salmon and Other Things*, 1923

XVI
Bait Fishing

PART THREE: THE PRAWN AND THE SHRIMP

Prawn fishing is a messy business. Fingers become sticky with salt and preservative, which climb all over your tackle, and after a time the stink gets tiresome. But if you don't mind this, the bait has much to offer—not least in the field of salmon behaviour.

Perhaps I should emphasize that although both prawn and shrimp are deadly at times, my motive in using them nowadays is not to make great bags of fish. Since my catch is never for sale, the size of the bag is of small importance. Most of the fun in fishing these baits—especially the prawn—comes from watching what the fish themselves get up to.

Chances of doing this today are far less frequent than they were. This is partly because of diminishing runs; partly because these baits have fallen out of favour. Unfortunately, in accordance with the less enviable characteristics of our human condition, some people derive perverse pleasure from trying to prevent others from doing things they have no desire to do themselves. As A. P. Herbert wrote sixty years ago:

> Let's find out what everyone is doing,
> And then stop everyone from doing it.

The grizzlers, who are forever seeking to stop their fellows enjoying themselves, have always been with us, and I suppose always will be. And of course, like other human activities, angling has its share of them. In consequence, together with the worm, prawn and shrimp are totally banned nowadays on many beats.

On some stretches, bait restrictions are understandable and, indeed, necessary. No matter whether prawn will drive a salmon from a pool, it will on occasion certainly drive him from his lie. Its indiscriminate

387

use on good fly water is foolish—and anyway, it is surely right in these times of shortage to place some sort of control on salmon-hungry "fish-mongers". But if I am to be honest and write from my own experience—which, after all, is what this book is based on—I can only repeat what I wrote in Chapter IV: that judicious use of prawn in the rivers where I have fished it, has not seemed seriously to have affected sport.

Apropos of this, some disparity between my experience and that of anglers on other rivers might be expected. Salmon reaction to similar lures sometimes seems to vary slightly from place to place. Returning mainly to their parent rivers, migratory fishes undoubtedly evolve along fractionally divergent paths. Although tiny, this difference may account for the variation in behaviour—if variation it really is.

There was a west coast beat where I used to stay as a guest long ago. We were permitted to try what baits we liked, provided only a fly rod, fly reel and fly line were used. I tended to fish fly in the mornings, worm after lunch and prawn after tea. This programme got switched about quite a bit, but that was the usual drill. I wasn't allowed to *spin* the prawn, but then I didn't want to. I vastly preferred fishing it like a fly, and always have done.

Drift-lining a prawn in this way was great fun. I would weight it by putting a twist of lead wire round the mount before wiring-on the prawn, then swing it out across the pool, shooting hand-held coils of line to get distance, and let it come round just like a big fly, but giving it a sharp jerk or two from time to time before working it through the slacker water by stripping-in line with my left hand. Very exciting, watching it come towards me in the clear water, sometimes followed by a big, grey shadow! Whatever tales of terror prawn may provoke in some places, it didn't do much harm in that pool.

It didn't on my own stretch of fishing twenty or thirty years ago, when the river was full of fish and I sometimes experimented with prawn every day for perhaps a week or so on end. Certainly, on the beat described above, the evening "do" with prawn never seemed to affect our chances the morning after. During one holiday there, when the autumn run was coming through, I caught twenty-six fish in nine days: twelve on fly; seven on worm; seven on prawn.

This varied attack of fly, worm and prawn was just for the hell of it. It was such fun fishing the different baits—especially since the water was clear and I could see most of what was going on. Fish would often "dog" the prawn, sometimes taking at the very moment of retrieve only a yard or two from my legs.

388

Mind you, that was many years ago in the golden age of innocence before some prodnose discovered the salmon's sea feeding grounds, and the professionals went to work with mile upon mile of nylon nets. There are far fewer fish to have a go at in the rivers these days, and feelings about the use of prawn run much higher than they did when I was young. Its use was quite common then. Nowadays, to mix fly-fishing with the prawn is practically unheard of.

And of course there is no excuse for doing so. As suggested in Chapter IV, the time to fish prawn is when weather and water conditions make fly-fishing chances virtually hopeless—as they are on many of our spate streams in summer.

But apart from this consideration, which accommodates the feelings and pleasure of anglers sharing the same water, there are no special times from about April onwards when prawn or shrimp is not likely to be worth a try. To the unrestricted angler fortunate to have his own stretch of some clearwater stream where, from time to time, the fish are visible, these baits offer a wealth of fascinating behaviour. Provided the water is holding fish and his primary interest is in their reactions, he will find plenty of opportunity for excitement.

A salmon may take a prawn in any height of water, whether clear or coloured. It may do so at any time of day, from dawn to dusk, and not by any means only the first time over.

It has been said, incorrectly, that if a salmon refuses a prawn on the first invitation he is unlikely to take it. As one writer put it:

It is generally accepted that a prawn is most likely to be taken by a salmon when it is first seen by the latter.

And he added:

No fish can be expected to look at an untidy prawn.

Prawn fishers believing this may enjoy a pleasant surprise, for the salmon will not only look at it, he will *take* it—sometimes, as described in the Introduction, after it has swung past him a hundred times. Moreover, although I am sure it pays to mount a prawn with great care and start fishing with an immaculate bait, I have caught salmon on only half a prawn, or even less. Their reactions to this bizarre form of attraction are far more subtle and unexpected than might be imagined. But it is only from watching them that one learns the truth. In salmon fishing, an ounce of observation is worth a ton of theory.

It was the boiled prawn's incongruity as a serious fishing bait that fired my enthusiasm to lie for hours on river banks and see what really happened when salmon were brought face to face with it.

Some of my happiest hours on fresh water have been spent crouched above a pool that, at times, held between half-a-dozen and twenty salmon, most of which could be recognized by their size and markings.

In addition to prawns and shrimps, I would offer these fish flies and spinners and maggots and worms—and sometimes strips of rubber and bacon rind and carrot, and other oddments. And highly fascinating it all was. But always I found myself returning to the prawn. This was simply because so often the reactions of the fish matched the ridiculous appearance of the bait.

After all, although there are certainly some oceanic crustaceans of similar colour, which the salmon probably encounters during his pelagic travels, who in sober mind could have imagined that he might take such a thing in the river? Well, somebody did—and hundreds of years ago at that. Richard Brookes mentioned it in 1740.*

Whoever it was, the first angler to catch a salmon on a boiled prawn may have got the idea accidentally, like the servant who, according to legend, dropped a spoon into the River Exe—and saw it seized by a fish. An incident said to have inspired the first spoon-bait.

Hoping to educe what colour of prawn was most likely to attract salmon, I sometimes went to the river in company with a box of oil paints and a brush. Surprisingly, although the salmon has an extremely acute sense of smell, he seems unaffected by oil pigment. At least, his interest is not diminished. A freshly-painted prawn is claggy to use, but a salmon has no objection to taking it.

And what did my research into Colour Response in Salmon achieve? Not a lot, I'm afraid. All I can claim is to have confirmed what other anglers had long suspected: that you can put your money on the nose of a dark, rich, purplish magenta, with a place bet on the boiled prawn's natural pinkness. None of the other make-up I used was conspicuously successful—apart from bright red, which gets a Mention in Despatches. Certainly, the colours given above got better marks than yellow or orange or green or blue or white or variegated polka dots and stripes—which, from what I remember, got little or no response.

So, there was no great discovery? Well, other than indicating that colour may occasionally play a part in attracting salmon—no, there

---

*In *The Art of Angling, Rock and Sea Fishing*, he wrote: ". . . a brother-angler caught a salmon with a prawn, without so much as using a single shot on his line: instead of that he drew his bait gently over the hole on the verge of the shallow, and at the same time kept out of sight." Other salmon baits mentioned by Brookes include cockle and mussel.

wasn't. But then, as I must confess, not always did my experiments attain that level of commitment demanded by the stricter canons of scientific research.

Perhaps the nearest I came to a break-through was on a sunny afternoon soon after an August spate. The pool was full of small, fresh-run fish. Having quickly caught two grilse on the magenta prawn, I was considering a bright cobalt blue with complementary orange spots, when an old friend and fellow wartime pilot arrived on the bank with a bottle.

This somewhat emotional reunion diverted my attention from the task in hand. Before I had recovered sufficiently to continue, some canoeists came paddling into the pool. While I was chasing them away, my Labrador polished off the prawns. After which the day degenerated into farce.

Now, alas, such golden opportunities for research have vanished with the vanished runs of salmon, and it is unlikely that I shall ever reopen the file. One day, perhaps, someone with suitable water and a plentiful stock of fish may care to carry on the work. Although I failed to make any shattering discoveries, the fish provided a feast of theatre—about which a few notes may not be unhelpful.

Reaction to Prawn

The behaviour of a salmon faced with a prawn can be summarized as follows:

1. He ignores the prawn completely. This response is by far the most common.

2. He swims up to the prawn, sometimes following it for several yards, but leaves it alone.

3. He sucks it in, then blows it out again, leaving no mark.

4. He gives it a nip, or "pecks" at it, often removing part of the head; or just the whiskers, which are sometimes sliced off as though with a razor. Or he gives the back of the prawn a little crunch.

5. He "chins" it, or hits it with his tail.

6. He rolls on it—if it is lying motionless.

7. He sucks out the eggs—if it is a "berried" prawn.

8. He crushes it in his mouth and then blows it out again, very fiercely.

9. He grabs it.

10. He chases across the pool to grab it.

11. He takes it the moment it hits the water.

12. He shows signs of increasing agitation as it approaches his lie. Then, when it enters his territory—comes, say, within a couple of feet or so—he turns and flees, often jumping after travelling very fast some distance up or down the pool. This fish is obviously frightened of the prawn. He may vacate his lie for as long as half-an-hour, although in my experience he usually returns within four or five minutes.

13. He starts to hop about as soon as the prawn is sighted.

Presumably this is the fish that writers have observed leaving a pool. Sometimes, it is said, a number of salmon will do so in unison. As mentioned in Chapter IV, although I have fished prawn for most of my life, this behaviour is something I have yet to see.

With regard to the way a bait is treated, I never cease to be astonished at the force a salmon can exert when sucking an object into his mouth, or blowing it out. For instance, a fish that has taken a worm presented on a leader weighted with twisted lead-wire, will often blow the worm right up *past* the weight. From what I have been able to see, the eggs on a gravid prawn, which salmon are very fond of, are not nipped but *sucked* from the prawn's belly. This is done with lightning speed, and so expertly that seldom does a single egg remain. Instantly, the prawn's underside is stripped clean.

Very little of this behaviour is transmitted to the angler. All he feels is a slight faltering of the bait, the suspicion of a nudge.* I once watched a salmon dealing with prawn after prawn fished by an angler who had no idea what was happening, and was at a complete loss to explain how the eggs kept disappearing. When I told him, he didn't believe me—until I persuaded him to change places and watch for himself.

Fish behaving like this are very difficult to hook. Strike as quickly as you may, invariably you will do so in vain.

It is a problem I have never really solved. Partial success was once achieved by setting up a mount with a small flying treble fastened, at right angles to the mount, in the middle of the eggs. But even this cunning device by no means always ensured a hooked fish. On one occasion I succeeded only in hooking myself. Forgetting the wretched little thing was buried in the eggs, I grabbed at the prawn preparatory to wading ashore—and drove one prong into my thumb!

Since that unhappy occasion I have learned a simple and far less painful method of hook removal. First, lessen the grip of the barb by pressing flat down on the back of the shank. Then, at the moment of maximum pressure, pluck the hook free with one quick, strong jerk. The barb will slide out cleanly with very little tearing of the flesh.

*See also *Salmon Reaction to Shrimp*, p. 393.

Reaction to Shrimp

As with prawn a salmon's reaction to shrimp—when the fish seems simply to toy with or nip the bait—is sometimes a take of extreme gentleness.

The picture shows a mounted shrimp that has been drift-lined on fly tackle and "taken" three times. On the first occasion the eggs were stripped clean from the belly. On the second, the head was nipped off. When the bait was cast a third time its back was crunched. On one occasion the angler felt a tiny nudge; otherwise only a momentary *slackening* of the line.

The photograph was shot during a morning's fishing when three salmon were landed—but over thirty shrimps treated in a similar manner!

Hooking

On the subject of hooking fish, what should we do when a salmon takes a bait? Well, on balance, I think the best course is to tighten at once.

If a fish takes avidly and sucks the bait right back into his throat, whatever you do will make no difference, he is already well hooked. If he takes the bait tentatively, preparatory to blowing it out again, your only chance of hooking him is to strike as quickly as you can. Which means that you can't go wrong by tightening the moment you suspect a take. If you are quick enough the "nudger" can sometimes be hooked.

Once when fishing for a confirmed whisker-nipper whose antics I had been watching, I contrived to hook him by keeping the rod pointing straight at the water. Next time round, just as the fish came up to nip the whiskers, I struck hard by pulling line back sharply with my left hand. There was immediate resistance, and I found myself fast in the fish. Instantly, it became clear that something odd had happened. He was struggling in a most extraordinary manner: writhing and twisting round and round, like an eel. As it transpired, this was not surprising. He was hooked right in the tip of the neb and unable to breathe properly, prongs of the treble hook having sunk into both jaws, holding them firmly together.

Reactions such as nipping or pecking at a bait; giving it a little crunch; sucking it in and blowing it out; bumping it with chin or tail;

or, more rarely, rolling on it with a flapping action reminiscent of redd-cutting, can happen naturally in the beaten way of angling. But the most dramatic response I have witnessed was in a contrived situation. Here, a prawn was manoeuvred into a position *behind* the fish, brought up close alongside and left lying motionless on the bottom just outside his edge of backward vision (see diagram).

I have managed this by myself when fishing for a salmon in view. But it is much more easily done by two people: one handling the rod while the other watches the fish and calls instructions.

The success of this little ploy depends on several factors. You need:

1. An overhanging bank on the deep side of a clear-water pool, with sufficient growth of long grass or bushes to conceal angler and observer— both of whom are on the same side of the pool, in tandem, the angler some dozen or fifteen yards upstream of the observer.

2. A moderate to sluggish current.

3. A fairly level bottom.

4. A weighted prawn that, despite the current, will lie motionless.

5. A complaisant salmon.

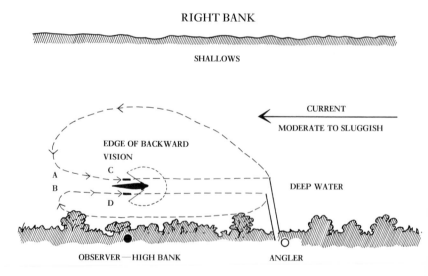

STATIONARY PRAWN PLOY

C.D. : RESTING PLACES FOR PRAWN

The object is to cast the prawn across the pool, or straight downstream very close to the bank, and bring it round to point A or B almost straight below the fish—as shown in the diagram. It is then drawn stealthily upstream along the bottom.

While doing this, great care must be taken to avoid touching the fish with the line, otherwise he will scoot off in alarm.

When the prawn arrives in position C or D, it is left lying there. The angler, maintaining a tight line, must hold the rod absolutely steady with its tip close to or just under the surface.

After a little while the salmon becomes conscious of something strange lying behind him, and starts to twist very slightly from side to side. Gradually the tempo of his movement quickens, and after a minute or so of increasing agitation as he swings more and more violently from side to side, each time catching a better glimpse of this pink interloper that has materialized inside his territory, he suddenly swirls round and grabs the prawn with such ferocity that a great cloud of sand or silt is thrown up from the bottom. All very exciting—and a fish that is invariably well-hooked and fights like fury.

I have caught salmon in this manner with shrimp and worm, but in neither case is the take quite so dramatic.

> *Note. Ploy fishing* such as this—when a particular salmon is kept in view
> and tempted with various lures in various ways—is a sport entirely of its
> own. Freshwater fishing offers nothing more fascinating.

Prawn Attachment (See diagrams overleaf)

There are three methods of attaching a prawn to a mount:

(a) With a criss-crossed rubber band.

(b) A length of nylon monofilament or thread with a tiny single or double hook at the end of it, as shown in fig. 1 p. 396. The thread, which is fastened to the tail treble of the mount, is wound round the prawn to the tail end, then criss-crossed back again to the head, where the little hook is embedded in the prawn's shell.

(c) With two lengths of fine copper wire as shown in fig. 2. The wires, which are fastened to the swivel ring at the upper end of the mount, are wound round the prawn from opposite sides. Two or three extra turns are made at the head of the prawn, then the ends of the wires are twisted together and laid back flat with the prawn. Although more fiddly I prefer this method. The wires hold the prawn together better during prolonged casting. And, who knows, the glint of the wire may add to the bait's attraction.

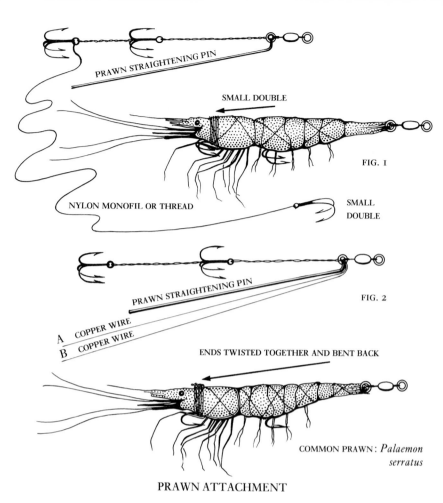

PRAWN STRAIGHTENING PIN

SMALL DOUBLE

FIG. I

NYLON MONOFIL OR THREAD

SMALL DOUBLE

SMALL DOUBLE

PRAWN STRAIGHTENING PIN

FIG. 2

A COPPER WIRE
B COPPER WIRE

ENDS TWISTED TOGETHER AND BENT BACK

COMMON PRAWN: *Palaemon serratus*

PRAWN ATTACHMENT

Lead wire is a good material for sinking the bait to a fishable depth. Weight can so easily be added or reduced according to the strength of current and depth of water.

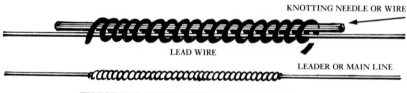

KNOTTING NEEDLE OR WIRE

LEAD WIRE

LEADER OR MAIN LINE

TWISTING LEAD WIRE ON LEADER OR LINE

When twisting lead wire round bait-mount or leader, hold your knotting-needle or a thin nail alongside as a stiffener and wind the lead wire round both. Then pull out the stiffener and tighten the turns of wire by twisting slightly.

396

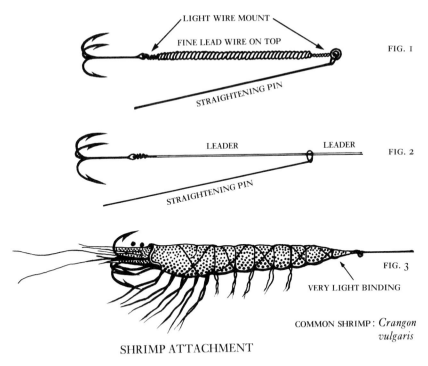

LIGHT WIRE MOUNT

FINE LEAD WIRE ON TOP

STRAIGHTENING PIN

FIG. 1

LEADER   LEADER

FIG. 2

STRAIGHTENING PIN

FIG. 3

VERY LIGHT BINDING

COMMON SHRIMP: *Crangon vulgaris*

SHRIMP ATTACHMENT

Lead wire comes in various thicknesses, usually wound round little cards. Keep several of these in your pocket.

Shrimp Attachment

For fishing shrimp in deep or very fast water it may be advisable to use a light wire mount weighted with fine lead wire (see fig. 1). Otherwise the rig shown in fig. 2 is simple and efficient: a straightening wire or "pin" is slipped up the leader on which a size 10 or 12 treble is then tied. The shrimp is held in position with a criss-crossed elastic band or light wire, (fig. 3).

Great care should be taken when mounting shrimp. Very fine binding wound so that the shrimp's legs hang naturally. If the shrimp is to be spun, the legs can be wound flat. When drift-lined the bait should swim on an even keel, without wobbling or rotating.

Shrimp fishing is a delicate technique. The take is usually extremely gentle. Often when the shrimp is fished on a float, the only sign of an offer is a slight dipping of the float tip as the bait is quietly sucked in *Strike at once.* Otherwise the chances are that a moment later it will be blown out.

Prawn and Shrimp fishing Methods and Tackles

There are seven methods of presenting prawn or shrimp. Apart from drift-lining, for which fly tackle can be used, they are best fished with fixed-spool reel and monofilament line.

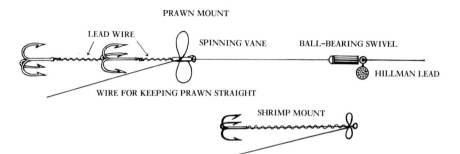

1. *Spinning*

Mounted with a spinning vane, baits can be fished across a pool in the same way as any other spinner.

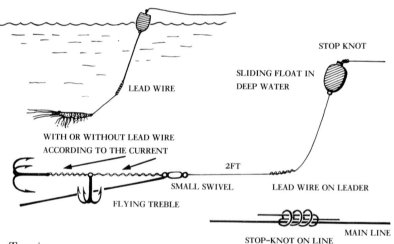

2. *Trotting*

Mounted without a vane, baits are set at a depth just above fish level and allowed to drift unimpeded down the pool. In deep water use a sliding float with stop-knot (see diagram). Compared with prawn, the shrimp is often taken very gently. Strike at the first dipping of the float.

Note. In shallow pools, a plain wine cork with a slit in it will serve as a float.

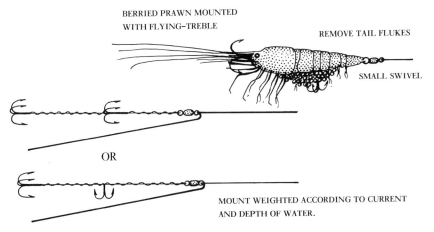

BERRIED PRAWN MOUNTED
WITH FLYING–TREBLE

REMOVE TAIL FLUKES

SMALL SWIVEL

OR

MOUNT WEIGHTED ACCORDING TO CURRENT
AND DEPTH OF WATER.

3. *Drift-lining*

Mounted without a vane and fished like a fly, baits can be drift-lined across a pool at any depth. Salmon will take anywhere between the bottom and the surface, but I prefer to get the bait well down to the fish.

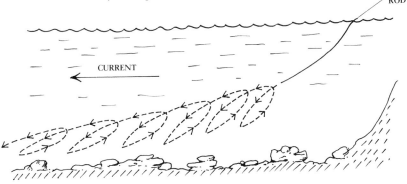

ROD

CURRENT

4. *Sink-and-draw*

An excellent method of fishing prawn. Mounted without a vane, the bait is cast out, brought up fairly quickly by winding in a yard or two of line; then allowed to sink again. This procedure continues "sink-and-draw" until the bait has swung round with the current into slack water under your own bank. It is then retrieved and cast again.

When fished from the deep side of the river, with some of the fish lying no more than a rod's length out, a bait can be let downstream from the head of the pool a yard or so at a time, checked, brought up a couple of yards, then allowed to drift down an extra couple of yards before being checked again and brought back as before. The bait is fished like this down the pool until the lies have been covered; then slowly retrieved foot by foot.

399

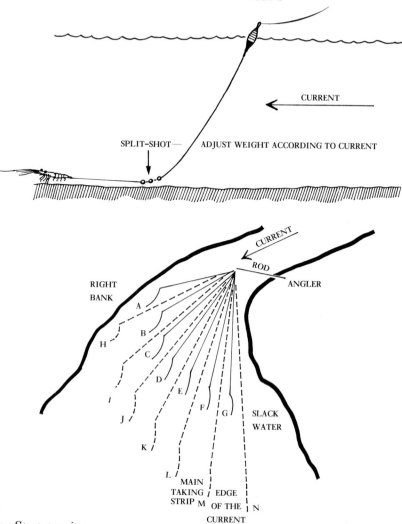

A LAYING-ON RIG FOR STRET-PEGGING

CURRENT

SPLIT-SHOT— ADJUST WEIGHT ACCORDING TO CURRENT

CURRENT

ROD

RIGHT
BANK

ANGLER

A

B

H

C

D

E

I

F

G

SLACK
WATER

J

K

L

MAIN
TAKING
STRIP M

EDGE
OF THE
CURRENT

N

5. *Stret-pegging*

This is a method of laying-on that can be used in running-water at long-range without the disturbance of long-range casting; but is possible only where the river bottom is of fine gravel, sand, or smooth rock. The bait, mounted without vane, not only covers a considerable area, but does so with very few casts—reaching the lies without breaking surface over-head or nearby. It works well with prawn and worm, but best of all with shrimp.

400

Instructions

1. Set the float deeper than the water depth by a foot to eighteen inches, according to the strength of current.

2. Cast at right-angles across the stream to a point just above A, then momentarily hold-back the float on a tight line. This induces the shotted leader and bait to sweep the bottom to A.

3. Release the float, letting out some line, and allow it to drift a yard or two downstream before again holding it back for a few seconds and fishing the bait as slowly as possible to B.

4. Carry on like this to C, D, E, F, each pause allowing the bait to cover a fresh arc of ground, and to rest on the bottom for short periods wherever there are little pockets of slack. Gradually the bait moves over in a crab-like manner to your own bank, ending up considerably farther downstream than when it started. When float and bait are nearing G, they make a quiet approach to the strip of water between current and slack. This is a favourite lie for salmon.

5. When the bait reaches G it will stop. Let it stay for a time. Then, to avoid disturbance, retrieve via the slack water very close to the bank.

6. Start again, this time casting slightly further downstream to just above H, and fishing round stage by stage to N.

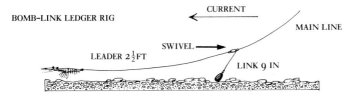

BOMB-LINK LEDGER RIG   CURRENT ← MAIN LINE   SWIVEL →   LEADER 2½FT   LINK 9 IN

6. *Ledgering*

A restful form of fishing. Very simple and, in essence, the same technique as described in chapter XV. Without vane, a prawn or shrimp is cast to where fish are lying and allowed to remain on or just off the bottom. A plain ledger rig with sliding lead is used in slackish water; a bomb-link rig in streamy water.

I have spent many peaceful hours in summer sunshine angling like this in locations similar to that depicted on p. 365. If other anglers who share the water want to fish other methods, they should of course be given priority. Speaking for myself, I only ledger when I have water to myself and conditions preclude the chance of sport with other methods. Most of the fun comes from watching the prawn—and the investigatory behaviour of the fish.

It was the prawn's incongruity as a bait that fired my enthusiasm to crouch for hours on river banks and watch what happened to it.

Fish lie like shadows on the gravel of a clearwater pool where I have fished many different baits and seen much salmon and sea trout taking behaviour.

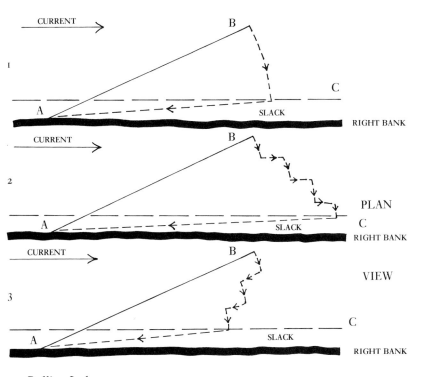

7. *Rolling Ledger*

A more active method than static ledgering, see diagram. Similar tackle
is used — pierced lead with running line, or bomb-link, but this time
fished in a stronger current. Provided the bottom is not too rough the
bait is kept on the move by casting across current to B and letting it
trundle slowly round to C (fig. 1). Variations worth trying are: lifting
the lead at intervals and letting the current work the bait crabwise downstream and across (fig. 2) (a form of stret-pegging minus float); or
upstream and across by drawing in line (fig. 3). (Both dependent on current strength.)

When the lead comes to a halt between current and slack at C, let
the bait lie for a time. Then, very gently inch it in towards you. While
you are doing this be careful to *keep out of sight*. Kneel down if necessary.
It is not uncommon for a fish to follow close behind and take just as
you are about to lift the bait from the water. When this happens *do
not strike*. Allow him to turn away with the bait before you tighten.

This parallels our reaction to a salmon taking the bob-fly when we
are fishing in stillwater — the subject of our next chapter.

There can be no question that the lady's place in angling is the very foremost rank . . . Whether by a stream in the midst of the meadows at eve, or cocked up in the bows of a Highland boat on a purple loch, no more graceful and harmonious picture can be imagined . . . Given a reasonably healthy physique, there is nothing to prevent the average girl becoming a competent angler on any kind of water at any season of the year.

Henry Lamond, *The Gentle Art*, 1911

XVII
Stillwater Fishing

Stillwaters differ so much in character that to do justice to them all in so short a space as this chapter is impossible. Nor need I try. There are several good books devoted to loch fishing for sea trout and salmon, and any beginner intending to fish stillwater will be sensible to read them first. The best I can do here is to outline a few general principles that hold good for most places; certainly all those I have fished myself.

Any English lake, Scottish loch or Irish lough that holds migratory fish (to avoid confusion, the term "lake" will be used throughout), is simply a big pool in the river that connects it—and perhaps other lakes in the same system—with the sea. To that extent, our approach to stillwater fishing is similar to that of the river.

As with a river pool, our first and most important task before starting to fish is to get some idea of the lake's underwater contours. The "taking" depth for salmon is roughly between two and ten feet (for fly fishing, two to six feet), and unless we establish exactly where these shallow stretches of water occur, a lot of fishing time will be wasted. It is commonplace to see anglers on some lakes beavering away over chasms perhaps ninety feet deep.

In this respect even the local boatmen can be fallible. I have known an experienced gillie confounded by the evidence of an echo-sounder when a windless day of bright sunshine was filled by taking lines of soundings across the lake. It is not surprising that a novice angler confronted with a strange lake is easily dispirited by the vast sheet of seemingly featureless water. There are, however, certain easily identified places common to all lakes where he can expect salmon to be lying.

When migratory fish first come into a lake, some lie for a time near the head of the river they have just run up. Later, these fish will join others that have pressed straight on round the edges of the lake to the mouths of feeder rivers in which most of them will ultimately spawn. If there is a chain of lakes higher up in the system, some fish will press on towards them without stopping. But if there is no further holding water, fish will gradually spread out along the margins of the lake they have run into.

Especially promising fly-fishing areas are formed by those long ridges of sand thrown out into the lake by river outflow. Such river "bars" stretch from shallows to deeps across the mouths of feeder streams and invariably provide good Taking-Strips. An example of this is the famous Endrick Bank, which stretches across the outflow of the River Endrick in Loch Lomond.

Other good taking spots are stony shallows dotted with big boulders, some barely awash, which form favourite lies for salmon. And those strips of water very close to shore where a steepish beach runs down into very deep water—the Taking-Strip being just before the break of the waves.

Other salmon lies are found in the shallow water formed by lines of rocks and stones stretching out into the lake. Salmon like big rocks. Such places are very exciting to fish, although great care must be taken in such shallow water: a long line cast, and the boat let back foot by foot by a skilful oarsman, and not a yard too far.

Islands, too, provide good lies—especially chains of small islands joined by shallow, underwater ridges of rock and boulders. Also, those rocky outcrops well out in the lake where the lake bottom comes almost to the surface, and indeed becomes visible when the water is very low.

Lies such as those described above, seldom more than three or four feet deep can afford salmon fly-fishing of the highest class. But they are extremely sensitive. They form the exceptions to my dictum—simply because, being so easily disturbed, they can easily be overfished. Such water should be used sparingly; never approached with the sun behind the rod, or with an outboard engine. And never on any account fished with the troll.

The Rod

The longer the rod, the further out from the boat a bob-fly can be kept dancing on the surface and furrowing along the edge of a wave—an action that salmon find very attractive.

There is a limit of course to what we can handle conveniently with one hand, although modern carbon has made it all comparatively easy. A twelve-foot carbon rod is no hardship. I have found the B. & W.

twelve-foot "Bob-Fly" ideal for the job.

Since fly-casting from a boat is made almost entirely downwind, a heavy line is not necessary. So, use the lightest you can conveniently throw, bearing in mind the need to roll cast. As I shall explain, this is a very practical cast to use from a boat.

Leader

Ten feet or so of monofilament: 10 lb–14 lb b.s., will suffice for most of our stillwater wet-fly fishing. On average, 12 lb b.s. will be about right. It should be made up with a dropper set three to four feet from the mainline to take the bob-fly.

Flies

Use anything you fancy. There is a huge number of lake patterns, but it is the *size* not the pattern that I think important.

Tail-fly: size 10 or 12. Stoat's tail and orange, or blue. Thunder and lightning. Yellow Dog. Connemara Black. Dunkeld.

Bob-Fly: size 6 or 8. Black Pennell, very bushy. Red Palmer. Zulu. Donegal Blue.

These are all good flies on their day. But they are only suggestions. *Put on whatever you have confidence in.* As for patterns, you never know what a salmon will or will not take. Forty-five years ago, on Lough Fern, having fished blank for two whole days of a precious week's leave, I suddenly struck it rich with a very anaemic-looking shrimp-fly, which caught me fish on four of my remaining five days. Those were the only times that pattern has ever caught me salmon in stillwater. I tried it many times since then, thinking that the day must come when salmon would fight to get at it again. But they never did. How do you account for such perverse behaviour?

Landing Net

There is no need to search far for a reliable net. It is pictured on p. 183.

Weather

I don't take much notice of it myself. If there's a bit of a wave, with fresh fish about, I know I'm always in with a chance. I don't care much for thunder storms because the lightning frightens me, as it does my old Labrador. But there isn't much else that will drive me off the water. Let those Jeremiah weather prophets get on top and you're half beaten before you start. As in the river, the most important factor in the fishing equation is the presence of fresh-run salmon. Given that, I will fish regardless of the temperature, or barometric pressure, or the light, or the amount of mist squatting on the hill.

If you really want to catch salmon, put the love of fishing first. Do that, and the fish will follow.

*　　　*　　　*

Safety

Not all sport in stillwater takes place afloat. Some parts of a lake, notably where a river flows into it, can be fished from the bank. But it is from a boat that most fish are caught. And so, before going further into fishing techniques, a word or two about boats and boating safety.

Unless you are an experienced boat handler and a powerful swimmer, it is worth remembering each time you go afloat that if things go wrong you can drown just as surely in stillwater as in the sea. And a lot of people do.

Most hired boats are sound, and professional boatmen reliable. But some are not. Again, some of the craft that anglers take with them on trailers and roof-racks are unsuitable for many of our bigger lakes. On numbers of occasions during my life I have rescued terrified holiday-makers in imminent danger of swamping who had gone afloat in unsuitable boats, only to be caught out by a rising wind and choppy water. The water can get dangerously rough in a very short time on some of our big lakes. Loch Lomond, for example. Such waters should be treated with respect.

And quite apart from the type of boat in use there are many other means of getting into trouble while afloat, and I have drawn attention to these in *Sea Trout Fishing* pages 403–407, but here are two of my *don'ts* in that book which I would like to stress:

1. *Don't* throw a rope to a person in the water without first tying a bowline in it. Failure to do this has cost a lot of lives. An exhausted person probably has numbed fingers and is unable to tie the knot. Without a loop in it, the rope is virtually useless.

A bowline is a loop that does not slip. The man in the water must be able to get his head and shoulders through it, so that it holds him under the arms. Once inside the loop he can be hauled to safety, even though he may have lost consciousness in the meantime.

If you cannot tie a bowline, learn to do so at once, and practise it.

It is the knot that saves lives. (See drawing of knot on page 175.)

2. *Don't* panic if the boat capsizes or gets swamped. Cling to the waterlogged hull or the oars or rubber rings until help arrives. But the colder the water the sooner you are likely to lose consciousness. If there is no help forthcoming, the sooner you start to swim for the shore the better. Don't undress if you have only a short distance to swim. Air trapped in your clothes will help to keep you afloat, as the clothes themselves will help keep your temperature up. But if you have far to go, strip off your clothes as quickly as possible. Do this while supporting yourself with the help of the boat.

When you reach shore, however tired you may be, force yourself to keep moving until you get help. If you become unconscious, you may die of exposure.

> *Note.* An alternative method of getting to safety, if the boat is not too big, is to swim the waterlogged hull ashore. This is not so difficult as it sounds. A friend and I used this method some years ago on a cold March morning after our boat had turned over—so I write from experience. We remained fully clothed and thigh-booted, held the boat's stern with outstretched hands, and swam with our legs, side by side. No story in it. One advantage of this method is that you have the hull to cling to when beginning to tire and needing a rest from time to time.

*   *   *

Wet-Fly Presentation

The area over which the boat travels while we fish the fly in stillwater is known as the "drift". The term is descriptive of a boat drifting in front of the wind, its anglers casting their flies downwind and drawing them in again faster than the speed of the drifting boat. And a lot of people fish like that.

It is a good enough method for catching trout. But not for salmon.

Drifting straight downwind is seldom so successful as fishing *across* the wind, the boat being held steady under oars on a course parallel to the Taking-Strip that is being fished. Casting straight downwind covers less water, gives the fish a less attractive view of the flies and increases the angler's tendency to pull a fly away from a fish's mouth. Far better is to cast the flies at an angle to the boat's path, so that as the boat moves forward across the wind, the flies move round astern of the boat and, still across wind, are then drawn in.

Alternatively, the flies can be kept moving at the speed of the boat, parallel to the boat's path, if the rod is held well up so that the wind bellies the line and allows the bob-fly to come tripping along the edge of a wave well out from the boat, the tail-fly following a few inches below the surface. With a fair wind blowing, this movement of the flies can be kept going almost indefinitely.

Both methods of working the flies are good, and when the wind is right an angler can vary his approach by trying each in turn. (See diagrams.)

Successful crosswind fishing depends, however, on two factors:

1. A fair breeze, with sufficient wave to diminish the movement of the oars.

2. An expert boatman who knows the water intimately and can hold the boat absolutely steady on the wind when certain hotspots are being fished.

Another advantage of crosswind fishing under oars is that if a salmon has risen but refused, the boat can be checked and held still while the lie is covered again, as often as the angler wishes. This is something that cannot be done on a downwind drift. Before such a fish can be covered twice, the boat has drifted over him. Nor can it be done if some form of lee-board is being used to induce a crosswind movement. A man at the oars is essential if the boat is suddenly to be checked and kept steady in one spot.

Achieving such control with little or no splash from the oars is difficult, but it can be done. And it *must* be done if we are to succeed at this form of fishing in the rocky shallows where so much of it takes place. As I have implied, almost everything depends on the boatman. The oarsman's thwart is no place for a beginner. With an expert who knows the lies, crosswind salmon fishing is a highly exciting and successful method. Without him, it is largely a waste of time. You may as well drift and have done with it. But what you will miss . . .

I have known boulder-strewn shores where taking salmon lay in water less than three feet deep, some in places where the breaking waves could scarcely cover them. You cannot drift among rocks half awash along a lee shore such as that. There is a hard wind blowing. A long line must be cast from a boat held against the gusts and let back foot by foot between the boulders, and then at the right moment checked as though at anchor so that the fly can go out straight downwind and fall like a feather. It has to, for it drops only an inch or two above a salmon's head . . .

To hook a fish in such a place; to lead him from that maze of rocks to fight it out offshore; that is as exciting as anything the sport of salmon fishing has to offer. But it is the oarsman who really catches the fish.

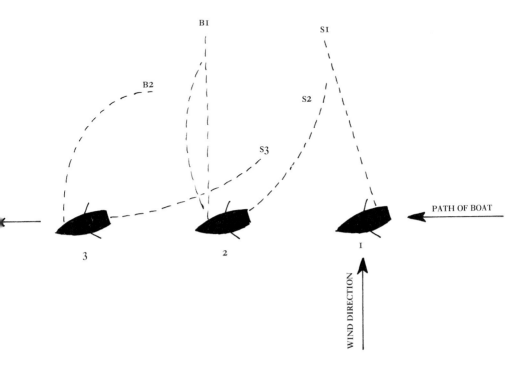

Crosswind Fishing
The boat is rowed slowly on a course at right-angles to the wind. To maintain this course the boat needs to head slightly into wind, as shown.

If the two rods are fishing, stern rod should cast first—to s1 as shown in Position 1. As the boat moves forward his flies will start to sink and then to swing round: s2 in Position 2.

Bow rod now casts to b1 and mends his line towards the bows.

In Picture 3, stern rod's flies—s3—have almost completed their swing and he is ready to start working them in towards the boat. Bow rod's flies—b2—are curving round, owing to the mended line and forward movement of the boat, and working along the line of the waves parallel to the boat's path.

This system of casting ensures that neither rod interferes with the other.

411

Be tidy in a boat. Don't leave pieces of tackle strewn about. They disappear under the floor-boards or get trodden on in the heat of action or caught up in loops of stripped line. And talking of stripping-in line to help work our flies, which happens during every cast, there are four ways of doing it.

1. Stripping it in and holding it in loops with the non-casting hand. These loops being shot again with the next cast.

2. Stripping it in and letting it fall between one's feet on the floor-boards, raising and lowering the rod-tip meanwhile to ensure a smooth recovery and avoid jerkiness. This is the easiest method, but results sometimes in loops getting caught up with the end of stretchers, buckles on tackle-bags or pieces of spare tackle. Better is to:

3. Strip in a yard or two, then draw the line right back with the non-casting hand to full extent of the arm, the line running under and controlled by the rod forefinger. Failing this, you may prefer to use a:

4. Figure-of-Eight Retrieve. in which case I recommend the "Finger-Ring" Figure-of-Eight. (See diagram.) Using forefinger and thumb as a line ring, and drawing in line right up close to it, makes retrieving much faster and easier than with the usual method—in which line is drawn direct from the butt ring. Keeping the line inside the rod forefinger enables us to control it instantly, when we wish, by trapping it against the rod. Very useful when we hit a fish.

During the retrieve, keep the rod point well up. This helps to keep the bob-fly working on the surface.

For casting from a boat I favour the roll cast, but aimed upwards so that the line extends in the air and not along the surface. Properly executed, it results in the line settling as gently as it will at the end of a good overhead cast.

I prefer this cast, especially in anything of a wind, because it is much safer than the overhead cast, both for the angler himself and other occupants of the boat—the boatman in particular. With long experience of indifferent fly-casters, many a veteran oarsman adopts a markedly hunched posture, head withdrawn tortoise-like into the shoulders, face twitching with the "boatman's wince" in apprehension of another wildly executed back-cast whistling past his ears. He will not comment, but he will appreciate your roll-casting.

Make sure you are throwing a long enough line; but, to maintain rhythm, keep it well within your range, so that you fish as comfortably as possible. In the shallows that many salmon inhabit, it is better to cast a canny line of moderate length than to strive for maximum distance

THE "FINGER-RING" FIGURE-OF-EIGHT RETRIEVE

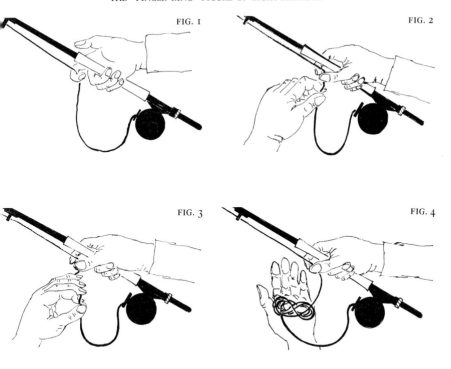

FIG. 1

FIG. 2

FIG. 3

FIG. 4

Having made a cast, grasp the rod only by the 3rd, 4th and 5th fingers of the right (or casting) hand and pass the line over the crook of the index finger (fig. 1). Drop the thumb until it touches the ball of the index finger. Thumb and index finger now perform the role of an extra rod ring.

Take hold of the fly line *behind* the right thumb with thumb and index finger of the left hand (fig. 2) and draw about 4 inches of line through the "finger ring".

Grab the line with the remaining fingers of the left hand (fig. 3). Allow the loop that has formed over the tip of the left forefinger to slip off into the palm as the hand moves back to its former position.

Repeat the procedure over and over again, with the wrist pivoting in a smooth figure-of-eight movement. It is important to keep the hands very close together; indeed, the angler should be conscious of his left little finger brushing his right thumb with each backward stroke.

Gradually, as the fly is worked towards the angler, coils of line are gathered up in the left hand. The gathered line is shown in fig. 4, with the hand displayed in an open position. This has been done purposely to reveal the coiled line. In practice, the hand merely opens sufficiently to grab each succeeding "bite" of line.

and cause disturbance. And on the subject of disturbance, remember that stealth is just as important in a boat as on the river bank. Keep still. Keep quiet. Don't rattle things about or thump with your feet. Boat bottoms are sounding boards, and sound travels a long way under water.

Hooking a Fish

Sometimes, in the wall of a wave, a fish can be seen coming to the fly, more especially the bob. But a fish taking the tail fly is by no mean always visible. We feel a pull—and the fish is either on or off. Apart from tightening too quickly if we see a swirl on the surface, there is little we can do about this fish except tighten as we feel him go down with the fly. But with a fish coming up to suck in the bob-fly off the surface, it is a different matter. We need to tighten on this fish, but our action must be carefully timed. Too quick, and we drag the fly out of the fish's mouth. Too slow, and the chances are he will eject it. Timing is all. It is a steady "One—two—tighten!"

What makes it difficult is one's impression that everything is happening in slow-motion—and one feels the urge to hurry it up! Fatal. When you see that big head coming up, *wait*. The mouth as likely as not is gaping wide open. Very exciting. There is a flurry of water and a big swirl. The fly has disappeared. The fish rolls over . . . *Now* is the moment. In one movement, raise the rod point and draw back line with the non-casting hand.

It sounds easy enough. It isn't. It takes a lot of practice to gain that control; to get that timing right. Don't worry. To start with, just try to do nothing until you feel a movement transmitted along the line. Then tighten. The fish will probably be hooked. Anyway, it's better to do nothing at all than react too quickly, because that is a certain way of missing the fish. After all, much depends on how the fish takes the fly. If he sucks it right down, the chances are he is going to be well hooked whatever you do, or don't do. If not, if he just sucks it part way in and holds it on a cushion of water, to be expelled a moment later like the fish playing blow-football, you *may* hook him by tightening. But, as with the fish coming to the dap, *never* if you tighten too soon.

I have described as simply as possible what I try to do myself when hooking a fish in stillwater. I realize it is all rather vague, and I'm sorry I can't be more explicit. But it is not possible to say exactly what should be done to hook a fish in every case. As described in earlier chapters, salmon have more ways than one of taking a fly, and nobody knows in advance what the next fish is going to do. However experienced he may be, no angler is going to hook every fish that takes.

A dark and cloudy day with a nice ripple on Loch Voshimid, Isle of Harris. Played out and ready to land, a salmon hooked by Grace Oglesby on a size 12 Connemara Black is being drawn in towards the net.

Grimersta

Many lakes are predominantly sea trout fisheries, so that much of our fishing is mainly for sea trout with the chance of hooking a salmon. There are, however, some river and lake systems in which the salmon takes precedence. The most famous of these is undoubtedly Grimersta on the Isle of Lewis, and we ought to have something about it in this book. Unhappily, I have never had the good fortune to fish there, but my friend Michael Daunt junior, an excellent fly-fisher who knows it well, has very kindly filled in for me.

415

Michael Daunt and gillies fishing no. 1 loch on the Grimersta system.
Double-figure catches are not at all unusual in a day.

It is, incidentally, a huge personal pleasure to include the name of
Daunt in this book. It gives me the opportunity of mentioning Michael's
father, Daunt senior, of the same christian name, and former chief test
pilot for the Gloster Aircraft Company—a man who treated me with
exceptional kindness many years ago when, as a very junior Royal Air
Force officer just out of the nest and feeling rather apprehensive, I turned
up at Gloster's to collect a new Gladiator.* Our meeting is stamped
on my memory.

"Mike's up checking your aircraft", said the company official who
greeted me on the tarmac. "Here he comes now."

A gleaming new silver Gladiator came zooming down, skimmed the
line of trees fringing the tiny Gloster airfield, and hurtled over the grass
at head height. As he went past, the pilot gave us a cheery wave. Michael
Daunt. Upside-down . . .

What a great flier he was, and how considerate and helpful to a young-

*The Gladiator—*pace* the Spitfire—was the last of the "gentleman's" aircraft.

ster for whom such dashing test pilots were like gods newly descended from Olympus.

But I must drag myself back from those wonderful fishing and flying pre-war dream days when the world was young, to the realities of this book, and Michael Daunt junior's account of fishing the Grimersta.

The salmon there tend to be very free-taking. The water is clear and pure and the lochs very shallow. Perhaps because of the shallowness of the water the fish, although generally small, fight harder than any I have met. For this reason I use a minimum of 12 lb breaking strain leader.

Fly pattern is unimportant. Generally, I have found that hair-wings are best. The size *is* important. The tail fly from June until the middle of September, no larger than size 8. I often use 10's or even 12's—tied on double hooks, as I find they work better in the water than singles. My preference, however, is for small tubes, the size being $\frac{3}{8}$ inch, very lightly dressed with the hair overlapping the tube by no more than $\frac{1}{4}$ inch. The whole fly being $\frac{5}{8}$ inch, the same as a size 10 double.

On these tubes I use size 14 or 16 trebles, the hooking qualities of which are excellent, producing such good holds that it is often necessary to use pliers to extract them.

I have had great success with these small tubes, and feel the mistake many people make is to use too large a tail fly. Even when fishing a good wave, it is not necessary to change to a larger fly. By contrast, the dropper fly *should* be large: size 4 or 2. On the Grimersta the fashion is to use Elver flies with Vulturine Guinea Fowl feathers of $1\frac{1}{2}$–2 inches in length; but I think that any large fly will do. Some people use a Muddler Minnow.

These large dropper flies, which are fished in the surface film, seem to act as *attractors*. Although they will sometimes catch fish, their effectiveness is in bringing a salmon up so that it will then take the tail fly.

Speed of fly retrieve depends on the wind. In a big wind the retrieve should be relatively slow, and the flies worked right up to the boat. In a light breeze, however, in that gin-clear water, a longer line should be thrown and the flies worked faster, with as much "swing" as possible on the line.

One point which I have found to be true time and time again is that, whether fast or slow, the retrieve must be at an even speed. Not jerky. This can be achieved by using the rod tip in conjunction with line stripping. Swing is achieved by bringing the rod tip over either the right or left shoulder.

Like the speed of fly-retrieve, speed of strike is all-important. Not too fast, not too slow. But it *is* a strike. The first time I fished Grimersta, having been warned to strike as quickly as possible, I was *too* quick. The first fish I rose came at me three times. I struck it as I would a trout with a small dry fly—and missed it each time. The ideal speed of strike, I soon found, is rather like that for hooking big rainbow trout taking nymph in the surface film.

Mike's advice holds good for nearly all the lakes I have fished. What I have never experienced, however, is the *shoaling* of salmon, which seems to be a feature of the shallow Grimersta fishery. Mike refers to this when writing about fishing the dry fly, for which he recommends a forward taper line.

The salmon in the Grimersta lochs tend to move in shoals, albeit in time-honoured lies. When you have spotted a shoal, get your gillie to row the boat very, very quietly towards it, and hold the boat no closer than 25 yards from the shoal. Any nearer and the fish will become frightened.

The take is sensational. You see the fish open its mouth, move forward . . . and then, suddenly, your fly is no longer there! *Don't strike*. The fish will continue to move forward—and eventually turn down. It is now that you strike.

The best conditions for fishing dry fly are those of flat or near flat calm. Provided salmon are present in good numbers and occasionally showing, they can be caught even though the surface is mirror-like and the sun blazing down.

Generally speaking, the type of fly is unimportant—except that it should be about the size of a Mayfly and, most important of all, should sit high on the water.

It seems strange that this method works best in a flat calm or tiny ripple, but not in a strong wind. And yet a bob-fly brought furrowing along the side of a wave is highly attractive in windy weather—as indeed is the dap itself.

Dapping

Dapping consists of tantalizing the fish by keeping a fly dancing on the surface like a piece of thistledown. With a bit of a breeze and a nice amount of wave it is effective for both salmon and sea trout and, if the fish are active, very exciting. One watches the fly quivering on the water with the tense expectancy that one watches a float, and the thrill of the rise is heart-stopping: usually every stage of the take can be seen.

But although dapping makes a pleasant enough change from the wet-fly, the fishing itself gets rather boring, since there is virtually nothing to do. Everything depends on the fish, and if they are reluctant to co-operate and time ticks by without an offer, dapping begins to pall. One has only to hold a rod reasonably steady, let the blowline waft out with the wind and keep the fly bouncing on the surface without getting waterlogged.

This ease of fishing makes dapping an ideal method for wives and camp followers, who know little about angling but fancy having a try themselves—and if they have good "hands" and can learn to make a fist of the strike, they have every chance of catching fish.

Tackle consists of a reel containing, say, 150 yards of 20 lb monofilament, ending in 12 to 15 yards of gossamer-light polypropylene dapping-line, or "blowline", which billows out with the breeze and keeps the fly well out from the boat. On the end of this blowline is about three feet of leader, say, 15 lb b.s. Polypropylene doesn't absorb water like the silk blowline of yesterday and, if one wishes, can be dapped in the slightest breeze—although as wind and wave diminish, so do the chances of catching fish.

A period of drought. The little river leading from the freshwater lochs is dead low. Where it flows into the sea loch, salmon and sea trout congregate in shoals, waiting for a spate. Some of the many fins breaking the surface can be clearly seen. This habit of waiting migratory fish to swim in shoals with their fins showing is mentioned by Mr Hansard as quoted in W. L. Calderwood's *Salmon Rivers and Lochs of Scotland*, 1909. (See p. 424)

There is nothing special about the rod except its length and lightness. Ideally, it should be sixteen to eighteen feet long. Shakespeare make a light collapsible dapping rod of 17 feet 3 inches that telescopes down to three feet for ease of stowing.

Hackled dapping-flies, mainly dressed palmer style, can be tied either on single hooks size 8 or thereabouts, or on $\frac{1}{2}-\frac{3}{4}$ in. tubes, armed with small trebles: size 14 or 16. The colour scheme can be anything you fancy. A mixture of black-and-yellow, or black-and-blue seems as good as anything.

As with river fishing, a small length of bicycle valve-tubing over the end of the tube and taking the head of the hook is essential. This prevents the treble slipping away from the floating tube and hanging some distance below—where it is not going to hook many fish!

Before use, flies should be soaked in Permaflote and allowed to dry.

If the fly is getting blown about too much in a high wind, lengthen the leader—which helps to hold the fly down on the water. Of course, you can simply put on a heavier fly. But generally, the lighter the fly the greater its attraction, since to do its job properly it needs to stand up on its hackles and "dance".

As always, it is essential to know the depth of water you are drifting across. For reasons I have never understood, sea trout will come up to the dap from greater depths than salmon—for which the ideal depth is from three to six feet.

The strike, which is all-important, needs to be very slow and deliberate. When you see a fish come open-mouthed to the fly, *do nothing. Wait.* This is not so easy, especially since everything seems to be happening in slow-motion and (as it always does) it takes you by surprise. But any premature reaction is disastrous. Invariably the fly is pulled away from the fish's mouth. Not until he has turned over and started to go down should one tighten.

Some anglers, on seeing a fish rolling over, chant: "God save the Queen. *Wow!*" Tightening on the "*Wow!*" This, besides showing a pleasing loyalty, seems to work well enough, and readers who have difficulty in timing their strike may find it helpful.

This is really just about all there is to dapping. It is a pleasant diversion; a change from waggling one's rod about. But much as the sight of a big fish rising to the dap excites me, the inaction becomes tedious when fish are dour.

A salmon leaps in a sunlit Hebridean sea loch. Until rain swells the tiny stream joining hill loch and sea, enabling fish to run, this salmon will be one of a shoal swimming close inshore near the freshwater outflow — in constant danger of attack by seals.

Mr Gerald Panchaud playing a salmon in the sea loch near Amhuinnsuidhe Castle, Isle of Harris. The fish, hooked in the freshwater outflow, has dashed straight out into the tide, an example of *Salmo*'s astonishing ability to make the instant physiological adjustment necessary for switching suddenly from one environment to another.

421

Trolling

But if dapping bores by its inaction, what of trolling? (It should be "trailing", see p. 323, but let that pass.)

As a method it is often described as dull and lacking in finesse. But an angler's pleasure in trolling comes largely from what he chooses to make of it.

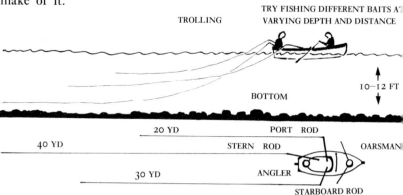

TRY FISHING DIFFERENT BAITS AT
VARYING DEPTH AND DISTANCE

TROLLING

BOTTOM

10–12 FT

20 YD PORT ROD
40 YD STERN ROD OARSMAN
30 YD ANGLER
STARBOARD ROD

When a lake is at good fishing height, and especially when a spate has brought in a fresh run from sea, fish are likely to be found mainly in the rocky shallows and along those sand bars off the mouths of feeder rivers. But when the weather turns hot during prolonged dry spells, fish move out into deeper water. Now, when chances of sport on fly are poor, trolling can be a profitable alternative. And it is worth observing that there is more skill in successful trolling than some critics may imagine. The angler who consistently takes fish from the depths of what appears to be a featureless expanse of water, is not haphazardly dragging a bait about. Over the years he has gradually built up a fascinating picture of the lake bottom, and has discovered the best taking spots. As a result, he will in the long term catch more fish than the angler who moves aimlessly about, never quite certain of the depth he is trolling in, and certainly not the depth at which his bait is fishing.

TURN OF FUSE WIRE

SWIVEL

SPLIT RING

Toby-type spoon with elasticum hook mount as suggested in Chap. XIV. The mount is fastened to the split-ring at head of bait, the treble hook held rigidly by turn of fuse wire through hole in tail of bait from which the split-ring has been removed.

The Toby is an excellent trolling lure, but the hooking qualities are improved by use of mount as shown above.

Note. For trolling at depth, see "Down-rigger", *Sea Trout Fishing* pp. 397–401.

422

Speaking for myself, as a rest and a change from fly-casting I enjoy a troll through some of the deeper water not otherwise fished, especially when going from one fly drift to another. Such use of bait harms no one. But otherwise the time I spend trolling is very limited. To catch the occasional fish is a bonus. But to make a killing on the troll would give me no pleasure.

But we are not all made alike. Far from being dedicated fly-fishers, some anglers have no wish to wave a rod about. For them, a day's pleasure is to sit in a boat with their baits trailing astern and enjoy the scenery. And provided they interfere with no one else's pleasure, who shall condemn them for that?

The sporting ethic of trolling as of any angling method, depends on the type of water, the time of year and how the method is used. Trolling during February, March and April in a big lake holding a run of spring fish is an entirely different proposition from dragging baits across good fly beats in a shallow western lake in summer.

On Loch Lomond, anyone handling his own boat in the driven hail and sleet of early spring, deserves his fish. More so, it might be argued, than the angler with his back to the wind, spinning a big bait down comparatively sheltered water from a gillie-handled boat on Tweed. The man on Lomond certainly works harder.

But when May arrives, and with it the chances of salmon on the small fly in the shallows—which gives pleasure to so many anglers—the situation changes with the changing behaviour of the fish. There is no doubt that in summer, indiscriminate trolling—all too often with outboard engines—can ruin good fly water. As, indeed, some of the best fly drifts on Loch Lomond have been spoiled during recent years.

Bill McEwan, who discusses trolling at length in his book *Angling on Lomond*, 1980, makes the comment:

> Many people decry and detest it, pointing out the very real damage it does to good fly water ... My trolling after mid-May is strictly limited until the end of the season, and during those summer months never across the fly drifts.

Anyone interested in fishing Loch Lomond, incidentally, would be foolish to go there without first consulting McEwan's excellent book. It gives everything one needs to know about the techniques of fishing that exciting water—with particular emphasis on the fly.

Strange Behaviour

But although, as we have seen, by choice of method it is possible to catch salmon in stillwater irrespective of the conditions, the presence of fish in the lake is essential. And the more recent their arrival from saltwater the better.

The outflow of a stream joining two lakes. The current continues for some distance into the lower lake like a little river and nearly always provides good "taking" water. Such outflows, however, are usually shallow and whether from boat or bank should be fished with great stealth.

Stillwater fishing, like that of summer spate streams, is very haphazard. Most lakes are dependent on flood water to bring their runs of fish up-river from the sea; so that, although when booking your fishing you choose what seems from the records a promising time, you are often thwarted by lack of salmon. But when a sudden rise follows weeks of dry weather as happened on that famous occasion on Grimersta, sport can sometimes be dramatic.

Grimersta was the fishery where during a week in August/September, 1888, three rods fishing fly caught 333 salmon and 71 sea trout.

This big catch, which was made almost entirely in one small loch as the result of an artificial spate following a long period of drought, would undoubtedly have been even bigger had the three rods not fished the loch in turn. The record bag, 54 salmon in the day, was made by a Mr Naylor. The second biggest, 46, by a Mr Hansard who, as recorded in *The Salmon Rivers and Lochs of Scotland*, 1909, by W. L. Calderwood, published an account in *The Field* of November 8th, 1902.

The chief reason why I allude to this account, however, is to draw attention to the curious behaviour of the fish.

Apparently after nearly four hours of non-stop activity on that long-ago Saturday morning when fish, it seems, were scrambling to get at the fly, the lake suddenly went *absolutely quiet*. Not a take. Not even a movement. And then, after a two-hour pause, the action re-started—and continued non-stop until the angler packed up at seven o'clock.

I find that extraordinarily interesting. The abrupt cessation of activity and equally sudden restart could not possibly have had any connection with fish movements. The artificial spate was long over. No fresh fish were entering the lake. For that matter, no fish were leaving it. They couldn't be, they were trapped. So—what happened? There were thousands of salmon in that one small, shallow stretch of water. What made them suddenly stop taking during those two hours when, as Mr Hansard wrote:

I literally flogged without rising, or, if I remember rightly, seeing a fish.

How can we account for behaviour as mysterious as that? It seems to defy analysis. And yet . . . I am struck by the similarity between the reaction of those salmon and the pattern of sea trout taking-behaviour at night.

So often, during what I call the "first-half"—that period from dusk until perhaps midnight or thereabouts, described fully in my book *Sea Trout Fishing*—there is a fine flurry of taking activity before, suddenly, the fish shut off completely. When this happens the river goes dead. There is no movement, no splashing about. The water seems lifeless and empty. And like that it stays, until perhaps two or two-thirty in the morning when, suddenly, the "second-half" starts and the fish come on the take again—often providing our best chance of catching a whopper.

What motivates such strange designs?

As suggested in Chapter II, the answer I believe lies hidden in the shifting curves of David Goldsborough's Hypothesis. For answer there *must* be, and no other solution I have ever heard comes anywhere near to fitting so many contradictory facts.

But even if I am right, until we can establish exactly what causes those physiological curves to shift so dramatically from side to side, we shall remain helplessly in the dark. With the fish themselves as gloriously unpredictable as ever.

425

On their way to the spawning redds, having escaped mile upon mile of monofilament netting and a host of predators, returning salmon leap in fresh water. A modern miracle of survival.

XVIII
The Future of *Salmo*

The history of angling offers no story so sad as the recent decline of *Salmo*. Although repercussions were not immediately noticeable, the unfortunate discovery of the salmon's Atlantic feeding grounds combined with the deadly monofilament nylon drift-net, made this decline inevitable.

On these grounds, mainly off the west coast of Greenland, a mushroom growth of commercial netting was soon responsible for huge catches. Greenland's rivers were incapable of producing such numbers and, as sea-caught salmon tagged as smolts quickly proved, most of them came from the spawning redds of Britain, Scandinavia, Canada and the USA. And as season followed season, the increasing catches made at sea began to be reflected inversely in the freshwater catches made with rod and line.

Although as a result of political intervention the growth of deep-sea salmon fishing was eventually checked, today's overall situation shows no improvement; anything gained on the swings of the ocean being lost on the roundabouts of our home waters. Large numbers of salmon homeward bound from the feeding grounds are intercepted by miles of nylon drift-nets off the Irish and British coasts, and finally by the estuarine nets that operate at the mouth of nearly every salmon river.

Nor is this the whole story. For the survivors of these three separate assaults by saltwater netsmen—in addition to a host of natural predators, notably the seal—the river is no sanctuary. Modern poaching has to be seen to be believed. Some gangs no longer wait for an angler to vacate a pool but march straight in and shoot their nets, and he interferes at his peril. Besides ruining his sport, some present-day poachers will damage his transport—and even his person. It is not only in the football stands and side-streets of our cities that violence abounds.

In Cumbria during the 1982 season, as reported by *The Whitehaven News* of October 28th, under the headline: "Poachers' Reign of Terror", anglers on the River Derwent were threatened, stoned and shot at, and their cars damaged.

Things have got so bad that some anglers are to be issued with walkie-talkie sets so that police and water bailiffs can be summoned quickly to their aid within a 25-miles radius.

Throughout Britain today, every known illicit method of taking salmon in quantity is being used, from systematic underwater killing in frogsuits to the use of nets, explosives and poison.

Poison most commonly used is the well-known Cymag, which inhibits fish from using the dissolved oxygen in the water and speedily chokes them. The overall effect is catastrophic. In addition to fish taken and sold by the poachers, poison can devastate a stretch of river for a long distance downstream.

82 salmon and 10 sea trout poisoned and netted out of a River Lune pool by two poachers surprised by the Lancashire Police. It is not known how many dead and dying fish were swept away by the current.

428

As an example: during the summer of 1982, a poaching gang poisoned a pool on the River Kent. Apart from fish removed by the gang, the following dead fish were recovered from more than a mile of water by members of the River Authority:

160 salmon, average 8 lb;
3,290 sea trout, average 3 lb;
780 brown trout, average $\frac{1}{4}$ lb.

Such was the result of a few minutes' ruthless poaching in just one pool on just one river!*

*   *   *

Together, over-fishing on the salmon's sea feeding grounds; interception on the return routes by fleets of monofilament nylon-using drift-netters; estuarine nets and traps, and organized poaching gangs netting and poisoning the rivers themselves, take a tremendous toll. But these are not the only threats to the future of *Salmo*. Hanging like a Damoclean sword above our heads is yet another form of commercial exploitation: *acid rain*.

Already in Britain this deadly type of pollution has accounted for a significant number of migratory and other species of fish. On the Cumbrian Esk during the third week of June, 1980, as I had the misfortune to witness, the early run of salmon and sea trout was almost totally destroyed; the fish dying within a few hours of their arrival in fresh water.

Together with employees of the North West Water Authority, I removed a number of dead sea trout of up to 12 lb and salmon to 20 lb. These fish had just run during a heavy spate and were covered with tide lice. Laboratory examination showed that death had been caused by excessive acidity.

Later, research by NWWA scientists confirmed that a number of the river's feeder streams, where much of the spawning took place, were "unexpectedly fishless" due to acidic pollution. Today in this once most prolific of rivers, the runs of migratory fish are minimal.

Acid rain is a result of fossil fuel combustion. The oxides of sulphur

---

*Poaching in Scottish coastal waters has increased enormously during recent years. From just a fourteen mile stretch of the Sutherland coast, no fewer than twenty-four monofilament-nylon gill-nets, the longest half-a-mile in length, were impounded by officers of the Northern Constabulary between January and July, 1984.

and nitrogen together with the other combustion products mix with moisture in the atmosphere. Circulating with the air masses that form our weather systems, they may travel for hundreds, even thousands of miles, changing as they go into deadly compounds that rain down as dilute solutions of sulphuric and nitric acids—killing fish, damaging crop lands, corroding buildings and causing human respiratory problems which in some cases have proved fatal.

This excessively acidic rainfall becomes even more lethal when it leaches aluminium from the granite rock that forms the watershed of many rivers. Apropos of which, the following brief extracts are from a recent report by the North West Water Authority's Rivers Division, Scientists Department, Biology North: *Juvenile Salmonid Populations and Biological Quality of Upland Streams in Cumbria with Particular References to Low pH Effects.** R. F. Prigg, 1983.

> Like extremely low pH stress, toxic levels of aluminium cause mucus clogging of the gills, and also induce ionic disequilibrium as measured by rapid loss of plasma salts . . . observations have shown a number of tributaries with *total aluminium levels between 200 and 500 mg/litre* and a negative correlation between pH and aluminium remarkably similar to that found for Swedish clearwater (i.e. non-dystrophic) lakes (Dickson, 1980). Aluminium toxicity is strongly pH dependent, being maximal around pH 5, and it may prove acutely lethal at levels *as low as 200 mg/litre* . . . It is suggested that pH depression to around 5 in the main river Esk, and elevated levels of mobilised aluminium from more acid tributaries, could account for the mortality in this clearwater system, under summer spate conditions. (My italics)

Since 1980, the Esk has been systematically monitored by NWWA scientists. During a period of heavy spate in the week 16–22 September, 1983, exceptionally high acidity caused another mass mortality of salmon and sea trout, this time among the greatly reduced autumn run. From this second disaster two very interesting facts emerge:

1. The period of peak acidity (pH 4.3 in the main river!) was of extremely short duration—a matter of an hour, or even less—and occurred when the river level was at its highest.

2. Contrary to general belief, the strongest concentration of acid is not necessarily during the spate following a long period of dry weather. Dur-

---

*pH is a quantitative measure of the acidity (or basicity) of a solution on a reciprocal logarithmic scale. For example: pH 5 is ten times more acid than pH 6. (Originally used by the Danish biochemist S. P. L. Sørenson to represent hydrogen ion concentration.)

ing the week in question, several spates had occurred in quick succession immediately prior to the spate that produced the sudden lethal slug of acid water.

These reports from the Rivers Division of the North West Water Authority emphasize the danger threatening some of our lakes and rivers. What can be done to avoid it?

In the long-term: the prevention of this pollution at source. But this is costly, and very much a political issue. Up to now the United Kingdom, reputedly one of the worst polluters in Europe, has shown no willingness to follow the lead of other European countries.

7 lb grilse with net marks.

In the short-term: much might be achieved by the liming of acidic and infertile uplands where these occur in river water-sheds. It is surely no coincidence that the 1980 Esk catastrophe followed close upon the cessation of liming four years earlier. Until September, 1976, when the removal of the agricultural subsidy put an end to nearly all hill-farm liming, this amount of alkali may have just sufficed to hold the balance of power; acidity becoming triumphant once it had gone.

The chief issues affecting *Salmo*'s future are clearly defined. First, commercial fishing on the Atlantic feeding grounds—a matter for international negotiation. Secondly, the domestic issue of netting, both legal and illegal, operating in our own rivers and coastal waters (and directly under our control), which accounts for so many salmon that survive the drift-nets and long-lines of the deep-sea fishermen.

The angler wants to see more of these fish in the river, and to support him he has a sound argument.

Man-made, stillwater, put-and-take salmon fishery at Upton Bishop near Ross-on-Wye. The fishery comprises two lakes of roughly fifteen acres each, separated by a small weir. Hatchery-bred salmon are transported from pens in Scottish sea lochs where the young fish are fattened, and make the transition from salt water to fresh without apparent distress.

On their transfer to fresh water the fish stop feeding and, judging by angling results so far, their taking-behaviour and the angler's chances of success seem similar to those relating to wild fish.

Much as some traditional salmon anglers may regret this manipulation of *Salmo*, the long-term effects of put-and-take salmon fishing might produce one benefit, at least. As the production of hand-reared fish increases, the market price must surely drop. This may well diminish the present-day intensive assault on wild fish by river poachers, and drift-netters at sea.

432

In the days prior to salmon fishing on the high seas, estuary netting had a valid function. Owing to the salmon's depressed appetite angling alone, no matter what methods were used, could never adequately harvest the big runs of returning fish. But with the vastly diminished runs of today, the estuarine net is an anachronism. Particularly is this true in Scotland, where salmon angling adds many millions of pounds to the economy. Whatever the value of a netted salmon today, there is not the slightest doubt that the value of a rod-caught salmon is many times greater.

The angler, moreover, is the salmon's chief benefactor. It is largely on his pocket that the procreation of this fish depends. So, too, does the huge sport-fishing interest—comprising tourism, the tackle-industry and a good deal of other employment, much of it in outlying country districts. From this viewpoint alone, the continuance of estuarine netting is a Carollian saga of economic absurdity.

One thing is certain. The situation as it exists cannot continue indefinitely. Unless the pressures of excessive netting and poaching are released and more fish made available, it is doubtful whether anglers will continue to pay such heavy bills. Disenchanted with flogging declining rivers at high cost, some are likely to resort to stillwaters where hand-reared salmon may provide cheaper opportunities. If so, some presently thriving but remote riverside villages may well become distressed areas.

Is this really what will happen to the great sport of salmon angling as we have known it? Is it in an artificial lake that the king of fish will end his days?

No, I am sure it is not. The stew-pond fish may well play a part in our angling future, but I cannot believe that *simply for want of sensible legislation* the unparalleled excitement of catching wild salmon will ever be lost. After all, as a glance at history confirms, this is not the first time that the future of *Salmo* has been threatened.

Not long ago, most if not all of our rivers had huge runs of migratory fish. Riverside farmers shovelled salmon fry to feed their swine. Salmon even figured in the commissariats for military campaigns: Edward II ordered thousands of dried salmon to feed his army. As late as the Reformation, salmon was only half the price of pike. Less than two hundred years ago, special teams of horses transported salmon from northern rivers to the London market.

Then came the ravages of water abstraction, river obstruction and pollution. Local rivers made handy drains. The Industrial Revolution destroyed their beauty. Manufacturers intent only on material wealth

Ulcerative dermal necrosis (UDN), the disease that ravaged our rivers after its appearance in the mid-sixties. If infected fish survive long enough to spawn, the eggs will hatch normally. But this salmon, its head almost totally smothered in fungus, is unlikely to reach the redds.

Many returning fish bear evidence of encounters with marine predators among whom the seal is probably the most destructive. It is not uncommon to find seals in fresh water pursuing salmon several miles upriver from the sea.

434

disposed of industry's filth in the easiest and cheapest way. The pollution of waste matter poured from factory and town along the river banks. Lower reaches became stinking sewers whose effluent vomited from estuary mouths to stain the tide.

The river flowing through Britain's capital city was no exception. Three hundred years ago, Izaak Walton wrote:

> There is no better salmon than in England; and that although some of our northern rivers have salmon as fat and as large as the River Thames, yet none are of so excellent a taste.

A century later the Thames was said to be:

> The greatest and chiefest of all the rivers in Britain—for the prodigious quantity of its fish, the variety of their sorts and the goodness of their kind, preferable to all the other rivers in Europe; and the prime of the English salmon is found in the Thames.

In 1816 the Thames had an exceptional run of salmon, so many being caught that they fetched only threepence a pound in Billingsgate market. Twenty years later the Thames salmon had almost vanished. As fast as that did they disappear. Locks and weirs that made the river navigable blocked the passage of salmon to their spawning redds, and pollution finished the job. For over a century-and-a-half like so many other rivers running as a smelly and highly toxic gutter, London's river was a national disgrace.

But in time commonsense prevailed. Now, almost unbelievably, as a result of the recent highly commendable drive against pollution, the Thames is once again clean enough to encourage a run of migratory fish. Already, returning sea trout and salmon have been recorded and even hooked in the upper reaches. Soon, perhaps sooner than one had ever dared to hope, an observer on the Embankment may see what Caesar's legions must have seen—the miracle of *Salmo* leaping on his way upstream in Chelsea Reach.

The Thames is a splendid example of what can be done. So, too, is the Clyde, to which salmon are returning after an absence of a hundred-and-thirty years. And there are many other victories that brighten the future.

Most migratory fish return from the sea to spawn in their rivers of origin. But not all. Each year, small but vital numbers find their ways to the redds of strange rivers. Quite apart from the introduction of fresh stocks, these wandering fish will explore and re-stock every barren river,

Robert Pashley of Ross-on-Wye with a 45 lb Wye fish. Between 1897 and 1951 this great angler caught more than 10,000 salmon, including 29 of over 40 lb. A catch not likely to be repeated in the light of present-day salmon runs.

if not repelled by an outflow of filth or destroyed by excessive acidity.

The safeguarding of salmon and sea trout angling, together with every-thing these sports entail, demands a reduction of commercial fishing; but this by itself is not enough. Our rivers are the breeding grounds essential to *Salmo*'s future. Efforts to improve and protect them must be redoubled. What has happened in the past must never be repeated.

It is sometimes said that our migratory fish are of importance only to wealthy anglers and gourmets. What an untruth! They are of paramount concern to everyone, and it is imperative that we ensure the future of these fish in their natural environment. Like the living canary that once proclaimed the safety of a mine, their presence in a river is proof of unpolluted water.

"Landscape", said Ruskin, "is part of a nation's wealth."

And who would not agree that clean water the life-blood of the countryside is an essential part of that landscape?

Thanks to the various Associations concerned with *Salmo*'s welfare much has been done, especially in the long and constant struggle against pollution. But the ogres of indifference and greed have still to be overcome.

This is the age of the contrived: of safari-parks and nature-trails and zoos and man-made lakes with stew-pond fish. And perhaps today there is a place for these. But vital to man's spirit is the challenge of the wilder-ness, with truly wild animals. Of all species, salmon and sea trout are certainly that.

We cannot afford to lose them.

Hugh Falkus
1984

Bibliography

ASHLEY-COOPER, John, *A Salmon Fisher's Odyssey*, 1982. *The Great Salmon Rivers of Scotland*, 1980.

BAINBRIDGE, George, *The Fly-fisher's Guide*, 1816.
BARKER, Thomas, *The Art of Angling*, 1651.
BERNERS, Dame Juliana, *A Treatyse of Fysshynge wyth an Angle*, 1496.
BICKERDYKE, John, *The Book of the All Round Angler*, 1888.
BOWLKER, Richard, *The Art of Angling Improved in all its Parts*, 1747.
BROOKES, Richard, *The Art of Angling, Rock and Sea Fishing*, 1740. *The Art of Angling*, 1766.

CALDERWOOD, W. L., *The Salmon Rivers and Lochs of Scotland*, 1909.
CHALMERS, Patrick, *The Angler's England*, 1938.
CHAYTOR, A. H., *Letters to a Salmon Fisher's Sons*, 1910.
CHETHAM, James, *The Angler's Vade Mecum*, 1681.
CHOLMONDELEY-PENNELL, H., *Fishing*, 1885.
COURTNEY WILLIAMS, A., *Angling Diversions*, 1945.

DAVY, Sir Humphry, *Salmonia*, 1828.
DAWSON, Kenneth, *Casts from a Salmon Reel*, no date [1948]. *Salmon and Trout in Moorland Streams*, 1928. Revised edition, 1947.
DENNYS, John, *The Secrets of Angling*, 1613.

FALKUS, Hugh, *Sea Trout Fishing*, revised second edition 1981.
FRANCIS, Francis, *A Book on Angling*, 1867.
FRANCK, Richard, *Northern Memoirs*, 1694.
FORTIN, Frère, François, *Les Ruses Innocentes*, 1660.

GILBERT, H. A., *The Tale of a Wye Fisherman*, 1929.
GRAY, L. R. N., *Torridge Fishery*, 1957.

HILLS, John Waller, *River Keeper*, 1934.
HOWLETT, Robert, *The Angler's Sure Guide*, 1706.
HUGHES-PARRY, J., *A Salmon Fisherman's Notebook*, 1955.
HUTTON, J. Arthur, *Rod Fishing for Salmon on the Wye*, 1920.

KELSON, George, *The Salmon Fly*, 1895.

LAMOND, Henry, *The Gentle Art*, 1911.

MARKHAM, Gervase, *The Pleasures of Princes*, 1614.
MASCALL, Leonard, *A Booke of Fishing with Hooke and Line*, 1590.
McEWAN, Bill, *Angling on Lomond*, 1980.

BIBLIOGRAPHY

MILLS, Derek, *Salmon and Trout*, 1971.

NICOLL, Henry, *Salmon and Other Things*, 1923.

OGLESBY, Arthur, *Salmon*, second edition, 1983.
O'GORMAN, *The Practice of Angling*, (Vol. 1), 1845.

PRIGG, R. F., *Juvenile Salmonid Populations and Biological Quality of Upland Streams in Cumbria with Particular References to Low pH effects*, 1983.

RAWLING, Tom, *Ghosts at my Back*, 1982.

SAMUEL, William, *The Arte of Angling*, 1577.
SCROPE, William, *Days and Nights of Salmon Fishing*, 1843.
STODDART, Thomas, Tod, *The Angler's Companion to the Rivers and Lochs of Scotland*, second edition, 1853.

TAVERNER, Eric, (and others), *Salmon Fishing*, 1931.

VENABLES, Robert, *The Experienc'd Angler*, 1662.

WADDINGTON, Richard, *Fly Fishing for Salmon*, 1951.
WALTON, Izaak, *The Compleat Angler*, 1653.
WULFF, Lee, *The Atlantic Salmon*, second edition, 1983.

YOUNG, J. Z., *The Life of Vertebrates*, second edition, 1966.
YOUNGER, John, *On River Angling for Salmon and Trout*, 1840.

Index